Perturbation Methods in Credit Derivatives

Founded in 1807, John Wiley & Sons is the oldest independent publishing company in the United States. With offices in North America, Europe, Australia and Asia, Wiley is globally committed to developing and marketing print and electronic products and services for our customers' professional and personal knowledge and understanding.

The Wiley Finance series contains books written specifically for finance and investment professionals as well as sophisticated individual investors and their financial advisors. Book topics range from portfolio management to e-commerce, risk management, financial engineering, valuation and financial instrument analysis, as well as much more.

For a list of available titles, visit our Web site at www.WileyFinance.com.

Perturbation Methods in Credit Derivatives

Strategies for Efficient Risk Management

COLIN TURFUS

WILEY

This edition first published 2021

Registered office
John Wiley & Sons Ltd, The Atrium, Southern Gate, Chichester, West Sussex PO19 8SQ, United Kingdom

For details of our global editorial offices, for customer services and for information about how to apply for permission to reuse the copyright material in this book please see our website at www.wiley.com.

Library of Congress Cataloging-in-Publication Data is available

Names: Turfus, Colin, author.
Title: Perturbation methods in credit derivatives : strategies for efficient risk management / Colin Turfus.
Description: Chichester, West Sussex, United Kingdom : John Wiley & Sons, 2021. | Series: Wiley finance series | Includes bibliographical references and index.
Identifiers: LCCN 2020029878 (print) | LCCN 2020029879 (ebook) | ISBN 9781119609612 (hardback) | ISBN 9781119609629 (adobe pdf) | ISBN 9781119609599 (epub)
Subjects: LCSH: Credit derivatives. | Financial risk management.
Classification: LCC HG6024.A3 T87 2021 (print) | LCC HG6024.A3 (ebook) | DDC 332.64/57–dc23
LC record available at https://lccn.loc.gov/2020029878
LC ebook record available at https://lccn.loc.gov/2020029879

Cover Design: Wiley
Cover Image: © MR.Cole_Photographer/Getty Images

Set in 10/12pt SabonLTStd by SPi Global, Chennai, India
Printed and bound by CPI Group (UK) Ltd, Croydon, CR0 4YY

Contents

Preface

This is a book about how to derive exact or approximate analytic expressions for semi-exotic credit and credit hybrid derivatives prices in a systematic way. It is aimed at readers who already have some familiarity with the concept of risk-neutral pricing and the associated stochastic calculus used to define basic models for pricing derivatives which depend on underlyings such as interest and FX rates, equity prices and/or credit default intensities, such as is provided by Hull [2018]. We shall set out models in terms of the stochastic differential equations which govern the evolution of the risk factors or market variables on which derivatives prices depend. However, we shall in the main seek to re-express the model as a pricing equation in the form of a linear partial differential equation (PDE), more specifically a second order diffusion equation, using the well known Feynman–Kac theorem, which we shall use without proof.

Our approach will be mathematical in terms of using mathematical arguments to derive solutions to pricing equations. However, we shall not be concerned here about the details of necessary and sufficient conditions for existence, uniqueness and smoothness of solutions. In the main we shall take advantage of the fact that the equations we are addressing are already known to have well-behaved solutions under conditions which have been well-documented. Our concern will be to use mathematical analysis to infer analytic representation, either exact or approximate, of solutions. We shall in some cases seek to offer more rigorous justification of the methods employed. But our general approach will be to demonstrate that the results are valid either in terms of satisfying the specified pricing equation (exactly or approximately), or else replicating satisfactorily prices derived by an established method such as Monte Carlo simulation.

Our method combines operator formalism with perturbation expansion techniques in a novel way. The focus is different from much of the work in the literature insofar as:

- Rather than deriving particular solutions for individual products with a specific payoff, we obtain first general solutions for pricing equations; in other words, pricing kernels. We then use these to produce prices for particular products simply by taking a convolution of the payoff function(s) with the kernel.
- Rather than focussing on products whose value is contingent on spot variables such as FX or inflation rates, or equity or commodity prices, and building expansions based on the assumption of low variability of local and/or stochastic volatility, we consider mainly rates-credit hybrid derivatives, taking the short rate and the instantaneous credit default intensity to be stochastic and building expansions based on the assumption of *low rates and/or intensities*. This latter assumption is almost always valid allowing simple expressions which are only first order, or at

most second order, to be used with very high accuracy. Implementation of the derived formulae typically involve nothing more complicated than quadrature in up to two dimensions and fixed point iterative solution of one-dimensional non-linear equations, so are well suited to scripting languages such as Python, which was indeed used for most of the calculations presented herein.

As a consequence, we are able to derive many new approximate but highly accurate expressions for hybrid derivative prices which have not been previously available in the literature. These approximations are furthermore uniformly valid in the sense that they remain valid over any trade time-scale unlike many other popular asymptotic methods such as the SABR approximation of Hagan et al. [2015], the accuracy of which depends on an assumption of short time-to-maturity (low term variance). We are also able to point the reader in the direction of how to derive further results for models and products other than those considered explicitly here.

The essence of our approach is that we focus on models where the stochastic factors approximate to a good degree to being normally distributed (or lognormally, which simply means that the logarithm of the variable in question is normally distributed) and where interest rates and credit default intensities are taken to be governed by short-rate models.[1] This means that the pricing kernel can to leading order be expressed as a multivariate gaussian distribution (multiplied by a discount factor). Corrections need to be applied to this base representation to obtain a sufficiently accurate result. We show how in many cases this can be done exactly. In other cases, in particular where rates or credit intensities are lognormal rather than normal, one or two correction terms need to be added to a leading order pricing kernel formula. The prices of derivatives are then obtained by taking a convolution of the pricing kernel with the associated payoff functions, which task is typically a standard one.

We start off in Chapter 1 by discussing why perturbation methods are not currently seen as "mainstream" quantitative finance, concluding that some of the reasons are seen on closer inspection to be invalid, while others, despite having some validity, do not apply to the methods set out in this book, which seeks to pioneer a new approach with wider applicability. We seek to justify this claim in the remainder of the book, starting with Chapter 2, which is dedicated to case studies illustrating how the approach we propose allows flexible response to evolving needs in a risk management context. In Chapter 3, we set out the mathematical approach and core tools which we will make use of throughout. We apply these in Chapters 4 and 5 to the construction of pricing kernels for the popular Hull–White and Black–Karasinski short-rate models, respectively, using these kernels to derive important derivative pricing formulae; as exact expressions in the former case and as perturbation expansions in the latter.

We then turn our attention to hybrid and multi-factor models, devoting Chapter 6 to setting out a generic framework for handling models with multiple factors following

[1] We exclude for the former reason rates (interest or credit) which are governed by a model of the CIR type defined by Cox et al. [1991) (where the underlying stochastic factor follows a χ^2 distribution), and for the latter reason rates which are governed by either a HJM model of the type defined by Heath et al. [1992) or a LIBOR market model. Most of the standard models for spot underlyings are encompassed within the framework, the main exceptions being Lévy models and rough volatility models.

the Ornstein–Uhlenbeck processes, the detailed calculation associated with which method turns out to depend only on the (stochastic) discounting model employed. We set out the details for both Hull–White and Black–Karasinski discounting models. The next four chapters deal with two-factor hybrid models: rates-equity; rates-credit; credit-equity; and credit-FX. Kernels are deduced, either exact or as perturbation expansions, and used to infer the prices of a number of semi-exotic derivatives in each case. Some evidence is provided of the favourable performance of approximate results against calculation performed by numerical schemes capable of delivering arbitrarily high precision.

Chapter 11 expands the envelope one step further, looking at a three-factor model incorporating an FX rate and two interest rates, deducing an exact pricing kernel and using this to infer option prices. It is noted that the model considered is of Jarrow–Yildirim type so is applicable also to the pricing of inflation derivatives. A further turn of the handle in Chapter 12 also brings credit risk into the mix, resulting in a four-factor model. A pricing kernel expansion is deduced and used to price a number of semi-exotic credit derivatives. Most notably we revisit quanto CDS pricing (covered in the first instance in Chapter 10), now allowing interest rates to be stochastic as well as credit and FX rates.

The next two chapters of the book take us off in slightly different directions. First we look forward to the new risk-free LIBOR replacement rates which are set in arrears on the basis of compounding daily (or overnight) rates (Chapter 13). This approach is intended to supplant the currently used multi-curve frameworks where LIBOR rates embed a tenor-dependent stochastic spread, the modelling of which is the subject of Chapter 14. In each of these cases we consider in the first instance how the pricing kernel for the short-rate model is affected then look at how the integration with a Black–Karasinski credit model impacts the resulting hybrid kernel and assess the consequent impact on credit derivatives formulae.

The remaining chapters are devoted to applications of the methods and results herein expounded in various areas of contemporary interest in a risk management context. Chapter 15 looks at scenario generation where interest rate and credit curves need to be evolved alongside spot processes to allow risk measures such as market risk, counterparty exposure and CVA, depending on a projected distribution of future prices, to be calculated. In Chapter 16 we look at model risk, noting that our methods have utility here too, both in providing useful, easily implemented benchmarks for model validation purposes and for making quantitative assessments of the influence of model parameters and modelling assumptions on portfolio evaluations. Finally the newly evolving application of machine learning to problems in quantitative finance and the question of how asymptotic methods could complement this approach in practice are addressed in Chapter 17.

C. Turfus
London, 2020

Acknowledgments

The author is grateful to co-researcher Alexander Shubert for his important contribution in implementing in Python the asymptotic formulae presented in Chapter 15 and in preparing the associated graphs.

Acronyms

ATM at the money
CCDS contingent credit default swap
CDS credit default swap
CDF cumulative distribution function
CMS constant maturity swap
CVA counterparty value adjustment
ITM in the money
OTM out of the money
PDE partial differential equation
PDF probability density function
FRTB Fundamental Review of the Trading Book
VaR value at risk
CCR counterparty credit risk
HJM Heath Jarrow Morton
LMM LIBOR Market Model

CHAPTER 1

Why Perturbation Methods?

1.1 ANALYTIC PRICING OF DERIVATIVES

How important are analytic formulae in the pricing of financial derivatives? The way you feel about this matter will probably determine to a large degree whether this book will be of interest to you. Current opinion is undoubtedly divided and perhaps for good reasons. On the one hand, presented with the challenge of some new financial calculation, financial engineers these days are likely to spend considerably less time looking for analytic solutions or approximations than, say, twenty years ago, citing the ever-increasing power and speed of computational resources at their disposal. On the other hand, where known analytic solutions exist, those same financial engineers are unlikely to eschew them and to persist doggedly in replicating the known solution using a Monte Carlo engine or a finite difference method.

So, it might be suggested, the resistance to analytic solutions that we observe is not to their use as such when they are already available, but to making the effort to find (and implement) them. One of the reasons for this is a perception that, given the huge amount of research effort that has been invested into finding solutions over the past few decades, most of the interesting and useful solutions have been found and published. It is the experience of the author that the reaction to the announcement of discovery of a new and interesting analytic solution tends to be indifference or scepticism rather than interest. At the same time, it is often assumed (correctly?) that such effort as is being invested into finding analytic solutions is these days directed mainly towards approximate solutions, most particularly using perturbation methods, which area continues to be a reasonably fertile ground for research effort, at least in academic institutions. We shall look more closely at the areas which are attracting attention below.

It is of interest to ask then why, despite the continuing effort being invested on the theoretical side into the development of analytic approximations, the take-up in practice appears to be relatively limited, certainly compared to the heyday of options pricing theory when the choice of models made by practitioners was significantly influenced by the availability of analytic solutions, even of analytic approximations such as SABR [Hagan et al., 2002]. For example Brigo and Mercurio [2006] observed of the short-rate model of Black and Karasinski [1991] that

> the rather good fitting quality of the model to market data, and especially to the swaption volatility surface, has made the model quite popular among practitioners and financial engineers. However, ... the Black–Karasinski (1991) model is not analytically tractable. This renders the model calibration to market data more burdensome than in the Hull and White (1990) Gaussian model, since no analytic formulae for bonds are available.

It is undoubtedly true that the relative tractability of the Hull–White model has been an important factor resulting in its much wider adoption as an industry standard.

No single reason can be cited to account for the relatively limited use to which analytic approximations are put. Practitioners' views vary greatly depending on the types of models they are looking at and what they are using them for. A number of factors can be pointed to, as we shall elaborate in the following section. For the moment we make the following observations, specifically comparing analytic pricing with a Monte Carlo approach.

- There is a general distrust by financial engineers of methods involving any kind of approximation. The fact that, if results involve power series-like constructions, it may not be possible to guarantee arbitrage-free prices in 100% of cases is often cited as a reason to avoid use of such approximations in pricing models intended for production purposes. Furthermore, it can be more work to assess the error implicit in a given approximation than it is to compute prices in the first place.
- While analytic methods are computationally more efficient, they appear to be intrinsically less scalable than Monte Carlo methods from a development and implementation standpoint. Whereas the Monte Carlo implementation of a model mainly involves the simulation of the underlying variables, with different products merely requiring different payoffs to be applied, each product variant tends to have a different analytic formula with limited scope for reuse with reference to other products. Also, if an additional stochastic factor is included in a Monte Carlo method, this can often be handled as an incremental change, while in the case of analytic methods, they will often break down completely when an additional risk factor is added.
- Another argument that is not infrequently heard against the introduction of new analytic results is that it is just too much trouble to integrate them into pricing libraries which are already quite mature. An accompanying argument may be that, since the libraries of financial institutions are already written in highly optimised C++ code, any gains that might be made are only likely to be marginal.
- There is also a suspicion concerning the utility of perturbation methods insofar as, while the most interesting and challenging problems in derivatives pricing occur where stochastic effects have a significant impact on the pricing, most perturbation approaches have some kind of reliance on the smallness of a volatility parameter, usually a term variance.[1] But, for this parameter to have a significant impact on

[1]Approximate solutions are sometimes presented as being valid for short times to maturity, but this limitation usually serves to limit the magnitude of the term variance which by construction tends to be a monotonically increasing function of time to maturity.

pricing it cannot be too "small", so we are led to the expectation that we will need a large number of terms in any approximating series to secure adequate convergence in many cases of importance.

- A more recent argument which the author has encountered in a number of conversations with fellow researchers is that, insofar as more efficient ways are sought to carry our repetitive execution of pricing algorithms, the strategy adopted in the future will increasingly be to replace the time-consuming solution of SDEs and PDEs not with analytic formulae but with machine-learned algorithms which can execute orders of magnitude faster (see for example Horvath et al. [2019]). The cost of adopting this approach is a large amount of up-front computational effort in the training phase where the full numerical algorithm is run multiple times over many market data configurations and product specifications to allow the machine-learning algorithm to learn what the "right answer" looks like so that it might replicate it. There will also be a concomitant loss of accuracy. But if, as is often the case, the requirement is to calculate prices for a given portfolio or the CVA associated with a given "netting set" of trades with a given counterparty over multiple scenarios for risk management or other regulatory purposes, the upfront cost can be amortised against a huge amount of subsequent usage of the machine-learned algorithm. Since machine-learning approaches are a fairly blunt instrument, there is not the need to customise the approach to the particular problem addressed, as would be necessary if perturbation methods were used instead as a speed-up strategy wherein some accuracy is traded for speed.
- Finally, there is not uncommonly a perception that, unlike with earlier analytic options pricing formulae which were deduced using suitable application of the Girsanov theorem, with which financial engineers tend to be familiar, perturbation-based methods are by comparison something of a dark art. Many of the results are derived using Malliavin calculus or Lie theory, with which relatively few financial engineers are familiar, and often presented in published research papers in notation which is relatively opaque and quite closely tied in to the method of derivation. Other derivations are performed using methodologies and notations borrowed from quantum mechanics or other areas of theoretical physics, areas with which a contemporary financial engineer is unlikely to be familiar. There is, furthermore, not a clearly defined body of theory which the practitioners of perturbation analysis seek to rely on; books which offer a unified approach to perturbation methods applicable to a range of problems in derivatives pricing such as Fouque et al. [2000], Fouque et al. [2011] and Antonov et al. [2019] are few and far between.

1.2 IN DEFENCE OF PERTURBATION METHODS

Although the arguments presented above challenging the merit of attempts to extend the range of analytic formulae available for derivatives pricing by means of perturbation expansion techniques may appear compelling, we suggest that, when they are unpicked a little, their apparent validity starts to unravel. More specifically they are seen to be premised on a view of what is possible with perturbation methods which is challengeable in the light of recent theoretical developments, in particular those set out in this book. They, furthermore, depend on a view of what practical purposes option pricing methods need to address in the industry and the consequent constraints they must satisfy which is likewise challengeable and not altogether up to date.

- While the development of derivatives pricing methods was based on the concept of risk-neutral pricing to guarantee the absence of arbitrage opportunities through which market makers could systematically lose money, the use of pricing models is increasingly in practice for risk management purposes, rather than the calculation of prices for market-making purposes. So, even if it is the case that an approximation method might technically give rise to arbitrage opportunities in a small number of extreme cases, provided no trading takes place at these prices this is not necessarily a problem. Indeed we are often in a risk management context more interested in real-world probabilities than in their risk-neutral counterparts, on account of the fact it is extreme real-world events and their frequency of occurrence in practice which can lead to the destabilisation or demise of a financial institution. For example, a report by Fintegral and IACPM [2015] surveying 37 global and regional financial institutions concludes that calculation of counterparty credit risk (CCR) tends to operate under "real-world" assumptions using historical volatilities to calibrate the Monte Carlo simulation.

  Also, since risk management is generally about portfolio aggregates rather than individual trades, and typically involves computing prices under hypothetical future scenarios, it is not so important to be able to estimate the size of errors associated with the pricing of individual trades as the expected aggregate error, which can often be estimated to a sufficient degree of accuracy by fairly heuristic methods. This is recognised in the Basel IV (FRTB) regulatory framework which has been proposed to replace VaR: internal models used for risk management purposes don't have to be validated in terms of their ability to price individual trades accurately, but rather the aggregate risk numbers produced need to be sufficiently close to those obtained using end-of-day pricing models in a back-testing exercise.

  Another factor is that, whereas the main criterion pricing models have to satisfy is accurate calculation of the first moment of a distribution, risk models are much more focussed on the *distribution* of prices, typically in the extreme quantiles where the greatest risk is usually deemed to lie, so their ability to give an accurate assessment of second and higher moments tends to be at least as important, if not more so. While, in the market, prices of a large number of traded financial securities can be considered known to a reasonable degree of accuracy (the bid–offer spread), this is not the case if one is asking about the distribution of those prices in the future, market information about which is typically much scarcer and the uncertainty about which is correspondingly much greater.
- One of the issues with the way in which perturbation expansions were derived and presented historically is that they were deduced as particular solutions

associated with a specific payoff structure: often this was a vanilla European-style payoff. Such results could not therefore be used for related problems like, say, forward-starting options. Likewise, restrictive assumptions were often made about market data, such as volatilities being constant, without clarification of how results could be generalised. We shall refer to such approaches to perturbation analysis as *first generation*. The last five years or so have seen focus shift more and more to deriving instead pricing kernels; in other words, general solutions to the pricing equation which can be used relatively straightforwardly to derive solutions for multiple payoff configurations. This approach to perturbation analysis we shall refer to as *second generation*. A good introduction to this subject is provided by Pagliarani and Pascucci [2012], where pricing kernels are referred to as transition densities.

The approach we shall take below is robustly second generation, seeking from the outset a pricing kernel associated with a given model before applying it to calculate derivative prices or risk measures. As we shall see, our approach has the further advantage that it provides a way not only to derive a pricing kernel (approximate or exact) systematically from a pricing equation, but also to extend it to include additional risk factors so that pricing kernels derived for simpler problems can be recycled in producing kernels for new and more complex problems. Indeed we will see (in Chapter 6) that, where risk factors do not impact on the discounting applied, they can often be included in a generic way using vectorised notation so that a single generic pricing kernel can present a unified solution to many different pricing equations. Also it will be seen that the resulting formulae all tend to have very similar structures so the coding effort involved in implementing them in a pricing library tends to be fairly light with significant code reuse possible.

In this way we will seek to go beyond existing second generation approaches and create the tools or frameworks from which pricing kernels can be constructed, rather than focussing on the pricing kernels themselves. In effect we are advocating for a Generation 2.5 approach.

- Although the requirements of investment banks have historically been the main driver of innovation in pricing methodologies, banks' pricing libraries are, in general, in a fairly mature and stable state: there is relatively little happening in the way of new product or model development. New implementation of pricing routines is much less likely to be happening in the front office of investment banks than in small investment houses, hedge funds, consultancies or other service providers. Rather than developing high-powered generic Monte Carlo engines in C++ code, they are more likely these days to be developing or buying-in more bespoke risk and pricing models, increasingly in more flexible scripting languages such as Python rather than in C++, since rapid development, easy maintenance and transparency are more likely to be at a premium. Further, the availability for more than a decade now of the Boost.Python C++ library allows routines and software objects written in C++ to be seamlessly accessed from or integrated into Python scripts, allowing the advantages of both worlds potentially to be enjoyed. It is in relation to such usage that we see the type of easily implemented perturbation solutions presented in this book as being most relevant.

- The great majority of work on derivatives pricing using perturbation expansions from the SABR model of Hagan et al. [2002] has been in the context of local and/or stochastic volatility (mainly the latter). Furthermore, relatively little attention has been paid to short-rate models, either for interest rates or for credit. One might ask why this is the case. This is a surprisingly difficult question to answer definitively because no one tends to report the reasons why they did *not* do research in a given area. The bias may in part be a consequence of the fact that short-rate models are considered to have been surpassed by other more flexible frameworks such as that of Heath et al. [1992] (HJM) and the LIBOR market model (LMM). There appears to be a sense that short-rate models are "harder" than models of spot processes on account of the non-linear interaction between the short rate appearing both in the payoff specification *and* in the discount factor. While this may limit considerably the scope for *exact* analytic solutions, it ought not to be considered overly problematic in relation to perturbation expansion approaches: the impact on the discount factor is invariably quite weak, which plays into a perturbation strategy. Much of the analysis in the present volume seeks to exploit precisely this fact, building rapidly convergent perturbation series in powers of the short rate(s). It remains unclear to the author why more advantage has not been taken of this possibility by other researchers.

  We shall, as indicated, focus on short-rate models at the expense of consideration of the HJM framework and the related LIBOR market model (although some short-rate models such as Hull–White can be derived from within a HJM framework). This is mainly because the latter do not lend themselves so well to analysis by the techniques we expound below. A word should be said in defence of this decision. In the first instance, as the book's title suggests, we are specifically interested in credit derivatives, and the HJM and LMM frameworks have far less utility in that space than do short-rate models. Further, insofar as our focus in the interest rate modelling we do perform is mainly on hybrid derivatives pricing rather than the types of interest rate option that tend to be the main targets of HJM and LMM approaches, short-rate modelling is what is likely already being used in practice in the contexts we address.
- The main shortcoming of the argument that traditional pricing libraries are about to be replaced by machine-learned versions of the algorithms they embody is that it currently lacks any real evidential basis. The strong recent interest in machine learning in the financial engineering community can be attributed to its increasingly being used, evidently to good effect, in devising and improving trading strategies by detecting signals in market data and trading patterns which a human observer might miss; and of course in algorithmic trading where the speed of the algorithm is key to profitability and even the latency of internet connections can have a significant impact. This has led to an upsurge of interest in this area, not only from those who already have relevant domain knowledge but also from many researchers who have established credentials in other areas, including I should add perturbation methods. But the colonisation by machine learning of the space currently occupied by pricing libraries is currently more an aspiration than a defined programme of research.

While it is probably too early to call how things will pan out in this area, we would venture that the future is best viewed not as a competition between analytic formulae and machine-learned alternatives but as an opportunity for mutually beneficial collaboration. For example, it is noteworthy that Horvath et al. [2019] in their highly influential paper target not option prices but Black-Scholes implied volatility in the learning process for a rough volatility model. So they are implicitly making use of the Black-Scholes pricing formula to provide an approximation for the rough volatility model price. Perhaps more interestingly, the recent work of Antonov et al. [2020] addresses the challenging problem of how to handle efficiently the outer limits of the (high-dimensional) phase space addressed by a machine-learned representation of a pricing algorithm, effectively by substituting in an asymptotic representation of the pricing algorithm for points outside a core region of the phase space which is sampled fairly exhaustively in the learning process. The utility of such an approach hinges crucially on the availability of an asymptotically valid approximate solution to the problem at hand, which can effectively be used as a control variate in the learning process.

- Finally, although it is true that there is a dearth of unified presentations of perturbation methodologies in the literature, we seek to address this in what follows by demonstrating how the particular second generation approach we advocate is applicable across a wide range of financial products, market underlyings and modelling assumptions for numerous tasks ranging from straightforward valuation to scenario generation, XVA and model risk quantification. We also seek to present results in a form which is at the same time transparent, so as to facilitate implementation, and fully general to allow real market data to be used without any modification or re-working of results.

CHAPTER 2

Some Representative Case Studies

Consider the following plausible scenarios where the methods set out in the remainder of this book are found to address the types of challenge faced by risk management groups, looking to capture risk more effectively and accurately under regulatory and other pressures without increasing computational overheads unduly or engaging in costly new model development.

2.1 QUANTO CDS PRICING

A Korean client of a US bank wishes to sell protection on KRW-denominated sovereign Korean debt and/or that of some systemically important Korean corporation. Providing a KRW-based CDS rate is available, this can be used to price the protection (in KRW) according to the well-known formula

$$V_P = (1 - R) \int_0^T B(0, u)\overline{\lambda}(u)du,$$

$$B(t_1, t_2) = e^{-\int_{t_1}^{t_2} (\overline{r}_f(u)+\overline{\lambda}(u))du}, \tag{2.1}$$

with $\overline{r}_f(\cdot)$ the KRW short rate, $\overline{\lambda}(\cdot)$ the instantaneous KRW-denominated credit spread and R the expected recovery level on the debt post-default. This can, if wished, be converted to a USD-based price at today's spot exchange rate.

However, it may be that the KRW-based spread is less liquid than the USD-based alternative and the desk (or risk management department) prefer to use the latter. There is likely to be a so-called quanto spread betweeen the USD CDS rate and the local KRW equivalent (reflecting the expected reduced value of a KRW protection payment after the default of a systemically important credit). This can be addressed by assuming a downwards jump-at-default in the value of KRW/USD exchange rate. Such remains amenable to analytic calculation. However, if the trader wants to take into account the additional possibility that the KRW/USD rate is negatively correlated with the credit spread, she appears to have no choice but to resort to Monte Carlo simulation of both the FX rate and the instantaneous credit spread (or credit default intensity).

However, referring to Chapter 10, she sees that a highly accurate modification to the above analytic formula is available for exactly this situation. This consists in simply replacing $\overline{\lambda}(\cdot)$ in the above with the effective credit intensity $\lambda_{\text{eff}}(\cdot)$ defined in (10.17).

If it happens that the coupons paid by the US bank are USD-denominated (as will often be the case), there is a quanto effect here also which prevents the coupon leg being priced straightforwardly by analytic means. However, recourse to Monte Carlo simulation can again be avoided if, in the discount factor $B(0, t_i)$ used to price the coupon payment at time t_i, $\overline{\lambda}(\cdot)$ is replaced by an effective credit intensity given this time by (10.9). In this way the trade can be priced and risk-managed entirely using analytic formulae.

2.2 WRONG-WAY INTEREST RATE RISK

Another issue arises shortly after at the same bank, this time raised by the market risk department. While the credit trading desk for developed markets uses analytic pricing for most vanilla credit products, the emerging markets desk, in recognition of the possibility of significant "wrong-way" risk associated with correlation between credit default risk and the local interest rate on foreign-denominated floating rate notes, uses a Monte Carlo approach with short-rate models representing both the credit intensity and the local rates processes. Market risk currently use the same (analytic pricing-based) risk engine for the trades of both desks. However, auditors have suggested, and market risk are now concerned, that there may be problems with back-testing of the Internal Model for market risk as a result of the discrepancy between the risk model and the emerging markets model, with only the latter capturing the wrong-way risk. They would prefer not to incur the significant cost of migrating part of the bank's credit portfolio to be priced by a Monte Carlo engine instead of an analytic approach.

However, it turns out that there is no need for the risk model to be changed to perform Monte Carlo pricing of floating rate notes. From results presented in Chapter 8, rather than (2.1), the protection leg can be priced using (8.54) which incorporates the wrong-way risk to a high degree of accuracy. Likewise the value of floating rate payments denominated in the local (foreign) currency can be priced using (8.58) to the same high level of accuracy. Here again, recourse to Monte Carlo simulation is avoided and computational resources are spared.

In the wake of this discussion, a question arises as to whether the quanto CDS trades currently priced with an analytic model taking account of FX-credit risk might likewise face the possibility of wrong-way rates-credit correlation risk, potentially in relation to both domestic and foreign currencies. It turns out from the extended calculations set out in Chapter 12 that the impact of wrong-way risk, from correlation of credit with the FX rate and with both interest rates on the value of a protection leg, can be taken into consideration by use of an effective credit intensity given by (12.46). Similarly the value of foreign currency coupon payments priced with a domestic currency credit curve can be obtained by making use of an effective credit intensity given by (12.38). Furthermore, it is seen that the value of a foreign currency float leg can be obtained to good accuracy by use of (12.39). In this case too, no recourse is needed to Monte Carlo methods.

2.3 CONTINGENT CDS PRICING AND CVA

Encouraged by the successful migration of a large number of trades away from Monte Carlo models to more efficient analytic models, attention falls on a portfolio of contingent CDS trades offering counterparty default protection on interest rate (including cross-currency) underlyings. Calculations for these are known to be very expensive on account of the need to integrate contributions from all possible default times in the exposure period, which requires in turn calculation of the value of the swap underlying at each such time for each Monte Carlo path. It is noted that analytic formulae for calculation of such protection are provided in §9.3.5 for single-currency interest rate swaps and in §10.4 and §12.4 for cross-currency swaps. The formulae are implemented and it is found that substantial speed-up is achieve in pricing, and particularly in risk-managing these trades.

The CVA desk hear about this and note that the CVA calculations they perform on interest rate portfolios are closely related to the contingent CDS protection pricing problem. They start looking into whether they could incorporate a similar analytic pricing approach into their workflow.

2.4 ANALYTIC INTEREST RATE OPTION PRICING

Another desk meanwhile trading hybrid products into emerging markets notices that the bank's pricing library now provides production-quality analytic methods for option pricing under the Black–Karasinski model. They frequently use this model in preference to Hull–White as an interest rate model, as they find it performs better in market conditions with high and volatile interest rates. They are interested in what analytic functions are available and see that in Chapter 5 there are explicit formulae for caplets, swaptions and zero coupon bonds (stochastic discount factors) which they consider could be useful, particularly in the process of model calibration, where pricing of calibration instruments must otherwise be done by repeated Monte Carlo simulation.

They note in addition that results in Chapter 14 allow calibration of the Black–Karasinski model in a multi-curve framework where the LIBOR spread(s) over the risk-free rate can be stochastic and potentially correlated with the risk-free rate. Furthermore, they note that results in Chapter 13 facilitate the extension of Black–Karasinski option pricing formulae enabling the model to be conveniently calibrated to caps referencing backward-looking risk-free rates, as and when a market in these inevitably appears in the post-IBOR world to which the finance industry is currently headed.

2.5 EXPOSURE SCENARIO GENERATION

Market risk management are in the throes of a comprehensive re-working of their risk framework to address the new Basel III regulations. Counterparty risk calculations are causing something of a headache. Previously interest rate and credit curves were evolved by identifying principal components, allowing each of these components to evolve along a Monte Carlo path, then reconstructing the implied shape of the curves at each exposure time of interest. The pricing engine can then be used taking the evolved curves along with the evolved values of other required spot variables (equity, FX, inflation, etc.) as input to obtain conditional prices for each relevant portfolio for each path at each exposure time. The distribution of positive exposure values can then be considered and expected positive exposures (EPE) and or potential future exposures (PFE) calculated by considering the tail of this distribution. Unfortunately, auditors are unhappy that a somewhat *ad hoc* method used for evolving the principal components hitherto is inadequately justified and would like to see something which is more industry-standard implemented in preference.

An option being considered is to try and evolve the curves in their entirety rather than just principal components. Standard models such as HJM-based or Black–Karasinski present themselves as candidates. But to be useful, there has to be a convenient mechanism for constructing the entire forward curve at each exposure time of interest, for use as input to the pricing model. The Black–Karasinski lognormal model is preferred to the simpler normal Hull–White alternative on the basis that, as the curve evolves upward or downward, lognormal volatilities rise or fall in proportion, which is intuitively sensible: if a Hull–White model is used instead, consideration would have to be given also to how the volatilities evolved as the associated curve moved up or down. Further, for the curve evolution to work in a credit curve context it must ensure positive values of all forward rates, which Black–Karasinski does, HJM-based models can, but Hull–White does not.

Encouragement is taken from the availability of the highly accurate analytic conditional bond formulae for the Black–Karasinski model set out in Chapter 5. But it is felt that the simple one-factor model does not do justice to the range of possible evolutions of the shape, not just the level, of interest rate and credit curves. Specifically, there should be fluctuations which impact mainly at the short end of the curve which decay relatively quickly (rapid mean reversion), whereas fluctuations affecting the long end are likely to be longer-lived (slow mean reversion). So the multi-factor Black–Karasinski model framework derived in §6.4 and expounded in greater detail in §15.5 is of interest. Work is initiated to implement the forward rate formula (15.49) to allow forward interest rate and credit curves to be generated from simple evolved Brownian variables, mutually correlated as necessary.

2.6 MODEL RISK

Model risk management faces a problem that one of the Monte Carlo pricing models used for credit derivatives pricing is found to manifest anomalous-looking behaviour when high volatility levels are used in conjunction with long times to maturity in the presence of significant rates-credit correlation. Auditors have asked for the situation to be investigated and an assessment made of what the correct behaviour should be, with the possibility of a reserve being set aside to take account of the risk of model error in the event that such large volatilities are observed in practice.

It is noted that the calculations set out in Chapter 8 illustrate how to price credit-contingent (default or survival) cash flows accurately under circumstances of relatively weak credit risk, with credit intensity represented by a Black–Karasinski short-rate model; further, that the relevant formulae are not limited in terms of the size of the credit volatility. The formula (8.54) for the value of protection payments is coded up and compared with the results from the Monte Carlo engine as the volatility level is increased. While the analytic results are seen to increase linearly with the credit volatility, the Monte Carlo results are found to deviate from this behaviour. It is concluded that there is likely model error resulting in this circumstance. A proposal is made that, in the event that volatility levels exceed a given threshold, a reserve should be set aside based on the difference between the Monte Carlo results and analytic results derived using the formulae presented in Chapter 8. A suggestion is also made that the front office quantitative analysts consider integrating a pricer based on the analytic formulae into the pricing library and migrating trades over from the Monte Carlo model.

Buoyed by this success, the model validation team within the model risk management department consider implementing more of the analytic formulae in their benchmark library for use as "challenger models" in the model validation process. In addition they note from the suggestions in Chapter 16 that in addition to providing alternative benchmarks, these analytic formulae upon differentiation are able to provide explicit formulae for the sensitivity of prices to model and market parameters. In this way model uncertainty calculations can be conveniently carried out, potentially at a large number of points in the product-model phase space. Thus the circumstances can be identified where the greatest model uncertainty is to be expected. In particular, model testing can be focussed on such "hot spots".

2.7 MACHINE LEARNING

A new project has started at the bank recently to look into the future prospect of replacing the internal model used for capital risk calculations with a more computationally efficient machine learning-based alternative. It is recognised that there are a number of unaddressed problems which currently prevent the realisation of such an ambition. One of these is that the training process for a machine learning-based algorithm which replicates pricing functionality is prohibitively high for the high-dimensional problem which is constituted by revaluing a bank's portfolio under diverse future market scenarios. Another problem is that the state space over which learning must take place is unbounded with respect to many of the relevant parameters, especially market parameters. Furthermore, regulators are very concerned that it be demonstrated in the model validation process that the internal model remains robust under extreme scenarios, such as those which occurred during the credit crunch of 2007. Consequently, a lot of effort is likely to have to be expended in the learning phase of the machine-learning process in relation to scenarios of marginal importance at the edge of the state space, which scenarios may contribute little to the overall risk numbers.

Encouragement is taken from the recent work of Antonov et al. [2020] which addresses the problem of how to handle the outer limits of the phase space in a machine-learned representation of a pricing algorithm, effectively by substituting in an asymptotic representation of the pricing algorithm, assuming such is available, for points outside a core region of the phase space which is sampled fairly exhaustively in the learning process.

The authors show how such asymptotic representations of the pricing function can be used effectively as a control variate for the learning process: rather than trying to learn the pricing algorithm itself, the learning process targets the difference between the exact pricing function and its asymptotic representation.

It is recognised by the team in the bank that, rather than seeing machine learning as an alternative to the use of analytic/asymptotic formulae to achieve speed-up of computational times, it would be potentially fruitful to view them as complementary partners. In particular, since some of the most challenging problems of implementing the machine learning strategy for real portfolios arise in addressing hybrid multi-asset derivatives whose value depends on market data including rates curves, possessed of many degrees of freedom, as well as just spot values, some of the formulae presented in the current book and the strategies used to obtain them could prove a useful adjoint to brute-force application of machine learning techniques.

2.8 INCORPORATING INTEREST RATE SKEW AND SMILE

Having successfully integrated analytic pricing functionality for Black–Karasinski rates modelling into the pricing library, in particular analytic formulae for cap, floor and swaption pricing, the hybrid derivatives traders are interested in whether it is possible also to incorporate interest rate skew and smile into analytic pricing formulae for rates options. They find that there are, unfortunately, no formulae in the book which address this problem, so they contact the author to ask if this is something that could be done. He informs them that, while this is difficult for the Black–Karasinski model, he has plans to extend the Hull–White model in precisely this way and hopes to publish analytic option pricing formulae in due course.[1]

[1]But if they are interested in expediting the calculation, he could consider offering consultancy services to that end.

CHAPTER 3

The Mathematical Foundations

3.1 THE PRICING EQUATION

We will be interested in this book in pricing derivatives of a semi-exotic nature using analytic formulae. We suppose that the derivative contract has a value at some time $t \geq 0$, with 0 the present time, dependent on the value of a number of risk factors $(x_{1t}, x_{2t}, \ldots, x_{nt}) =: \boldsymbol{x}_t$, stochastic processes which capture the fluctuation of market variables. We write the (stochastic) value of the derivative contingent on $\boldsymbol{x}_t = \boldsymbol{x}$ symbolically as $f(\boldsymbol{x}, t)$. In general we shall adopt the convention of representing stochastic processes as indexed with time as a subscript. Deterministic functions of time will be denoted in the standard way with time as an argument. The present value, or PV, of the derivative will be $f(0, 0)$, i.e. it is a deterministic function, the parameters on which the price depends being those specified in the derivative contract and through current market data, gleaned from available price or other observable data used for model calibration.

All pricing will be in what we will refer to as the domestic currency with instantaneous interest rate $r_{dt} = r_d(\boldsymbol{x}_t, t)$. For simplicity we shall usually ignore spreads associated with different LIBOR tenors, although we will relax this assumption in Chapter 14, showing there how stochastic spreads can be incorporated, if wished, into the framework. There will on occasion be payments made in (or market variables referenced in terms of) another currency which we shall refer to as the foreign currency, with instantaneous interest rate $r_{ft} = r_f(\boldsymbol{x}_t, t)$. Where payments are contingent on default or survival of a named issuer of debt or credit, we shall represent the default risk using a reduced-form model whereby the instantaneous default rate is given by $\lambda_t = \lambda(\boldsymbol{x}_t, t)$. We will not consider here cases involving more than one named credit.[1]

In the main we will assume all processes to be of the Itô type, writing symbolically

$$d\boldsymbol{x}_t = \boldsymbol{\mu}(\boldsymbol{x}_t, t)dt + \boldsymbol{\sigma}(t)d\boldsymbol{W}_t. \tag{3.1}$$

[1]This is because, where cash flows are potentially impacted by more than one credit issuer, the correlation between default events becomes important to consider. To that end a copula linking the default times is usually specified. The inclusion of such a copula unfortunately prevents the type of analysis we shall pursue throughout this book from being performed.

Here $\boldsymbol{\mu} : \mathbb{R}^n \times \mathbb{R}^+ \to \mathbb{R}^n$ is an L^1-integrable vector-valued function representing the drift; $\boldsymbol{\sigma} : \mathbb{R}^+ \to \mathbb{R}^n \times \mathbb{R}^n$ is an L^2-integrable matrix-valued function (typically of full rank) representing the diffusion; and $\mathbf{W}_t = (W_t^1, \ldots, W_t^n)^T$ is a vector of independent Wiener processes (Brownian motion) under the equivalent martingale measure $\mathbb{Q}$. It may be considered that this specification, constraining us as it does to normally distributed risk factors, is unduly restrictive. However, we shall allow market variables to be deterministic functions of the risk factors, typically linear or exponential functions, allowing in particular the representation of lognormally distributed market variables. We shall consider one important exception to the specification (3.1), in that we will on occasions allow jumps of a predetermined relative magnitude to occur in relation to one or other process contingent on a credit default event.[2]

We shall also usually assume that $\boldsymbol{\mu}(\boldsymbol{x}_t, t)$ is an affine function of the state variables x_{it}. But for the moment we shall keep the more general form. The fair value at time $t \geq 0$ of a contingent payment $P(\boldsymbol{x}_T)$ at some time $T > t$ is then given by

$$f_0(\boldsymbol{x}_t, t) = E\left[e^{-\int_t^T r_d(x_u, u)du} P(\boldsymbol{x}_T) \middle| \mathcal{F}_t \right], \tag{3.2}$$

where $\mathcal{F}_t$ is the filtration associated with $\boldsymbol{x}_t$. Suppose further that a default event occurs at a stopping time τ driven by a credit default intensity $\lambda(\boldsymbol{x}_t, t)$ and denote the filtration associated with the default process $\mathcal{H}_t$, assumed independent of $\mathcal{F}_t$. If the previously considered payment is also contingent on no default having occurred, its fair value will be instead

$$\begin{aligned} f(\boldsymbol{x}_t, t) &= E\left[e^{-\int_t^T r_d(x_u, u)du} \mathbb{1}_{\tau > T} P(\boldsymbol{x}_T) \middle| \mathcal{F}_t \vee \mathcal{H}_t \right], \\ &= \mathbb{1}_{\tau > t} E\left[e^{-\int_t^T (r_d(x_u, u) + \lambda(x_u, u))du} P(\boldsymbol{x}_T) \middle| \mathcal{F}_t \right]. \end{aligned} \tag{3.3}$$

See for example Ehlers and Schönbucher [2004] for a more detailed discussion.

It is well known (see for example Chapter 9.4 of Pascucci, 2011) that, under mild assumptions, $f(\cdot)$ as given by (3.3) satisfies the following Kolmogorov backward equation

$$\left(\frac{\partial}{\partial t} + \mathcal{L}(t) + \mathcal{V}(t) \right) f(\boldsymbol{x}, t) = 0; \qquad f(\boldsymbol{x}, T) = P(\boldsymbol{x}), \tag{3.4}$$

where

$$\begin{aligned} \mathcal{L}(t) &= \frac{1}{2} \sum_{i=1}^n \sum_{j=1}^n \left\{ \boldsymbol{\sigma}(t) \boldsymbol{\sigma}^T(t) \right\}_{ij} \frac{\partial^2}{\partial x_i \partial x_j} \\ &= \frac{1}{2} \sum_{i=1}^n \sum_{j=1}^n \sum_{k=1}^n \sigma_{ik}(t) \sigma_{jk}(t) \frac{\partial^2}{\partial x_i \partial x_j}, \end{aligned} \tag{3.5}$$

$$\mathcal{V}(t) = \sum_{i=1}^n \mu_i(\boldsymbol{x}, t) \frac{\partial}{\partial x_i} - r_d(\boldsymbol{x}, t) - \lambda(\boldsymbol{x}, t), \tag{3.6}$$

and $\sigma_{ij}(t)$ and $\mu_i(\boldsymbol{x}, t)$ are the component functions of $\boldsymbol{\sigma}(t)$ and $\boldsymbol{\mu}(\boldsymbol{x}, t)$, respectively.

---

[2] As we shall see, the impact of this in the pricing equation is to require a compensating affine drift, which can be incorporated into $\boldsymbol{\mu}(\boldsymbol{x}, t)$. The impact of the jump itself will only be on the payoff at default, which effect will be addressed in more detail later.

Notational Convention We shall throughout make use of calligraphic script representation such as $\mathcal{L}(t)$ to represent linear operators. These will involve functions of the state variables and of time, which functions are coefficients of derivatives w.r.t the state variables. The dependence on the time variable controlling the evolution we shall always make explicit, but the dependence on state variables in the operator representation will always be implicit. The general form for a linear operator will be

$$\mathcal{L}(t) \equiv \sum_{i_1=0} \cdots \sum_{i_N=0} f_{i_1 \ldots i_N}(x,t) \frac{\partial^{i_1+\ldots+i_N}}{\partial x_i^{i_1} \ldots x_N^{i_N}},$$

where in most cases the order $i_1 + \cdots + i_N$ of the derivative will not exceed 2, at least in the defining equation, although it may in the process of deriving solutions be allowed to approach infinity.

We mention that, where a linear operator arises directly in the context of a pricing equation, it will almost always be the case that the relevant function $f_{i_1 \ldots i_N}(x,t)$ is separable in respect of the time dependence. This means that we can think of $\mathcal{L}(t) + \mathcal{V}(t)$ as a linear sum of time-independent linear operators multiplied by time-dependent coefficients. However, other linear operators which arise in the manipulations required to solve the said pricing equation may turn out not to be separable in this way.

The evolution equation analogous to (3.4) in the absence of credit risk is of course obtained simply by letting $\lambda(\cdot,\cdot) \to 0$ in (3.6). Since one of the market drivers x_i will typically be associated with the credit default intensity, the sum in (3.5) will in the risk-free case usually only involve $n-1$ risk factors. The corresponding result for the risk-free derivative price $f_0(x,t)$ is thus straightforwardly obtained by analogy.

We look now at strategies and methodologies for solving (3.4). Key to our investigations will be the concept of a pricing kernel.

3.2 PRICING KERNELS

3.2.1 What Is a Kernel?

A kernel is a ubiquitous concept in mathematics which goes by a number of names, depending on the context in which it is applied and the purpose to which it is put. For our purposes we can think of it as a general solution to an equation of evolution such as (3.4) such that the particular solution associated with some given final condition is given by taking a convolution-style integral of the kernel over the function $P(\xi)$ determining the final state of the evolved property. The kernel or *integral kernel* is thus a function of the form $G(x,t;\xi,T)$, $t \leq T$, such that

$$f(x,t) = \int_{\mathbb{R}^n} G(x,t;\xi,T)P(\xi)d\xi. \tag{3.7}$$

The function $G(\cdot)$ with this property is also commonly referred to as a *Green's function*. Let us make this more concrete with an example.

Example 3.1 ***(Mean-reverting Evolution):*** *Consider the following simple problem*

$$\left(\frac{\partial}{\partial t} + (\theta(t) - \alpha(t)x)\frac{\partial}{\partial x}\right) f(x,t) = 0; \qquad f(x,T) = P(x). \tag{3.8}$$

Use of the substitution $y = \phi_\alpha(t,T)x$ *with* $\phi_\alpha(t,T) := e^{-\int_t^T \alpha(u)du}$ *reduces the original problem to*

$$\left(\frac{\partial}{\partial t} + \theta(t)\frac{\partial}{\partial y}\right) g(y,t) = 0; \qquad g(y,T) = P(y), \tag{3.9}$$

with $f(x,t) \equiv g(\phi_\alpha(t,T)x, t)$. *Further substitution of* $z = y + w_\theta(t,T)$ *with* $w_\theta(t,T) := \int_t^T \theta(u)du$ *results in*

$$\frac{\partial}{\partial t} h(z,t) = 0; \qquad h(z,T) = P(z), \tag{3.10}$$

with $g(y,t) \equiv h(y + w_\theta(t,T), t)$. *This equation has a self-evident solution*

$$h(z,t) = P(z).$$

Thus, the solution to our original problem is

$$f(x,t) = P(\phi_\alpha(t,T)x + w_\theta(t,T)).$$

The (integral) kernel for (3.8) *is a function of the form* $G(x,t;\xi,T)$ *such that*

$$f(x,t) = \int_{\mathbb{R}} G(x,t;\xi,T)P(\xi)d\xi.$$

Clearly by inspection we must choose

$$G(x,t;\xi,T) = \delta(\phi_\alpha(t,T)x + w_\theta(t,T) - \xi),$$

where $\delta(\cdot)$ *is the Dirac delta function.*

Essentially $G(\boldsymbol{x},t;\boldsymbol{\xi},T)$ can be thought of as a weight function specifying the degree of influence which the value of the terminal function at time T associated with a state $\boldsymbol{\xi}$ has on $f(\boldsymbol{x},t)$. The linearity of the governing equation means that the solution is constructed as a weighted sum of all contributions from all possible $\boldsymbol{\xi}$. For this reason $G(\boldsymbol{x},t;\boldsymbol{\xi},T)$ is also often referred to as a *transition density* in relation to the Kolmogorov backward equation (3.4) or the system of stochastic differential equations (3.1) from which it derives. Clearly, in the above example the relationship is very simple: in the absence of diffusion, the density function is singular and the value of $f(x,t)$ is completely determined by the value of $P(\cdot)$ associated with a terminal value of $\xi = \phi_\alpha(t,T)x + w_\theta(t,T)$.

Example 3.2 *(Heat Kernel): Consider next the simplification which occurs when $\mathcal{V}(x,t) = 0$ in (3.4). This problem is known to have a trivial Green's function solution, the well-known heat kernel. This is basically a (multivariate) Gaussian density function, expressible as*

$$G_0(x,t;\xi,T) = \frac{e^{-\frac{1}{2}(\xi - x)^T \Sigma^{-1}(t,T)(\xi - x)}}{\sqrt{(2\pi)^n\ |\Sigma(t,T)|}}, \tag{3.11}$$

with

$$\Sigma(t,T) = \int_t^T \sigma(u)\sigma^T(u)du. \tag{3.12}$$

In the one-dimensional case, this reduces to

$$\begin{aligned} G_0(x,t;\xi,T) &= \frac{1}{\sigma} N\left(\frac{x - \xi}{\sigma}\right), \\ N(x) &= \frac{1}{\sqrt{2\pi}} e^{-\frac{x^2}{2}}. \end{aligned} \tag{3.13}$$

We will make frequent use of these expressions in the remainder of this book, our main task being to consider the impact of the additional term $\mathcal{V}(t)$ for various choices.

3.2.2 Kernels in Financial Engineering

The situation we are interested in is where $f(x,t)$ represents the time-t price of a derivative given by (3.2) or (3.3) and satisfies a pricing equation in the form of (3.4). In this case we will refer to the associated Green's function or integral kernel $G(x,t;\xi,T)$ as a *pricing kernel*. This is slightly different from the typical usage of this term in financial engineering, where the relevant "kernel" considered is that associated with the expectation (3.3) rather than the integral (3.7). Frequently also the measure considered for the expectation is the real-world measure $\mathbb{P}$ rather than the risk-neutral measure $\mathbb{Q}$. Specifically the kernel definition would in this understanding be the $K(x,t;\xi,T)$ satisfying the condition that

$$\begin{aligned} f(x_t,t) &= E^{\mathbb{P}}[K(x_t,t;x_T,T)P(x_T)|\mathcal{F}_t], \\ &= \int K(x_t,t;x_T,T)P(x_T)d\mathbb{P}, \\ &= \int_{\mathbb{R}^n} K(x_t,t;\xi,T)\frac{\partial \mathbb{P}}{\partial \xi}P(\xi)d\xi, \end{aligned} \tag{3.14}$$

for a terminal payoff $P(x_T)$ at T. Comparing now (3.14) with (3.7), we see the two notions of kernels are related through

$$G(x,t;\xi,T) = K(x,t;\xi,T)\frac{\partial \mathbb{P}}{\partial \xi}; \tag{3.15}$$

i.e. effectively a change of co-ordinates. Given that we shall not in the context of the present work give explicit consideration to the real-world measure $\mathbb{P}$, we shall not either look to use (3.15) to produce $K(\cdot)$ explicitly and shall instead simply use the integral kernel $G(\cdot)$ as an equivalent representation.

We note that the concept of a pricing kernel is also commonly denoted in practice as an *Arrow–Debreu* state price or as the price of an Arrow–Debreu security. Again there is ambiguity around the state co-ordinates relative to which this is defined. To avoid such ambiguity, we shall consider Arrow–Debreu prices like pricing kernels to be synonymous with our integral kernel $G(\cdot)$.

3.2.3 Why Use Pricing Kernels?

Our intention in this book is to provide a methodology for pricing credit-rates (and other) hybrid derivatives analytically, either exactly where possible or as an efficient and accurate approximation based on perturbation theory. The main focus of our work will be to produce formulae for standard derivative products under suitably realistic modelling assumptions. At the same time, a key part of our effort will be to do this in such a way as to facilitate extension of the calculations to address a wider range of products incorporating:

- alternative payoff profiles, associated either with contractual payment dates or contingent on default events;
- additional market underlyings on which the payoffs might depend.

We would also like the flexibility to incorporate additional risk factors into the model if needed.

To achieve this end, we will have to depart from the approach generally taken in much of the financial engineering literature hitherto in deriving and presenting analytic pricing formulae. Specifically we will adopt three key strategies:

- We will seek to derive pricing kernels from which pricing formulae for multiple diverse payoffs can be derived, rather than seeking to derive these formulae directly on a case-by-case basis.
- We will look to provide a systematic approach to deriving such pricing kernels from pricing equations across as wide as possible a range of modelling approaches.
- We will look to identify a mechanism through which the assumptions involved in deriving a pricing kernel can be loosened, new risk factors or market underlyings added and/or, when two or more component pricing models are combined in a hybrid model, a hybrid pricing kernel can be formulated conveniently out of the (known) pricing kernels for the component models.

In this regard, we follow in the footsteps of Lorig et al. [2017] (see also references therein) in their work deriving implied volatility approximations for options on spot underlyings under diverse local stochastic volatility modelling assumptions. We hope to attain in this way maximum reuse of results obtained, both within the context of this book and in further use which is made of the methodology beyond the limited realm of what is presented here. We shall elaborate on the pursuit of these three strategies in a general framework in the present chapter before applying the proposed approach in subsequent chapters to the more specific task of obtaining derivatives pricing formulae and other important results of practical importance.

The reader is advised at this stage that the remainder of the chapter may at first encounter make for quite heavy reading, particularly if the reader is not familiar with evolution operator formalism. However, once a degree of mastery has been achieved over the ideas here presented, the remainder of the book can be seen in the main as simply illustrating the application of these ideas to a multiplicity of problems of varying degrees of complexity.

3.3 EVOLUTION OPERATORS

Closely related to the idea of an integral kernel is that of an *evolution operator*. In the classical perturbation theory for linear operators (see for example Kato [1995]), it is noted that, subject to certain technical conditions, a (time-independent) linear operator $\mathcal{L}$ gives rise to a semigroup of bounded linear evolution operators of the form $\mathcal{U}(\tau) = e^{\tau\mathcal{L}}$, where $\tau := T - t$ and we define the exponential of an operator by

$$e^{\tau\mathcal{L}} := I + \sum_{n=1}^{\infty} \frac{\tau^n}{n!}\mathcal{L}^n, \tag{3.16}$$

with I the identity operator. This evolution operator has the convenient property that $f(x,t) := \mathcal{U}(T-t)P(x)$ is formally a solution to the following Cauchy problem

$$\left(\frac{\partial}{\partial t} + \mathcal{L}\right) f(x,t) = 0; \qquad f(x,T) = P(x). \tag{3.17}$$

This fact can be seen by observing from differentiation of (3.16) that that $\mathcal{U}(\tau)$ satisfies the following operator equation[3]

$$\left(\frac{\partial}{\partial t} + \mathcal{L}\right) \mathcal{U}(T-t) = 0; \qquad \mathcal{U}(0) = I. \tag{3.18}$$

In such circumstances we refer to $\mathcal{L}$ as the (parabolic) generator of the operator $\mathcal{U}(\tau)$. We say it is "formally" a solution because we need to be able to interpret the application of the exponentiated operator to $P(\cdot)$, which may not be a trivial matter. Here the concept of an integral kernel comes in useful. If we can obtain a suitable kernel expression for $\mathcal{U}(\tau)$, we can use it in (3.7) to obtain a solution for (3.17). It turns out that it is often possible to make good progress in this way.

[3]Consideration of whether an evolution operator satisfies a given equation or not requires prior specification of the space of functions on which the operator is permitted to act, which space will depend on the definition of both $\mathcal{L}$ and $P(\cdot)$. We shall in general avoid consideration of such matters, assuming that the cases we are considering will in practice have well-enough behaved solutions.

3.3.1 Time-Ordered Exponential

Although our focus in the above has been on the case of time-independent operators, this was not because our real interest lies there, but rather because of the incidental complexity which time dependence brings. We observe that even the simple examples 3.1 and 3.2 considered above involved time-dependent operators $\mathcal{L}(t)$. The most immediately pressing issue is that the obvious extension to (3.16); namely, defining

$$\mathcal{U}(t,T) = e^{\int_t^T \mathcal{L}(u)du} = I + \sum_{n=1}^{\infty} \frac{\left(\int_t^T \mathcal{L}(u)du\right)^n}{n!}, \tag{3.19}$$

does not in general provide a solution to (3.17) with $\mathcal{L} \equiv \mathcal{L}(t)$. The reason for this is that operators do not in general commute under composition in the way that functions do under multiplication; specifically, we cannot in general assume that $\mathcal{L}\mathcal{V} = \mathcal{V}\mathcal{L}$ or indeed that $\mathcal{U}(t_1,T)\mathcal{U}(t_2,T) = \mathcal{U}(t_2,T)\mathcal{U}(t_1,T)$. The way to work around this problem is to work not with the exponential function but its generalisation to operators as a Neumann expansion, which we denote $\mathcal{E}_t^T(\mathcal{L}(\cdot))$ and define as follows.

Definition 3.1 *The* time-ordered exponential *or* Dyson series *defined for a linear operator $\mathcal{L}(t)$ by*

$$\begin{aligned}
\mathcal{E}_t^T(\mathcal{L}(\cdot)) &= I + \sum_{n=1}^{\infty} \int_{t \le t_1 \le \dots \le t_n \le T} \mathcal{L}(t_1)\dots\mathcal{L}(t_n)dt_1\dots dt_n, \\
&= I + \sum_{n=1}^{\infty} \int_t^T \int_{t_1}^T \cdots \int_{t_{n-1}}^T \mathcal{L}(t_1)\mathcal{L}(t_2)\dots\mathcal{L}(t_n)dt_n\dots dt_2 dt_1, \\
&= I + \sum_{n=1}^{\infty} \int_t^T \int_t^{t_n} \cdots \int_t^{t_2} \mathcal{L}(t_1)\mathcal{L}(t_2)\dots\mathcal{L}(t_n)dt_1 dt_2\dots dt_n,
\end{aligned} \tag{3.20}$$

generalises the exponentiation of the integral of a function $f(t)$ to the case of a time-dependent linear operator $\mathcal{L}(t)$.

Notes:

1. The third line of (3.20) follows naturally from the second by application of Fubini's theorem.
2. The time-ordered exponential is usually defined with the integrals expressed over $[0, t_i]$, rather than over $[t_i, T]$ as here. Our formulation can conveniently be transformed into the standard one by a change of variable $t \to \tau = T - t$.

It is a straightforward matter to check, defining $\mathcal{U}(t,T) = \mathcal{E}_t^T(\mathcal{L}(\cdot))$ and differentiating (3.20) w.r.t. t, that it satisfies for $t \le T$ the following operator equation

$$\left(\frac{\partial}{\partial t} + \mathcal{L}(t)\right)\mathcal{U}(t,T) = 0; \qquad \mathcal{U}(T,T) = I, \tag{3.21}$$

and by that token is the natural generalisation of (3.16) to the case of a time-dependent operator. The solution to (3.17) in the more general case when $\mathcal{L} \equiv \mathcal{L}(t)$ is then given by $f(x, t) = \mathcal{U}(t, T)P(x)$.

Of course, it is a lot more convenient to deal with standard exponentials than with the time-ordered variety. It is therefore important to know under what circumstances we are entitled to replace the latter with the former. The answer is obtained by consideration of the important Magnus expansion, which shows how a time-ordered exponential can be re-written as a standard exponential.

3.3.2 Magnus Expansion

The problem of re-expressing a time-ordered exponential of the form (3.20) in the more convenient form

$$\mathcal{E}_t^T(\mathcal{L}(\cdot)) = e^{\Omega(t,T)}, \tag{3.22}$$

for some linear operator $\Omega(t, T)$ was first addressed by Magnus [1954]. ($\Omega(t, T)$ is effectively the logarithm of the time-ordered exponential.) Magnus found that $\Omega(t, T)$ can be expanded in powers of $\mathcal{L}(\cdot)$, whence we can write

$$\Omega(t, T) = \sum_{i=1}^{\infty} \Omega_i(t, T). \tag{3.23}$$

To state his result for the dependence of the $\Omega_i(t, T)$ on $\mathcal{L}(t)$ we need to introduce the concept of the commutatator of two operators.

Definition 3.2 *We define the* commutator *of an operator $\mathcal{L}(t)$ with an operator $\mathcal{V}(t)$ where both operators act on the same function space by the following operator*

$$\mathrm{ad}_{\mathcal{L}(t_1)}(\mathcal{V}(t_2)) := \mathcal{L}(t_1)\mathcal{V}(t_2) - \mathcal{V}(t_2)\mathcal{L}(t_1). \tag{3.24}$$

This expression is often, particularly in the context of quantum mechanics, written using the more symmetric notation $[\mathcal{L}(t_1), \mathcal{V}(t_2)]$. We prefer the so-called adjoint notation, emphasising as it does the privileged role of $\mathcal{L}(t_1)$ as an operator with $\mathcal{V}(t_2)$ as an operand. This will be a recurring theme in the analysis below.

The first two terms in the Magnus series are in our notation found to be

$$\begin{aligned}\Omega_1(t, T) &= \int_t^T \mathcal{L}(u)du, \\ \Omega_2(t, T) &= \frac{1}{2}\int_t^T \mathrm{ad}_{\Omega_1(u,T)}(\mathcal{L}(u))du.\end{aligned} \tag{3.25}$$

For an up-to-date survey with extensive references, the reader is referred to Arnal et al. [2018], who provide a useful explicit formula for $\Omega_i(t, T)$, valid for any i. Higher terms in the series can all be expressed as iterations on $\Omega_2(t, T)$. We infer that $\Omega_2(t, T)$, and consequently all higher-order terms, will be zero if and only if the condition $[\mathcal{L}(u), \mathcal{L}(t)] = 0$ for $t, u \in [0, T]$. In summary we have

Proposition 3.3.1 The condition

$$[\mathcal{L}(u), \mathcal{L}(t)] = 0 \qquad \forall t, u \in [0, T] \tag{3.26}$$

is a necessary and sufficient condition for us to make the simplification

$$\mathcal{E}_t^T(\mathcal{L}(\cdot)) \to e^{\int_t^T \mathcal{L}(u)du} \quad \text{for} \quad t \in [0, T]. \tag{3.27}$$

We will make frequent use of this simplification subsequently. We note in passing that one of the simplest and commonest ways in which condition (3.26) can be satisfied is if $\mathcal{L}(t)$ is separable into a product of a time-dependent function and a time-independent operator, as we have indicated will often be the case; however, a linear sum of two such operators will *not* in general satisfy the condition unless the time-independent operators themselves commute.

3.4 OBTAINING THE PRICING KERNEL

Our approach to solving (3.4) will be to exploit the fact that, for the case $\mathcal{V}(t) = 0$, the formal evolution operator has solution (3.11). $\mathcal{V}(t)$ can then be treated as a perturbation on $\mathcal{L}(t)$ and perturbation theory used to determine how it impacts on the known solution. Our approach is akin to but differs in terms of methodology from that of Lorig et al. [2017] who sought to build a perturbation expansion for the pricing kernel starting with the heat kernel (3.11) as an initial approximation. This is quite different from the approach taken by Fouque et al. [2000, 2011] and most other authors who sought to obtain analytic pricing formulae by using the heat kernel as an approximate representation of the pricing kernel, then correcting the pricing formula iteratively, effectively as a Dyson expansion (see below); under this approach no pricing kernel is produced.

The approach we take was first expounded in a financial engineering context by Hagan et al. [2015] in the process of deriving their renowned asymptotic formula for option pricing under the SABR model.[4] They obtained a formal operator-based solution by direct integration of the operator equation (3.4) and applying perturbation theory to this, rather than to its kernel.[5] We find in this way the perturbation that needs to be applied to the known heat kernel solution to convert it into a solution to the full (perturbed) problem, in other words, to give us the pricing kernel we seek. If the pricing kernel obtained can be written $G(x, t; \xi, T)$, the solution to the initial value

[4]The paper was actually written and made available as a pre-print ten years before it was formally published.

[5]As has been pointed out by Gulisashvili et al. [2016], the SABR expansion of Hagan et al. [2015] is flawed insofar as it omits an additional term representing absorption at zero of the evolving pricing function. This shortcoming is a consequence of the fact that the SABR volatility is not lognormal but proportional to a power $\beta < 1$ of the diffused variable. The issue consequently does not arise in any of the contexts we shall address below.

problem (3.4) is given by (3.7). If payments at default are involved in the derivative contract, this can also be handled with a little extra work using the same pricing kernel (see §8.1.4 in Chapter 8).

We now present the key results which we shall use to achieve this. Most of what follows is not new, certainly not in a general mathematical context, nor indeed in a financial engineering context. However, insofar as results have been presented in the latter context, this tends to have been with the evolution operators assumed time-independent. The generalisation to time-dependent evolution operators was set out in a financial engineering by Lorig et al. [2017].

3.4.1 Duhamel–Dyson Expansion Formula

We start by noting that use of Duhamel's principle allows us to infer (Lorig et al., 2017) that the evolution operator providing a formal solution to our pricing equation (3.4) can be expressed using our time-ordered exponential terminology (3.20) as

$$\mathcal{E}_t^T(\mathcal{L}(\cdot)+\mathcal{V}(\cdot)) = \mathcal{E}_t^T(\mathcal{L}(\cdot)) + \int_t^T \mathcal{E}_t^{t_1}(\mathcal{L}(\cdot))\mathcal{V}(t_1)\mathcal{E}_{t_1}^T(\mathcal{L}(\cdot)+\mathcal{V}(\cdot))dt_1. \tag{3.28}$$

A Dyson expansion for this solution is obtained by replacing $\mathcal{L}(\cdot)+\mathcal{V}(\cdot)$ with $\mathcal{L}(\cdot)$ on the r.h.s. to obtain a first-order approximation for $\mathcal{E}_t^T(\mathcal{L}(\cdot)+\mathcal{V}(\cdot))$. This approximation can then be back-substituted for $\mathcal{E}_{t_1}^T(\mathcal{L}(\cdot)+\mathcal{V}(\cdot))$ on the r.h.s. of (3.28) to obtain a second-order approximation and so on recursively to yield the Duhamel–Dyson expansion formula

$$\begin{aligned}\mathcal{E}_t^T(\mathcal{L}(\cdot)+\mathcal{V}(\cdot)) &= \mathcal{E}_t^T(\mathcal{L}(\cdot)) + \int_t^T \mathcal{E}_t^{t_1}(\mathcal{L}(\cdot))\mathcal{V}(t_1)\mathcal{E}_{t_1}^T(\mathcal{L}(\cdot))dt_1,\\ &+ \int_t^T\int_{t_1}^T \mathcal{E}_t^{t_1}(\mathcal{L}(\cdot))\mathcal{V}(t_1)\mathcal{E}_{t_1}^{t_2}(\mathcal{L}(\cdot))\mathcal{V}(t_2)\mathcal{E}_{t_2}^T(\mathcal{L}(\cdot))dt_2dt_1 + \dots.\end{aligned} \tag{3.29}$$

This formula was used successfully by Lorig et al. [2017] to obtain approximate expressions for vanilla equity option prices for a number of local-stochastic volatility models and implicitly by Horvath et al. [2017] to derive approximate caplet prices for a family of short-rate models including that of Black and Karasinski [1991]. Here we will not use the Duhamel–Dyson formula directly but instead follow Grishchenko et al. [2014] in applying to it the celebrated Baker–Campbell–Hausdorff expansion formula to obtain a more powerful result.

3.4.2 Baker–Campbell–Hausdorff Expansion Formula

Theorem 3.1 *(Baker–Campbell–Hausdorff): For uniformly bounded L^1 linear operators $\mathcal{L}(t)$ and $\mathcal{V}(t)$ acting on a suitably restricted function space and a suitable operator norm, the following result holds for $t_1, t_2 \in [0, T]$*

$$\mathcal{E}_{t_1}^{t_2}(\mathcal{L}(\cdot))\mathcal{V}(t_2) \sim \mathcal{E}_{t_1}^{t_2}(ad_{\mathcal{L}(\cdot)})(\mathcal{V}(t_2))\mathcal{E}_{t_1}^{t_2}(\mathcal{L}(\cdot)). \tag{3.30}$$

Observe that, combining Definitions 3.1 and 3.2, we can write more concretely

$$\mathcal{E}_t^u(\mathrm{ad}_{\mathcal{L}(\cdot)})(\mathcal{V}(u)) = \mathcal{V}(u) + \int_t^u \mathrm{ad}_{\mathcal{L}(t_1)}(\mathcal{V}(u))dt_1 + \int_t^u\int_{t_1}^u \mathrm{ad}_{\mathcal{L}(t_1)}(\mathrm{ad}_{\mathcal{L}(t_2)}(\mathcal{V}(u)))dt_2 dt_1 + \dots. \tag{3.31}$$

The result (3.30) can be applied successively to each term in (3.29) to drive all the $\mathcal{E}_{u_1}^{u_2}(\mathcal{L}(\cdot))$ terms, proceeding from right to left, over to the r.h.s. of the respective integrals. We obtain in this way

$$\mathcal{E}_t^T(\mathcal{L}(\cdot) + \mathcal{V}(\cdot)) = \left(I + \int_t^T \mathcal{E}_t^{u_1}(\mathrm{ad}_{\mathcal{L}(\cdot)})(\mathcal{V}(u_1))du_1, \right.$$
$$\left. + \int_t^T\int_{u_1}^T \mathcal{E}_t^{u_1}(\mathrm{ad}_{\mathcal{L}(\cdot)})(\mathcal{V}(u_1))\mathcal{E}_t^{u_2}(\mathrm{ad}_{\mathcal{L}(\cdot)})(\mathcal{V}(u_2))du_2 du_1 + \dots \right)\mathcal{E}_t^T(\mathcal{L}(\cdot). \tag{3.32}$$

This result was applied by Grishchenko et al. [2014] to deduce vanilla option prices for a λ-SABR stochastic volatility model and by Turfus [2019] to derive an exact pricing kernel for the short-rate model of Hull and White [1990]. Note that the term in brackets is precisely in the form of a time-ordered exponential, a fact we shall make use of below.

We are now in a position to state formally our fundamental result which we shall use in subsequent chapters to derive exact or approximate pricing kernels for multiple models and so to obtain option prices for a wide range of hybrid derivative products. Note: we make mention of Lie algebras and Banach spaces in the statement of the theorem and the subsequent proof, as these concepts are helpful in stating the formal conditions under which the infinite sums which appear in the formula are guaranteed to converge. However, an understanding of the significance of these concepts is not vital to understanding either the result or the essence of the proof of its validity.

3.4.3 Exponential Expansion Formula

Theorem 3.2 ***(Exponential Expansion Formula):*** *Suppose that the initial-boundary value problem*

$$\left(\frac{\partial}{\partial t} + \mathcal{L}(t) + \mathcal{V}(t)\right) g(y,t) = 0,$$
$$g(y,T) = f(y), \tag{3.33}$$
$$g(y,t) \to 0 \quad as \quad \| y \| \to \infty, \quad t > 0$$

is known to have a unique C^∞ solution $g : \mathbb{R}^n \times [0,T] \to \mathbb{R}$ for linear operators $\mathcal{L}(t)$ and $\mathcal{V}(t)$ depending continuously on the parameters t and T and some L^1 function $f : \mathbb{R}^n \to \mathbb{R}$. Denote by $\mathfrak{g}$ the (possibly infinite-dimensional) Lie algebra generated by operation of Lie generators $\mathcal{L}(t)$ and $\mathcal{V}(t)$ with Lie bracket $[\mathcal{L}(t_1), \mathcal{V}(t_2)] = ad_{\mathcal{L}(t_1)}(\mathcal{V}(t_2))$ on the vector space span$\{g\}$ taken over the field $\mathbb{R}$. Denote by $\mathfrak{g}_M$ the corresponding Lie algebra resulting when the domain of $f(\cdot)$ is restricted to $[-M,M]^n$. Suppose further *that this Lie algebra is a Banach space under some suitable norm with reference to which $\mathcal{L}(t)$ and $\mathcal{V}(t)$ are uniformly bounded over $\mathfrak{g}_M$ for $t \in [0, T]$. Then:*

1. *There exists a linear evolution operator $\mathcal{U}(t, T)$ acting on $\mathfrak{g}$ for $t \leq T$, which satisfies the initial value problem*

$$\begin{aligned} \left(\frac{\partial}{\partial t} + \mathcal{L}(t) + \mathcal{V}(t)\right) \mathcal{U}(t, T) &= 0, \\ \mathcal{U}(T, T) &= I. \end{aligned} \tag{3.34}$$

2. *This operator can be expressed as*

$$\mathcal{U}(t, T) = \mathcal{E}_t^T(\mathcal{W}(t, \cdot))\mathcal{E}_t^T(\mathcal{L}(\cdot)), \tag{3.35}$$

where

$$\mathcal{W}(t, u) = \mathcal{E}_t^u(ad_{\mathcal{L}(\cdot)})(\mathcal{V}(u)). \tag{3.36}$$

Proof: A stand-alone proof of this result following that provided by Turfus [2019] is provided for completeness in §3.6.1 below.

We make the following observations:

1. In most cases the Lie elements which make up the Lie algebra will be time-separable, i.e. can be written as $\mathcal{L}(t) = f(t)\mathcal{L}$, in which case we can consider $\mathcal{L}$ to be the Lie generator giving rise to all such elements, rather than there being a family of generators for all possible t. But this is not a necessary condition for the applicability of our theorem.
2. Although the technical conditions for validity are quite intricately expressed, they need not concern the reader unduly, as they are unlikely to be an obstacle to usage of the theorem's main result, namely that (3.35) and (3.36) together provide a solution for (3.34).

More formally, we propose

Proposition 3.4.1 It is expected that the required conditions of $\mathcal{L}(t)$ and $\mathcal{V}(t)$ being uniformly bounded on the Lie algebra $\mathfrak{g}_M$ will be satisfied in almost all practical circumstances where the above theorem is applied in a derivatives pricing context.

3.4.4 Exponentials of Derivatives

3.4.4.1 First-order Derivatives It is often the case that use of Theorem 3.2 to derive pricing kernels gives rise to expressions involving exponentials of linear operators. Therefore, we need to be able to make sense of expressions such as

$$\begin{aligned} g(\mathbf{x}, t) &= \exp\left(\sum_{i=0}^{n} a_i(t)\frac{\partial}{\partial x_i}\right) f(\mathbf{x}, t), \\ &= \exp(\mathbf{a}(t).\nabla_{\mathbf{x}})\, f(\mathbf{x}, t). \end{aligned} \tag{3.37}$$

Using Proposition 3.3.1 we can write

$$g(x,t) = \prod_{i=0}^{n} \exp\left(a_i(t)\frac{\partial}{\partial x_i}\right) f(x,t). \tag{3.38}$$

The exponential is defined in this context in terms of its formal power series, whence

$$\begin{aligned} g(x,t) &= \prod_{i=0}^{n}\left(\sum_{r=0}^{\infty}\frac{a_i^r(t)}{r!}\frac{\partial^r}{\partial x_i^r}\right) f(x,t), \\ &= f(x + a(t), t), \end{aligned} \tag{3.39}$$

the last line following from the fact that the operator in brackets gives rise to a Taylor–Maclaurin series and is applied n times, once for each dimension. In other words, the application of an operator which has the form of an exponential of a first-order linear differential operator serves merely to shift the value of x at which the function it operates on is evaluated.

Specifically, (3.11) becomes on transformation

$$\begin{aligned} G(x,t;\xi,T) &= \exp(a(t).\nabla_x)G_0(x,t;\xi,T), \\ &= G_0(x + a(t), t;\xi,T). \end{aligned} \tag{3.40}$$

3.4.4.2 Higher-order Derivatives The corresponding problem for second-order differential operators is less tractable in general, but the task is much simplified if they are operating on a Gaussian kernel. Suppose $\mathcal{L}(t)$ is given by (3.5), the associated kernel for which is Gaussian, given by (3.11). We are interested in computing expressions like

$$\exp\left(\frac{1}{2}\sum_{i=0}^{n}\sum_{j=0}^{n}\Delta\Sigma_{ij}(t,T)\frac{\partial^2}{\partial x_i \partial x_j}\right) G_0(x,t;\xi,T). \tag{3.41}$$

This is most easily handled by considering the evolution operator equation (3.4) where the linear operator $\mathcal{V}(\cdot)$ is such that

$$\int_t^T \mathcal{V}(u)du = \frac{1}{2}\sum_{i=0}^{n}\sum_{j=0}^{n}\Delta\Sigma_{ij}(t,T)\frac{\partial^2}{\partial x_i \partial x_j}. \tag{3.42}$$

We already have that

$$\int_t^T \mathcal{L}(u)du = \frac{1}{2}\sum_{i=0}^{n}\sum_{j=0}^{n}\Sigma_{ij}(t,T)\frac{\partial^2}{\partial x_i \partial x_j},$$

with $\mathbf{\Sigma}(t,T)$ given by (3.12). We conclude on this basis that the solution to the evolution operator equation (3.34) is

$$\mathcal{U}(t,T) = \exp\left(\frac{1}{2}(\Sigma_{ij}(t,T) + \Delta\Sigma_{ij}(t,T))\frac{\partial^2}{\partial x_i \partial x_j}\right),$$

which has integral kernel

$$\begin{aligned} G(x,t;\xi,T) &= \frac{e^{-\frac{1}{2}(\xi-x)^T(\mathbf{\Sigma}(t,T)+\Delta\mathbf{\Sigma}(t,T))^{-1}(\xi-x)}}{\sqrt{(2\pi)^d \det(\mathbf{\Sigma}(t,T)+\Delta\mathbf{\Sigma}(t,T))}} \\ &= N(\xi - x; \mathbf{\Sigma}(t,T) + \Delta\mathbf{\Sigma}(t,T)), \end{aligned}$$

with $N(\cdot;\mathbf{\Sigma})$ a multivariate Gaussian distribution with covariance $\mathbf{\Sigma}$. But trivial application of Theorem 3.2 shows (3.41) to be a solution to the same problem. Equating the two expressions, we conclude

$$\begin{aligned} \exp\left(\frac{1}{2}\sum_{i=0}^{n}\sum_{j=0}^{n}\Delta\Sigma_{ij}(t,T)\frac{\partial^2}{\partial x_i \partial x_j}\right) G_0(x,t;\xi,T) &= \frac{e^{-\frac{1}{2}(\xi-x)^T(\mathbf{\Sigma}(t,T)+\Delta\mathbf{\Sigma}(t,T))^{-1}(\xi-x)}}{\sqrt{(2\pi)^d \det(\mathbf{\Sigma}(t,T)+\Delta\mathbf{\Sigma}(t,T))}} \\ &= N(\xi - x; \mathbf{\Sigma}(t,T) + \Delta\mathbf{\Sigma}(t,T)) \quad (3.43) \end{aligned}$$

We conclude that the impact on the Gaussian kernel of an operator $\mathcal{V}(t)$ satisfying (3.42) is simply to shift the correlation matrix from $\mathbf{\Sigma}(t,T)$ to $\mathbf{\Sigma}(t,T) + \Delta\mathbf{\Sigma}(t,T)$. This is to be compared with the previous result which is that the impact of the exponential of a first-order derivative is to shift the *first* moment of a Gaussian kernel. In what follows, we shall usually make use of (3.43) only implicitly, letting $\mathbf{\Sigma}(t,T) \to \mathbf{\Sigma}(t,T) + \Delta\mathbf{\Sigma}(t,T)$ in the Gaussian kernel from the outset.

Although we shall have little need to consider in what follows operators higher than second order, we mention that higher-order derivatives can be handled by considering their impact not on the pricing kernel but on its Fourier transform. The resulting kernel expressions will in that case be in the form of an inverse transform or convolution integral, which will naturally be less pleasant to work with than the simpler results presented above for the first and second-order cases.

3.4.5 Example – The Black–Scholes Pricing Kernel

We start off with a rather simple example with which the reader is likely to have some familiarity, demonstrating the construction of a pricing kernel for equity options under the Black–Scholes framework. Suppose an equity process S_t is given by

$$\frac{dS_t}{S_t} = (\overline{r}_d(t) - q(t))dt + \sigma_z(t)dW_{1t}, \tag{3.44}$$

with $\bar{r}_d(t)$ and $q(t)$ the (deterministic) interest rate and dividend rate, respectively. Define a new stochastic variable z_t such that

$$S_t = F(t)e^{z_t - \frac{1}{2}\mathrm{var}(z_t)},$$
$$F(t) = S_0 e^{\int_0^t (\bar{r}_d(u) - q(u))du}. \tag{3.45}$$

It follows from Itô's lemma that

$$dz_t = \sigma_z(t)dW_{1t}. \tag{3.46}$$

The pricing equation (3.4) will then have

$$\mathcal{L}(t) = \frac{1}{2}\sigma_z^2(t)\frac{\partial^2}{\partial z^2}$$
$$\mathcal{V}(t) = -\bar{r}_d(t), \tag{3.47}$$

with a trivial formal solution

$$\mathcal{U}(t,T) = e^{\int_t^T (\mathcal{L}(u) + \mathcal{V}(u))du}$$
$$= D_d(t,T)e^{\int_t^T \mathcal{L}(u)du}, \tag{3.48}$$
$$D_d(t,T) = e^{-\int_t^T \bar{r}_d(u)du}. \tag{3.49}$$

The pricing kernel is simply the well-known heat kernel, discounted for interest rates, whence we have

$$G(z,t;\zeta,T) = \frac{D_d(t,T)}{\sqrt{\Sigma_{zz}(t,T)}}N\left(\frac{z-\zeta}{\sqrt{\Sigma_{zz}(t,T)}}\right),$$
$$\Sigma_{zz}(t,T) = \int_t^T \sigma_z^2(u)du, \tag{3.50}$$

where $N(\cdot)$ represents a standard unit normal distribution

$$N(x) = \frac{1}{\sqrt{2\pi}}e^{-x^2/2} \tag{3.51}$$

See Melnikov and Melnikov [2007] for an alternative, more detailed derivation and discussion. It is a straightforward matter to substitute (3.50) into (3.7) with payoff $P(\zeta) = [F(T)e^{\zeta - \frac{1}{2}\Sigma_{zz}(0,T)} - K]^+$ for a call option or $P(\zeta) = [K - F(T)e^{\zeta - \frac{1}{2}\Sigma_{zz}(0,T)}]^+$ for a put to obtain the standard Black–Scholes option pricing formulae [Black and Scholes, 1973] from

$$V(x,t) = \frac{D_d(t,T)}{\sqrt{\Sigma_{zz}(t,T)}}\int_{\mathbb{R}} P(\zeta)N\left(\frac{z-\zeta}{\sqrt{\Sigma_{zz}(t,T)}}\right)d\zeta \tag{3.52}$$

We see that the simplification in the above was possible because the operator $\mathcal{V}(\cdot)$ commuted with $\mathcal{L}(\cdot)$. Our main interest will of course be in circumstances where this is *not* the case, most specifically where the interest rate, and therefore the drift term, is stochastic. If the underlying we are primarily interested in is the interest rate itself, we are led to consider the class of short-rate models. This will be the subject of the next two chapters. Alternatively we can consider the extension of the Black–Scholes model to include stochastic rates, whence it becomes a two-factor model. The extension of our approach to such multi-factor models will be our focus in the remainder of the book.

Before embarking on this project, let us first consider the application of Theorem 3.2 to another more tractable but less trivial problem, namely the impact of mean reversion on a diffusion.

3.4.6 Example – Mean-Reverting Diffusion

We look to infer the impact of mean reversion on a diffusion by finding an integral kernel for (3.4) with

$$\mathcal{L}(t) = \frac{1}{2}\sigma_d^2(t)\frac{\partial^2}{\partial x_d^2}, \tag{3.53}$$

$$\mathcal{V}(t) = -\alpha_d(t)x_d\frac{\partial}{\partial x_d} \tag{3.54}$$

Our strategy will be as always to seek first an evolution operator $\mathcal{U}(t,T)$ satisfying (3.34). The following lemmas will prove useful here and subsequently.

Lemma 3.1 *For $\mathcal{V}(t)$ as defined in* (3.54) *and*

$$\phi_d(t,v) := e^{-\int_t^v \alpha_d(u)du}, \tag{3.55}$$

the following hold

$$\mathcal{E}_t^u(ad_{\mathcal{V}(\cdot)})\left(\frac{\partial^n}{\partial x_d^n}\right) = \frac{1}{\phi_d^n(t,u)}\frac{\partial^n}{\partial x_d^n}, \tag{3.56}$$

$$\mathcal{E}_t^u(ad_{\mathcal{V}(\cdot)})(f(x_d)) = f(\phi_d(t,u)x_d). \tag{3.57}$$

Proof: The proof of these results is presented in §3.6.2 below.

The solution for $\mathcal{U}(t,T)$ satisfying (3.34) is given formally by

$$\mathcal{U}(t,T) = \mathcal{E}_t^T(\mathcal{L}(\cdot) + \mathcal{V}(\cdot)))$$

We expand this by applying Theorem 3.2, to which end we must compute $\mathcal{W}(t,u)$ as given by (3.36). Using the first result of Lemma 3.1, we conclude that $\mathcal{W}(t,u)$ is given by

$$\mathcal{E}_t^u(\mathrm{ad}_{\mathcal{V}(\cdot)}(\mathcal{L}(u))) = \phi_d^{-2}(t,u)\mathcal{L}(u),$$

whence we infer from (3.35) that

$$\begin{aligned}\mathcal{U}(t,T) &= \mathcal{E}_t^T\left(-\frac{1}{2}\frac{\sigma_d^2(.)}{\phi_d^2(t,\cdot)}\frac{\partial^2}{\partial x_d^2}\right)\mathcal{E}_t^T(\mathcal{V}(\cdot))\\ &= \mathcal{E}_t^T\left(-\frac{1}{2}\frac{\phi_d^2(\cdot,T)\sigma_d^2(.)}{\phi_d^2(t,T)}\frac{\partial^2}{\partial x_d^2}\right)\mathcal{E}_t^T(\mathcal{V}(\cdot))\\ &= e^{-\frac{1}{2}\frac{\Sigma_{dd}(t,T)}{\phi_d^2(t,T)}\frac{\partial^2}{\partial x_d^2}}e^{-\int_t^T\alpha_d(u)du\, x_d\frac{\partial}{\partial x_d}}, \end{aligned}\tag{3.58}$$

where we have defined

$$\Sigma_{dd}(t,v) := \int_t^v \phi_d^2(u,v)\sigma_d^2(u)du. \tag{3.59}$$

However, we know how to compute integral kernels for each of the two terms in (3.58). The first is simply a Gaussian

$$\frac{\phi_d(t,T)}{\sqrt{\Sigma_{dd}(t,T)}}N\left(\frac{\phi_d(t,T)(x_d-\xi_d)}{\sqrt{\Sigma_{dd}(t,T)}}\right),$$

whereas, from Example 3.1, the second is a δ-function

$$\delta(\phi_d(t,T)x_d-\xi_d).$$

Combining these in a convolution, we conclude that the integral kernel for $\mathcal{U}(t,T)$ is

$$\begin{aligned}G(x_d,t;\xi_d,T) &= \frac{1}{\sqrt{\Sigma_{dd}(t,T)}}\int_{\mathbb{R}}N\left(\frac{\phi_d(t,T)(x_d-\xi_d')}{\sqrt{\Sigma_{dd}(t,T)}}\right)\delta(\phi_d(t,T)\xi_d'-\xi_d)\phi_d(t,T)d\xi_d'\\ &= \frac{1}{\sqrt{\Sigma_{dd}(t,T)}}N\left(\frac{\phi_d(t,T)x_d-\xi_d}{\sqrt{\Sigma_{dd}(t,T)}}\right).\end{aligned}\tag{3.60}$$

In other words, the impact of mean reversion on a diffusion is a) to modify the variance appearing in the Gaussian kernel and b) to replace x_d by $\phi_d(t,T)x_d$ in the numerator. Now it might (rightly) be argued that we could have saved ourselves a lot of effort by proceeding as we did in Example 3.1 and making the substitution $y_d = \phi_d(t,T)x_d$ at the outset. We would offer two reasons why the above calculation was nonetheless worth working through, in addition to the obvious advantage of avoiding the proliferation of notation which results from a co-ordinate shift.

First, it provided us with a nice illustration of the utility of the operator expansion machinery we developed in the previous section on a problem whose solution was already well understood, which experience should stand us in good stead when we tackle more complex problems which take us into uncharted territory. It might also be argued that, whereas the substitution argument is a trick which can be seen with hindsight to work, the brute-force application of Theorem 3.2 provided a turn-the-handle approach which, combined with some basic knowledge of how to combine kernels, yielded the result without need for any tricks or insights. This is a theme which will be seen to play greatly to our advantage in the remainder of this book. Interestingly, it is one which was presaged by Sophus Lie whose name is associated with the Lie algebra framework within which we are implicitly working. The question he asked in 1874 was "How can the knowledge of a stability group for a differential equation be utilized towards its integration?" (Helgason, 1994). Lie went on in the following years to derive a systematic way of uncovering symmetries in differential equations and exploiting them to infer co-ordinate transformations which rendered the equations integrable.

Secondly, our calculation showed us how we can straightforwardly dispense with mean reversion terms in an evolution equation by treating them as $\mathcal{V}(t)$ and the remainder of the evolution operator as $\mathcal{L}(t)$ in an application of Theorem 3.2 to isolate them on the right-hand side of the final expression for $\mathcal{U}(t, T)$, where their impact can be easily taken into account by applying a shift to the relevant mean-reverting co-ordinate(s). This will prove of great utility when we move in Chapter 8 to consider how to extend solutions for simpler models to cases incorporating additional mean-reverting factors.

3.5 CONVOLUTIONS WITH GAUSSIAN PRICING KERNELS

Having successfully derived the required pricing kernel for a given pricing equation using the above methods, it remains to apply it to a payoff function $P(\cdot)$ using the convolution expression (3.7). In all the instances we shall consider below, the form of the pricing kernel will be a variant of the Gaussian kernel represented in (3.11), possibly with a linear operator (depending on the n-dimensional vector $\boldsymbol{x}$) acting on it. The variants we shall deal with will essentially take the form of linear mappings of variables, something which will cause little obstacle to the use of the results below. The impact of linear operators can conveniently be handled by applying them to $G_0(\cdot)$ *after* its convolution with $P(\cdot)$ has been calculated in accordance with (3.7), effectively taking the linear operator outside the integral.

To facilitate the work in the sequel of calculating convolutions involving such Gaussian kernels (particularly multi-factor), we now state and offer self-contained sketch proofs of a number of useful results. Our starting point will be the generic multi-factor Gaussian density function $G_0(\boldsymbol{x}, t; \boldsymbol{\xi}, T)$ in (3.11). For convenience, we shall drop the explicit dependence on t and T which does not affect our calculations and re-express this as

$$\begin{aligned} G_0(\boldsymbol{x}; \boldsymbol{\xi}) &= \frac{e^{-\frac{1}{2}(\boldsymbol{x}-\boldsymbol{\xi})^T \boldsymbol{\Sigma}^{-1}(\boldsymbol{x}-\boldsymbol{\xi})}}{\sqrt{(2\pi)^n\,|\boldsymbol{\Sigma}|}} \\ &=: g(\boldsymbol{x}-\boldsymbol{\xi}). \end{aligned} \tag{3.61}$$

We are therefore interested in being able to calculate convolution integrals of the form

$$V(x) = \int_{\mathbb{R}^n} g(x-\xi)P(\xi)d\xi. \tag{3.62}$$

It turns out that the easiest way to proceed with multiple integrals over a multivariate Gaussian is to perform the integration(s) in Fourier space, where the operations of integration and differentiation become algebraic manipulations which are easier to process. To that end, let us define the Fourier transform of a multivariate function $f(x)$ by

$$\tilde{f}(\boldsymbol{k}) := \frac{1}{(2\pi)^n}\int_{\mathbb{R}^n} f(x)e^{-ik.x}dx, \tag{3.63}$$

from which the original function can be recovered by the inverse transform relationship

$$f(x) = \int_{\mathbb{R}^n} \tilde{f}(\boldsymbol{k})e^{ik.x}d\boldsymbol{k}. \tag{3.64}$$

Here the binary operator . denotes the Cartesian scalar product between two vectors.

A key result we shall make use of is that the transform of the convolution of two functions is the product of their transforms. Thus, from (3.62)

$$\tilde{V}(\boldsymbol{k}) = \tilde{g}(\boldsymbol{k})\tilde{P}(\boldsymbol{k}), \tag{3.65}$$

Now it is well known that

$$\tilde{g}(\boldsymbol{k}) = \frac{1}{2\pi}e^{-\frac{1}{2}k^T\Sigma k},$$

whence

$$V(x) = \frac{1}{2\pi}\int_{\mathbb{R}^n} \tilde{P}(\boldsymbol{k})e^{-\frac{1}{2}k^T\Sigma k+ik.x}d\boldsymbol{k}. \tag{3.66}$$

We will commonly encounter payoff expressions of the form

$$P(x) = e^{\alpha.x} \tag{3.67}$$

In this case we have

Theorem 3.3 *For $P(x)$ given by* (3.67), *the convolution* (3.62) *can be expressed as*

$$V(x) = e^{\alpha.x+\frac{1}{2}\alpha^T\Sigma\alpha}. \tag{3.68}$$

Proof: From the definition (3.63), a straightforward calculation leads to

$$\tilde{P}(\boldsymbol{k}) = \frac{1}{(2\pi i)^n\prod_{j=1}^{n}(k_j+i\alpha_j)}.$$

Substituting into (3.66), we obtain

$$V(\boldsymbol{x}) = \frac{1}{(2\pi i)^n}\int_{\mathbb{R}^n}\frac{e^{-\frac{1}{2}\boldsymbol{k}^T\boldsymbol{\Sigma}\boldsymbol{k}+i\boldsymbol{k}.\boldsymbol{x}}}{\prod_{j=1}^{n}(k_j+i\alpha_j)}d\boldsymbol{k}$$

Defining $\boldsymbol{k}' = \boldsymbol{k} + i\boldsymbol{\alpha}$, we can write

$$V(\boldsymbol{x}) = \frac{e^{\boldsymbol{\alpha}.\boldsymbol{x}+\frac{1}{2}\boldsymbol{\alpha}^T\boldsymbol{\Sigma}\boldsymbol{\alpha}}}{(2\pi i)^n}\int_{\mathbb{R}^n}\frac{e^{-\frac{1}{2}\boldsymbol{k}'^T\boldsymbol{\Sigma}\boldsymbol{k}'+i\boldsymbol{k}'.(\boldsymbol{x}+\boldsymbol{\Sigma}\boldsymbol{\alpha})}}{\prod_{j=1}^{n}k_j'}d\boldsymbol{k}$$

But the integral expression here is precisely the result obtained by taking $P(\cdot) \equiv 1$, namely $\int_{\mathbb{R}^n} g(\boldsymbol{x}+\boldsymbol{\Sigma}\boldsymbol{\alpha}-\boldsymbol{\xi})d\boldsymbol{\xi} \equiv 1$ independently of $\boldsymbol{x}$, since $g(\cdot)$ is by assumption a probability density. This completes the proof.

The following result will prove useful.

Theorem 3.4 *For $g(\cdot)$ defined by* (3.61), *we have*

$$\int_{\mathbb{R}}\xi_1 g(\boldsymbol{x}-\boldsymbol{\xi})d\xi_1 = \left(x_1 + \sum_{j=2}^{n}\Sigma_{1j}\frac{\partial}{\partial x_j}\right)\int_{\mathbb{R}} g(\boldsymbol{x}-\boldsymbol{\xi})d\xi_1. \tag{3.69}$$

Proof: We start by noting the self-evident fact that the inverse Fourier transform of the one-dimensional Dirac delta function $\delta(k_1)$ is unity, whence the Fourier transform of unity is $\delta(k_1)$. It follows that the Fourier transform of ξ_1 is

$$\begin{aligned}\frac{1}{2\pi}\int_{\mathbb{R}}\xi_1 e^{-ik_1\xi_1}d\xi_1 &= \frac{i}{2\pi}\frac{\partial}{\partial k_1}\int_{\mathbb{R}} e^{-ik_1\xi_1}d\xi_1\\ &= i\delta'(k_1).\end{aligned}$$

We note that in (3.69) we have again a convolution, this time one-dimensional. It is a convolution of the function $g(\boldsymbol{u})$, where

$$\boldsymbol{u}(\boldsymbol{x},\boldsymbol{\xi}) := (x_1, x_2-\xi_2,\ldots,x_n-\xi_n).$$

We deduce that its Fourier transform will be given by the product of the transforms

$$\tilde{V}(\boldsymbol{k}) = i\delta'(k_1)\tilde{g}(\boldsymbol{k}),$$

whence, using (3.64) and integration by parts w.r.t. k_1

$$\begin{aligned}\int_{\mathbb{R}}\xi_1 g(\boldsymbol{x}-\boldsymbol{\xi})d\xi_1 &= \int_{\mathbb{R}^n}\tilde{V}(\boldsymbol{k})e^{i\boldsymbol{k}.\boldsymbol{u}}d\boldsymbol{k}\\ &= \frac{1}{i}\int_{\mathbb{R}^n}\delta(k_1)\frac{\partial}{\partial k_1}(\tilde{g}(\boldsymbol{k})e^{i\boldsymbol{k}.\boldsymbol{u}})d\boldsymbol{k}\\ &= \int_{\mathbb{R}^{n-1}}\left(x_1 + i\sum_{j=2}^{n}\Sigma_{1j}k_j\right)e^{-\frac{1}{2}\boldsymbol{k}^T\boldsymbol{\Sigma}\boldsymbol{k}+i\boldsymbol{k}.\boldsymbol{u}}\bigg|_{k_1=0}dk_2\ldots dk_n\\ &= \left(x_1 + \sum_{j=2}^{n}\Sigma_{1j}\frac{\partial}{\partial x_j}\right)\int_{\mathbb{R}^{n-1}}e^{-\frac{1}{2}\boldsymbol{k}^T\boldsymbol{\Sigma}\boldsymbol{k}+i\boldsymbol{k}.(\boldsymbol{x}-\boldsymbol{\xi})}\bigg|_{k_1=0}dk_2\ldots dk_n.\end{aligned}$$

Since the integral in the last expression is nothing other than the $(n-1)$-dimensional multivariate distribution of $\xi_2 - x_2, \ldots, \xi_n - x_n$, which is equally obtained by integrating the full distribution over ξ_1, this expression is seen to be equivalent to the r.h.s. of (3.69) as required. This completes the proof.

Example 3.3 *Using this result we are able to deduce straightforwardly the expected value of ξ_2 conditional on ξ_1 exceeding some threshold*

$$\int_{\mathbb{R}^n} \xi_2 \mathbb{1}_{\xi_1 > K}\, g(\boldsymbol{x} - \boldsymbol{\xi}) d\boldsymbol{\xi} = x_2 \Phi(d(x_1, K, \Sigma_{11})) + \frac{\Sigma_{12}}{\sqrt{\Sigma_{11}}} N(d(x_1, K, \Sigma_{11})), \tag{3.70}$$

where $\Phi(\cdot)$ is a cumulative Gaussian distribution function and

$$d(x, K, \Sigma) := \frac{x - K}{\sqrt{\Sigma}}. \tag{3.71}$$

From the previous theorem

$$\begin{aligned}
\int_{\mathbb{R}^n} \xi_2 \mathbb{1}_{\xi_1 > K}\, g(\boldsymbol{x} - \boldsymbol{\xi}) d\boldsymbol{\xi} &= \left(x_2 + \Sigma_{12} \frac{\partial}{\partial x_1} \right) \int_{\mathbb{R}^n} \mathbb{1}_{\xi_1 > K}\, g(\boldsymbol{x} - \boldsymbol{\xi}) d\boldsymbol{\xi} \\
&= \int_K^\infty \left(x_2 - \Sigma_{12} \frac{\partial}{\partial \xi_1} \right) \frac{e^{-\frac{1}{2}(\xi_1 - x_1)^2/\Sigma_{11}}}{\sqrt{2\pi\Sigma_{11}}} d\xi_1 \\
&= x_2 \int_K^\infty \frac{e^{-\frac{1}{2}(\xi_1 - x_1)^2/\Sigma_{11}}}{\sqrt{2\pi\Sigma_{11}}} d\xi_1 - \Sigma_{12} \left[\frac{e^{-\frac{1}{2}(\xi_1 - x_1)^2/\Sigma_{11}}}{\sqrt{2\pi\Sigma_{11}}} \right]_{\xi_1 = K}^{\xi_1 = \infty} \\
&= x_2 \Phi(d(x_1, K, \Sigma_{11})) + \frac{\Sigma_{12}}{\sqrt{\Sigma_{11}}} N(d(x_1, K, \Sigma_{11})).
\end{aligned}$$

Extending the result of Theorem 3.3 likewise to incorporate a conditional variable, we have

Theorem 3.5 *For $g(\boldsymbol{x})$ given by (3.61) and $P(\boldsymbol{x}) = e^{\boldsymbol{\alpha}.\boldsymbol{x}}$, we have*

$$\int_{\mathbb{R}^n} P(\boldsymbol{\xi}) \mathbb{1}_{\xi_1 > K}\, g(\boldsymbol{x} - \boldsymbol{\xi}) d\boldsymbol{\xi} = e^{\boldsymbol{\alpha}.\boldsymbol{x} + \frac{1}{2}\boldsymbol{\alpha}^T \boldsymbol{\Sigma} \boldsymbol{\alpha}} \Phi\left(d\left(x_1 + \sum_{j=1}^n \alpha_j \Sigma_{1j}, K, \Sigma_{11} \right) \right), \tag{3.72}$$

with $d(\cdot)$ given by (3.71).

Proof: This result is proved along the same lines as Example 3.3 above, except that, in place of $\int_{\mathbb{R}^n} g(\boldsymbol{x} + \boldsymbol{\Sigma\alpha} - \boldsymbol{\xi}) d\boldsymbol{\xi} \equiv 1$, we have

$$\int_{\mathbb{R}^n} \mathbb{1}_{\xi_1 > K} g(\boldsymbol{x} + \boldsymbol{\Sigma\alpha} - \boldsymbol{\xi}) d\boldsymbol{\xi} = \Phi\left(d\left(x_1 + \sum_{j=1}^n \alpha_j \Sigma_{1j}, K, \Sigma_{11} \right) \right),$$

from which observation (3.72) follows.

A related result which will also prove useful in the event that a pricing kernel has to be applied twice in succession to a vanilla option payoff is the following:

Theorem 3.6 *For $g(x)$ given by* (3.61), $P(x) = e^{\alpha.x}$ *and* $d(\cdot)$ *given by* (3.71), *we have*

$$\int_{\mathbb{R}^n} P(\xi)\Phi(d(\xi_1, K, \Sigma_0))g(x-\xi)d\xi = e^{\alpha.x+\frac{1}{2}\alpha^T\Sigma\alpha}\Phi\left(d\left(x_1 + \sum_{j=1}^{n}\alpha_j\Sigma_{1j}, K, \Sigma_0 + \Sigma_{11}\right)\right). \tag{3.73}$$

Proof: This result is effectively an extension of Theorem 3.5. We note first the well-known result for the Fourier transform of an integral

$$\frac{1}{2\pi}\int_{\mathbb{R}}\int_{-\infty}^{x_1} f(x)dx\, e^{-ik_1x_1}dx_1 = \frac{\tilde{f}(k_1)}{ik_1},$$

whence it follows that the Fourier transform of $\Phi(d(\xi_1, K, \Sigma_0))$ is

$$\frac{e^{-iKk_1-\frac{1}{2}\Sigma_0k_1^2}}{2\pi ik_1}.$$

It follows that the convolution $\int_{\mathbb{R}^n}\Phi(d(\xi_1, K, \Sigma_0))g(x-\xi)d\xi$ has transform

$$e^{-\frac{1}{2}k^T\Sigma k}\frac{e^{-iKk_1-\frac{1}{2}\Sigma_0k_1^2}}{2\pi ik_1} = \frac{e^{-iKk_1-\frac{1}{2}k^T\Sigma^+k}}{2\pi ik_1},$$

where $\Sigma^+_{ij} = \Sigma_{ij} + \Sigma_0\mathbb{1}_{i=j=1}$. It follows that

$$\int_{\mathbb{R}^n}\Phi(d(\xi_1, K, \Sigma_0))g(x-\xi)d\xi = \Phi(d(x_1, K, \Sigma_0 + \Sigma_{11})).$$

An extension to the above argument along the lines of that used in Theorem 3.5 establishes (3.73).

3.6 PROOFS FOR CHAPTER 3

3.6.1 Proof of Theorem 3.2

$\mathfrak{g}_M$ with the assumed norm is by assumption a Banach space. The convergence in $\mathfrak{g}_M$ of the Neumann series in (3.36) and in (3.74) below is thus guaranteed by the boundedness of $\mathcal{L}(t)$, of $\mathcal{V}(t)$ and (consequently) of $\mathrm{ad}_{\mathcal{L}(u)}(\mathcal{V}(t))$. We conclude that the operator $\mathcal{U}(t,T)$ acting on $\mathfrak{g}_M$ specified by (3.35) is well-defined. We will show below that it satisfies (3.34). Since the solution to (3.33) generated by $\mathcal{U}(t,T)$ exists and is unique by assumption, it must emerge as the limit as $M \to \infty$ of the solution $g_M(x,t)$

obtained by restricting the domain of $f(\cdot)$ to $[-M, M]^n$. We can therefore consider our solution (3.35) of (3.34) to act on $\mathfrak{g}$ as stated.

Let us define

$$\mathcal{U}_0(t,T) = \mathcal{E}_t^T(\mathcal{L}(\cdot)), \tag{3.74}$$

$$\mathcal{Q}(t,T) = \mathcal{E}_t^T(\mathcal{W}(t,\cdot)), \tag{3.75}$$

in terms of which we can express

$$U(t,T) = \mathcal{Q}(t,T)\mathcal{U}_0(t,T).$$

Clearly from the definition (3.35), $\mathcal{U}(T,T) = I$ as required. Differentiating w.r.t. t, we find

$$\begin{aligned}\frac{\partial \mathcal{U}}{\partial t} &= \frac{\partial \mathcal{Q}}{\partial t}\mathcal{U}_0 + \mathcal{Q}\frac{\partial \mathcal{U}_0}{\partial t} \\ &= \left(\frac{\partial \mathcal{Q}}{\partial t} + \mathcal{Q}\mathcal{L}\right)\mathcal{U}_0 \\ &= \left(\frac{\partial \mathcal{Q}}{\partial t} - \mathrm{ad}_{\mathcal{L}}(\mathcal{Q}) - \mathcal{V}\mathcal{Q}\right)\mathcal{U}_0 + (\mathcal{L}+\mathcal{V})\mathcal{Q}\mathcal{U}_0. \end{aligned} \tag{3.76}$$

Using again (3.35) we infer

$$\frac{\partial \mathcal{U}}{\partial t} = (\mathcal{L}+\mathcal{V})\mathcal{U} \Longleftrightarrow \frac{\partial \mathcal{Q}}{\partial t} = \mathrm{ad}_{\mathcal{L}}(\mathcal{Q}) + \mathcal{V}\mathcal{Q}. \tag{3.77}$$

It remains to validate the latter identity.

Differentiating (3.75) using the defining property of $\mathcal{E}_t^T(\cdot)$ we see

$$\frac{\partial}{\partial t}\mathcal{Q}(t,T) = \mathcal{W}(t,t)\mathcal{Q}(t,T) + \sum_{n=1}^{\infty}\int_{t\le t_1\le\dots\le t_n\le T}\frac{\partial}{\partial t}(\mathcal{W}(t,t_1)\dots\mathcal{W}(t,t_n))dt_1\dots dt_n. \tag{3.78}$$

Observe that

$$\frac{\partial}{\partial t}\mathcal{W}(t,t_i) = \mathrm{ad}_{\mathcal{L}(t)}(\mathcal{W}(t,t_i)). \tag{3.79}$$

Applying the product rule to the integrand in (3.78) and using (3.79), we see that the result is of the form

$$B_n = \sum_{i=1}^{n} A_1\dots\mathrm{ad}_L(A_i)\dots A_n$$

with $L \equiv \mathcal{L}(t)$ and $A_i \equiv \mathcal{W}(t,t_i)$. We propose that

$$B_n = \mathrm{ad}_L\left(\prod_{i=1}^{n} A_i\right).$$

The proof is by induction. The result is trivially true for $n = 1$. Next, suppose it is true for $n = k - 1$, $k > 1$. We infer

$$
\begin{aligned}
B_k &= \mathrm{ad}_L\left(\prod_{i=1}^{k-1} A_i\right)A_k + \left(\prod_{i=1}^{k-1} A_i\right)\mathrm{ad}_L(A_k) \\
&= \left(L\left(\prod_{i=1}^{k-1} A_i\right) - \left(\prod_{i=1}^{k-1} A_i\right)L\right)A_k + \left(\prod_{i=1}^{k-1} A_i\right)(LA_k - A_kL) \\
&= L\left(\prod_{i=1}^{k-1} A_i\right)A_k - \left(\prod_{i=1}^{k-1} A_i\right)A_kL \\
&= \mathrm{ad}_L\left(\prod_{i=1}^{k} A_i\right),
\end{aligned}
$$

so the result is true also for $n = k$, as required. Applying this result and the fact that $\mathcal{W}(t,t) = \mathcal{V}(t)$ to (3.78), we obtain

$$
\begin{aligned}
\frac{\partial}{\partial t}\mathcal{Q}(t,T) &= \mathcal{V}(t)\mathcal{Q}(t,T) + \sum_{n=1}^{\infty}\int_{t\le t_1\le\ldots\le t_n\le T} \mathrm{ad}_{\mathcal{L}(t)}(\mathcal{W}(t,t_1)\ldots\mathcal{W}(t,t_n))dt_1\ldots dt_n \\
&= \mathcal{V}(t)\mathcal{Q}(t,T) + \mathrm{ad}_{\mathcal{L}(t)}(\mathcal{Q}(t,T) - I) \\
&= \mathrm{ad}_{\mathcal{L}(t)}(\mathcal{Q}(t,T)) + \mathcal{V}(t)\mathcal{Q}(t,T).
\end{aligned} \tag{3.80}
$$

The identities in (3.77) are seen to hold as required. This completes our proof.

3.6.2 Proof of Lemma 3.1

We prove (3.56) by letting $\mathcal{L} = \frac{\partial^n}{\partial x_d^n}$. To obtain $\mathcal{E}_t^u(\mathrm{ad}_{\mathcal{V}(\cdot)}(\mathcal{L}))$ we must compute

$$
\begin{aligned}
\int_t^u \mathrm{ad}_{\mathcal{V}(t_1)}(\mathcal{L})dt_1 &= \int_t^u (\mathcal{V}(t_1)\mathcal{L} - \mathcal{L}\mathcal{V}(t_1))dt_1 \\
&= n\int_t^u \alpha_d(t_1)dt_1\mathcal{L}.
\end{aligned}
$$

Similarly

$$
\int_t^u\int_{t_2}^u \mathrm{ad}_{\mathcal{V}(t_2)}(\mathrm{ad}_{\mathcal{V}(t_1)}(\mathcal{L}))dt_1dt_2 = \frac{1}{2}\left(n\int_t^u \alpha_d(t_1)dt_1\right)^2\mathcal{L},
$$

and so on. Proceeding inductively, we obtain

$$
\int_t^u\cdots\int_{t_k}^u \mathrm{ad}_{\mathcal{V}(t_k)}(\ldots\mathrm{ad}_{\mathcal{V}(t_1)}(\mathcal{L})\ldots)dt_1\ldots dt_k = \frac{1}{k!}\left(n\int_t^u \alpha_d(t_1)dt_1\right)^k\mathcal{L}.
$$

Performing the required infinite sum, we conclude that

$$\mathcal{E}_t^u(\mathrm{ad}_{\mathcal{V}(\cdot)}(\mathcal{L})) = \phi_d^{-n}(t,u)\mathcal{L},$$

as required.

For the proof of (3.57), we observe first that, setting $z = \ln x_d$, we have

$$x_d \frac{\partial}{\partial x_d} f(x_d) = \frac{\partial}{\partial z} f(e^z).$$

We observe in turn that

$$\int_t^u \mathrm{ad}_{\mathcal{V}_0}(t_1)(f(x_d))dt_1 = -\int_t^u \alpha_d(t_1)dt_1 \frac{\partial}{\partial z} f(e^z),$$

$$\int_t^u \int_{t_2}^u \mathrm{ad}_{\mathcal{V}_0(t_2)}(\mathrm{ad}_{\mathcal{V}_0(t_1)}(f(x_d)))dt_1 dt_2 = \frac{1}{2}\left(-\int_t^u \alpha_d(t_1)dt_1\right)^2 \frac{\partial^2}{\partial z^2} f(e^z),$$

$$\int_t^u \cdots \int_{t_k}^u \mathrm{ad}_{\mathcal{V}_0(t_k)}(\ldots \mathrm{ad}_{\mathcal{V}_0(t_1)}(f(x_d))\ldots)dt_1 \ldots dt_k = \frac{1}{k!}\left(-\int_t^u \alpha_d(t_1)dt_1\right)^k \frac{\partial^k}{\partial z^k} f(e^z).$$

Performing the required infinite sum over k, we conclude that

$$\begin{aligned}\mathcal{E}_t^u(\mathrm{ad}_{\mathcal{V}_0(\cdot)}(f(x_d))) &= \sum_{k=1}^{\infty} \frac{\left(-\int_t^u \alpha_d(t_1)dt_1\right)^k}{k!} \frac{\partial^k}{\partial z^k} f(e^z) = e^{-\int_t^u \alpha_d(t_1)dt_1 x_d \frac{d}{dx_d}} f(x_d) \\ &= \int_{\mathbb{R}} \delta(\phi_d(t,u)x_d - \xi_d) f(\xi_d) d\xi_d = f(\phi_d(t,u)x_d),\end{aligned}$$

as required, where we have used the integral kernel derived in §3.1 above. This completes our proof.

CHAPTER 4

Hull–White Short-Rate Model

The first problem we shall seek to apply our pricing kernel methodology to is the well-known short-rate model of Hull and White [1990]. This has the felicitous property that it possesses an exact pricing kernel. We deduce below a formula for this pricing kernel, then demonstrate how it can be used to derive some important derivatives pricing formulae, basing our derivations on the work of Turfus [2019].

Rather than the short rate r_{dt} itself, we shall find it convenient to work with an auxiliary process x_{dt} satisfying the following canonical Ornstein–Uhlenbeck process

$$dx_{dt} = -\alpha_d(t)x_{dt}dt + \sigma_d(t)dW_t, \tag{4.1}$$

where $\alpha_d, \sigma_d : \mathbb{R}^+ \to \mathbb{R}^+$ are piecewise continuous functions, the former L_1- and the latter L_2-integrable, and W_t is a Brownian motion under the risk-neutral measure for $t \geq 0$. Under the Hull–White model, this auxiliary process x_{dt} is related to the instantaneous short rate r_{dt} by

$$r_{dt} = r_d(x_{dt}, t), \tag{4.2}$$

$$r_d(x, t) := \bar{r}_d(t) + r_d^*(t) + x, \tag{4.3}$$

with $r_d^* : \mathbb{R}^+ \to \mathbb{R}$ an (L_1-integrable) function to be determined by calibration to fit the instantaneous forward curve given by the (L_1-integrable) function $\bar{r}_d : \mathbb{R}^+ \to \mathbb{R}$. We seek to obtain an exact pricing kernel for European-type securities whose contingent payoff at some future time v depends upon the short rate r_v at that time.[1]

We shall go on in the following chapter to consider the alternative postulate that r_{dt} is given by an exponential rather than a linear function of x_{dt}. This gives rise to the

[1]In practice, a LIBOR or swap rate is usually fixed for payment at time $v = T$ at some fixing time $T - \tau$. The value of such a payment can be determined as of time $T - \tau$ using the pricing kernel with $v = T$. A second application using the effective payoff expressed as a function of the rate fixed at $T - \tau$, which payoff is a function of $x_{T-\tau}$, then allows the value as of some earlier time t to be determined.

important Black–Karasinski model. As we shall see, the calculation is more involved in that case, although many of the features of the present calculation will recur there, and indeed throughout the remainder of this book. For that reason we shall go through the derivation of the Hull–White result in rather careful detail.

4.1 BACKGROUND OF HULL–WHITE MODEL

The short-rate model of Hull and White [1990] was introduced by those authors as a natural extension of the short-rate model of Vasicek [1977]. Whereas the latter author assumed that $r_d^*(t)$ in our notation was constant, Hull and White [1990] showed how a judicious choice of this function allows the model to be fitted to an arbitrary term structure of interest rates.

The problem of obtaining an analytic pricing kernel for the Hull–White model has been considered by a number of authors. It was first solved by Jamshidian [1989] for the specialised Vasicek case (with constant coefficients). His paper focussed on bond option pricing but included a derivation of a closed-form pricing kernel in an appendix. The derivation for the generalised Hull–White case with time-dependent coefficients appears to be attributable to Van Steenkiste and Foresi [1999]. They presented a closed-form solution for a multi-factor Hull–White model, based on a method extending the state space to cover both the interest rate and its integral. Their result appears not to be well known on account of the fact that a) it was only ever made available as a working paper, and b) the authors mainly sought to demonstrate the applicability of their method to more intractable problems involving jump-diffusions and non-linear payoffs.

A number of other authors have carried out derivations using asymptotic analysis. Tourrucôo et al. [2007] considered the Hull–White model as a special case of a generalised Black–Karasinski family of models they proposed, using a small volatility assumption and an approach borrowed from geometrical optics similar to that used in the derivation of the authors' previous asymptotic expansion for the SABR model—see Hagan et al. [2015]. They employed a change of variable from a mean-reverting normal variable to one which is seen to follow instead a simple Brownian motion, rendering the dynamics simpler, as we shall do below. Horvath et al. [2017] adopted a similar approach with a slightly different family of models incorporating both the Hull–White model and that of Black and Karasinski [1991]. They find that the required pricing kernel can be written asymptotically under the assumption of small deviations on average of the short rate from the forward rate curve as an asymptotic expansion, deriving explicitly all terms up to second order. They do not provide the Hull–White results explicitly but only as a limiting case. They demonstrate how to price caps and floors to good accuracy using the pricing kernel, focussing on the important Black–Karasinski case.

Our approach is closely related to that of Horvath et al. [2017] and enjoys a number of its advantages. First, we allow the instantaneous volatility and the mean reversion rate and level to be fully time-dependent, unlike many Fourier transform approaches which make the assumption of constant coefficients (see for example Beyna and Wystup [2011] and references therein); likewise for the exponent expansion technique propounded by Capriotti [2006] and applied to the Black–Karasinski model by Capriotti and Stehlíkova [2014], and for the method proposed by Daniluk and Muchorski [2016] based on the Karhunen–Loève representation of the Ornstein–Uhlenbeck process using Hermite polynomials.

Secondly, while many approaches such as the Black–Karasinski expansion proposed by Antonov and Spector [2010] depend on a small term variance assumption, the relevant "small" expansion parameter appearing in our series representations reflects the smallness of absolute rather than relative deviations of the short rate from its forward value, so for low rates will converge rapidly. Although this is not an issue in the present calculation where rates are normal and the result obtained exact, it is an import consideration for models such as Black–Karasinski, where rates are log-normal, volatilities consequently not particularly small, and results invariably used in truncated or other approximate form (see following chapter).

Having established our pricing kernel, we use it to derive analytic formulae for caplet and European swaption prices, as well as results for delayed LIBOR payments and CMS indices. The caplet and swaption formulae were originally presented by Jamshidian [1989], although expressed there as bond option formulae. They were set out more explicitly by Henrard [2003]. Constant model coefficients (local volatility and mean reversion rate) were assumed in all these calculations, but in the following we make the more general assumption of time-dependent model coefficients.

4.2 THE PRICING KERNEL

Here we look to derive in closed form an exact pricing kernel solution for the Hull–White model specified by (4.1) and (4.2). Denoting the price of a European-type security depending for its payout amount on the realised short rate at maturity T by $f(x_{dt}, t)$, this will be given by

$$f(x_{dt}, t) = \mathbb{E}^{\mathbb{Q}}\left[e^{-\int_t^T r_{ds} ds} P(x_{dT}) \middle| \mathcal{F}_t \right], \tag{4.4}$$

with $\mathbb{Q}$ the relevant martingale measure and $P(\cdot)$ the payoff function. By the Feynman–Kac theorem, the function $f(x_d, t)$ emerges as the solution to the following Kolmogorov backward diffusion equation

$$\frac{\partial f}{\partial t} - \alpha_d(t) x_d \frac{\partial f}{\partial x_d} + \frac{1}{2}\sigma_d^2(t)\frac{\partial^2 f}{\partial x_d^2} - r_d(x_d, t) f = 0, \quad t \geq 0 \tag{4.5}$$

subject to the final condition $\lim_{t\to T^-} f(x_d, t) = P(x_d)$, with $r_d(\cdot)$ given by (4.3).

Theorem 4.1 ***(Hull–White Pricing Kernel):*** *The pricing kernel for* (4.5) *can be expressed straightforwardly as the product of the v-maturity zero coupon bond price and a Gaussian probability density function* N(·) *as follows*

$$G(x_d, t; \xi_d, v) = \frac{D_d(t, v) e^{-\mu_d^*(x_d, t, v)}}{\sqrt{\Sigma_{dd}(t, v)}} N\left(\frac{\phi_d(t, v) x_d - I_{dd}^*(t, v) - \xi_d}{\sqrt{\Sigma_{dd}(t, v)}} \right), \tag{4.6}$$

with

$$D_d(t,v) = e^{-\int_t^v \bar{r}_d(s)ds}, \tag{4.7}$$

$$\phi_d(t,v) = e^{-\int_t^v \alpha_d(u)du}, \tag{4.8}$$

$$B_d^*(t,v) = \int_t^v \phi_d(t,u)du, \tag{4.9}$$

$$\Sigma_{dd}(t,v) = \int_t^v \phi_d^2(u,v)\sigma_d^2(u)du, \tag{4.10}$$

$$I_{dd}^*(t,v) = \int_t^v \phi_d(u,v)\Sigma_{dd}(t,u)du, \tag{4.11}$$

$$K_{dd}^*(t,v) = \int_t^v I_{dd}^*(t,u)du, \tag{4.12}$$

$$\mu_d^*(x_d,t,v) = B_d^*(t,v)(x_d + r_d^*(t)) + \tfrac{1}{2}B_d^{*2}(t,v)\Sigma_{dd}(0,t), \tag{4.13}$$

$$r_d^*(t) = I_{dd}^*(0,t). \tag{4.14}$$

The choice of $r_d^*(t)$ in (4.14) *follows from the requirement of calibration of the model to the instantaneous forward curve $D_d(0,t)$.*

Proof: We show in §4.4 below how this result can be derived using the tools developed in Chapter 3.

4.3 APPLICATIONS

4.3.1 Zero Coupon Bond Pricing

Applying our general pricing kernel to a payoff of $P(\xi_d) = 1$ at time T reveals that the T-maturity Hull–White zero coupon bond price can be written

$$F^T(x_d,t) = D_d(t,T)e^{-\mu_d^*(x_d,t,T)}. \tag{4.15}$$

We demonstrate now the tower property in relation to this price by replicating it as the time-t price of a contract to receive the same bond at time $v \in (t,T)$. In other words we seek to demonstrate that

$$D_d(v,T)\int_{\mathbb{R}} e^{-\mu_d^*(\xi_d,v,T)}G(x_d,t;\xi_d,v)d\xi_d = D_d(t,T)e^{-\mu_d^*(x_d,t,T)}. \tag{4.16}$$

From the definitions of the various terms in (4.16), applying Theorem 3.3 and making use of (4.38)–(4.40) and the definition (4.14) of $r_d^*(v)$, we have

$$
\begin{aligned}
\ln(\text{l.h.s.}/D_d(t,T)) &= -\mu_d^*(x_d,t,v) - \mu_d^*(\phi_d(t,v)x_d - I_{dd}^*(t,v),v,T) + \frac{1}{2}B_d^{*2}(v,T)\Sigma_{dd}(t,v) \\
&= -B_d^*(t,v)(x_d + I_{dd}^*(0,t)) - \frac{1}{2}B_d^{*2}(t,v)\Sigma_{dd}(0,t) \\
&\quad - B_d^*(v,T)(\phi_d(t,v)x_d - I_{dd}^*(t,v) + I_{dd}^*(0,v)) \\
&\quad - \frac{1}{2}B_d^{*2}(v,T)(\Sigma_{dd}(0,v) - \Sigma_{dd}(t,v)) \\
&= -B_d^*(t,v)(x_d + I_{dd}^*(0,t)) - \frac{1}{2}B_d^{*2}(t,v)\Sigma_{dd}(0,t) \\
&\quad - B_d^*(v,T)\phi_d(t,v)(x_d + I_{dd}^*(0,t) + B_d^*(t,v)\Sigma_{dd}(0,t)) \\
&\quad - \frac{1}{2}B_d^{*2}(v,T)\ \phi_d^2(t,v)\Sigma_{dd}(0,t) \\
&= -(B_d^*(t,v) + \phi_d(t,v)B_d^*(v,T))(x_d + r_d^*(t)) \\
&\quad - \frac{1}{2}(B_d^*(t,v) + \phi_d(t,v)B_d^*(v,T))^2\Sigma_{dd}(0,t) \\
&= -B_d^*(t,T)(x_d + r_d^*(t)) - \frac{1}{2}B_d^{*2}(t,T)\Sigma_{dd}(0,t) \\
&= -\mu_d^*(x_d,t,T) \\
&= \ln(\text{r.h.s.}/D_d(t,T)),
\end{aligned}
$$

as required.

4.3.2 LIBOR Pricing

As is well known, the LIBOR rate for the payment period $[T_1, T_2]$ fixing at T_1 and paying at T_2 can, under the assumption that there is no LIBOR spread over the risk-free rate,[2] be expressed as $L(x_{dT_1}, T_1, T_2)$, where

$$L(x_d, T_1, T_2)\delta(T_1, T_2) = \frac{1}{F^{T_2}(x_d, T_1)} - 1, \tag{4.17}$$

and $\delta(\cdot,\cdot)$ represents the relevant year fraction. The value as of time T_1 of the LIBOR payoff (4.17) will thus be

$$V_{\text{LIBOR}}(x_d, T_1) = 1 - F^{T_2}(x_d, T_1).$$

Making use of the tower property, we deduce

$$V_{\text{LIBOR}}(x_d, t) = F^{T_1}(x_d, t) - F^{T_2}(x_d, t). \tag{4.18}$$

[2]The argument can be easily modified if it is desired to address the case where a deterministic spread is present by adding the spread into the definition (4.17). The more intricate problem of dealing with stochastic spreads is addressed in Chapter 14.

Adjusted Payment Date. We consider next the case where the LIBOR payment date is adjusted to be not T_2, the end of the payment period, but $T_2 + \Delta T$, with ΔT allowed to be positive or negative. Thus the payoff (4.17) is made at time $T_2 + \Delta T$. We value this as of time T_1 as follows

$$V_L(x_d, T_1) \sim F^{T_2+\Delta T}(x_d, T_1)\left(\frac{1}{F^{T_2}(x_d, T_1)} - 1\right). \tag{4.19}$$

To obtain the price for $t < T_1$, we find the second term in brackets is easily handled using again the tower property. In the case of the first term we note that

$$\frac{F^{T_2+\Delta T}(x_d, T_1)}{F^{T_2}(x_d, T_1)} = D_d(T_2, T_2+\Delta T)e^{-(B_d^*(T_1,T_2+\Delta T)-B_d^*(T_1,T_2))(\psi_d(x_d,T_1,T_1)+B_d^*(T_1,T_2)\Sigma_{dd}(0,T_1))},$$

with $\psi_d(\cdot)$ defined as in (4.54) below. Applying our pricing kernel, making use of Theorem 3.3 and (4.40), we obtain

$$V_L(x_d, t) = F^{T_1}(x_d,t)D_d(T_2, T_2+\Delta T)e^{-(B_d^*(T_1,T_2+\Delta T)-B_d^*(T_1,T_2))(\psi_d(x_d,t,T_1)+B_d^*(T_1,T_2)\Sigma_{dd}(0,T_1))} - F^{T_2+\Delta T}(x_d, t). \tag{4.20}$$

Note that (4.20) reduces to the simpler expression (4.18) in the event that $\Delta T = 0$. Finally, setting $x_d = t = 0$ yields the following expression for the PV of the adjusted LIBOR payment

$$V_L = D_d(0, T_2+\Delta T)\left(\frac{F_{\text{convexity}}(T_1, T_2, T_2+\Delta T)}{D_d(T_1, T_2)} - 1\right). \tag{4.21}$$

where

$$F_{\text{convexity}}(T_1, T_2, v) := e^{-B_d^*(T_1,T_2)(B_d^*(T_1,v)-B_d^*(T_1,T_2))\Sigma_{dd}(0,T_1)}. \tag{4.22}$$

We note also for reference that we can express, using (4.38)

$$B_d^*(T_1, v) - B_d^*(T_1, T_2) = \begin{cases} -\phi_d(T_1, v)B_d^*(v, T_2), & v \le T_2, \\ \phi_d(T_1, T_2)B_d^*(T_2, v), & v > T_2. \end{cases} \tag{4.23}$$

4.3.3 Caplet Pricing

We are particularly interested in applying our pricing kernel to option pricing problems, the most important being LIBOR caps and floors, to price which we need to be able to calculate the impact of capping/flooring a future LIBOR payment (or payments) at a given level. In terms of the above notation, the payoff at time T_2 for a LIBOR caplet with strike K will be

$$P(x_{dT_1}) = [L(x_{dT_1}, T_1, T_2) - K]^+ \delta(T_1, T_2),$$

From the perspective of time T_1, this can be viewed as a fixed payment and priced accordingly. The value as of time T_1 will thus be

$$V_{\text{Caplet}}(x_d, T_1) = F^{T_2}(x_d, T_1)[L(x_d, T_1, T_2) - K]^+ \delta(T_1, T_2),$$

where the superscript + indicates the positive part. This expression can then be used in turn as input to the pricing kernel. Suppose now that the critical value at which the payoff comes into the money is denoted by x_d^*, viz. we have $L(x_d^*, T_1, T_2) = K$, or alternatively $F^{T_2}(x_d^*, T_1) = \kappa$, where

$$\kappa := \frac{1}{1 + K\delta(T_1, T_2)}. \tag{4.24}$$

Then the time-t caplet value will be given from (3.7) and (4.17) by

$$V_{\text{Caplet}}(x_d, t) = \int_{x_d^*}^{\infty} (1 - \kappa^{-1} F^{T_2}(\xi_d, T_1)) G(x_d, t; \xi_d, T_1) d\xi_d \tag{4.25}$$

We observe here that, to compute (4.25) and the similar expressions we shall encounter below, it is sufficient to be able to price as of time t a payoff at T_1 of the form $P(\xi_d) = F^{T_2}(\xi_d, T_1)\mathbb{1}_{\xi_d > x_d^*}$. This price can be calculated making use of Theorem 3.5 as

$$\begin{aligned}\int_{x_d^*}^{\infty} P(\xi_d) G(x_d, t; \xi_d, T_1) d\xi_d &= \frac{F^{T_1}(x_d, t)}{\sqrt{\Sigma_{dd}(t, T_1)}} \int_{x_d^*}^{\infty} F^{T_2}(\xi_d, T_1) \\ &\quad N\left(\frac{\xi_d + I_{dd}^*(t, T_1) - \phi_d(t, T_1) x_d}{\sqrt{\Sigma_{dd}(t, T_1)}}\right) d\xi_d \\ &= F^{T_2}(x_d, t)\Phi(-d_1(x_d, t, T_1, T_2)),\end{aligned} \tag{4.26}$$

$$d_1(x_d, t, T_1, T_2) = \frac{x_d^* - \phi_d(t, T_1) x_d + I_{dd}^*(t, T_1) + B_d^*(T_1, T_2)\Sigma_{dd}(t, T_1)}{\sqrt{\Sigma_{dd}(t, T_1)}} \tag{4.27}$$

with $\Phi(x_d) := \int_{-\infty}^{x} N(\xi_d) d\xi_d$ a cumulative normal distribution. For a fixed unit payoff we need only take the limit of the above as $T_2 \to T_1$, viz.

$$\int_{x_d^*}^{\infty} G(x_d, t; \xi_d, T_1) d\xi_d = F^{T_1}(x_d, t)\Phi(-d_2(x_d, t, T_1)), \tag{4.28}$$

where we define

$$d_2(x_d, t, T_1) := d_1(x_d, t, T_1, T_1)$$
$$= \frac{x_d^* - \phi_d(t, T_1)x_d + I_{dd}^*(t, T_1)}{\sqrt{\Sigma_{dd}(t, T_1)}}. \tag{4.29}$$

Combining these terms in accordance with (4.25), we find the caplet price to be

$$V_{\text{caplet}}(x_d, t) = F^{T_1}(x_d, t)\Phi(-d_2(x_d, t, T_1)) - \kappa^{-1}F^{T_2}(x_d, t)\Phi(-d_1(x_d, t, T_1, T_2)). \tag{4.30}$$

Similarly or making use of put–call parity, we find the floorlet price to be

$$V_{\text{floorlet}}(x_d, t) = \kappa^{-1}F^{T_2}(x_d, t)\Phi(d_1(x_d, t, T_1, T_2)) - F^{T_1}(x_d, t)\Phi(d_2(x_d, t, T_1)). \tag{4.31}$$

Letting $x_d, t \to 0$ in (4.30) and (4.31), the familiar option pricing formulae are reproduced.

4.3.4 European Swaption Pricing

As demonstrated by Henrard [2003], it is a straightforward matter following Jamshidian [1989] to extend our caplet calculation to allow us to price swaptions. Let us suppose that the swap underlying the swaption has payment periods $[T_{i-1}, T_i]$ for $i = 1, 2, \ldots, n$ with fixed and floating cash flows in opposite directions at time T_i and exercise date $t_0 \in [0, T_0]$. The exercise value of the swaption will then be the positive part of the time-t_0 value of the swap underlying, namely for a payer swaption

$$P_{\text{payer}}(x_d) = \sum_{i=1}^{n} [F^{T_{i-1}}(x_d, t_0) - \kappa^{-1}F^{T_i}(x_d, t_0)]\mathbb{1}_{x_d > x_d^*}, \tag{4.32}$$

with x_d^* now redefined to denote the value of x_d at which the swap underlying comes into the money. Following a calculation exactly analogous to that for the caplet, we can write the payer swaption value for $0 \le t < t_0$ as

$$V_{\text{payer}}(x_d, t) = \sum_{i=1}^{n} (F^{T_{i-1}}(x_d, t)\Phi(-d_1(x_d, t, t_0, T_{i-1})) - \kappa^{-1}F^{T_i}(x_d, t)\Phi(-d_1(x_d, t, t_0, T_i))), \tag{4.33}$$

The corresponding result for a receiver swaption is

$$V_{\text{receiver}}(x_d, t) = \sum_{i=1}^{n} (\kappa^{-1}F^{T_i}(x_d, t)\Phi(d_1(x_d, t, t_0, T_i)) - F^{T_{i-1}}(x_d, t)\Phi(d_1(x_d, t, t_0, T_{i-1}))), \tag{4.34}$$

with the same definition of x_d^* used.

4.4 PROOF OF THEOREM 4.1

4.4.1 Preliminary Results

For our proof of Theorem 4.1, we establish first the following preliminary results.

Lemma 4.1 *Defining*

$$\mathcal{L}(t,u) = \frac{1}{2}\frac{\sigma_d^2(u)}{\phi_d^2(t,u)}\frac{\partial^2}{\partial x_d^2}, \tag{4.35}$$

$$\mathcal{V}(t,u) = \phi_d(t,u)x_d. \tag{4.36}$$

the following holds

$$\mathcal{E}_t^u(ad_{\mathcal{L}(t,\cdot)})(\mathcal{V}(t,u)) = \phi_d(t,u)x_d + \frac{\Sigma_{dd}(t,u)}{\phi_d(t,u)}\frac{\partial}{\partial x_d}, \tag{4.37}$$

where we have made use of the notation of Definitions 3.1 and 3.2.

Proof: We prove (4.37) in the usual way by applying Theorem 3.2. To obtain $\mathcal{E}_t^u(\mathrm{ad}_{\mathcal{L}(t,\cdot)}(\mathcal{V}(t,u)))$ we must compute

$$\begin{aligned}\int_t^u \mathrm{ad}_{\mathcal{L}(t,t_1)}(\mathcal{V}(t,u))dt_1 &= \int_t^u (\mathcal{L}(t,t_1)\mathcal{V}(t,u) - \mathcal{V}(t,u)\mathcal{L}(t,t_1))dt_1 \\ &= \phi_d(t,u)\int_t^u \frac{\sigma_d^2(t_1)}{\phi_d^2(t,t_1)}dt_1\frac{\partial}{\partial x_d} \\ &= \frac{\Sigma_{dd}(t,u)}{\phi_d(t,u)}\frac{\partial}{\partial x_d},\end{aligned}$$

where we have used the definition (4.10) and the fact that $\phi_d(t,u) = \phi_d(t,t_1)\phi_d(t_1,u)$. Further application of the commutator operator gives a null result. Adding then the two non-zero terms yields (4.37) as required.

Lemma 4.2 *The following identities hold for $t \le u \le v$ from the definitions in* (4.7)–(4.13)

$$B_d^*(t,v) = B_d^*(t,u) + \phi_d(t,u)B_d^*(u,v) \tag{4.38}$$

$$\Sigma_{dd}(t,v) = \Sigma_{dd}(u,v) + \phi_d^2(u,v)\Sigma_{dd}(t,u) \tag{4.39}$$

$$I_{dd}^*(t,v) = r_d^*(v) - \phi_d(t,v)(r_d^*(t) + B_d^*(t,v)\Sigma_{dd}(0,t)) \tag{4.40}$$

$$K_{dd}^*(t,v) = \int_t^v r_d^*(u)du - B_d^*(t,v)r_d^*(t) - \frac{1}{2}B_d^{*2}(t,v)\Sigma_{dd}(0,t). \tag{4.41}$$

Proof: Identities (4.38) and (4.39) follow directly from the definitions. To prove (4.40), we observe from the definition (4.11) and making use of identity (4.39) that

$$
\begin{aligned}
I^*_{dd}(0,v) &= \int_0^v \phi_d(u,v)\Sigma_{dd}(0,u)du \\
&= \int_0^t \phi_d(u,v)\Sigma_{dd}(0,u)du + \int_t^v \phi_d(u,v)\Sigma_{dd}(t,u)du \\
&\quad + \int_t^v \phi_d(u,v)(\Sigma_{dd}(0,u) - \Sigma_{dd}(t,u))du \\
&= \phi_d(t,v)\int_0^t \phi_d(u,t)\Sigma_{dd}(0,u)du + I^*_{dd}(t,v) + \phi_d(t,v)\Sigma_{dd}(0,t)\int_t^v \phi_d(t,u)du \\
&= I^*_{dd}(t,v) + \phi_d(t,v)(I^*_{dd}(0,t) + B^*_d(t,v)\Sigma_{dd}(0,t)).
\end{aligned}
$$

The identity (4.40) follows from use of (4.14). The further identity (4.41) follows from straightforward integration of (4.40) and use of the definition (4.9).

4.4.2 Turn the Handle!

We look to derive our pricing kernel by finding first an evolution operator $\mathcal{U}(t,T)$ satisfying

$$
\begin{aligned}
\left(\frac{\partial}{\partial t} + \mathcal{L}_1(t) + \mathcal{L}_2(t) + \mathcal{V}_1(t)\right)\mathcal{U}(t,T) = 0,& \\
\mathcal{U}(T,T) = I.&
\end{aligned}
\tag{4.42}
$$

with

$$
\mathcal{L}_1(t) = -\alpha_d(t)x_d\frac{\partial}{\partial x_d} \tag{4.43}
$$

$$
\mathcal{L}_2(t) = \frac{1}{2}\sigma_d^2(t)\frac{\partial^2}{\partial x_d^2}, \tag{4.44}
$$

$$
\mathcal{V}_1(t) = -(\overline{r}_d(t) + r^*_d(t) + x_d). \tag{4.45}
$$

Making use of Theorem 3.2 and Lemma 3.1, we can write the solution of (4.42) as

$$
\begin{aligned}
\mathcal{U}(t,T) &= \mathcal{E}_t^T(\mathcal{W}(t,\cdot))\mathcal{E}_t^T(\mathcal{L}_1(\cdot)), \\
\mathcal{W}(t,u) &= \mathcal{E}_t^u(\mathrm{ad}_{\mathcal{L}_1(\cdot)})(\mathcal{L}_2(u) + \mathcal{V}_1(u)) \\
&= \frac{1}{2}\frac{\sigma_d^2(u)}{\phi_d^2(t,u)}\frac{\partial^2}{\partial x_d^2} - \overline{r}_d(u) - r^*_d(u) - x_d\phi_d(t,u).
\end{aligned}
\tag{4.46}
$$

Considering $\mathcal{L}(.) \equiv \frac{1}{2}\frac{\sigma_d^2(\cdot)}{\phi_d^2(t,\cdot)}\frac{\partial^2}{\partial x_d^2}$ and applying Theorem 3.2 again then Lemma 4.1 in the calculation of $\mathcal{E}_t^T(\mathcal{W}(t,\cdot))$, we obtain

$$\begin{aligned}\mathcal{E}_t^T(\mathcal{W}(t,\cdot)) &= \mathcal{E}_t^T\left(-\bar{r}_d(\cdot) - r_d^*(\cdot) - \phi_d(t,\cdot)x_d - \frac{\Sigma_{dd}(t,\cdot)}{\phi_d(t,\cdot)}\frac{\partial}{\partial x_d}\right) e^{\frac{\frac{1}{2}\Sigma_{dd}(t,T)}{\phi_d^{2}(t,T)}\frac{\partial^2}{\partial x_d^2}} \\ &= e^{-R^*(t,T)}\mathcal{E}_t^T(\mathcal{W}_1(t,\cdot))e^{\frac{\frac{1}{2}\Sigma_{dd}(t,T)}{\phi_d^{2}(t,T)}\frac{\partial^2}{\partial x_d^2}}.\end{aligned} \tag{4.47}$$

where we define

$$R^*(t,T) = \int_t^T (\bar{r}_d(u) + r_d^*(u))du, \tag{4.48}$$

$$\mathcal{W}_1(t,u) = -\phi_d(t,u)x_d - \frac{\Sigma_{dd}(t,u)}{\phi_d(t,u)}\frac{\partial}{\partial x_d}. \tag{4.49}$$

Applying Theorem 3.2 a third time to the calculation of $\mathcal{E}_t^T((\mathcal{W}_1(\cdot))$ with $\mathcal{L}(.) \equiv -\frac{\Sigma_{dd}(t,\cdot)}{\phi_d(t,\cdot)}\frac{\partial}{\partial x_d}$ and noting from (4.11) that

$$\phi_d(t,u)\int_t^u \frac{\Sigma_{dd}(t,w)}{\phi_d(t,w)}dw = I_{dd}^*(t,u)$$

yields

$$\begin{aligned}\mathcal{E}_t^T(\mathcal{W}_1(\cdot)) &= \mathcal{E}_t^T(-\phi_d(t,\cdot)x_d + I_{dd}^*(t,\cdot))\mathcal{E}_t^T\left(-\frac{\Sigma_{dd}(t,\cdot)}{\phi_d(t,\cdot)}\frac{\partial}{\partial x_d}\right) \\ &= e^{-B_d^*(t,T)x_d + K_{dd}^*(t,T)}e^{-\frac{I_{dd}^*(t,T)}{\phi_d(t,T)}\frac{\partial}{\partial x_d}}.\end{aligned} \tag{4.50}$$

Putting everything together we thus obtain

$$\mathcal{U}(t,T) = e^{-B_d^*(t,T)x_d + K_{dd}^*(t,T) - R^*(t,T)}e^{-\frac{I_{dd}^*(t,T)}{\phi_d(t,T)}\frac{\partial}{\partial x_d}}e^{\frac{\frac{1}{2}\Sigma_{dd}(t,T)}{\phi_d^{2}(t,T)}\frac{\partial^2}{\partial x_d^2}}e^{-\int_t^T \alpha_d(u)du\, x_d\frac{\partial}{\partial x_d}} \tag{4.51}$$

Using now the result of Example 3.4.2 and (3.40) we find the required pricing kernel is given by

$$\begin{aligned}G(x_d,t;\xi_d,T) &= \frac{e^{-B_d^*(t,T)x_d + K_{dd}^*(t,T) - R^*(t,T)}}{\sqrt{\Sigma_{dd}(t,T)}}e^{-\frac{I_{dd}^*(t,T)}{\phi_d(t,T)}\frac{\partial}{\partial x_d}}\mathrm{N}\left(\frac{\phi_d(t,T)x_d - \xi_d}{\sqrt{\Sigma_{dd}(t,T)}}\right) \\ &= \frac{e^{-B_d^*(t,T)x_d + K_{dd}^*(t,T) - R^*(t,T)}}{\sqrt{\Sigma_{dd}(t,T)}}\mathrm{N}\left(\frac{\phi_d(t,T)x_d - I_{dd}^*(t,T) - \xi_d}{\sqrt{\Sigma_{dd}(t,T)}}\right)\end{aligned} \tag{4.52}$$

It remains to calibrate the model to render it consistent with the market-observed forward curve $D_d(0, t)$.

We apply our pricing kernel in the form (4.52) to a payoff of $P(\xi_d) = 1$ at time T with $(x_d, t) = (0, 0)$, making use of (3.7) to obtain

$$\int_{\mathbb{R}} G(x_d, t; \xi_d, T) d\xi = e^{K^*_{dd}(0,T) - R^*(0,T)}.$$

Applying the condition that the result must be $D_d(0, T)$ yields the requirement that

$$K^*_{dd}(0, T) - R^*(0, T) = -\int_0^T \bar{r}_d(u) du \tag{4.53}$$

for any $T > 0$, whence we deduce the calibration condition (4.14). Making use also of identity (4.41) of Lemma 4.2, we obtain (4.6). This completes our derivation.

We note out of interest that, defining

$$\psi_d(x_d, t, v) := \phi_d(t, v)(x_d + r^*_d(t) + B^*_d(t, v)\Sigma_{dd}(0, t)) \tag{4.54}$$

and using (4.40), we have

$$\phi_d(t, v)x_d - I^*_{dd}(t, v) - \xi_d = \psi_d(x_d, t, v) - \psi_d(\xi_d, v, v),$$

which better brings out the symmetry in (4.6) with respect to x_d and ξ_d.

CHAPTER 5

Black–Karasinski Short-Rate Model

We consider next the short-rate model of Black and Karasinski [1991]. We shall start, as in the Hull–White case, with an auxilary process x_{dt} defined by (4.1). Under the Black–Karasinski model, this auxiliary process x_t is related to the instantaneous short rate r_t by

$$r_{dt} = \tilde{r}(t)e^{x_{dt}-\frac{1}{2}\Sigma_{dd}(0,t)}, \tag{5.1}$$

with $\tilde{r} : \mathbb{R}^+ \to \mathbb{R}^+$ an (L_1-integrable) function to be determined by calibration to fit the instantaneous forward curve and $\Sigma_{dd}(\cdot)$ given by (4.10) above. We shall again seek to obtain an exact Green's function solution. On this occasion, a closed form solution turns out not to be possible; instead, the result obtained takes the form of a perturbation expansion in powers of the short rate. As we shall see, only the first one or two correction terms are ever likely to be needed, so the solution enjoys most of the advantages of a closed form solution in practice.

5.1 BACKGROUND OF BLACK–KARASINSKI MODEL

The problem of finding analytic solutions to the Black–Karasinski equation has been considered by a number of authors starting with Tourrucôo et al. [2007] who addressed it as a special case of the "generalized Black–Karasinski" family of models they proposed, using a small-term variance assumption and an approach borrowed from geometrical optics similar to that used in the derivation of the asymptotic expansion for the SABR model – see Hagan et al. [2015]. They employed a change of variable, effectively from x to $x' = x/\phi_r(0, T)$, which, as we have seen in §3.4.2, effectively allows the impact of mean reversion to be factored out of the calculation. They considered three distinct cases: Hull–White, Black–Karasinski and an intermediate square-root volatility case closely related to the CIR model of Cox et al. [1991]. They derived zero coupon bond formulae for all three cases expressing these effectively as an exponential function of a power series in the term variance. They produce a general formula for terms up to second order in the term variance (the Hull–White series terminating after the first-order term) and go on to present explicit formulae for the square-root volatility case, although not for the Black–Karasinski case.

A number of variations on this approach have been proposed since by other authors, most of whom went on also to derive option prices. A small-term variance assumption was employed by Antonov and Spector [2010] who, like Tourrucôo et al. [2007], considered the Black–Karasinski model in a slightly wider context, in this case of a family of multi-factor models. They considered not only zero coupon bond prices but also the form of the pricing kernel, deriving in both cases the leading order term and first-order correction of an implied power series expansion in the term variance. Using their pricing kernel result they derived an asymptotic formula for swaption prices, and demonstrated good agreement of implied volatilities with Monte Carlo simulations over a wide range of strikes.

An exponent expansion technique originally propounded by Capriotti [2006] was subsequently applied to the Black–Karasinski model by Capriotti and Stehlíkova [2014]. Like Antonov and Spector [2010], they derived asymptotic formulae both for zero coupon bond prices and for the pricing kernel. The exponent expansion technique they used is based on a small time-to-maturity assumption and involves expansions in powers of the time to maturity. It requires the further assumption that the local volatility is constant. As they state, it "can be seen as a semi-classical (high-temperature) approximation of the quantum gas of particles which was the context in which it was originally introduced". They suggest how the small time-to-maturity limitation can be overcome by dividing the relevant time period into a series of shorter time intervals and applying the technique successively over each such interval, effectively performing a series of convolutions to join the sub-solutions into a more accurate unified solution, albeit at the expense of some analytic tractability. They produce terms up to sixth order in the expansion for the pricing kernel, which they use to infer zero coupon bond prices, demonstrating high accuracy even with only a few terms in the expansion, but they do not derive any option pricing formulae.

Another method again is that proposed by Daniluk and Muchorski [2016] based on the Karhunen–Loève representation of the Ornstein–Uhlenbeck process which gives rise to a small term variance expansion in terms of Hermite polynomials. This they use to infer, like Antonov and Spector [2010], expressions for zero coupon bond and swaption prices. Their approximation consists in truncating the Gauss-Hermite series after a finite number of terms: in practice they suggest the use of five terms, $k = 5$ in their terminology. The final result is obtained by computing a nested kth order convolution-type integral over an exponential function of the kth order Gauss-Hermite representation. They demonstrated good agreement with Monte Carlo simulations for both zero coupon bond and swaption prices.

More recently Horvath et al. [2017] adopted yet another approach with a "beta blend" family of models incorporating both Hull–White and Black–Karasinski models as limiting cases. They find that the required pricing kernel can be written asymptotically under the assumption of small deviations on average of the short rate from the forward rate curve as an asymptotic series, deriving explicitly all terms up to second order. They demonstrate how to price caps and floors to good accuracy under the Black–Karasinski model using their second-order pricing kernel, obtaining good accuracy even using just the first-order expansion. Our calculation here effectively replicates the Black–Karasinski results of Horvath et al. [2017], so benefiting from the advantages this approach enjoys over others in terms of combining tractability with applicability over a wide range of pricing contexts, while offering a high degree of accuracy even with a lower order expansion.

An extension of the Horvath et al. [2017] calculation of the Black–Karasinski pricing kernel was performed by Turfus [2018b]. The asymptotic series was in this instance extended to all orders with a general expression given for the nth order term. Conditions were also found for the calibration condition of fitting the forward curve to be satisfied at each order of approximation. The calculation presented below is based on that of Turfus [2018b], presented in the first instance to second-order accuracy, since that is all we shall make use of here, but with a summary of the full result presented in §5.6.

5.2 THE PRICING KERNEL

We infer, following the same argument as used in Chapter 4, that if interest rates are governed by (5.1) and the Ornstein–Uhlenbeck equation (4.1) and the price of a European-type security depending for its payout amount at time $v > t$ on the realised short rate is expressed as $f(x_d, t)$, this price is governed by the following Kolmogorov backward diffusion equation

$$\frac{\partial f}{\partial t} - \alpha_d(t)x_d\frac{\partial f}{\partial x_d} + \frac{1}{2}\sigma_d^2(t)\frac{\partial^2 f}{\partial x_d^2} - \tilde{r}(t)e^{x_d - \frac{1}{2}\Sigma_{dd}(0,t)}f = 0, \quad t \geq 0 \tag{5.2}$$

(cf. (4.5) for the Hull–White case), subject to the final condition $\lim_{t\to v^-} f(x_d, t) = P(x_d)$ for some payoff function $P(\cdot)$. We shall reuse directly the notation introduced in §4.2 above, subject to the reinterpretation of r_{dt} and $\tilde{r}(t)$.

In this case we are unable to derive a pricing kernel in closed form but instead as an asymptotic expansion valid in the limit of low rates:

Theorem 5.1 *(Black–Karasinski Pricing Kernel): Suppose that* $\| \tilde{r}(\cdot) \| = \mathcal{O}(\epsilon)$[1] *in* (5.2) *under some suitable norm as* $\epsilon \to 0$. *The pricing kernel for* (5.2) *can then be written*

$$G(x_d, t; \xi_d, v) = D_d(t, v) \sum_{n=0}^{\infty} G_n(x_d, t; \xi_d, v) \tag{5.3}$$

with $D_d(t, v)$ *given by (4.7), where* $\| G_n(\cdot) \| = \mathcal{O}(\epsilon^n)$. *Further the requirement that the model be calibrated to fit the forward interest rate curve implied by* $D_d(t, v)$ *is met by*

[1] In practice the small parameter can be considered less stringently to be $\| r_\cdot - \bar{r}_d(\cdot) \|$, but this is only evident with hindsight.

specifying a suitable asymptotic series for $\tilde{r}(\cdot)$ as follows

$$\tilde{r}(t) = \sum_{n=1}^{\infty} \tilde{r}_n(t) \tag{5.4}$$

with $\| \tilde{r}_n(\cdot) \| = \mathcal{O}(\epsilon^n)$. A solution to second order in ϵ is provided by choosing

$$G_0(x_d, t; \xi_d, v) = \frac{1}{\sqrt{\Sigma_{dd}(t,v)}} N\left(\frac{\xi_d - \phi_d(t,v)x_d}{\sqrt{\Sigma_{dd}(t,v)}}\right), \tag{5.5}$$

$$G_1(x_d, t; \xi_d, v) = -\int_t^v (R_1(x_d, t, t_1)\mathcal{M}(t, t_1) - \overline{r}(t_1))G_0(x_d, t; \xi_d, v)dt_1, \tag{5.6}$$

$$\begin{aligned} G_2(x_d, t; \xi_d, v) = & \int_t^v (R_1(x_d, t, t_1)\mathcal{M}(t, t_1) - \overline{r}(t_1)) \\ & \times \int_{t_1}^v (R_1(x_d, t, t_2)\mathcal{M}(t, t_2) - \overline{r}(t_2))G_0(x_d, t; \xi_d, v)dt_2 dt_1 \\ & - \int_t^v R_2(x_d, t, t_1)\mathcal{M}(t, t_1)G_0(x_d, t; \xi_d, v)dt_1, \end{aligned} \tag{5.7}$$

where we define

$$R_n(x_d, t, t_1) := \tilde{r}_n(t_1)e^{\theta_d(x_d, t, t_1)}, \quad n = 1, 2, \ldots \tag{5.8}$$

$$\theta_d(x_d, t, t_1) := \phi_d(t, t_1)x_d - \frac{1}{2}\phi_d^2(t, t_1)\Sigma_{dd}(0, t), \tag{5.9}$$

$$\mathcal{M}(t, t_1)f(x_d, \ldots) := f(x_d + \Delta_{dd}(t, t_1), \ldots), \tag{5.10}$$

$$\Delta_{dd}(t, t_1) := \frac{\Sigma_{dd}(t, t_1)}{\phi_d(t, t_1)}. \tag{5.11}$$

Truncation of (5.4) at $n = 2$ and the choice

$$\tilde{r}_1(t) = \overline{r}_d(t), \tag{5.12}$$

$$\tilde{r}_2(t) = \tilde{r}_1(t) \int_0^t \tilde{r}_1(t_1)(e^{\phi_d(t_1, t)\Sigma_{dd}(0, t_1)} - 1)dt_1 \tag{5.13}$$

ensures exact calibration of the second-order Green's function to the forward curve represented by $D_d(0, t)$.

Proof: We show in §5.5 below how this result can be derived using the tools developed in Chapter 3.

5.3 APPLICATIONS

Since, as noted in a similar context by Pagliarani and Pascucci [2012], our pricing kernel expansion takes the form of a series of linear operators w.r.t. x_d acting on a Gaussian distribution $G_0(x_d, t; \xi_d, v)$, application of the pricing kernel to a given payoff $P(\xi_d)$ requires at leading order a convolution w.r.t. ξ_d of $G_0(\cdot)$ with $P(.)$. This is for many practical problems analytically tractable and leads to Black-type expressions involving cumulative Gaussian distribution functions. No further such convolutions need be calculated since higher-order terms are obtained straightforwardly by applying the linear operators w.r.t. x_d to the leading order result. In practice the situation is complicated by the fact that the effective payoff function for LIBOR-based options (valued as of the fixing date) will take the form of an asymptotic series, so that calculations to order n accuracy will typically require $\mathcal{O}(n)$ convolutions to be performed.

The numerical work will in general then be limited to the calculation of nested integrals w.r.t. time, one level of integration for each level of approximation. With an efficient quadrature algorithm, this approach can be orders of magnitude faster than, say, Monte Carlo simulation or a lattice approach for a given required level of accuracy in option pricing.

5.3.1 Zero Coupon Bond Pricing

We apply our second-order representation of (5.3) to a unit payoff at time T to obtain the following second-order accurate expression for the zero coupon bond price at time $T_1 < T$

$$F^T(x_d, T_1) = D_d(T_1, T) + F_1^T(x_d, T_1) + F_2^T(x_d, T_1) + \mathcal{O}(\epsilon^3), \tag{5.14}$$

$$F_1^T(x_d, T_1) = -D_d(T_1, T) \int_{T_1}^{T} (R_1(x_d, T_1, t_1) - \bar{r}_d(t_1))dt_1, \tag{5.15}$$

$$\begin{aligned} F_2^T(x_d, T_1) = {} & D_d(T_1, T) \int_{T_1}^{T} (R_1(x_d, T_1, t_1) - \bar{r}_d(t_1)) \int_{t_1}^{T} (R_1(x_d, T_1, t_2) - \bar{r}_d(t_2))dt_2 dt_1 \\ & + D_d(T_1, T) \int_{T_1}^{T} R_1(x_d, T_1, t_1) \int_{t_1}^{T} R_1(x_d, T_1, t_2) \\ & \times (e^{\phi_d(t_1, t_2)\Sigma_{dd}(T_1, t_1)} - 1)dt_2 dt_1 \\ & - D_d(T_1, T) \int_{T_1}^{T} R_2(x_d, T_1, t_1)dt_1. \end{aligned} \tag{5.16}$$

As a consistency check we test the tower property by calculating the time-t expectation of the time-T_1 price, applying the second order representation of (5.3) again to (5.16). This process will naturally generate terms up to $\mathcal{O}(\epsilon^4)$ which we cannot expect to match the time-t price calculated directly from the second order expansion, so we make a point of retaining only those terms which are explicitly $\mathcal{O}(\epsilon^2)$ or less. It will be useful to first prove the following lemma:

Lemma 5.1

$$\int_{\mathbb{R}} G_0(x_d, t; \xi_d, v) R_i(\xi_d, v, w) d\xi_d = R_i(x_d, t, w). \tag{5.17}$$

Proof: Making use of Theorem 3.3 and (4.43), we obtain

$$\begin{aligned}
\text{l.h.s.} &= R_i(x_d, v, w) e^{\frac{1}{2}\phi_d^2(v,w)\Sigma_{dd}(t,v)} \\
&= \tilde{r}_i(w) e^{\theta_d(x_d,v,w)+\frac{1}{2}\phi_d^2(v,w)\Sigma_{dd}(t,v)} \\
&= \tilde{r}_i(w) e^{\phi_d(t,w)x_d-\frac{1}{2}\phi_d^2(v,w)\Sigma_{dd}(0,v)+\frac{1}{2}\phi_d^2(v,w)\Sigma_{dd}(t,v)} \\
&= \tilde{r}_i(w) e^{\theta_d(x_d,t,w)} \\
&= \text{r.h.s.},
\end{aligned}$$

as required. This completes the proof.

Applying the second order representation of $G(\cdot)$ to $D_d(T_1, T)$ and making use of Lemma 5.1 with $v \equiv T_1$, we obtain

$$\begin{aligned}
&D_d(t,T) - D_d(t,T) \int_t^{T_1} (R_1(x_d,t,t_1) - \overline{r}_d(t_1)) dt_1 \\
&+ D_d(t,T) \int_t^{T_1} (R_1(x_d,t,t_1) - \overline{r}_d(t_1)) \int_{t_1}^{T_1} (R_1(x_d,t,t_2) - \overline{r}_d(t_2)) dt_2 dt_1 \\
&+ D_d(t,T) \int_t^{T_1} R_1(x_d,t,t_1) \int_{t_1}^{T_1} R_1(x_d,t,t_2)(e^{\phi_d(t_1,t_2)\Sigma_{dd}(t,t_1)} - 1) dt_2 dt_1 \\
&- D_d(t,T) \int_t^{T_1} R_2(x_d,t,t_1) dt_1 + \mathcal{O}(\epsilon^3).
\end{aligned}$$

Next applying the first-order representation of $G(\cdot)$ to $F_1^T(x_d, T_1)$, we obtain

$$\begin{aligned}
&- D_d(t,T) \int_{T_1}^{T} (R_1(x_d,t,t_1) - \overline{r}_d(t_1) dt_1 \\
&+ D_d(t,T) \int_t^{T_1} (R_1(x_d,t,t_1) - \overline{r}_d(t_1)) \int_{T_1}^{T} (R_1(x_d,t,t_2) - \overline{r}_d(t_2)) dt_2 dt_1 \\
&+ D_d(t,T) \int_t^{T_1} R_1(x_d,t,t_1) \int_{T_1}^{T} R_1(x_d,t,t_2)(e^{\phi_d(t_1,t_2)\Sigma_{dd}(t,t_1)} - 1) dt_2 dt_1 + \mathcal{O}(\epsilon^3).
\end{aligned}$$

Finally, applying the zeroth order representation of $G(\cdot)$ to $F_2^T(x_d, T_1)$, we obtain

$$D_d(t,T)\int_{T_1}^{T}(R_1(x_d,t,t_1)-\overline{r}_d(t_1))\int_{t_1}^{T}(R_1(x_d,t,t_2)-\overline{r}_d(t_2))dt_2dt_1$$
$$+D_d(t,T)\int_{T_1}^{T}R_1(x_d,t,t_1)\int_{t_1}^{T}R_1(x_d,t,t_2)(e^{\phi_d(t_1,t_2)\Sigma_{dd}(t,t_1)}-1)dt_2dt_1$$
$$-D_d(t,T)\int_{T_1}^{T}R_2(x_d,t,t_1)dt_1.$$

Combining all contributions, we obtain $D_d(t,T)+F_1^T(x_d,t)+F_2^T(x_d,t)+\mathcal{O}(\epsilon^3)$ as expected.

5.3.2 Caplet Pricing

We consider next the pricing of caplets, first reported in a more general context by Horvath et al. [2017]. We will make use here of the following extension of Lemma 5.1.

Lemma 5.2

$$\int_{x_d^*}^{\infty}G_0(x_d,t;\xi_d,T_1)d\xi_d=\Phi(-d_1(x_d^*-\phi_d(t,v)x_d,t,T_1)), \tag{5.18}$$

$$\int_{x_d^*}^{\infty}G_0(x_d,t;\xi_d,T_1)R_i(\xi_d,T_1,w)d\xi_d=R_i(x_d,t,w)\Phi(-d_2(x_d^*-\phi_d(t,v)x_d,t,T_1,w)) \tag{5.19}$$

where we define, for $t \le T_1$

$$d_1(\xi_d,t,T_1):=\frac{\xi_d}{\sqrt{\Sigma_{dd}(t,T_1)}} \tag{5.20}$$

$$d_2(\xi_d,t,T_1,w):=d_1(\xi_d-\phi_d(T_1\wedge w,T_1\vee w)\Sigma_{dd}(t,T_1\wedge w)) \tag{5.21}$$

with $\Phi(\cdot)$ representing a Gaussian cumulative distribution function and the binary operators $\wedge$ and $\vee$ denoting min *and* max, *respectively.*[2]

Proof: The proof is similar to that of Lemma 5.1 except in that use is made of Theorem 3.5 rather than Theorem 3.3. We omit the details.

By the same process as described in §4.3.3 above in relation to the Hull–White model, we seek to derive a second-order accurate expression for the time-t price of a caplet based on a LIBOR payment fixed at time T_1 for payment at time T_2 and strike K. We shall suppose here that $K=\mathcal{O}(\epsilon)$ so that the strike is commensurate with

[2]We will subsequently make use of the definition (5.21) in the case also when $w < T_1$.

the referenced LIBOR payment. Following the same process as in §4.3.3, this will be given again by (4.25), with the notation suitably reinterpreted for the Black–Karasinski context. The critical value x_d^* will in this context be the highest value which causes the payoff *calculated to second order* to have zero value. Specifically, x_d^* satisfies

$$D_d(T_1, T_2) + \sum_{i=1}^{2} F_i^{T_2}(x_d^*, T_1) = \kappa. \tag{5.22}$$

The caplet price can then be written to the same degree of accuracy as

$$\begin{aligned} V_{\text{caplet}}(x_d, t) = D_d(t, T_1) \int_{-\infty}^{\infty} & G_0(x_d, t; \xi_d, T_1) P_1(\xi_d) d\xi_d \\ + D_d(t, T_1) \int_{-\infty}^{\infty} & (G_1(x_d, t; \xi_d, T_1) P_1(\xi_d) \\ & + G_0(x_d, t; \xi_d, T_1) P_2(\xi_d)) d\xi_d + \mathcal{O}(\epsilon^3). \end{aligned} \tag{5.23}$$

where

$$\begin{aligned} P_1(\xi_d) &:= (1 - \kappa^{-1} D_d(T_1, T_2)(1 + F_1^{T_2}(\xi_d, T_1))) \mathbb{1}_{\xi_d > x_d^*}, \\ P_2(\xi_d) &:= -\kappa^{-1} D_d(T_1, T_2) F_2^{T_2}(\xi_d, T_1) \mathbb{1}_{\xi_d > x_d^*}, \end{aligned} \tag{5.24}$$

with $P_n(\xi_d) = \mathcal{O}(\epsilon^n)$, since $1 - \kappa^{-1} D_d(T_1, T_2) = \mathcal{O}(\epsilon)$ by assumption. Application of $G_j(\cdot)$ for $j > 1$ clearly gives rise to negligible terms of $\mathcal{O}(\epsilon^3)$. Integration over the Gaussian distribution making use of Lemma 5.2 yields for the first-order term

$$\begin{aligned} D_d(t, T_1) & \int_{-\infty}^{\infty} G_0(x_d, t; \xi_d, T_1) P_1(\xi_d)\, d\xi_d \\ &= (D_d(t, T_1) - \kappa^{-1} D_d(t, T_2)) \Phi(-d_1(x_d^* - \phi_d(t, T_1) x_d, t, T_1)) \\ &\quad + \kappa^{-1} D_d(t, T_2) \int_{T_1}^{T_2} (R_1(x_d, t, u) \Phi(-d_2(x_d^* - \phi_d(t, T_1) x_d, t, T_1, u)) \\ &\qquad - \bar{r}(u) \Phi(-d_1(x_d^* - \phi_d(t, T_1) x_d, t, T_1))) du. \end{aligned}$$

Similarly we obtain at second order

$$\begin{aligned} D_d(t, T_1) & \int_{-\infty}^{\infty} (G_1(x_d, t; \xi_d, T_1) P_1(\xi_d) + G_0(x_d, t; \xi_d, T_1) P_2(\xi_d)) d\xi_d \\ &= -(D_d(t, T_1) - \kappa^{-1} D_d(t, T_2)) \int_t^{T_1} (R_1(x_d, t, u) \Phi(-d_2(x_d^* - \phi_d(t, T_1) x_d, t, T_1, u)) \\ &\qquad - \bar{r}(u) \Phi(-d_1(x_d^* - \phi_d(t, T_1) x_d, t, T_1))) du \end{aligned}$$

$$
\begin{aligned}
&- \kappa^{-1} D_d(t, T_2) \int_{T_1}^{T_2} R_1(x_d, t, v) \int_t^v (e^{\phi_d(u,v)\Sigma_{dd}(t,u)} R_1(x_d, t, u) \\
&\qquad\qquad \times \Phi(-d_2^*(x_d^* - \phi_d(t, T_1)x_d, t, T_1, u, v)) \\
&\qquad\qquad - \bar{r}(u)\Phi(-d_1^*(x_d^* - \phi_d(t, T_1)x_d, t, T_1, u, v)))dudv \\
&+ \kappa^{-1} D_d(t, T_2) \int_{T_1}^{T_2} R_1(x_d, t, v) \int_t^v (R_1(x_d, t, u)\Phi(-d_2(x_d^* - \phi_d(t, T_1)x_d, t, T_1, u)) \\
&\qquad\qquad - \bar{r}(u)\Phi(-d_1(x_d^* - \phi_d(t, T_1)x_d, t, T_1)))dudv \\
&+ \kappa^{-1} D_d(t, T_2) \int_{T_1}^{T_2} R_2(x_d, t, v)\Phi(-d_2(x_d^* - \phi_d(t, T_1)x_d, t, T_1, v))dv,
\end{aligned}
$$

where we define, for $v \geq T_1$ and $u \in (t, v]$

$$
d_1^*(\xi_d, t, T_1, u, v) := d_1(\xi_d - \phi_d(T_1, v)\Sigma_{dd}(u \wedge T_1, T_1), t, T_1), \tag{5.25}
$$

$$
d_2^*(\xi_d, t, T_1, u, v) := d_2(\xi_d - \phi_d(T_1, v)\Sigma_{dd}(u \wedge T_1, T_1), t, T_1, u) \tag{5.26}
$$

Setting $x = t = 0$, we find the caplet PV has the following form.

Theorem 5.2 *For a Black–Karasinski short rate process governed by* (5.1)*, the PV of a caplet with a LIBOR underlying, strike K and payment period* $[T_1, T_2]$ *is given in the limit of low rates by*

$$
\begin{aligned}
PV_{caplet} &= (D_d(0, T_1) - \kappa^{-1} D_d(0, T_2))\Phi(-d_1(x_d^*, 0, T_1)) \\
&\quad - D_d(0, T_1) \int_0^{T_1} \bar{r}(u)(\Phi(-d_2(x_d^*, 0, T_1, u)) - \Phi(-d_1(x_d^*, 0, T_1)))du \\
&\quad + \kappa^{-1} D_d(0, T_2) \int_0^{T_2} \bar{r}(u)(\Phi(-d_2(x_d^*, 0, T_1, u)) - \Phi(-d_1(x_d^*, 0, T_1)))du \\
&\quad - \kappa^{-1} D_d(0, T_2) \int_{T_1}^{T_2} \bar{r}(v) \int_0^v \bar{r}(u) e^{\phi_d(u,v)\Sigma_{dd}(0,u)}(\Phi(-d_2^*(x_d^*, 0, T_1, u, v)) \\
&\qquad\qquad - \Phi(-d_2(x_d^*, 0, T_1, v)))dudv \\
&\quad + \kappa^{-1} D_d(0, T_2) \int_{T_1}^{T_2} \bar{r}(v) \int_0^v \bar{r}(u)(\Phi(-d_1^*(x_d^*, 0, T_1, u, v)) \\
&\qquad\qquad - \Phi(-d_2(x_d^*, 0, T_1, v)) \\
&\qquad + \Phi(-d_2(x_d^*, 0, T_1, u)) - \Phi(-d_1(x_d^*, 0, T_1)))dudv + \mathcal{O}(\epsilon^3),
\end{aligned} \tag{5.27}
$$

using the notation defined above with $\epsilon = \| \tilde{r}(\cdot) \|$.

The corresponding floorlet PV is easily obtained from the principle of put–call parity

$$
\begin{aligned}
PV_{\text{floorlet}} &= (\kappa^{-1}D_d(0,T_2) - D_d(0,T_1))\Phi(d_1(x_d^*,0,T_1)) \\
&\quad + D_d(0,T_1)\int_0^{T_1}\overline{r}(u)(\Phi(d_2(x_d^*,0,T_1,u)) - \Phi(d_1(x_d^*,0,T_1)))du \\
&\quad - \kappa^{-1}D_d(0,T_2)\int_0^{T_2}\overline{r}(u)(\Phi(d_2(x_d^*,0,T_1,u)) - \Phi(d_1(x_d^*,0,T_1)))du \\
&\quad + \kappa^{-1}D_d(0,T_2)\int_{T_1}^{T_2}\overline{r}(v)\int_0^{v}\overline{r}(u)e^{\phi_d(u,v)\Sigma_{dd}(0,u)}(\Phi(d_2^*(x_d^*,0,T_1,u,v)) \\
&\qquad - \Phi(d_2(x_d^*,0,T_1,v)))dudv \\
&\quad - \kappa^{-1}D_d(0,T_2)\int_{T_1}^{T_2}\overline{r}(v)\int_0^{v}\overline{r}(u)(\Phi(d_1^*(x_d^*,0,T_1,u,v)) - \Phi(d_2(x_d^*,0,T_1,v)) \\
&\qquad + \Phi(d_2(x_d^*,0,T_1,u)) - \Phi(d_1(x_d^*,0,T_1)))dudv + \mathcal{O}(\epsilon^3),
\end{aligned}
\tag{5.28}
$$

The corresponding first-order results are obtained in each case by omitting the terms in the formulae involving double integrals. In this case of course the $i = 2$ term in (5.22) should for consistency also be ignored in calculating x_d^* to first-order accuracy.

5.3.3 European Swaption Pricing

The calculation for European swaption prices, first presented by Turfus [2018a], proceeds in a similar manner. We consider the same swaption as was discussed in §4.3.4 above, which at t_0 will have the same payoff function (4.32) subject to the bond price expressions being reinterpreted appropriately. We find following a calculation analogous to the above that the payer swaption PV is given by

$$
PV_{\text{payer}} = \sum_{i=1}^{n} PV_{\text{payer}}^{(i)} + \mathcal{O}(\epsilon^3) \tag{5.29}
$$

where

$$
\begin{aligned}
PV_{\text{payer}}^{(i)} &:= (D_d(0,T_{i-1}) - \kappa^{-1}D_d(0,T_i))\Phi(-d_1(x_d^*,0,t_0)) \\
&\quad - D_d(0,T_{i-1})\int_0^{T_{i-1}}\overline{r}(u)(\Phi(-d_2(x_d^*,0,t_0,u)) - \Phi(-d_1(x_d^*,0,t_0)))du \\
&\quad + \kappa^{-1}D_d(0,T_i)\int_0^{T_i}\overline{r}(u)(\Phi(-d_2(x_d^*,0,t_0,u)) - \Phi(-d_1(x_d^*,0,t_0)))du
\end{aligned}
$$

$$
\begin{aligned}
&- \kappa^{-1} D_d(0,T_i) \int_{t_0}^{T_i} \bar{r}(v) \int_0^v \bar{r}(u) e^{\phi_d(u,v)\Sigma_{dd}(0,u)} (\Phi(-d_2^*(x_d^*, 0, t_0, u, v)) \\
&\qquad - \Phi(-d_2(x_d^*, 0, t_0, v)))dudv \\
&+ \kappa^{-1} D_d(0,T_i) \int_{t_0}^{T_i} \bar{r}(v) \int_0^v \bar{r}(u)(\Phi(-d_1^*(x_d^*, 0, t_0, u, v)) - \Phi(-d_2(x_d^*, 0, t_0, v)) \\
&\qquad + \Phi(-d_2(x_d^*, 0, t_0, u)) - \Phi(-d_1(x_d^*, 0, t_0)))dudv.
\end{aligned} \tag{5.30}
$$

Here x_d^* is defined as in §4.3.4, with the Hull–White zero coupon bond formulae $F_T(x_d, t_0)$ replaced by its (second-order accurate) Black–Karasinski equivalent. The result for the receiver swaption is easily obtained through the put–call parity principle as

$$
PV_{\text{receiver}} = PV_{\text{payer}} - \sum_{i=1}^{n} (D_d(0, T_{i-1}) - \kappa^{-1} D_d(0, T_i)). \tag{5.31}
$$

5.4 COMPARISON OF RESULTS

In the following, reproduced from Horvath et al. [2017], we focus on the pricing of caps: from put–call parity, the error associated with the asymptotic approximation in the corresponding floor prices is guaranteed to be identical, so does not merit separate investigation.

Calculations were done using a first-order asymptotic representation. That is, we ignored the contribution from F_2^T in (5.14) and used only the first three lines of (5.27). Comparisons were made with a Monte Carlo simulation using a conservative 500,000 simulations, ensuring any Monte Carlo error did not impact significantly on the quality of the comparison. The instantaneous forward rate is taken to follow the profile of the USD market for January 2017 rising from around 1% to around 3% over a five-year period. The (lognormal) local volatility is taken to be 30%, with a (constant) mean reversion rate of 25%. The results are illustrated in Fig. 5.1 for various moneyness levels. As can be seen, they are indistinguishable to visual accuracy.

We consider next how the asymptotic expansion performs in the case of different maturities up to 20y. For the purposes of allowing comparative analysis across different maturities, we focus on ATM options by moving the strike of the caps appropriately. Results are shown in Fig. 5.2. They remain fairly indistinguishable to visual accuracy. As is evident, the error increases with maturity but of course so does the cap value. Overall the relative error increases, so the approximation does deteriorate slightly for longer maturities.

Next we consider the variation of cap prices with the volatility $\sigma_d(t)$. Results are shown in Fig. 5.3. As with time to maturity, the error is seen to grow as volatility increases, as does the price, both approximately linearly in the high volatility limit. Even at the very high level of 50% volatility the error is still only about 0.4% in relative terms.

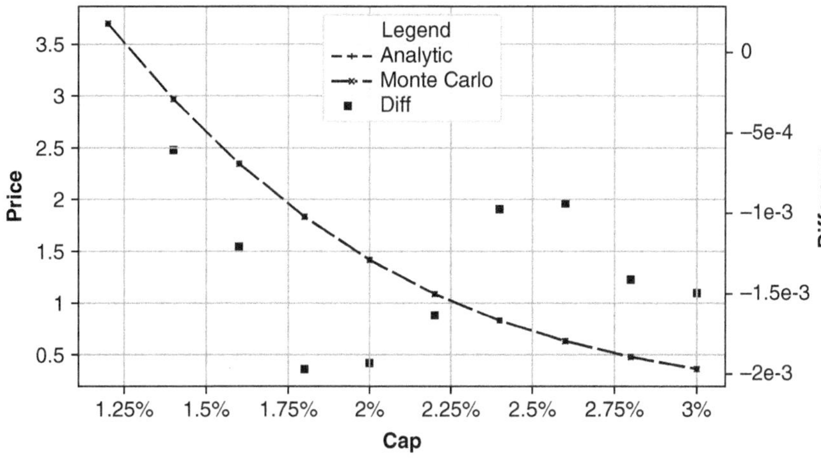

FIGURE 5.1 Black–Karasinski prices for 5y maturity cap with 6m LIBOR tenor

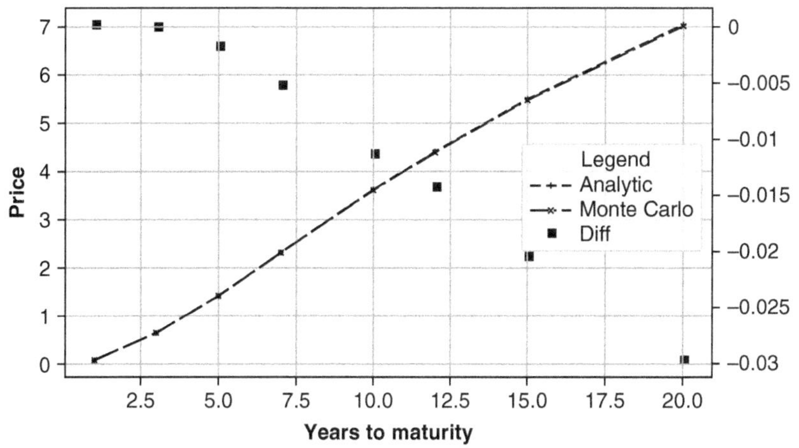

FIGURE 5.2 Black–Karasinski prices for caps with different maturities

A similar comparison is illustrated in Fig. 5.4 of the dependency of 5y cap prices on the assumed volatility mean reversion rate $\alpha_d(t)$. Not surprisingly, as the mean reversion rate approaches zero allowing the volatility to grow without bound as T increases, the errors in the asymptotic approximation become larger, but even in such circumstances no greater in relative terms than those observed in Fig. 5.3.

Given that our asymptotic expansion is based on an assumption of small fluctuations in the rates in absolute terms, it is to be expected that the accuracy will be lessened as the level of the yield curve is raised with fixed lognormal volatility levels. The impact of such a change is considered in Fig. 5.5, where the yield curve is parallel-bumped upward by up to 8%. To enable a fair comparison, the strike is raised by the same amount in each case, ensuring that options remained roughly at the money. As can be

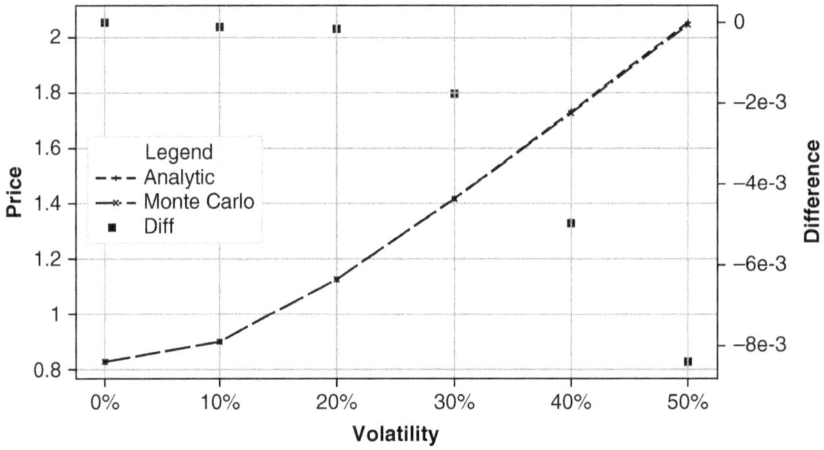

FIGURE 5.3 Dependence of Black–Karasinski prices for 5y caps on volatility level

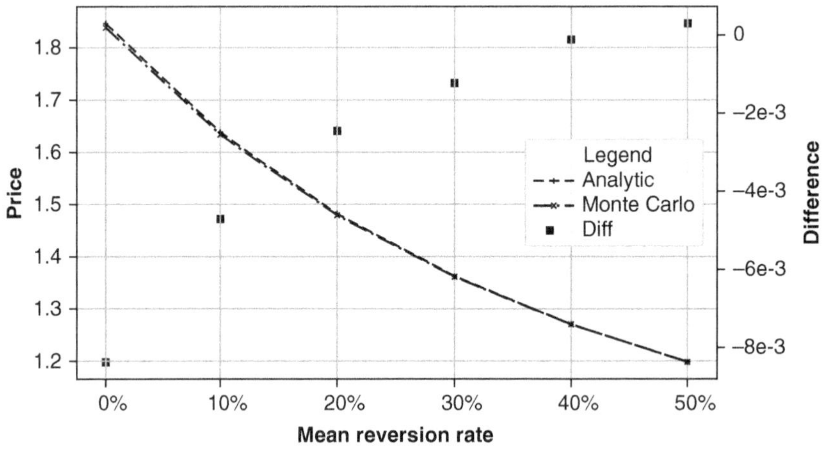

FIGURE 5.4 Dependence of Black–Karasinski prices for 5y caps on volatility mean reversion rate α_d

seen, the option value increases due to the (fixed) lognormal volatility having greater PV impact for higher rates. As expected, the error also increases, roughly in proportion. Even in the fairly extreme case of a 10% interest rate, the relative error in the 5y cap PV was seen to be only 0.5% in relative terms.

In conclusion, we infer that even our rather simple first-order approximations ought to be usable for many practical purposes, particularly calibration and risk management where exact reproduction of market prices is less essential than in pricing for trading purposes. If greater accuracy is required, particularly in the Black–Karasinski case, the inclusion of second order terms ought easily to provide enough accuracy with very little additional computational burden.

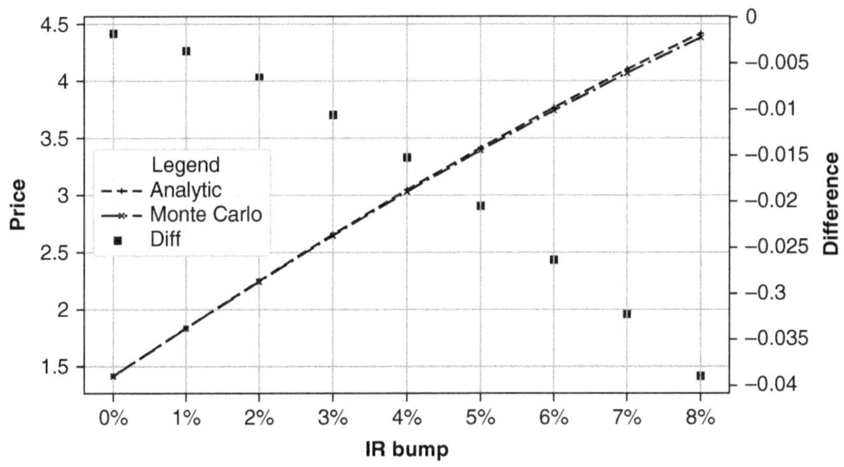

FIGURE 5.5 Dependence of ATM Black–Karasinski prices for 5y caps on IR curve level

5.5 PROOF OF THEOREM 5.1

5.5.1 Preliminary Result

For our proof of Theorem 5.1, we establish first the following lemma.

Lemma 5.3 *Defining*

$$\mathcal{L}(t,u) = \frac{1}{2}\frac{\sigma_d^2(u)}{\phi_d^2(t,u)}\frac{\partial^2}{\partial x_d^2}, \tag{5.32}$$

$$\mathcal{V}(t,u) = -\tilde{r}(u)e^{\phi_d(t,u)x_d - \frac{1}{2}\Sigma_{dd}(0,u)}. \tag{5.33}$$

the following holds

$$\mathcal{E}_t^u(ad_{\mathcal{L}(t,\cdot)})(\mathcal{V}(t,u)) = \mathcal{V}(t,u)\exp\left(\Sigma_{dd}(t,u)\left(\frac{1}{2} + \frac{1}{\phi_d(t,u)}\frac{\partial}{\partial x_d}\right)\right). \tag{5.34}$$

Proof: We prove (5.34) inductively. To obtain $\mathcal{E}_t^u(\mathrm{ad}_{\mathcal{L}(t,\cdot)}(\mathcal{V}(t,u)))$ we must compute

$$\begin{aligned}\int_t^u \mathrm{ad}_{\mathcal{L}(t,t_1)}(\mathcal{V}(t,u))dt_1 &= \int_t^u (\mathcal{L}(t,t_1)\mathcal{V}(t,u) - \mathcal{V}(t,u)\mathcal{L}(t,t_1))dt_1 \\ &= \mathcal{V}(t,u)\int_t^u \frac{\sigma_d^2(t_1)}{\phi_d^2(t,t_1)}dt_1\left(\frac{1}{2}\phi_d^2(t,u) + \phi_d(t,u)\frac{\partial}{\partial x_d}\right) \\ &= \mathcal{V}(t,u)\Sigma_{dd}(t,u)\left(\frac{1}{2} + \frac{1}{\phi_d(t,u)}\frac{\partial}{\partial x_d}\right),\end{aligned}$$

Further application of the commutator operator and integration yields

$$\int_t^u \int_{t_1}^v \mathrm{ad}_{\mathcal{L}(t,t_1)}(\mathrm{ad}_{\mathcal{L}(t,t_2)}(\mathcal{V}(t,u)))dt_2dt_1 = \mathcal{V}(t,u)\frac{\Sigma^2_{dd}(t,u)}{2!}\left(\frac{1}{2}+\frac{1}{\phi_d(t,u)}\frac{\partial}{\partial x_d}\right)^2, \tag{5.35}$$

and similarly for higher terms. Summing over all terms yields (5.34) as required.

5.5.2 Turn the Handle!

As in the Hull–White case, we seek to prove Theorem 5.1 by first deriving an evolution operator $\mathcal{U}(t,T)$ satisfying

$$\begin{aligned}\left(\frac{\partial}{\partial t}+\mathcal{L}_1(t)+\mathcal{L}_2(t)+\mathcal{V}_1(t)\right)\mathcal{U}(t,T) &= 0,\\ \mathcal{U}(T,T) &= I,\end{aligned} \tag{5.36}$$

with in this case

$$\mathcal{L}_1(t) = -\alpha_d(t)x_d\frac{\partial}{\partial x_d} \tag{5.37}$$

$$\mathcal{L}_2(t) = \frac{1}{2}\sigma_d^2(t)\frac{\partial^2}{\partial x_d^2}, \tag{5.38}$$

$$\mathcal{V}_1(t) = -\tilde{r}_d(t)e^{x_d-\frac{1}{2}\Sigma_{dd}(0,t)}. \tag{5.39}$$

Making use of Theorem 3.2 and Lemma 3.1 as we did in the Hull–White case, we can write the solution of (5.36) as

$$\mathcal{U}(t,T) = \mathcal{E}_t^T(\mathcal{L}(t,\cdot)+\mathcal{V}(t,\cdot))\mathcal{E}_t^T(\mathcal{L}_1(\cdot)), \tag{5.40}$$

with $\mathcal{L}(t,u)$ and $\mathcal{V}(t,u)$ as defined in (5.32) and (5.33), respectively, in Lemma 5.3. Making use of this lemma and (4.43), we obtain

$$\mathcal{U}(t,T) = \mathcal{E}_t^T(\mathcal{W}(t,\cdot))\mathcal{E}_t^T(\mathcal{L}(t,\cdot))\mathcal{E}_t^T(\mathcal{L}_1(\cdot)), \tag{5.41}$$

$$\begin{aligned}\mathcal{W}(t,t_1) &= \mathcal{E}_t^{t_1}(\mathrm{ad}_{\mathcal{L}(t,\cdot)}(\mathcal{V}(t,t_1)))\\ &= -\tilde{r}(t_1)e^{\phi_d(t,t_1)x_d-\frac{1}{2}\phi_d^2(t,t_1)\Sigma_{dd}(0,t)}\exp\left(\Delta_{dd}(t,t_1)\frac{\partial}{\partial x_d}\right),\end{aligned} \tag{5.42}$$

with $\Delta_{dd}(t,t_1)$ as defined in (5.11). Taking the integral kernel of $\mathcal{U}(t,T)$ in the same manner as in the Hull–White case using the result of §3.4.2 and (3.40), we obtain the following expression for the pricing kernel

$$G(x_d,t;\xi_d,v) = \mathcal{E}_t^v(\mathcal{W}(t,\cdot))G_0(x_d,t;\xi_d,v). \tag{5.43}$$

To facilitate calibration, it is convenient to make an adjustment at this stage, factoring out $D_d(t,v)$ from the definition of $\mathcal{E}_t^v(\mathcal{W}(t,\cdot))$. To that end let us define

$$\mathcal{W}_1(t,t_1) = \overline{r}_d(t_1)+\mathcal{W}(t,t_1), \tag{5.44}$$

using which we can write (5.43) as

$$G(x_d, t; \xi_d, v) = \mathcal{E}_t^v(-\bar{r}_d(\cdot))\mathcal{E}_t^v(\mathcal{W}_1(t,\cdot))G_0(x_d, t; \xi_d, v)$$
$$= D_d(t,v)\mathcal{E}_t^v(\mathcal{W}_1(t,\cdot))G_0(x_d, t; \xi_d, v). \quad (5.45)$$

Finally, unpacking $\mathcal{E}_t^T(\mathcal{W}_1(t,\cdot))$ using Definition 3.1 and (3.39) to interpret the exponential of a derivative, we deduce that $G(\cdot)$ has the structure of (5.3) and that (5.5) and (5.6) represent the zeroth and first-order contributions, respectively.

Obtaining higher terms in the expansion requires a little extra care to take account of the fact that $\mathcal{W}_1(t, t_1)$ does not commute with $\mathcal{W}_1(t, t_2)$. We see that the result for $G_2(x_d, t; \xi_d, v)$ is obtained by consideration of:

- products of the $R_1(\cdot)$ and $\bar{r}_d(\cdot)$ terms arising in $\int_t^v \int_{t_1}^v \mathcal{W}_1(t,t_1)\mathcal{W}_1(t,t_2)G_0(x_d, t; \xi_d, v)dt_2 dt_1$, and
- the $R_2(\cdot)$ term arising in $-\int_t^v \mathcal{W}_1(t,t_1)G_0(x_d, t; \xi_d, v)dt_1$.

The former results in the first line of (5.7) and the latter in the second line.

It remains to specify the required form of the function $\tilde{r}(t)$ to be commensurate with the instantaneous forward curve at $t = 0$. We require that the zero coupon bond PV inferred from the Green's function is $D_d(0, v)$, with $D_d(t, v)$ given by (3.49). Applying (5.3) to a unit payoff at $t = 0$, we conclude:

$$D_d(0,v)^{-1}\int_{\mathbb{R}} G(0,0;\xi_d,v)d\xi_d = 1$$
$$\Rightarrow \mathcal{E}_0^v(\mathcal{W}_1(0,\cdot))\int_{\mathbb{R}} G_0(x_d, 0; \xi_d, v)d\xi_d\bigg|_{x_d=0} = 1 \quad (5.46)$$

At first order in ϵ this gives rise to

$$\int_0^v (\tilde{r}_1(t_1) - \bar{r}_d(t_1))dt_1,$$

which is satisfied by the choice (5.12). At second order in ϵ we have

$$\int_0^v \left(\tilde{r}_2(t_1) - \tilde{r}_1(t_1)\int_{t_1}^v \tilde{r}_1(t_2)(e^{\phi_d(t_1,t_2)\Sigma_{dd}(0,t_1)} - 1)dt_2\right)dt_1 = 0.$$

Applying Fubini's theorem we deduce

$$\int_0^v \left(\tilde{r}_2(t_2) - \tilde{r}_1(t_2)\int_0^{t_2} \tilde{r}_1(t_1)(e^{\phi_d(t_1,t_2)\Sigma_{dd}(0,t_1)} - 1)dt_1\right)dt_2 = 0,$$

which is satisfied by the choice (5.13). This completes the proof.

5.6 EXACT BLACK–KARASINSKI PRICING KERNEL

For completeness we include here the derivation of an exact representation of the Black–Karasinski pricing kernel to arbitrary order of accuracy. Our presentation is based broadly on that of Turfus [2018b]. Our starting point is to take the pricing kernel in the form (5.43). Rather than factoring out $D_d(t, T)$ as previously and representing $\tilde{r}(t)$ as an asymptotic series, it is more expeditious to compute (5.43) directly.[3] Analogous to (5.8) we define

$$R(x_d, t, t_1) := \tilde{r}(t_1) e^{\theta_d(x_d, t, t_1)}, \tag{5.47}$$

in terms of which we deduce

$$G(x_d, t; \xi_d, v) = G_0(x_d, t; \xi_d, v) + \sum_{n=1}^{\infty} G_n^*(x_d, t; \xi_d, v), \tag{5.48}$$

where for $n \geq 1$

$$\begin{aligned} G_n^*(x_d, t; \xi_d, v) &= (-1)^n \int_t^v \int_t^{t_n} \dots \int_t^{t_2} \prod_{i=1}^{n} R(x_d, t, t_i) \mathcal{M}(t, t_i) G_0(x_d, t; \xi_d, v) dt_1 \dots dt_n \\ &= (-1)^n \int_t^v \int_t^{t_n} \dots \int_t^{t_2} \prod_{i=1}^{n} R(x_d, t, t_i) G_0(x_d, t; \xi_d, v) dt_1 \dots dt_n \\ &+ (-1)^n \int_t^v \int_t^{t_n} \dots \int_t^{t_2} \left(\prod_{i=1}^{n} R(x_d, t, t_i) \mathcal{M}(t, t_i) - \prod_{i=1}^{n} R(x_d, t, t_i) \right) \\ &\qquad G_0(x_d, t; \xi_d, v) dt_1 \dots dt_{n-1} dt_n. \end{aligned} \tag{5.49}$$

Here we have used the second version of the time-ordered exponential formula in (3.20). Substituting back, we can write

$$\begin{aligned} G(x_d, t; \xi_d, v) &= e^{-\int_t^v R(x_d, t, t_1) dt_1} G_0(x_d, t; \xi_d, v) \\ &+ \sum_{n=1}^{\infty} (-1)^n \int_t^v \int_t^{t_n} \dots \int_t^{t_2} \left(\prod_{i=1}^{n} R(x_d, t, t_i) \mathcal{M}(t, t_i) - \prod_{i=1}^{n} R(x_d, t, t_i) \right) \\ &\qquad G_0(x_d, t; \xi_d, v) dt_1 \dots dt_{n-1} dt_n. \end{aligned} \tag{5.50}$$

Making use of this representation, the exact calibration condition (5.46) can be written as

$$\begin{aligned} \sum_{n=2}^{\infty} (-1)^n \int_0^v \int_0^{t_n} \dots \int_0^{t_2} \left(\prod_{i=2}^{n} \tilde{r}(t_i) e^{\phi_d(t_{i-1}, t_i) \Sigma_{dd}(0, t_{i-1})} - \prod_{i=2}^{n} \tilde{r}(t_i) \right) dt_1 \dots dt_{n-1} dt_n \\ = D_d(0, v) - e^{-\int_0^v \tilde{r}(t_1) dt_1} \\ = \sum_{n=1}^{\infty} (-1)^n \frac{\left(\int_0^v \bar{r}(t_1) dt_1\right)^n - \left(\int_0^v \tilde{r}(t_1) dt_1\right)^n}{n!}. \end{aligned}$$

[3] This is not necessary but results in a more transparent process for extraction of the $\tilde{r}_n(t)$ subsequently.

Substituting in from (5.4) and satisfying this equality for successive powers of ϵ allows the required form for each of the $\tilde{r}_n(t)$ to be obtained in turn as previously. The process for the elucidation of the general formula for arbitrary n is a little involved, but it is demonstrated by Turfus [2018b] that, for $n > 1$

$$\tilde{r}_n(t) = \sum_{i=1}^{n-1} \int_0^t \int_0^{t_i} \cdots \int_0^{t_2} \sum_{p \in P(i+1,n)} R_{[p]}(t, t_1, \ldots, t_i)$$
$$\left(\exp\left(\sum_{j=1}^{i-1} \phi_d(t_j, t_{j+1}) \Sigma_{dd}(0, t_j) + \phi_d(t_i, t) \Sigma_{dd}(0, t_i) \right) - 1 \right) dt_1 \ldots dt_{i-1} dt_i, \tag{5.51}$$

where, for $1 \leq i \leq n$, $P(i, n)$ is the set of all permutations of positive integers of the form $p = (k_1, k_2, \ldots, k_i)$ with $\sum_{j=1}^{i} k_j = n$ and we define

$$\tilde{R}_{[k_1,k_2,\ldots,k_j]}(t_1, t_2, \ldots, t_j) = \prod_{i=1}^{j} \tilde{r}_{k_i}(t_i). \tag{5.52}$$

By way of illustration we have for $n = 4$

$$P(1, 4) = \{(4)\}$$
$$P(2, 4) = \{(1, 3), (2, 2), (3, 1)\}$$
$$P(3, 4) = \{(1, 1, 2), (1, 2, 1), (2, 1, 1)\}$$
$$P(4, 4) = \{(1, 1, 1, 1)\}.$$

It can be seen that this process is consistent with the results for $\tilde{r}_1(t)$ and $\tilde{r}_2(t)$ obtained above. Turfus [2018b] also states explicitly the form of the third order expansion, including the fact that

$$\tilde{r}_3(t) = \int_0^t (\tilde{r}_1(t)\tilde{r}_2(t_1) + \tilde{r}_2(t)\tilde{r}_1(t_1))(e^{\phi_r(t_1,t)\Sigma_r(0,t_1)} - 1) dt_1$$
$$+ \int_0^t \int_0^{t_2} \tilde{r}_1(t)\tilde{r}_1(t_2)\tilde{r}_1(t_1)(e^{\phi_r(t_1,t_2)\Sigma_r(0,t_1)+\phi_r(t_2,t)\Sigma_r(0,t_2)} - 1) dt_1 dt_2. \tag{5.53}$$

We can further use (5.50) to establish the following useful *exact* representation of the conditional bond price

$$F^T(x_d, t) = e^{-\int_t^T R(x_d,t,t_1) dt_1} + \sum_{n=2}^{\infty} (-1)^n \int_t^T \int_0^{t_n} \cdots \int_0^{t_2} \left(\prod_{i=2}^{n} R(x_d, t, t_i) e^{\phi_d(t_{i-1},t_i)\Sigma_{dd}(t,t_{i-1})} \right.$$
$$\left. - \prod_{i=2}^{n} R(x_d, t, t_i) \right) dt_1 \ldots dt_{n-1} dt_n \tag{5.54}$$

since $\tilde{r}(t)$, and therefore $R(x_d, t, t_1)$, can be considered known on the basis of the above.

CHAPTER 6

Extension to Multi-Factor Modelling

6.1 MULTI-FACTOR PRICING EQUATION

Having demonstrated successfully how the methods we introduced in Chapter 3 can be used to derive pricing kernels for one-factor short-rate models, and further how these pricing kernels can be used to calculate derivative prices, we turn our attention to multi-factor modelling, where our real interest lies in the context of the present work. There are four different ways which we can consider additional stochastic factors as influencing the calculations we performed in the previous two chapters.

Multi-factor yield curve. It may be that the rate used for discounting, instead of being a function of a single stochastic variable, is a function of several stochastic variables (which, without loss of generality, can be considered as independent).

Additional factors not impacting rates. The pricing equation we consider, and therefore the pricing kernel produced, may specify the co-evolution of other stochastic variables which evolve without impacting on the evolution of the rate itself. The co-evolution may be trivial, but usually there is at least the potential for correlated diffusion. An example here would be a diffusion for which the governing diffusion was correlated with the risk-free interest rate, and the drift of which depended on the same. Equally, we could consider LIBOR of a given tenor being given by the risk-free rate plus an additional stochastic spread. This spread impacts the LIBOR rates which appear in payoff expressions, but not the discounting applied thereto, which is typically considered to be driven by the (instantaneous) risk-free rate.

Additional factors impacting rates. On occasions an interest rate may have no direct functional dependence on an additional factor, yet this factor may impact on the evolution of that rate. An example of this would be if the factor were driving a stochastic volatility representation for the rate (a possibility we shall not seek to address explicitly in the following). Another case of relevance would be if the interest rate was in a foreign currency, i.e. one other than that in which the prices calculated are denominated. Then there would be an additional drift associated with the change of numéraire from foreign to domestic currency, which change would affect the evolution of the foreign rate, specifically its drift.

Additional factors capturing default risk. A final possibility, the one with which we shall mainly be concerned throughout the remainder of this book, is that an additional factor may appear in the role of driving a stochastic credit intensity which, like the risk-free interest rate, impacts on the discounting which has to be applied to any payoffs, to ascertain the present value of the payment.

Of course, these four categories are not mutually exclusive; indeed, factors of all four types can be present simultaneously in a pricing context. For that reason, we shall look to address them all in a single unified framework. It turns out that this is adequate for all the situations we shall be interested in below.

In the first instance we shall consider multi-factor short-rate models, which can be taken as describing the evolution of interest rate or credit default intensity curves. Mathematically, this problem is not distinct from the multi-asset problem, so no new mathematical innovation will be needed for that purpose. We shall be interested in hybrid modelling where there may be other market underlyings on which derivative prices depend, such as equity prices, inflation indices, FX rates and/or commodity prices. In addition we will be interested in multi-currency instruments and derivatives involving credit risk, more generally credit hybrid derivatives.

Our aim will therefore be to extend the work we did in Chapter 3 for the one-factor short-rate modelling problem to provide a more general foundation for obtaining pricing kernels in the case of multi-factor models. We will take advantage of the fact that most of the problems we are interested in can be considered as instances of (3.4) and look for a general solution to that problem. As we shall see, the further work needed to find pricing kernels for specific multi-asset models is thereby reduced to considering the impact of the (standard) drift and diffusion terms on the discount rate (r_{dt} or $r_{dt} + \lambda_t$). In this way, we shall maximise reuse of those parts of previous calculations which are generic and in each case home in on only those parts which are specific to the problem at hand, and of course on the application of the derived pricing kernels to specific problems.

We shall restrict our attention to the case of multi-variate Ornstein–Uhlenbeck processes, following the lead of Meucci [2010] who took a similar approach in his paper on the use of multivariate Ornstein–Uhlenbeck processes in analyzing statistical arbitrage. He argued that the Ornstein–Uhlenbeck process is parsimonious, and yet general enough to cover a broad range of processes, so that by studying the multivariate Ornstein–Uhlenbeck process we gain insight into the properties of the main multivariate features used daily by econometricians.

Thus, we consider the multivariate Ornstein-Uhlenback process specified by (3.1), where the drift $\boldsymbol{\mu}(x, t)$, considered as a column vector, is an affine function of x with, specifically

$$\mu_i(x, t) = \beta_i(t) - \sum_{j=1}^{n} \kappa_{ij}(t) x_j, \tag{6.1}$$

or more compactly $\boldsymbol{\mu}(x, t) = \boldsymbol{\beta}(t) - \boldsymbol{\kappa}(t)x$. We follow Meucci [2010] in making the further assumption that all eigenvalues of $\boldsymbol{\kappa}(t)$ have non-negative real parts, so ensuring that the drift is not mean-fleeing, as is commonly postulated with the type of market-driven processes we are interested in. We shall make the further assumption that all are real. Whereas Meucci [2010] obtained an analytic representation of the joint distribution function, we shall look to obtain one for the pricing kernel in the case of a general $r(x, t)$. We will go on to deduce explicit representations in the particular cases of Hull–White rates and Black–Karasinski rates or credit default intensity.

Consider, therefore, the (stochastic) time-t price of a European-style security which pays a cash amount $P(x_T)$ at maturity T, denoting this as previously by $f_t = f(x_t, t)$. We infer as a consequence of the Feynman–Kac theorem that, in the general case, $f(x, t)$ emerges as the solution of the following Kolmogorov backward diffusion equation

$$\left(\frac{\partial}{\partial t} + \sum_{j=1}^{n} [\beta(t) - \kappa(t)x]_i \frac{\partial}{\partial x_i} + \frac{1}{2}\sum_{i=1}^{n}\sum_{j=1}^{n} [\sigma(t)\sigma^T(t)]_{ij} \frac{\partial^2}{\partial x_i \partial x_j} - r(x, t)\right) f(x, t) = 0. \tag{6.2}$$

subject to the final condition $f(x, T) = P(x)$.

Change of Co-ordinates. We next introduce an affine co-ordinate change to remove the x-dependence from the drift term in (6.2). To this end, following §12.1 of Andersen and Piterbarg [2010] or §9.5 of Pascucci [2011], we note that an integrating factor for (6.2) is given by the matrix function $\mathbf{\Phi}(t)$ satisfying the following Cauchy problem

$$\begin{cases} \mathbf{\Phi}'(t) = -\boldsymbol{\kappa}(t)\mathbf{\Phi}(t), \\ \mathbf{\Phi}(0) = I_N, \end{cases} \tag{6.3}$$

where I_N is the $N \times N$ identity matrix. Considering the matrix $\boldsymbol{\kappa}(t)$ as a linear operator, the solution can be expressed as the following time-ordered exponential

$$\mathbf{\Phi}(t) = \mathcal{E}_0^t(-\boldsymbol{\kappa}(\cdot)). \tag{6.4}$$

Making the transformation from (x, t) to (y, t) with $y = \mathbf{\Phi}^{-1}(t)x$ and writing $g(y, t) \equiv f(x, t)$, (6.2) becomes, using operator notation

$$\left(\frac{\partial}{\partial t} + \mathcal{L}(t) + \mathcal{V}(t)\right) g(y, t) = 0, \tag{6.5}$$

with

$$\mathcal{L}(t) = \sum_{i=1}^{n} \beta_i^*(t)\frac{\partial}{\partial y_i} + \frac{1}{2}\sum_{i=1}^{n}\sum_{j=1}^{n} \sigma_{ij}^*(t)\frac{\partial^2}{\partial y_i \partial y_j} - \bar{r}_d(t), \tag{6.6}$$

$$\mathcal{V}(t) = \bar{r}_d(t) - r(\mathbf{\Phi}(t)y, t), \tag{6.7}$$

where $\bar{r}_d(t)$ is the instantaneous forward rate as previously, $\sigma_{ij}^*(t)$ are the components of the matrix-valued function

$$\boldsymbol{\sigma}^*(t) := \mathbf{\Phi}^{-1}(t)\boldsymbol{\sigma}(t)(\mathbf{\Phi}^{-1}(t)\boldsymbol{\sigma}(t))^T, \tag{6.8}$$

and $\beta_i^*(t)$ are the components of the vector-valued function

$$\boldsymbol{\beta}^*(t) := \mathbf{\Phi}^{-1}(t)\boldsymbol{\beta}(t)). \tag{6.9}$$

Computation of $\mathbf{\Phi}(t)$ and Its Inverse. We observe that the calculation of the expression in (6.4) is not trivial insofar as the definition (3.20) requires summation of an infinite series. However, in the event that $\boldsymbol{\kappa}(t)$ is lower triangular (which is often the case), $\mathbf{\Phi}(t)$ will also be lower triangular, so a simpler recursive procedure is available, which we now describe. Starting with the diagonal terms, we see

$$\begin{cases} \Phi'_{ii}(t) = -\kappa_{ii}(t)\Phi_{ii}(t), \\ \Phi_{ii}(0) = 1, \end{cases} \tag{6.10}$$

with solution

$$\Phi_{ii}(t) = e^{-\int_0^t \kappa_{ii}(u)du}.$$

For off-diagonal terms with $j < i$, we have

$$\begin{cases} \Phi'_{ij}(t) = -\kappa_{ii}(t)\Phi_{ij}(t) + \theta_{ij}(t), \quad i = 1, \ldots, n \\ \Phi_{ij}(0) = 0, \end{cases} \tag{6.11}$$

with

$$\theta_{ij}(t) := -\sum_{k=j}^{i-1} \kappa_{ik}(t)\Phi_{kj}(t)$$

known if the subdiagonals are addressed in turn in increasing order of $i - j$. The Cauchy problem (6.11) has an integrating factor $\Phi_{ii}^{-1}(t)$ and consequently a solution

$$\Phi_{ij}(t) = \Phi_{ii}(t) \int_0^t \Phi_{ii}^{-1}(u)\theta_{ij}(u)du.$$

The terms on successive subdiagonals of $\mathbf{\Phi}(t)$ can on this basis be computed in turn. The full solution will in general required nested n-dimensional quadrature to be performed, but as n is not likely to be too large in practice, this should not prove to be a significant computational burden. A similar recursive procedure is available for the subsequent calculation of $\mathbf{\Phi}^{-1}(t)$.

6.2 DERIVATION OF PRICING KERNEL

6.2.1 Preliminaries

We start by solving (6.5) for the special case $\mathcal{V}(t) = 0$, before considering in the following subsection the impact of $\mathcal{V}(t) \neq 0$. From §9.5 of Pascucci [2011], (6.5) has a Green's function solution given in this instance by

$$G_0(\mathbf{y}, t; \boldsymbol{\eta}, v) = D_d(t, v)N(\mathbf{y} + \boldsymbol{\gamma}^*(t, v) - \boldsymbol{\eta}; \mathbf{\Sigma}^*(t, v)), \tag{6.12}$$

where $N(., \mathbf{\Sigma})$ is a multivariate Gaussian density with covariance $\mathbf{\Sigma}$, $D_d(t, v)$ is given by (3.49) and we define

$$\gamma^*(t, v) := \int_t^v \beta^*(u)du. \tag{6.13}$$

$$\mathbf{\Sigma}^*(t, v) := \int_t^v \sigma^*(u)du. \tag{6.14}$$

We look to establish the general form of the Green's function solution, or pricing kernel, for (6.5), and thereby for (6.2); specifically its dependence on the functional form of $r(\boldsymbol{x}, t)$. As previously, we consider the semigroup of evolution operators $\mathcal{U}(t, T)$, seeking in the first instance an evolution operator solution to the following Cauchy problem

$$\begin{aligned} \left(\frac{\partial}{\partial t} + \mathcal{L}(t) + \mathcal{V}(t)\right) \mathcal{U}(t, T) &= 0, \\ \mathcal{U}(T, T) &= I. \end{aligned} \tag{6.15}$$

The integral kernel associated with this evolution operator $\mathcal{U}(t, T)$ is precisely the pricing kernel we seek. We have already established in closed form the integral kernel (6.12) associated with the case $\mathcal{V}(t) = 0$. The full solution can be obtained formally therefrom using linear operator theory for a generic representation of $r(\boldsymbol{x}, t)$. Finally, explicit formulae can be obtained for the important Hull–White and Black–Karasinski cases, and indeed for a hybrid two-factor model, as we shall see in the following sections.

6.2.2 Full Solution Using Operator Expansion

The solution to the evolution operator equation (6.15) can be formally written as

$$\mathcal{U}(t, T) = \mathcal{E}_t^T(\mathcal{L}(\cdot) + \mathcal{V}(\cdot)), \tag{6.16}$$

with $\mathcal{L}(t)$ and $\mathcal{V}(t)$ given by (6.6) and (6.7). Applying Theorem 3.2, we obtain

$$\mathcal{U}(t, T) = \mathcal{E}_t^T(\mathcal{W}(t, \cdot))\mathcal{E}_t^T(\mathcal{L}(\cdot)), \tag{6.17}$$

with

$$\mathcal{W}(t, u) := \mathcal{E}_t^u(\mathrm{ad}_{\mathcal{L}(\cdot)})(\overline{r}_d(u) - r^*(\boldsymbol{y}, u)), \tag{6.18}$$

$$r^*(\boldsymbol{y}, t) := r(\mathbf{\Phi}(t)\boldsymbol{y}, t). \tag{6.19}$$

We next look to derive the associated pricing kernel. We take advantage of the fact we have established that (6.12) is the kernel associated with the evolution operator (6.6) to obtain the integral kernel associated with (6.17). We deduce

Theorem 6.1 *The pricing kernel associated with (6.5) is*

$$G(y, t; \boldsymbol{\eta}, v) = \mathcal{E}_t^v(\mathcal{W}(t, \cdot))G_0(y, t; \boldsymbol{\eta}, v), \tag{6.20}$$

with $\mathcal{W}(t, u)$ given by (6.18) and $G_0(y, t; \boldsymbol{\eta}, v)$ by (6.12).

We now seek to elucidate the expression (6.18) further for some specific choices of $r(x, t)$. We will make the assumption that the dependence is on the first m components of x, with $1 \leq m \leq n$.

In the case of a Hull–White model we will typically take

$$r(x, t) = \tilde{r}(t) + \sum_{k=1}^{m'} x_k \tag{6.21}$$

with $m' \leq m$, while for a Black–Karasinski model we will take

$$r(x, t) = \tilde{r}(t)e^{\sum_{k=1}^{m'} x_k - \frac{1}{2}\mathrm{var}\left(\sum_{k=1}^{m'} x_{kt}\right)} + s(t), \tag{6.22}$$

where $s(t)$ is a displacement factor which would typically be chosen to be negative to allow of the possibility of the short rate becoming negative, as may be required to facilitate calibration to the forward curve.

We shall also be interested below in the situation alluded to above where we have risky discounting involving both a short rate *and* a credit intensity. In these circumstances we shall usually represent the short rate with a Hull–White model and the credit intensity with a Black–Karasinski model. The discount rate $r(x, t)$ will then typically be a linear combination of (6.21) and (6.22), typically both taken to be one-factor ($m = m' = 1$).

6.3 EXACT EXPRESSION FOR HULL–WHITE MODEL

We consider next the particular case of a multi-factor Hull–White model, writing (6.21) in terms of y co-ordinates as

$$r^*(y, t) = \tilde{r}(t) + \sum_{k=1}^{m'} \sum_{l=1}^{m} \Phi_{kl}(t)y_l. \tag{6.23}$$

Note that, in general, there will be dependence here on all components of y up to the mth, even if $m' < m$. From (6.6), we then have

$$\mathrm{ad}_{\mathcal{L}(t_1)}(r^*(y, u)) = \sum_{k=1}^{m'} \sum_{l=1}^{m} \Phi_{kl}(u) \left(\beta_l^*(t_1) + \frac{1}{2} \sum_{j=1}^{n} (\sigma_{jl}^*(t_1) + \sigma_{lj}^*(t_1)) \frac{\partial}{\partial y_j} \right).$$

We note from the structure of our pricing equations that the stochastic variables x_k involved in defining the discounting (with $k \leq m$) can have no influence from other stochastic variables (with $k > m$). Consequently we must have $\Phi_{kl}(\cdot) = 0$ for $l > m$, whence the sum over l in the above can be taken up to $l = n$ without impacting on the result. Making use of this fact and the symmetry of $\boldsymbol{\sigma}^*(\cdot)$, we can write more compactly

$$\mathrm{ad}_{\mathcal{L}(t_1)}(r^*(y,u)) = \sum_{k=1}^{m'} \left([\boldsymbol{\Phi}(u)\boldsymbol{\beta}^*(t_1)]_k + \sum_{j=1}^{n} [\boldsymbol{\Phi}(u)\boldsymbol{\sigma}^*(t_1)]_{kj} \frac{\partial}{\partial y_j} \right).$$

Further application of the commutator delivers a null result. We obtain from (6.18)

$$\mathcal{W}(t,u) = \bar{r}_d(u) - r^*(y,u) + \mathcal{L}_1(t,u), \tag{6.24}$$

$$\mathcal{L}_1(t,u) := -\sum_{k=1}^{m'} \left([\boldsymbol{\Phi}(u)\boldsymbol{\gamma}^*(t,u)]_k + \sum_{j=1}^{n} [\boldsymbol{\Phi}(u)\boldsymbol{\Sigma}^*(t,u)]_{kj} \frac{\partial}{\partial y_j} \right). \tag{6.25}$$

Using again Theorem 3.2, we can write

$$\mathcal{E}_t^T(\mathcal{W}(t,\cdot)) = \mathcal{E}_t^T\left(\mathcal{W}_1(t,\cdot)\right) \mathcal{E}_t^T(\mathcal{L}_1(t,\cdot)), \tag{6.26}$$

with

$$\mathcal{W}_1(t,u) := \mathcal{E}_t^u(\mathrm{ad}_{\mathcal{L}_1(t,\cdot)})(\bar{r}_d(u) - r^*(y,u))$$

For future notational convenience, let us also define at this point

$$\boldsymbol{\Theta}(t,u) := \boldsymbol{\Phi}(u)\boldsymbol{\Sigma}^*(t,u), \tag{6.27}$$

$$F^*(t,u) := \sum_{i=1}^{m'} \sum_{k=1}^{m'} \left[\int_t^u \boldsymbol{\Theta}(t,t_1)\boldsymbol{\Phi}^T(u) dt_1 \right]_{ik}, \tag{6.28}$$

in terms of which we find

$$\begin{aligned}
\mathrm{ad}_{\mathcal{L}_1(t,t_1)}(\bar{r}_d(u) - r^*(y,u)) &= \sum_{i=1}^{m'} \sum_{j=1}^{n} [\boldsymbol{\Theta}(t,t_1)]_{ij} \frac{\partial}{\partial y_j} \sum_{k=1}^{m'} \sum_{l=1}^{n} \Phi_{kl}(u) y_l \\
&= \sum_{i=1}^{m'} \sum_{j=1}^{n} [\boldsymbol{\Theta}(t,t_1)]_{ij} \sum_{k=1}^{m'} \Phi_{kj}(u) \\
&= \sum_{i=1}^{m'} \sum_{k=1}^{m'} [\boldsymbol{\Theta}(t,t_1)\boldsymbol{\Phi}^T(u)]_{ik}
\end{aligned}$$

and so deduce

$$\int_t^u \mathrm{ad}_{\mathcal{L}_1(t,t_1)}(\bar{r}_d(u) - r^*(y,u)) dt_1 = F^*(t,u).$$

Further application of the commutator operation yields a null result, whence we conclude

$$\mathcal{W}_1(t,u) = \bar{r}_d(u) - r^*(y,u) + F^*(t,u),$$

and consequently, using (6.26)

$$\mathcal{E}_t^T(\mathcal{W}(t,\cdot)) = e^{\int_t^T(\bar{r}_d(u)-r^*(y,u)+F^*(t,u))du} e^{-\sum_{i=1}^{m'}[\mathbf{\Phi}(T)\gamma^*(t,T)]_i - \sum_{j=1}^{n}\Delta y_j(t,T)\frac{\partial}{\partial y_j}}, \tag{6.29}$$

where we define a vector $\Delta y(t,T)$ through

$$\Delta y_j(t,T) := \sum_{i=1}^{m'} \int_t^T \Theta_{ij}(t,u)du. \tag{6.30}$$

Finally substituting back into (6.20) and making use of (3.39), we obtain

$$G_{\text{H-W}}(y,t;\boldsymbol{\eta},v) = D_d(t,v)e^{\int_t^v(\bar{r}_d(u)-r^*(y,u)+F^*(t,u))du} N(y - \Delta y(t,v) + \gamma(t,v) - \boldsymbol{\eta}; \boldsymbol{\Sigma}^*(t,v))$$

Calibration. To calibrate our model, we observe that the PV of a unit cash flow at time v is given by

$$\int_{\mathbb{R}^n} G_{\text{H-W}}(0,0;\boldsymbol{\eta},v)d\boldsymbol{\eta} = D_d(0,v)e^{\int_0^v(\bar{r}_d(u)-r^*(0,u)+F^*(0,u))du}. \tag{6.31}$$

Calibration to the forward curve requires that this be equal to $D_d(0,v)$. Noting that $r^*(0,u) = \tilde{r}(u)$, we infer that this condition is uniquely satisfied by the choice

$$\tilde{r}(t) = \bar{r}_d(t) + F^*(0,t). \tag{6.32}$$

The corresponding expression for the time-t price of the unit cash flow can on this basis be written

$$F^v(y,t) = D_d(t,v)e^{-\sum_{i=1}^{m'}[\mathbf{\Psi}(t,v)y]_i - \int_t^v(F^*(0,u)-F^*(t,u))du}, \tag{6.33}$$

where

$$\mathbf{\Psi}(t,v) := \int_t^v \mathbf{\Phi}(u)du. \tag{6.34}$$

Observing that

$$\mathbf{\Theta}^T(0,u) - \mathbf{\Theta}^T(t,u) = \mathbf{\Theta}^T(0,t) + \boldsymbol{\Sigma}^*(0,t)\mathbf{\Psi}^T(t,u), \tag{6.35}$$

we can re-express

$$F^v(y,t) = D_d(t,v)e^{-\sum_{k=1}^{m'}\left([\mathbf{\Psi}(t,v)(y+\Delta y(0,t))]_k + \frac{1}{2}\sum_{i=1}^{m'}[\mathbf{\Psi}(t,v)\boldsymbol{\Sigma}^*(0,t)\mathbf{\Psi}^T(t,v)]_{ki}\right)}, \tag{6.36}$$

which is more convenient for computational purposes. Also, comparing with (4.13) for the one-factor case, we see that the first term in the exponent is equivalent to $B_d^*(t,v)(x_d + I_{dd}^*(0,t))$ and the second to $\frac{1}{2}B_d^{*2}(t,v)\Sigma_{dd}(0,t)$. We can also obtain straightforwardly the instantaneous T-forward rate $f^T(y,t)$, using the well known result that

$$f^T(y,t) = -\frac{\partial}{\partial T}\ln F^T(y,t).$$

We obtain

$$f^T(y,t) = \sum_{k=1}^{m'}\left([\mathbf{\Phi}(T)(y+\Delta y(0,t))]_k + \sum_{i=1}^{m'}[\mathbf{\Phi}(T)\mathbf{\Sigma}^*(0,t)\mathbf{\Psi}^T(t,T)]_{ki}\right). \tag{6.37}$$

In summary, we have demonstrated

Theorem 6.2 *The pricing kernel associated with* (6.5) *in the case that the function* $r(x,t)$ *follows the Hull–White specification* (6.21) *is*

$$G_{H\text{-}W}(y,t;\boldsymbol{\eta},v) = F^v(y,t)N(y - \Delta y(t,v) + \gamma(t,v) - \boldsymbol{\eta};\mathbf{\Sigma}^*(t,v)), \tag{6.38}$$

with $F^v(y,t)$ *given by* (6.36). *The required functional form of* $\tilde{r}(t)$ *in* (6.21) *is given by* (6.32). *The corresponding pricing kernel associated with* $f(x,t) \equiv g(y,t)$ *where* $\boldsymbol{x} = \Phi(t)y$ *is*

$$G(x,t;\xi,v) = |\mathbf{\Phi}^{-1}(v)|G_{H\text{-}W}(\mathbf{\Phi}^{-1}(t)x,t;\mathbf{\Phi}^{-1}(v)\xi,v). \tag{6.39}$$

Finally, it should be noted that, although we allow more than one state variable to be used in (6.21), viz. $m' > 1$, it is desirable to work if possible with $m' = 1$. This is because, in the event that interest rate option prices are to be calculated, greater analytic tractability is secured if we have to integrate the payoff over only one state variable. Of course, a sum of variables x_k can be redefined to be the first variable and the problem re-cast in the resulting modified co-ordinates. The cost of this, however, would be that a matrix $\boldsymbol{\kappa}(t)$ which was lower triangular will typically cease to be so, with the result that the convenient explicit production of the matrix $\Phi(t)$ detailed at the end of the previous section will not be available: this may or may not be considered a price worth paying, depending on the kind of problem one wished to address.

6.4 ASYMPTOTIC EXPANSION FOR BLACK–KARASINSKI MODEL

As with the Hull–White case, we shall seek a solution for the Black–Karasinski case (6.22) by expanding the exponential operator in (6.18). We start by noting in this case that we can write

$$r^*(y,t) = \tilde{r}(t)e^{\sum_{k=1}^{m'}[\mathbf{\Phi}(t)y]_k - \frac{1}{2}\Gamma^*(0,t)} + s(t), \tag{6.40}$$

where we take the normalising function $\Gamma^*(0,t)$ to be as defined in (6.43) below. Since our main interest here will be in providing a formulation for a multi-factor short rate kernel (see Chapter 15), rather than a more general multi-asset kernel, we shall assume in the following that $\boldsymbol{\beta}^*(t) = 0$ in (6.6).[1] It follows that

$$
\begin{aligned}
&\mathrm{ad}_{\mathcal{L}(t_1)}(r^*(\mathbf{y},u)) \\
&= \frac{1}{2}(r^*(\mathbf{y},u) - s(u)) \sum_{k=1}^{m'} \sum_{l=1}^{m} \Phi_{kl}(u) \left(\sum_{j=1}^{n} (\sigma^*_{jl}(t_1) + \sigma^*_{lj}(t_1)) \frac{\partial}{\partial y_j} + \sum_{j=1}^{m} \sigma^*_{lj}(t_1) \sum_{i=1}^{m'} \Phi_{ij}(u) \right) \\
&= (r^*(\mathbf{y},u) - s(u)) \sum_{k=1}^{m'} \left(\sum_{j=1}^{n} [\boldsymbol{\Phi}(u)\boldsymbol{\sigma}^*(t_1)]_{kj} \frac{\partial}{\partial y_j} + \frac{1}{2} \sum_{i=1}^{m'} [\boldsymbol{\Phi}(u)\boldsymbol{\sigma}^*(t_1)\boldsymbol{\Phi}^T(u)]_{ki} \right),
\end{aligned}
$$

where we have made use again of the symmetry of $\boldsymbol{\sigma}^*(\cdot)$ and the fact that $\Phi_{kl}(\cdot) = 0$ for $l > m$. Consequently

$$
\int_t^u \mathrm{ad}_{\mathcal{L}(t_1)}(r^*(\mathbf{y},u))dt_1 = (r^*(\mathbf{y},u) - s(u))\mathcal{L}_2(t,u),
$$

with

$$
\mathcal{L}_2(t,u) := \sum_{j=1}^{n} \Delta y_j(t,u) \frac{\partial}{\partial y_j} + \frac{1}{2}\Gamma^*(t,u), \tag{6.41}
$$

$$
\Delta y_j(t,u) := \sum_{k=1}^{m'} \Theta_{kj}(t,u). \tag{6.42}
$$

$$
\Gamma^*(t,u) := \sum_{k=1}^{m'} \sum_{i=1}^{m'} [\boldsymbol{\Theta}(t,u)\boldsymbol{\Phi}^T(u)]_{ki}. \tag{6.43}
$$

Here the definition of $\Delta y_j(t,u)$ in (6.42) supersedes that in (6.30). Repeating this procedure and summing all terms in the infinite expansion which arises, we obtain from (6.18)

$$
\mathcal{W}(t,u) = \overline{r}_d(u) - s(u) - \tilde{r}(u) e^{\sum_{k=1}^{m'} [\boldsymbol{\Phi}(u)\mathbf{y}]_k - \frac{1}{2}\Gamma^*(0,u)} e^{\mathcal{L}_2(t,u)}. \tag{6.44}
$$

Substitution of (6.44) into (6.17) does not give rise to an analytically tractable expression. So we must again compute the time-ordered exponential as an explicit power series in ϵ defined as $\| \tilde{r}(\cdot) + s(\cdot) - \overline{r}_d(\cdot) \|$ for some suitable norm. Considering then the limit as $\epsilon \to 0$, we pose the following perturbation expansion representation of our solution

$$
\begin{aligned}
G_{\text{B-K}}(\mathbf{y},t;\boldsymbol{\eta},v) &= D_d(t,v) \sum_{n=0}^{\infty} \mathcal{M}_n(t,v) N(\mathbf{y} - \boldsymbol{\eta}; \boldsymbol{\Sigma}^*(t,v)), \\
&= \sum_{n=0}^{\infty} G_n(\mathbf{y},t;\boldsymbol{\eta},v)
\end{aligned}
\tag{6.45}
$$

[1] The impact of non-zero $\boldsymbol{\beta}^*(t)$ can be reinstated by replacing $\mathbf{y}$ with $\mathbf{y} + \mathbf{y}^*(t,v)$ in (6.45) below.

for operators $\mathcal{M}_n(t,T)$ with $\| \mathcal{M}_n(t,T) \| = \mathcal{O}(\epsilon^n)$, again for some suitable (operator) norm, with in particular $\mathcal{M}_0(t,T) = I$, the identity operator. We pose also

$$\tilde{r}(t) = \sum_{n=1}^{\infty} \tilde{r}_n(t), \tag{6.46}$$

with $\tilde{r}_n(\cdot) = \mathcal{O}(\epsilon^n)$ and define

$$R_n(y,t,t_1) := \tilde{r}_n(t_1) e^{\sum_{k=1}^{m'} [\boldsymbol{\Phi}(t)y]_k - \frac{1}{2}(\Gamma^*(0,t_1) - \Gamma^*(t,t_1))}, \tag{6.47}$$

noting that $R_n(0,0,t_1) = \tilde{r}_n(t_1)$. Substituting into (6.45), we see at $\mathcal{O}(1)$ that the implicit choice of $G_0(y,t;\boldsymbol{\eta},v) := D_d(t,v)N(y-\boldsymbol{\eta};\boldsymbol{\Sigma}^*(t,v))$ is a consistent one. At $\mathcal{O}(\epsilon)$ we have

$$\mathcal{M}_1(t,v) = \int_t^v \left(\bar{r}_d(t_1) - s(t_1) - R_1(y,t,t_1) e^{\sum_{j=1}^{n} \Delta y_j(t,t_1) \frac{\partial}{\partial y_j}} \right) dt_1,$$

whence we obtain, using again the fact that $e^{a \frac{\partial}{\partial x}} f(x) = f(x+a)$

$$G_1(y,t;\boldsymbol{\eta},v) = \Delta(t,v) G_0(y,t;\boldsymbol{\eta},v) - \int_t^v R_1(y,t,t_1) G_0(y + \Delta y(t,t_1), t; \boldsymbol{\eta}, v) dt_1, \tag{6.48}$$

$$\Delta(t,v) := \int_t^v (\bar{r}_d(t_1) - s(t_1)) dt_1. \tag{6.49}$$

Similarly, at $\mathcal{O}(\epsilon^2)$ we have

$$\mathcal{M}_2(t,v) = \int_t^v \left(\bar{r}_d(t_2) - s(t_2) - R_1(y,t,t_2) e^{\sum_{j=1}^{n} \Delta y_j(t,t_2) \frac{\partial}{\partial y_j}} \right) \int_t^{t_2} \left(\bar{r}_d(t_1) - s(t_1) - R_1(y,t,t_1) e^{\sum_{j=1}^{n} \Delta y_j(t,t_1) \frac{\partial}{\partial y_j}} \right) dt_1 dt_2$$
$$- \int_t^v R_2(y,t,t_1) e^{\sum_{j=1}^{n} \Delta y_j(t,t_1) \frac{\partial}{\partial y_j}} dt_1,$$

whence we deduce

$$\begin{aligned} G_2(y,t;\boldsymbol{\eta},v) = {} & \frac{1}{2}\Delta^2(t,v) G_0(y,t;\boldsymbol{\eta},v) - \Delta(t,v) \int_t^v R_1(y,t,t_1) G_0(y + \Delta y(t,t_1), t; \boldsymbol{\eta}, v) dt_1 \\ & + \int_t^v R_1(y,t,t_1) \int_t^{t_2} R_1(y,t,t_2) e^{F_2(t,t_1,t_2)} G_0\Big(y + \sum_{i=1}^{2} \Delta y(t,t_i), t; \boldsymbol{\eta}, v\Big) dt_1 dt_2 \\ & - \int_t^v R_2(y,t,t_1) G_0(y + \Delta y(t,t_1), t; \boldsymbol{\eta}, v) dt_1, \end{aligned} \tag{6.50}$$

where

$$F_2(t,t_1,t_2) = \sum_{k=1}^{m'} [\mathbf{\Phi}(t_1)\Delta y(t,t_2)]_k. \tag{6.51}$$

Finally, matching the T-maturity zero coupon bond price requires

$$\iint_{\mathbb{R}^2} G(0,0;\boldsymbol{\eta},T)d\xi d\eta = D_d(0,T)$$

for any $T > 0$. This is satisfied to $\mathcal{O}(\epsilon^2)$ by the choice

$$\begin{aligned}\tilde{r}_1(t) &= \overline{r}_d(t) - s(t),\\ \tilde{r}_2(t) &= \tilde{r}_1(t)\int_0^t \tilde{r}_1(t_1)\left(e^{F_2(0,t_1,t)} - 1\right)dt_1.\end{aligned} \tag{6.52}$$

In summary, we have demonstrated

Theorem 6.3 *The pricing kernel associated with* (6.5) *in the case that the function* $r(\boldsymbol{x},t)$ *follows the Black–Karasinski specification* (6.22) *is given asymptotically to second order in the limit as* $\epsilon = \| \tilde{r}(\cdot) + s(\cdot) - \overline{r}_d(\cdot) \| \to 0$ *by* (6.45), *where the first three terms needed for the second order expansion are given by* (6.12), (6.48) *and* (6.50). *The required functional form of* $\tilde{r}(t)$ *in* (6.22) *is given by* (6.46), *where the first two terms needed for the second order expansion are given by* (6.52). *The corresponding pricing kernel associated with* $f(\boldsymbol{x},t) \equiv g(y,t)$ *where* $\boldsymbol{x} = \Phi(t)y$ *is*

$$G(\boldsymbol{x},t;\boldsymbol{\xi},v) = |\mathbf{\Phi}^{-1}(v)|G_{B\text{-}K}(\mathbf{\Phi}^{-1}(t)\boldsymbol{x},t;\mathbf{\Phi}^{-1}(v)\boldsymbol{\xi},v). \tag{6.53}$$

The following corollary immediately follows

Corollary 6.1 *The* T*-maturity zero coupon bond price satisfying* (6.5) *in the case that the function* $r(\boldsymbol{x},t)$ *follows the Black–Karasinski specification* (6.22) *with payoff* $P(y) \equiv 1$ *at time* T *is given asymptotically in the limit as* $\epsilon = \| \tilde{r}(\cdot) + s(\cdot) - \overline{r}_d(\cdot) \| \to 0$ *by*

$$\begin{aligned}F^T(y,t) = D_d(t,T)\Bigg(&1 - \int_t^T (R_1(y,t,t_1) + s(t_1) - \overline{r}_d(t_1))dt_1\\ &+ \frac{1}{2}\left(\int_t^T (R_1(y,t,t_1) + s(t_1) - \overline{r}_d(t_1))dt_1\right)^2\\ &+ \int_t^T \left(R_1(y,t,t_2)\int_t^{t_2} R_1(y,t,t_1)\left(e^{F_2(t,t_1,t_2)} - 1\right)dt_1 - R_2(y,t,t_1)\right)dt_2\\ &+ \mathcal{O}(\epsilon^3)\Bigg).\end{aligned} \tag{6.54}$$

Noting that the first three terms of the above expansion represent the initial part of an expansion of an exponential function, it is possible to complete the series as was done in §5.6 and obtain the following alternative representation

Corollary 6.2 *The expression* (6.54) *can be written to the same degree of asymptotic accuracy as*

$$F^T(y,t) = e^{-\int_t^T (R_1(y,t,t_1)+s(t_1)+\Delta R_2(y,t,t_1))dt_1} + \mathcal{O}(\epsilon^3), \tag{6.55}$$

with

$$\Delta R_2(y,t,T) := R_2(y,t,T) - R_1(y,t,T)\int_t^T R_1(y,t,t_1)\left(e^{F_2(t,t_1,T)} - 1\right)dt_1. \tag{6.56}$$

Note that conveniently $\Delta R_2(0,0,T) = 0$, so the calibration to the forward curve remains exact.

These results can be given the following alternative interpretation.

Proposition 6.4.1 If $r(x,t)$ in (6.22) is taken instead to be the instantaneous default intensity of a named debt issuer, (6.54) and (6.55) can be taken as giving the survival probability of this issuer from t to T.

We can again also obtain straightforwardly the instantaneous T-forward rate. The best result is probably obtained by using (6.55):

$$f^T(y,t) = R_1(y,t,T) + s(T) + \Delta R_2(y,t,T) + \mathcal{O}(\epsilon^3), \tag{6.57}$$

6.5 FORMAL SOLUTION FOR RATES-CREDIT HYBRID MODEL

We also consider the case of a rates-credit hybrid model where the discounting is taken to be governed by

$$r(x,t) = \tilde{r}(t) + x_d + \lambda^*(t)e^{x_\lambda}. \tag{6.58}$$

We infer immediately from our analysis in Chapter 4 that we must choose

$$\tilde{r}(t) = \overline{r}_d(t) + r_d^*(t), \tag{6.59}$$

with $r_d^*(t)$ given by (4.14). We defer until Chapter 8 below the specification of $\lambda^*(t)$. We consider the vector $\boldsymbol{x}$ on this occasion to be of the form $\boldsymbol{x} = (x_d, x_\lambda, \dots, x_n)^T$, with $n \geq 2$. In other words we equate x_1 with x_d and x_2 with x_λ.

Under transformed co-ordinates, the pricing equation will again be given by (6.5), except in that we replace (6.6) and (6.7) with

$$\mathcal{L}(t) = \sum_{i=1}^{n} \beta_i^*(t)\frac{\partial}{\partial y_i} + \frac{1}{2}\sum_{i=1}^{n}\sum_{j=1}^{n} \sigma_{ij}^*(t)\frac{\partial^2}{\partial y_i \partial y_j} - \overline{r}_d(t) - \overline{\lambda}(t), \tag{6.60}$$

$$\mathcal{V}(t) = \overline{r}_d(t) + \overline{\lambda}(t) - r(\boldsymbol{\Phi}(t)y, t), \tag{6.61}$$

respectively. The solution is obtained as in the preceding cases, as the integral kernel associated with the operator $\mathcal{U}(t, T)$ given by (6.17), subject to reinterpreting (6.18) as

$$\mathcal{W}(t, u) := \mathcal{E}_t^u(\text{ad}_{\mathcal{L}(\cdot)})(\overline{r}_d(u) + \overline{\lambda}(u) - r^*(y, u)). \tag{6.62}$$

In this case we have

$$r^*(y, t) = \tilde{r}(t) + [\Phi(t)y]_1 + \lambda^*(t)e^{[\Phi(t)y]_2}, \tag{6.63}$$

whence

$$\overline{r}_d(u) + \overline{\lambda}(u) - r^*(y, u) = -r_d^*(u) - [\Phi(u)y]_1 + \overline{\lambda}(u) - \lambda^*(u)e^{[\Phi(u)y]_2}. \tag{6.64}$$

It follows that

$$\begin{aligned}
\text{ad}_{\mathcal{L}(t_1)}(r^*(y,u)) &= \frac{1}{2}\sum_{l=1}^{n}\Phi_{1l}(u)\left(2\beta_l^*(t_1) + \sum_{i=1}^{n}\sigma_{il}^*(t_1)\frac{\partial}{\partial y_i} + \sum_{j=1}^{n}\sigma_{lj}^*(t_1)\frac{\partial}{\partial y_j}\right) \\
&\quad + \frac{1}{2}\lambda^*(u)e^{[\Phi(u)y]_2}\left(\sum_{l=1}^{n}\Phi_{2l}(u)\left(2\beta_l^*(t_1) + \sum_{i=1}^{n}\sigma_{il}^*(t_1)\frac{\partial}{\partial y_i}\right.\right. \\
&\quad \left.\left. + \sum_{j=1}^{n}\sigma_{lj}^*(t_1)\frac{\partial}{\partial y_j}\right) + \sum_{i=1}^{n}\sum_{j=1}^{n}\sigma_{ij}^*(t_1)\Phi_{2i}(u)\Phi_{2j}(u)\right) \\
&= [\boldsymbol{\Phi}(u)\boldsymbol{\beta}^*(t_1)]_1 + \sum_{j=1}^{n}[\boldsymbol{\Phi}(u)\boldsymbol{\sigma}^*(t_1)]_{1j}\frac{\partial}{\partial y_j} \\
&\quad + \lambda^*(u)e^{[\Phi(u)y]_2}\left([\boldsymbol{\Phi}(u)\boldsymbol{\beta}^*(t_1)]_2 + \sum_{j=1}^{n}[\boldsymbol{\Phi}(u)\boldsymbol{\sigma}^*(t_1)]_{2j}\frac{\partial}{\partial y_j}\right. \\
&\quad \left. + \frac{1}{2}[\boldsymbol{\Phi}(u)\boldsymbol{\sigma}^*(t_1)\boldsymbol{\Phi}^T(u)]_{22}\right),
\end{aligned}$$

where we have made use in the second expression of the symmetry of $\boldsymbol{\sigma}^*(\cdot)$. Consequently,

$$\int_t^u \text{ad}_{\mathcal{L}(t_1)}(r^*(y,u))dt_1 = \mathcal{L}_1(t,u) + \lambda^*(u)e^{[\Phi(u)y]_2}\mathcal{L}_2(t,u),$$

with

$$\mathcal{L}_1(t,u) := [\mathbf{\Phi}(u)\boldsymbol{\gamma}^*(t,u)]_1 + \sum_{j=1}^{n} \Theta_{1j}(t,u)\frac{\partial}{\partial y_j}, \tag{6.65}$$

$$\mathcal{L}_2(t,u) := [\mathbf{\Phi}(u)\boldsymbol{\gamma}^*(t,u)]_2 + \sum_{j=1}^{n} \Theta_{2j}(t,u)\frac{\partial}{\partial y_j} + \frac{1}{2}[\mathbf{\Theta}(t,u)\mathbf{\Phi}^T(u)]_{22}, \tag{6.66}$$

where $\mathbf{\Theta}(t,u)$ is given by (6.27) above. Application of the commutator operator to $\mathcal{L}_1(t,u)$ yields a null result. Further application of the commutator operator to the term involving $\mathcal{L}_2(t,u)$ is handled in the same manner as in the previous section. We obtain

$$\mathcal{E}_t^u(\mathrm{ad}_{\mathcal{L}(\cdot)})(r^*(y,u)) = \tilde{r}(u) + [\Phi(u)y]_1 + \mathcal{L}_1(t,u) + \lambda^*(u)e^{[\Phi(u)y]_2}e^{\mathcal{L}_2(t,u)},$$

Hence, analogous to (6.44), we obtain

$$\mathcal{W}(t,u) = -[\Phi(u)y]_1 - r_d^*(u) - \mathcal{L}_1(t,u) - \lambda^*(u)e^{[\Phi(u)y]_2}e^{\mathcal{L}_2(t,u)} + \overline{\lambda}(u). \tag{6.67}$$

We conclude, taking the integral kernel of $\mathcal{U}(t,v)$ as previously and recalling the definitions (6.13) and (6.14), that the required pricing kernel is of the form

$$G_{\text{R-C}}(y,t;\boldsymbol{\eta},v) = B(t,v)\mathcal{E}_t^v(\mathcal{W}(t,\cdot))N(y + \boldsymbol{\gamma}^*(t,v) - \boldsymbol{\eta}; \boldsymbol{\Sigma}^*(t,v)), \tag{6.68}$$

where

$$B(t,v) := e^{-\int_t^v (\overline{r}_d(s)+\overline{\lambda}(s))ds}, \tag{6.69}$$

is the risky discount factor.

Since the various terms in (6.67) do not commute with each other, we face a choice as to which one(s) to separate out first. It turns out that separating out the term involving $\mathcal{L}_2(t,u)$ does not give rise to a convenient analytic expression, so we deal first with the $\mathcal{L}_1(t,u)$ term. Isolating $\mathcal{L}_1(t,u)$ in the usual way, we can write

$$\mathcal{E}_t^v(\mathcal{W}(t,\cdot)) = \mathcal{E}_t^v(\mathcal{W}_2(t,\cdot))\mathcal{E}_t^v(-\mathcal{L}_1(t,\cdot)), \tag{6.70}$$

$$\mathcal{W}_2(t,u) = \mathcal{E}_t^u(\mathrm{ad}_{-\mathcal{L}_1(t,\cdot)})\left(-[\Phi(u)y]_1 - r_d^*(u) - \lambda^*(u)e^{[\Phi(u)y]_2}e^{\mathcal{L}_2(t,u)} + \overline{\lambda}(u)\right). \tag{6.71}$$

We obtain straightforwardly

$$\int_t^u \mathrm{ad}_{-\mathcal{L}_1(t,t_1)}(-[\Phi(u)y]_1)dt_1 = \int_t^u [\mathbf{\Theta}(t,t_1)\mathbf{\Phi}^T(u)]_{11}dt_1,$$

$$\int_t^u \mathrm{ad}_{-\mathcal{L}_1(t,t_1)}(-\lambda^*(u)e^{[\Phi(u)y]_2}e^{\mathcal{L}_2(t,u)})dt_1 = \lambda^*(u)e^{[\Phi(u)y]_2}e^{\mathcal{L}_2(t,u)}\int_t^u [\mathbf{\Theta}(t,t_1)\mathbf{\Phi}^T(u)]_{12}dt_1.$$

Application of the commutator operator to the first term yields a null result, while further application to the second term is handled in the same manner as previously. We obtain

$$\mathcal{W}_2(t,u) = \mathcal{G}_1(t,u) + \mathcal{G}_2(t,u), \tag{6.72}$$

$$\mathcal{G}_1(t,u) = -[\Phi(u)y]_1 - r_d^*(u) + \int_t^u [\boldsymbol{\Theta}(t,t_1)\boldsymbol{\Phi}^T(u)]_{11}dt_1, \tag{6.73}$$

$$\mathcal{G}_2(t,u) = -\lambda^*(u)e^{[\Phi(u)y]_2 - \int_t^u [\boldsymbol{\Theta}(t,t_1)\boldsymbol{\Phi}^T(u)]_{12}dt_1}e^{\mathcal{L}_2(t,u)} + \overline{\lambda}(u). \tag{6.74}$$

Finally we isolate $\mathcal{G}_1(t,u)$, writing

$$\mathcal{E}_t^v(\mathcal{W}_2(t,\cdot)) = \mathcal{E}_t^v(\mathcal{G}_3(t,\cdot))\mathcal{E}_t^v(\mathcal{G}_1(t,\cdot)), \tag{6.75}$$

$$\mathcal{G}_3(t,u) = \mathcal{E}_t^u(\mathrm{ad}_{\mathcal{G}_1(t,\cdot)})(\mathcal{G}_2(t,u)). \tag{6.76}$$

We observe, using again the fact that $e^{a\frac{\partial}{\partial x}}(f(x)) = f(x+a)$, that

$$\int_t^u \mathrm{ad}_{\mathcal{G}_1(t,t_1)}\left(e^{\mathcal{L}_2(t,u)}\right)dt_1 = \int_t^u [\boldsymbol{\Theta}(t,u)\boldsymbol{\Phi}^T(t_1)]_{21}dt_1 e^{\mathcal{L}_2(t,u)}.$$

Applying this result recursively, we deduce

$$\mathcal{G}_3(t,u) = \overline{\lambda}(u) - \lambda^*(u)e^{[\Phi(u)y]_2 - \int_t^u [\boldsymbol{\Theta}(t,t_1)\boldsymbol{\Phi}^T(u)]_{12}dt_1}e^{\mathcal{L}_2(t,u) + \int_t^u [\boldsymbol{\Theta}(t,u)\boldsymbol{\Phi}^T(t_1)]_{21}dt_1}. \tag{6.77}$$

Further simplification is not possible. We conclude from back-substitution into (6.68) that

$$G_{\text{R-C}}(y,t;\boldsymbol{\eta},v) = B(t,v)\mathcal{E}_t^v(\mathcal{G}_3(t,\cdot))\mathcal{E}_t^v(\mathcal{G}_1(t,\cdot))\mathcal{E}_t^v(-\mathcal{L}_1(t,\cdot))N(y+\boldsymbol{\gamma}^*(t,v)-\boldsymbol{\eta};\boldsymbol{\Sigma}^*(t,v)). \tag{6.78}$$

Here the first two operators acting successively on the normal distribution can be applied analytically, the first incorporating a shift operation on y with $y_j \to y_j - \Theta_{1j}(t,u)$. However, the operator involving $\mathcal{G}_3(t,\cdot)$ can only be applied term-by-term using the definition of the time-ordered exponential, on this occasion incorporating a shift from $y_j \to y_j + \Theta_{2j}(t,u)$. The transformation back to the variable x is through a transformation of the form set out in (6.53) above. We defer further details until Chapter 8, where we derive an asymptotic expansion for a two-factor rates-credit pricing kernel, and Chapter 12, where we extend this result to the (four-factor) multi-currency situation.

CHAPTER 7

Rates-Equity Hybrid Modelling

7.1 STATEMENT OF PROBLEM

Having derived the general form of multi-factor pricing kernels in the preceding chapter, we look now to apply this knowledge first to a relatively simple problem, considering the joint distribution of equity and rates with a view to calculating a pricing kernel for rates-equity hybrid derivatives. For rates we assume the short-rate model of Hull and White [1990], as described in Chapter 4, using the notation there introduced. We suppose the equity process S_t to be given by

$$\frac{dS_t}{S_t} = (r_{dt} - q(t))dt + \sigma_z(t)dW_t^z, \tag{7.1}$$

with r_{dt} given by (4.2), $q(t)$ the dividend rate and W_t^z a Brownian motion. Further, take this Brownian motion to be correlated with that driving the Hull–White rates model, with

$$\text{corr}(W_t, W_t^z) = \rho_{dz}. \tag{7.2}$$

As previously, define an auxiliary process z_t implicitly by (3.45). It follows from Itô's lemma that

$$dz_t = (r_d^*(t) + x_{dt})dt + \sigma_z(t)dW_t^z. \tag{7.3}$$

We seek to obtain an exact pricing kernel for European-type securities whose contingent payoff at some predetermined future time $t = v$ depends upon the equity price and/or the short rate at that time. In the following section we describe previous related work, before going on to derive the kernel and illustrate its application to vanilla equity option pricing.

7.2 PREVIOUS WORK

The problem we consider here of deriving a pricing kernel appears to have been first considered by Van Steenkiste and Foresi [1999], but without correlation between the equity and the rates. Mallier and Deakin [2002] attempted to solve the problem using the simpler Vasicek version of the rates model, assuming the mean reversion rate and the mean reversion level to be constant rather than time-dependent. They perform Kummer and Laplace transforms on the relevant pricing PDE and deduce a closed form representation of the associated Green's function as the difference between two Gaussian distributions. They suggest that this can be used for pricing convertible bonds but do not attempt to do so. There is an inconsistency evident in their result insofar as it does not appear to reduce to the single Gaussian shown in Chapter 4 above in the event that there is no dependence on the equity in the payoff.

Other authors have considered the narrower problem of finding analytic pricing formulae for vanilla equity options subject to stochastic interest rates. In his pioneering paper, Merton [1973] set out a method for deriving closed form solutions for vanilla option pricing where the interest rate model was of the Ho–Lee variety, i.e. Gaussian rates with no mean reversion – see Ho and Lee [1986]. This work was generalised by Amin and Jarrow [1992] to cover interest rate models of the Heath–Jarrow–Morton (HJM) type, see Heath et al. [1992]. Their solution includes the (constant-volatility) Hull–White model as a special case.

Other extensions were made to address the important CIR model of Cox et al. [1991] with a square root dependence of the volatility on the interest rate. While this model has closed-form bond prices, closed-form solutions have been derived for the situation when the model is used in the context of equity option pricing only in the form of asymptotic approximation, for example by Kim and Kunitomo [1999]. Analytic formulae have been presented which make use of Fourier analysis, but results are in this event expressed as an (inverse) Fourier integral which must be evaluated numerically. For example Bakshi and Chen [1997] analyse a general modelling approach where both rates and the equity volatility can be considered to be stochastic.

We restrict ourselves here to the Hull–White case of Gaussian rates with the equity volatility a deterministic function of time and derive a closed form solution for the pricing kernel.

7.3 THE PRICING KERNEL

7.3.1 Main Result

If the price of a European-type security depending for its payout amount on the spot price of an equity is expressed as $f(x_d, z, t)$, this price is governed under the rates-equity hybrid model specified above for $t \geq 0$ by the following Kolmogorov backward diffusion equation

$$\frac{\partial f}{\partial t} - \alpha_d(t)x_d\frac{\partial f}{\partial x_d} + (r_d^*(t) + x_d)\frac{\partial f}{\partial z} + \frac{1}{2}\left(\sigma_d^2(t)\frac{\partial^2 f}{\partial x_d^2} + 2\rho_{dz}\sigma_d(t)\sigma_z(t)\frac{\partial^2 f}{\partial x_d \partial z} + \sigma_z^2(t)\frac{\partial^2 f}{\partial z^2}\right) - (\bar{r}(t) + r_d^*(t) + x_d)f = 0 \tag{7.4}$$

subject to the final condition $\lim_{t\to v^-} f(x_d, z, t) = P(z)$ for some payoff function $P(\cdot)$. This is of the form of (6.2). Here we look to derive in closed form an exact Green's function solution for this pricing equation. In terms of the notation introduced in the previous chapter, we have $\boldsymbol{x} = (x_d, z)^T$, $\boldsymbol{\beta}(t) = (0, r_d^*(t))^T$ and

$$\boldsymbol{\kappa}(t) = \begin{pmatrix} \alpha_d(t) & 0 \\ -1 & 0 \end{pmatrix}. \tag{7.5}$$

Using the method set out in §6.1, we obtain

$$\boldsymbol{\Phi}(t) = \begin{pmatrix} \phi_d(0,t) & 0 \\ B_d^*(0,t) & 1 \end{pmatrix}; \qquad \boldsymbol{\Phi}^{-1}(t) = \begin{pmatrix} \phi_d(0,t)^{-1} & 0 \\ -\phi_d(0,t)^{-1} B_d^*(0,t) & 1 \end{pmatrix} \tag{7.6}$$

and

$$\boldsymbol{\Psi}(t,v) = \begin{pmatrix} \phi_d(0,t) B_d^*(t,v) & 0 \\ \int_t^v B_d^*(0,u)du & v-t \end{pmatrix}, \tag{7.7}$$

in terms of which we define $\boldsymbol{y} = \boldsymbol{\Phi}^{-1}(t)\boldsymbol{x}$. The required pricing kernel can then be derived using the results of Chapter 6.

Theorem 7.1 *(Rates-Equity Pricing Kernel): The pricing kernel for (7.4) is seen to consist of the zero coupon bond formula multiplied by the joint distribution function of x_d and z with the mean and covariance parameters shifted by given time-dependent amounts as follows*

$$G(\boldsymbol{x}, t; \boldsymbol{\xi}, v) = D(t,v) e^{-\mu_d^*(x_d,t,v)} N\left(\boldsymbol{\xi} + \Delta\boldsymbol{\xi}(t,v) - \boldsymbol{\Phi}(v)\boldsymbol{\Phi}^{-1}(t)\boldsymbol{x}; \boldsymbol{\Sigma}^+(t,v)\right), \tag{7.8}$$

where $\boldsymbol{\xi} = (\xi_d, \zeta)^T$ and we define

$$\Delta\boldsymbol{\xi}(t,v) = \begin{pmatrix} I_{dd}^*(t,v) \\ I_{zd}^*(t,v) + K_{dd}^*(t,v) - B_d^*(t,v) r_d^*(t,v) - \frac{1}{2} B_d^{*2}(t,v)\Sigma_{dd}(0,t) \end{pmatrix}, \tag{7.9}$$

$$\boldsymbol{\Sigma}^+(t,v) = \begin{pmatrix} \Sigma_{dd}(t,v) & \Sigma_{dz}(t,v) + I_{dd}^*(t,v) \\ \Sigma_{dz}(t,v) + I_{dd}^*(t,v) & \Sigma_{zz}(t,v) + 2(I_{zd}^*(t,v) + K_{dd}^*(t,v)) \end{pmatrix}, \tag{7.10}$$

$$\Sigma_{dz}(t,v) = \rho_{dz} \int_t^v \phi_d(u,v)\sigma_d(u)\sigma_z(u)du, \tag{7.11}$$

$$\Sigma_{zz}(t,v) = \int_t^v \sigma_z^2(u)du, \tag{7.12}$$

$$I_{zd}^*(t,v) = \int_t^v \Sigma_{dz}(t,u)du. \tag{7.13}$$

with other functions as defined previously, in particular $K_{dd}^*(t,v)$ given by (4.12).

Proof: We observe from (6.8) and (6.9) that

$$\boldsymbol{\sigma}^*(t) = \begin{pmatrix} \frac{\sigma_d^2(t)}{\phi_d^2(0,t)} & \rho_{dz}\frac{\sigma_d(t)\sigma_z(t)}{\phi_d(0,t)} - \frac{B_d^*(0,t)\sigma_d^2(t)}{\phi_d^2(0,t)} \\ \rho_{dz}\frac{\sigma_d(t)\sigma_z(t)}{\phi_d(0,t)} - \frac{B_d^*(0,t)\sigma_d^2(t)}{\phi_d^2(0,t)} & \sigma_z^2(t) - 2\rho_{dz}\frac{B_d^*(0,t)\sigma_d(t)\sigma_z(t)}{\phi_d(0,t)} + \frac{B_d^{*2}(0,t)\sigma_d^2(0,t)}{\phi_d^2(0,t)}, \end{pmatrix}, \tag{7.14}$$

$$\boldsymbol{\beta}^*(t,v) = \begin{pmatrix} 0 \\ r_d^*(t) \end{pmatrix}. \tag{7.15}$$

Integrating these expressions (by parts where necessary) yields, respectively

$$\boldsymbol{\Sigma}^*(t,v) = \begin{pmatrix} \frac{\Sigma_{dd}(t,v)}{\phi_d^2(0,v)} & \frac{\Sigma_{dz}(t,v)}{\phi_d(0,v)} - \frac{B_d^*(0,v)\Sigma_{dd}(t,v)}{\phi_d^2(0,v)} + \frac{I_{dd}^*(t,v)}{\phi_d(0,v)} \\ \frac{\Sigma_{dz}(t,v)}{\phi_d(0,v)} - \frac{B_d^*(0,v)\Sigma_{dd}(t,v)}{\phi_d^2(0,v)} + \frac{I_{dd}^*(t,v)}{\phi_d(0,v)} & \Sigma_{zz}^*(t,v) \end{pmatrix},$$

$$\boldsymbol{\gamma}^*(t,v) = \begin{pmatrix} 0 \\ \int_t^v r_d^*(u)du \end{pmatrix},$$

with

$$\begin{aligned} \Sigma_{zz}^*(t,v) := \Sigma_{zz}(t,v) - 2\frac{B_d^*(0,v)\Sigma_{dz}(t,v)}{\phi_d(0,v)} + 2I_{zd}^*(t,v) + \frac{B_d^{*2}(0,v)\Sigma_{dd}(t,v)}{\phi_d^2(0,v)} \\ - 2\frac{B_d^*(0,v)I_{dd}^*(t,v)}{\phi_d(0,v)} + 2K_{dd}^*(t,v), \end{aligned}$$

from which we infer by construction that

$$\boldsymbol{\Phi}(v)\boldsymbol{\Sigma}^*(t,v)\boldsymbol{\Phi}^T(v) = \boldsymbol{\Sigma}^+(t,v),$$

$$\int_t^T [\boldsymbol{\Phi}(u)\boldsymbol{\Sigma}^*(0,t)\boldsymbol{\Psi}^T(t,u)]_{11}\, du = \tfrac{1}{2}B_d^{*2}(t,T)\Sigma_{dd}(0,t).$$

The derivation of the pricing kernel proceeds along the lines of that in §6.3.The only significant difference is that the drift term involving $\boldsymbol{\gamma}^*(t,v)$ in (6.12) is not zero in this case. However, we see it yields no influence on any of the above results, or on the calculation of $\mathcal{L}_1(t,u)$ from (6.25). Using (6.30) we infer

$$\Delta y_1(t,v) = \frac{I_{dd}^*(t,v)}{\phi_d(0,v)}$$

$$\begin{aligned} \Delta y_2(t,v) &= I_{zd}^*(t,v) + K_{dd}^*(t,v) - \int_t^v \frac{B_d^*(0,u)\Sigma_{dd}(t,u)}{\phi_d(0,u)} du - \int_t^v r_d^*(u)du \\ &= I_{zd}^*(t,v) + K_{dd}^*(t,v) - \frac{B_d^*(0,v)I_{dd}^*(t,v)}{\phi_d(0,v)} - B_d^*(t,v)r_d^*(t) - \tfrac{1}{2}B_d^{*2}(t,v)\Sigma_{dd}(0,t), \end{aligned}$$

where in the final line we have employed integration by parts and used (4.45). We infer

$$[\boldsymbol{\Psi}(t,v)\Delta y(0,t)]_1 = B_d^*(t,v)r_d^*(t).$$

We deduce that the pricing kernel has the form

$$G_{\text{R-E}}(y,t;\boldsymbol{\eta},v) = F^v(y,t)N(y - \Delta y(t,v) - \boldsymbol{\eta}; \boldsymbol{\Sigma}^*(t,v)), \tag{7.16}$$

with $F^v(y,t)$ given by (6.36). Substituting using the expressions set out above, reverting to the original variable $\boldsymbol{x}$, making the transformation

$$\Delta\boldsymbol{\xi}(t,v) = \boldsymbol{\Phi}(v)\Delta y(t,v)$$

to obtain (7.9), we arrive at (7.8). This completes the proof.

We note for reference that in (7.8) the argument

$$\boldsymbol{\xi} + \Delta\boldsymbol{\xi}(t,v) - \boldsymbol{\Phi}(v)\boldsymbol{\Phi}^{-1}(t)\boldsymbol{x} \equiv \begin{pmatrix} \xi_d + I_{dd}^*(t,v) - x_d\phi_d(t,v) \\ \zeta + I_{zd}^*(t,v) + K_{dd}^*(t,v) - \mu_d^*(x_d,t,v) - z \end{pmatrix}. \tag{7.17}$$

7.4 VANILLA OPTION PRICING

It is now a straightforward matter using (7.8) to calculate the price of European-style equity options. For example a call option with strike K and maturity T will have time-t price given by

$$\begin{aligned} V_{\text{Call}}^{K,T}(x_d,z,t) &= \iint_{\mathbb{R}^2} G(\boldsymbol{x},t;\boldsymbol{\xi},T)[F(T)e^{\zeta-\frac{1}{2}\Sigma_{zz}(0,T)} - K]^+ d\boldsymbol{\xi} \\ &= D(t,T)e^{-\mu_d^*(x_d,t,T)}\left(F(T)e^{z-\frac{1}{2}\Sigma_{zz}(0,t)}\Phi(d_1^{K,T}(x_d,z,t)) - K\Phi(d_2^{K,T}(x_d,z,t))\right), \end{aligned} \tag{7.18}$$

with $\Phi(\cdot)$ a Gaussian cumulative distribution function and

$$d_1^{K,T}(x_d,z,t) = \frac{\ln\frac{F(T)}{K} + z - \frac{1}{2}\Sigma_{zz}(0,t) + \mu_d^*(x_d,t,T) + \frac{1}{2}\Sigma_{zz}^+(t,T)}{\sqrt{\Sigma_{zz}^+(t,T)}}, \tag{7.19}$$

$$d_2^{K,T}(x_d,z,t) = d_1^{K,T}(x_d,z,t) - \sqrt{\Sigma_{zz}^+(t,T)}, \tag{7.20}$$

$$\Sigma_{zz}^+(t,v) = \Sigma_{zz}(t,v) + 2(I_{zd}^*(t,v) + K_{dd}^*(t,v)). \tag{7.21}$$

This can be compared with the conclusions of Amin and Jarrow [1992]. Although their results were derived for an HJM interest rate model, the use of an HJM volatility of the form $\sigma(t,T) = \sigma_0 \phi_d(t,T)$ can be shown to be equivalent to our Hull–White model for the case of constant $\sigma_d(\cdot)$. In that case, their (3.22) can be seen to be equivalent to our (7.18).

Essentially, the impact of the stochastic rates here is that the volatility appearing in the standard Black–Scholes formula is the term volatility not of the equity but of the discounted forward equity price, for the reasons elucidated by Merton [1973]. We see that the pricing kernel specifies in addition a modification to the covariance terms in (7.10) which will impact in cases where the payoff depends on both the equity price *and* the interest rate: essentially, the rates-equity covariance is incremented by the covariance between the interest rate and the reciprocal of the zero coupon bond price.

CHAPTER 8

Rates-Credit Hybrid Modelling

8.1 BACKGROUND

8.1.1 Black–Karasinski as a Credit Model

We introduced the Black–Karasinski short-rate model in Chapter 5 as an interest rate model. Its main advantage over the Hull–White model in that respect is that it preserves positive rates, the price we must pay for that convenience being that the resultant pricing kernel is not in closed form but is available only as an asymptotic series. Since, for interest rates, the convenience of being able to ensure positive rates is not, particularly under current market conditions, considered to be a necessary feature of a model we shall tend to use Hull–White as our default interest rate model.

However, our interest in the present context is not only in modelling interest rate dynamics but particularly in capturing credit default risk. Our approach to this will be through the reduced-form modelling approach pioneered by Merton [1976], wherein the assets and liabilities of a borrower are not considered explicitly, so allowing an insolvency event to be modelled and a default consequently predicted (the so-called structural modelling approach). Rather, we look to model the occurrence as a Poisson process[1] with a stochastic process λ_t representing the intensity (probability per unit time) of a default event occurring at time t. Notably this probability is *not* conditioned on survival of the debt-issuing institution until time t, although for the event to be financially meaningful it would usually have to be the first (and only) such event in the life of the institution.[2]

[1]The representation of the default process we shall use here, with the default intensity driving the stochastic default events itself assumed to be a stochastic process, is more accurately referred to as a *Cox process*.

[2]It might be noted that sovereign debt issuers will survive even an insolvency event and ultimately recommence issuing debt after a hiatus, usually under some conditions imposed by the IMF or other such international bodies. However, credit derivative contracts citing sovereign debt usually reference only the first such default, so the subsequent re-emergence of the sovereign as a debt issuer is immaterial to the derivatives pricing tasks we will be concerned with here.

It is our contention that, for a number of reasons which we shall elaborate on below, the Black–Karasinski short-rate model is a good candidate as a model for the stochastic credit default intensity process.

8.1.2 Analytic Pricing of Rates-Credit Hybrid Products

There is little previous work has been done in the area of analytic pricing of hybrid rates-credit products, most calculations of this kind having been performed numerically, using Monte Carlo, finite difference or lattice techniques, or else under the assumption of no correlation, which often allows volatility effects to be ignored. Pioneering work was done in this regard by Schönbucher [2002] who took both processes to be normal mean-reverting diffusions, in other words governed by the Hull–White short-rate model. Solutions were in his case found by constructing a two-dimensional lattice. Exact analytic solutions of this model were reported for defaultable bonds by Tchuindjo [2007]. He derives the PDE satisfied by the bond price and solves this using separation of variables to obtain an analytic expression for the bond price. This work was recently extended by Russo et al. [2020] to provide analytic expressions for the case of defaultable options on coupon bonds. We observe there that, because of the symmetric role of the interest rate and the credit spread, the model and associated PDE are essentially equivalent to the two-factor Hull-White interest rate model which we consider in more detail in Chapter 15. As was pointed out by Schönbucher [2002], it is a straightforward matter to extend his model to non-Gaussian processes.

A number of authors have followed this suggestion taking the credit process to be lognormal, governed by a Black–Karasinski short-rate model, which, although less tractable than the Hull–White model, ensures that credit spreads stay positive (and thus that survival probabilities are decreasing functions of time). Jobst and Zenios [2001] sought to price portfolios of bonds, modelling the credit spread for securities in a given rating class in this way, coupled with a Hull–White interest rate model, but also allowing rating class migrations to take place. A similar approach with only rates and credit default risk was used by Cortina [2007] to provide analytic solutions for the prices of defaultable bonds in the assumed absence of correlation, and by Pan and Singleton [2007] who considered the joint distribution of credit spreads and default loss rates implied by CDS market data.

Subsequently Ng [2013] set out a similar model where the Hull–White interest rate model was allowed to be multi-factor. The model was implemented on a trinomial tree, but approximate solutions were also provided for pricing of CDS options and single swap contingent CDS contracts. We consider the latter problem in §8.3.5 below, providing an asymptotic representation, showing clearly how the wrong-way risk impacts on the result.

An alternative approach by Schönbucher [2001] was to model both LIBOR rates and credit spreads as lognormal variables in a hybrid extension of the LIBOR market model of Brace et al. [1997], Jamshidian [1997] and Miltersen et al. [1997]. Analytic pricing formulae were deduced for standard credit derivatives including credit default swaps and swaption and asset swaps. These formulae were exact in the case of zero rates-credit correlation with approximate expressions in the case of non-zero correlation.

An analytic pricing kernel was presented by the author [Turfus, 2018e] combining the exact Hull–White pricing kernel presented in Chapter 4 for the Hull–White interest rate model with the asymptotically accurate expansion for the Black–Karasinski pricing kernel presented in Chapter 5 to obtain an asymptotic expansion for the hybrid model. The pricing kernel was used to estimate analytically the prices of extinguisher interest rate swaps and contingent credit default swaps. We present below a derivation of the pricing kernel based on the results we derived in Chapter 6 and use it to reproduce and extend the results of Turfus [2018e].

8.1.3 Mathematical Definition of the Model

We consider the joint distribution of interest rates r_{dt} and the credit default intensity λ_t associated with a risky issuer of debt with a view to calculating a pricing kernel for rates-credit hybrid derivatives. For rates we assume a Hull–White short-rate model and for credit default intensity a Black–Karasinski short-rate model. In place of r_{dt} and λ_t we shall work with auxiliary processes x_{dt} and $x_{\lambda t}$ satisfying the following canonical Ornstein–Uhlenbeck processes

$$dx_{dt} = -\alpha_d(t)x_{dt}dt + \sigma_d(t)dW_t^1, \tag{8.1}$$

$$dx_{\lambda t} = -\alpha_\lambda(t)x_{\lambda t}dt + \sigma_\lambda(t)dW_t^2, \tag{8.2}$$

where $\alpha_d, \alpha_\lambda, \sigma_d, \sigma_\lambda : \mathbb{R}^+ \to \mathbb{R}^+$ are piecewise continuous functions, the first two L^1- and the second two L^2-integrable, and W_t^1 and W_t^2 are Brownian motions under their respective equivalent martingale measures for $t \geq 0$, with

$$\text{corr}(W_t^1, W_t^2) = \rho_{d\lambda} \tag{8.3}$$

assumed and $x_{d0} = x_{\lambda 0} = 0$. Under the Hull–White model, x_{dt} is related to the instantaneous short rate r_{dt} by (4.2) and for our Black–Karasinski stochastic credit model, we relate $x_{\lambda t}$ to the instantaneous credit default intensity λ_t as previously in Chapter 6 through

$$\lambda_t = \lambda^*(t)e^{x_{\lambda t}}. \tag{8.4}$$

8.1.4 Pricing Credit-Contingent Cash Flows

In essence the credit-contingent cash flows we are interested in are of two types:

- cash flows contingent on survival of a named debt issuer up to a specified date;
- cash flows contingent on default of a named debt issuer before some specified date.

The debt issuer will often, particularly in a counterparty value adjustment (CVA) context, be the counterparty of the derivative whose value is being assessed. We write the pricing kernel for the hybrid model as $G(x_d, x_\lambda, t; \xi_d, \xi_\lambda, v)$. Following (3.7), the value of a derivative contract paying $P(\xi_d)$ at time T contingent on survival of the debt issuer until that date will be

$$f(x_d, x_\lambda, t) = \iint_{\mathbb{R}^2} P(\xi_d) G(x_d, x_\lambda, t; \xi_d, \xi_\lambda, T) d\xi_d d\xi_\lambda. \tag{8.5}$$

Consider next a derivative contract that, contingent on default at time τ in the range $[0, T]$, pays $P_{\text{def}}(x_d)$ at some subsequent time $T_{\text{pay}}(\tau)$.[3] Writing the credit intensity specified by (8.4) as $\lambda(x_\lambda, t)$, we can express the probability of a default in the period $[t, t + dt)$ as $\lambda(x_\lambda, t)dt$. Weighting all payoff contributions $P_{\text{def}}(x_d)$ with their probability of occurrence and summing/integrating all contribution from 0 to T, we arrive at a derivative price of

$$g(x_d, x_\lambda, t) = \int_0^T \iint_{\mathbb{R}^2} \lambda(\xi_\lambda, v) P_{def}(\xi_d) G(x_d, x_\lambda, t; \xi_d, \xi_\lambda, T_{\text{pay}}(v)) d\xi_d d\xi_\lambda dv. \tag{8.6}$$

Equipped with the above two formulae and the expression we shall now derive for $G(\cdot)$, we will be in a position to price rates-credit hybrid derivatives with payments contingent either on survival or on default.

8.2 THE PRICING KERNEL

Let the price of a European-type security depending for its payout amount on the instantaneous short rate value (or, equivalently, zero coupon bond price) and the survival of a named debt issuer (possibly the derivative counterparty) be expressed as $f(x_d, x_\lambda, t)$. This price is seen, by application of the Feynman–Kac theorem, to emerge under the rates-credit hybrid model specified above as the solution for $t \geq 0$ to the following Kolmogorov backward equation

$$\frac{\partial f}{\partial t} - \alpha_d(t) x_d \frac{\partial f}{\partial x_d} - \alpha_\lambda(t) x_\lambda \frac{\partial f}{\partial x_\lambda} + \frac{1}{2}\left(\sigma_d^2(t) \frac{\partial^2 f}{\partial x_d^2} + 2\rho_{d\lambda}\sigma_d(t)\sigma_\lambda(t) \frac{\partial^2 f}{\partial x_d \partial x_\lambda} + \sigma_\lambda^2(t) \frac{\partial^2 f}{\partial x_\lambda^2} \right) - (r_d(x_d, t) + \lambda(x_\lambda, t)) f = 0, \tag{8.7}$$

with $r_d(x_d, t)$ given by (4.3) and

$$\lambda(x_\lambda, t) := \lambda^*(t) e^{x_\lambda}, \tag{8.8}$$

subject to the final condition $\lim_{t \to v^-} f(x_d, t) = P(x_d)$ for some payoff function $P(\cdot)$. Here we look to derive an asymptotically valid pricing kernel for this pricing equation. As we shall see, it is also possible using the pricing kernel to value payments made contingent on default of the same issuer in accordance with some default payoff function $P_{\text{def}}(x_d)$. Analogous to our Black–Karasinski short rate result, which is asymptotically valid for low interest rates, our result here is expressed asymptotically as a perturbation expansion valid for small credit spreads to second order accuracy in (8.14) below. The method can in principle be extended to higher order but we suggest this is unlikely to be necessary.

[3]We shall usually simply assume that $T_{\text{pay}}(\tau) = \tau$.

We define here the following additional notation

$$\phi_\lambda(t,v) = e^{-\int_t^v \alpha_\lambda(u)du}, \tag{8.9}$$

$$\Sigma_{\lambda\lambda}(t,v) = \int_t^v \phi_\lambda^2(u,v)\sigma_\lambda^2(u)du, \tag{8.10}$$

$$\Sigma_{d\lambda}(t,v) = \rho_{d\lambda}\int_t^v \phi_d(u,v)\phi_\lambda(u,v)\sigma_d(u)\sigma_\lambda(u)du, \tag{8.11}$$

$$I^*_{\alpha d}(t,v) = \int_t^v \phi_\alpha(u,v)\Sigma_{d\alpha}(t,u)du, \quad \alpha \in \{d,\lambda\}, \tag{8.12}$$

$$\mathbf{\Sigma}(t,v) = \begin{pmatrix} \Sigma_{dd}(t,v) & \Sigma_{d\lambda}(t,v) \\ \Sigma_{d\lambda}(t,v) & \Sigma_{\lambda\lambda}(t,v) \end{pmatrix}. \tag{8.13}$$

We take $B(t,v)$ to be as defined by (6.69), specifying the term structure of risky bond prices, i.e. $B(t,v)$ represents the t-forward price of a risky unit cash flow at time $v \geq t$. It will be a requirement of our model that it be calibrated (through suitable choice of $\lambda^*(t)$) to reproduce this term structure. Equation (6.69) can therefore be taken to define implicitly the instantaneous credit spread $\overline{\lambda}(t)$ as that required to reproduce the (known) risky bond prices. We now state our main result as follows:

Theorem 8.1 ***(Rates-Credit Hybrid Pricing Kernel):*** *The required pricing kernel for* (8.7) *can be expressed asymptotically for some parameter ϵ representing the smallness of the credit default intensity by*

$$G(x_d,x_\lambda,t;\xi_d,\xi_\lambda,v) = f^v(x_d,t)\sum_{j=0}^{\infty} G_j(x_d,x_\lambda,t;\xi_d,\xi_\lambda,v) \tag{8.14}$$

where we define

$$f^v(x_d,t) := e^{-\mu_d^*(x_d,t,v)} \tag{8.15}$$

with $\mu_d^*(x_d,t,v)$ given by (4.13), *the $G_j(\cdot)$ are $\mathcal{O}(\epsilon^j)$ and the first three terms in the series are given by* (8.41)*–*(8.43) *below.*

Furthermore, to fit the risk-free forward curve, we must choose $r_d^*(t)$ to be given by (4.14) *and, to fit the risky curve*

$$\lambda^*(t) = \tilde{\lambda}(t)e^{I^*_{\lambda d}(0,t)-\frac{1}{2}\Sigma_{\lambda\lambda}(0,t)}, \tag{8.16}$$

$$\tilde{\lambda}(t) = \sum_{j=1}^{\infty} \tilde{\lambda}_j(t), \tag{8.17}$$

where the first two terms[4] *in the series are given in the limit of low credit default intensity by* (8.46) *and* (8.47) *below.*

---

[4]Only two terms are needed to match the second order accuracy achieved by using three terms in the expansion (8.14).

Proof: The starting point in our calculation is the knowledge from (6.78) that the pricing kernel can be expressed for $x = (x_d, x_\lambda)$ as

$$\begin{aligned}G(x, t; \xi, v) &= |\Phi^{-1}(v)|G_{\text{R-C}}(\Phi^{-1}(t)x, t; \Phi^{-1}(v)\xi, v)\\ &= B(t, v)\mathcal{E}_t^v(\mathcal{G}_3(t, \cdot))\mathcal{E}_t^v(\mathcal{G}_1(t, \cdot))\mathcal{E}_t^v(-\mathcal{L}_1(t, \cdot))|\Phi^{-1}(v)|N(\Phi^{-1}(t)x\\ &\quad - \Phi^{-1}(v)\xi; \Sigma^*(t, v)).\end{aligned} \tag{8.18}$$

We proceed by re-expressing the operators in the above in terms of the variable x and then simplifying. We start by noting that in this instance

$$\kappa(t) = \begin{pmatrix} \alpha_d(t) & 0 \\ 0 & \alpha_\lambda(t) \end{pmatrix}, \tag{8.19}$$

whence

$$\Phi(t) = \begin{pmatrix} \phi_d(0, t) & 0 \\ 0 & \phi_\lambda(0, t) \end{pmatrix}; \qquad \Phi^{-1}(t) = \begin{pmatrix} \phi_d(0, t)^{-1} & 0 \\ 0 & \phi_\lambda(0, t)^{-1} \end{pmatrix}, \tag{8.20}$$

and furthermore $\beta^*(\cdot) = \gamma^*(\cdot) = 0$. It follows that

$$\Sigma^*(t, v) = \begin{pmatrix} \frac{\Sigma_{dd}(t,v)}{\phi_d^2(0,v)} & \frac{\Sigma_{d\lambda}(t,v)}{\phi_d(0,v)\phi_\lambda(0,v)} \\ \frac{\Sigma_{d\lambda}(t,v)}{\phi_d(0,v)\phi_\lambda(0,v)} & \frac{\Sigma_{\lambda\lambda}(t,v)}{\phi_\lambda^2(0,v)} \end{pmatrix}, \tag{8.21}$$

$$\Theta(t, v) = \begin{pmatrix} \frac{\Sigma_{dd}(t,v)}{\phi_d(0,v)} & \frac{\Sigma_{d\lambda}(t,v)}{\phi_\lambda(0,v)} \\ \frac{\Sigma_{d\lambda}(t,v)}{\phi_d(0,v)} & \frac{\Sigma_{\lambda\lambda}(t,v)}{\phi_\lambda(0,v)} \end{pmatrix}. \tag{8.22}$$

In addition we find

$$\int_t^u [\Theta(t, t_1)\Phi^T(u)]_{11} dt_1 = I_{dd}^*(t, u), \tag{8.23}$$

$$\int_t^u [\Theta(t, t_1)\Phi^T(u)]_{12} dt_1 = I_{d\lambda}^*(t, u), \tag{8.24}$$

$$\int_t^u [\Theta(t, u)\Phi^T(t_1)]_{21} dt_1 = B_d^*(t, u)\frac{\Sigma_{d\lambda}(t, u)}{\phi_d(t, u)}, \tag{8.25}$$

$$[\Theta(t, u)\Phi^T(u)]_{22} = \Sigma_{\lambda\lambda}(t, u), \tag{8.26}$$

and

$$\sum_{j=1}^{2} \Theta_{1j}(t,u)\frac{\partial}{\partial y_j} = \sum_{k=1}^{2} \left[\mathbf{\Theta}(t,u)\mathbf{\Phi}^T(t)\right]_{1k}\frac{\partial}{\partial x_k}$$
$$= \frac{\Sigma_{dd}(t,v)}{\phi_d(t,v)}\frac{\partial}{\partial x_d} + \frac{\Sigma_{d\lambda}(t,v)}{\phi_\lambda(t,v)}\frac{\partial}{\partial x_\lambda} \tag{8.27}$$

$$\sum_{j=1}^{2} \Theta_{2j}(t,u)\frac{\partial}{\partial y_j} = \sum_{k=1}^{2} \left[\mathbf{\Theta}(t,u)\mathbf{\Phi}^T(t)\right]_{2k}\frac{\partial}{\partial x_k}$$
$$= \frac{\Sigma_{d\lambda}(t,v)}{\phi_d(t,v)}\frac{\partial}{\partial x_d} + \frac{\Sigma_{\lambda\lambda}(t,v)}{\phi_\lambda(t,v)}\frac{\partial}{\partial x_\lambda}. \tag{8.28}$$

Making use of (4.45) and (4.13), we conclude

$$\mathcal{E}_t^v(\mathcal{G}_1(t,\cdot)) = e^{-\mu_d^*(x_d,t,v)}$$
$$\mathcal{E}_t^v(-\mathcal{L}_1(t,\cdot)) = e^{-\frac{I_{dd}^*(t,v)}{\phi_d(t,v)}\frac{\partial}{\partial x_d} - \frac{I_{d\lambda}^*(t,v)}{\phi_\lambda(t,v)}\frac{\partial}{\partial x_\lambda}}. \tag{8.29}$$

Substituting into (8.18) and applying the shift operators to the normal distribution, we obtain

$$G(x_d,x_\lambda,t;\xi_d,\xi_\lambda,v) = B(t,v)\mathcal{E}_t^v(\mathcal{G}_3(t,\cdot))e^{-\mu_d^*(x_d,t,v)}$$
$$N_2(\phi_d(t,v)x_d - I_{dd}^*(t,v) - \xi_d, \phi_\lambda(t,v)x_\lambda - I_{\lambda d}^*(t,v) - \xi_\lambda; \mathbf{\Sigma}(t,v)), \tag{8.30}$$

where under $\boldsymbol{x}$ coordinates we have

$$\mathcal{G}_3(t,u) = \overline{\lambda}(u) - \lambda^*(u)e^{\phi_\lambda(t,u)x_\lambda - I_{\lambda d}^*(t,u) + \frac{1}{2}\Sigma_{\lambda\lambda}(t,u)}e^{\frac{\Sigma_{d\lambda}(t,u)}{\phi_d(t,u)}\left(B_d^*(t,u)+\frac{\partial}{\partial x_d}\right)+\frac{\Sigma_{\lambda\lambda}(t,u)}{\phi_\lambda(t,u)}\frac{\partial}{\partial x_\lambda}}. \tag{8.31}$$

We make use of the fact that

$$e^{\frac{\Sigma_{d\lambda}(t,u)}{\phi_d(t,u)}\left(B_d^*(t,u)+\frac{\partial}{\partial x_d}\right)}e^{-\mu_d^*(x_d,t,v)} = e^{-\mu_d^*(x_d,t,v)}e^{\frac{\Sigma_{d\lambda}(t,u)}{\phi_d(t,u)}\left(B_d^*(t,u)-B_d^*(t,v)+\frac{\partial}{\partial x_d}\right)}$$
$$= e^{-\mu_d^*(x_d,t,v)}e^{-B_d^*(u,v)\Sigma_{d\lambda}(t,u)+\frac{\Sigma_{d\lambda}(t,u)}{\phi_d(t,u)}\frac{\partial}{\partial x_d}}$$

to invert the order of the shift operator(s) and the exponential and allow the time-ordered exponential operator in (8.30) to act directly on the normal distribution, resulting in

$$G(x_d,x_\lambda,t;\xi_d,\xi_\lambda,v) = B(t,v)f^v(x_d,t)\mathcal{E}_t^v(\overline{\lambda}(\cdot) - e^{-B_d^*(\cdot,v)\Sigma_{d\lambda}(t,\cdot)}\mathcal{M}(t,\cdot))$$
$$N_2(\phi_d(t,v)x_d - I_{dd}^*(t,v) - \xi_d, \phi_\lambda(t,v)x_\lambda - I_{\lambda d}^*(t,v) - \xi_\lambda; \mathbf{\Sigma}(t,v)), \tag{8.32}$$

where we define, making use of (8.16),

$$\mathcal{M}(t,t_1) := \Lambda(x_\lambda,t,t_1)e^{\frac{\Sigma_{d\lambda}(t,t_1)}{\phi_d(t,t_1)}\frac{\partial}{\partial x_d}+\frac{\Sigma_{\lambda\lambda}(t,t_1)}{\phi_\lambda(t,t_1)}\frac{\partial}{\partial x_\lambda}}. \tag{8.33}$$

$$\begin{aligned}\Lambda(x_\lambda,t,t_1) &:= \lambda^*(t_1)e^{\phi_\lambda(t,t_1)x_\lambda - I^*_{\lambda d}(t,t_1)+\frac{1}{2}\Sigma_{\lambda\lambda}(t,t_1)}\\ &= e^{I^*_{\lambda d}(0,t_1)-\frac{1}{2}\Sigma_{\lambda\lambda}(0,t_1)}\tilde{\lambda}(t_1)e^{\phi_\lambda(t,t_1)x_\lambda - I^*_{\lambda d}(t,t_1)+\frac{1}{2}\Sigma_{\lambda\lambda}(t,t_1)}\\ &= \tilde{\lambda}(t_1)e^{\theta_\lambda(x_\lambda,t,t_1)},\end{aligned} \tag{8.34}$$

with

$$\theta_\lambda(x_\lambda,t,t_1) := \phi_\lambda(t,t_1)(x_\lambda + I^*_{\lambda d}(0,t) + B^*_d(t,t_1)\Sigma_{d\lambda}(0,t)) - \tfrac{1}{2}\phi^2_\lambda(t,t_1)\Sigma_{\lambda\lambda}(0,t) \tag{8.35}$$

(cf. the corresponding expression (5.9) for the short-rate model wherein the cross-terms are absent). In deriving (8.34) we have made use of the identities that for $t \le u \le v$

$$\Sigma_{\alpha\beta}(t,v) - \Sigma_{\alpha\beta}(u,v) = \phi_\alpha(u,v)\phi_\beta(u,v)\Sigma_{\alpha\beta}(t,u), \quad \alpha,\beta \in \{d,\lambda\}, \tag{8.36}$$

$$I^*_{\lambda d}(t,v) - I^*_{\lambda d}(u,v) = \phi_\lambda(u,v)(I^*_{\lambda d}(t,u) + B^*_d(u,v)\Sigma_{d\lambda}(t,u)), \tag{8.37}$$

these expressions being obtained in the same way as (4.43) and (4.44). We observe for future reference that by this definition $\Lambda(x_\lambda,t,t) = \lambda(x_\lambda,t)$, the instantaneous default intensity, and further $\Lambda(0,0,t_1) = \tilde{\lambda}(t_1)$.

Calibration. The calibration of the model to the term structure of credit spreads requires an asymptotic representation of the function $\tilde{\lambda}(t)$. To that end suppose $\tilde{\lambda}(t)$ has an expansion of the form of (8.17) with $\tilde{\lambda}_j(\cdot) = \mathcal{O}(\epsilon^j)$. We can re-write (8.34) correspondingly as

$$\Lambda(x_\lambda,t,t_1) = \sum_{j=1}^{\infty}\Lambda_j(x_\lambda,t,t_1) \tag{8.38}$$

$$\Lambda_j(x_\lambda,t,t_1) := \tilde{\lambda}_j(t_1)e^{\theta_\lambda(x_\lambda,t,t_1)}. \tag{8.39}$$

and define analogously

$$\mathcal{M}_j(t,t_1) := \Lambda_j(x_\lambda,t,t_1)e^{\frac{\Sigma_{d\lambda}(t,t_1)}{\phi_d(t,t_1)}\frac{\partial}{\partial x_d}+\frac{\Sigma_{\lambda\lambda}(t,t_1)}{\phi_\lambda(t,t_1)}\frac{\partial}{\partial x_\lambda}}, \tag{8.40}$$

so that $\mathcal{M}_j(t,t_1)$ maps $x_d \to x_d + \frac{\Sigma_{d\lambda}(t,t_1)}{\phi_d(t,t_1)}$ and $x_\lambda \to x_\lambda + \frac{\Sigma_{\lambda\lambda}(t,t_1)}{\phi_\lambda(t,t_1)}$. We deduce that there will be an asymptotic expansion for $G(\cdot)$ in the form of (8.14). Matching terms at successive powers of ϵ, we obtain

$$G_0(x_d, x_\lambda, t; \xi_d, \xi_\lambda, v) = B(t,v) N_2(\phi_d(t,v)x_d - I^*_{dd}(t,v) - \xi_d, \phi_\lambda(t,v)x_\lambda - I^*_{\lambda d}(t,v) - \xi_\lambda; \mathbf{\Sigma}(t,v)), \tag{8.41}$$

$$G_1(x_d, x_\lambda, t; \xi_d, \xi_\lambda, v) = B(t,v) \int_t^v \left(\overline{\lambda}(t_1) - e^{-B^*_d(t_1,v)\Sigma_{d\lambda}(t,t_1)} \mathcal{M}_1(t,t_1)\right) \times G_0(x_d, x_\lambda, t; \xi_d, \xi_\lambda, v) dt_1, \tag{8.42}$$

$$G_2(x_d, x_\lambda, t; \xi_d, \xi_\lambda, v) = B(t,v) \int_t^v \int_t^{t_2} \left(\overline{\lambda}(t_1) - e^{-B^*_d(t_1,v)\Sigma_{\lambda d}(t,t_1)} \mathcal{M}_1(t,t_1)\right) \left(\overline{\lambda}(t_2) - e^{-B^*_d(t_2,v)\Sigma_{d\lambda}(t,t_2)} \mathcal{M}_1(t,t_2)\right) G_0(x_d, x_\lambda, t; \xi_d, \xi_\lambda, v) dt_1 dt_2 - B(t,v) \int_t^v \mathcal{M}_2(t,t_1) G_0(x_d, x_\lambda, t; \xi_d, \xi_\lambda, v) dt_1. \tag{8.43}$$

Higher order terms can be derived in a similar manner but are likely to be of limited use in practice.

It remains to ensure that the risky coupon bond PV inferred from the pricing kernel is $B(0,v)$ as required, by suitable specification of the $\tilde{\lambda}_i(\cdot)$. Applying (8.14) to a unit payoff at time v evaluated as of time $t = 0$, we deduce

$$\iint_{\mathbb{R}^2} G(0,0,0; \xi_d, \xi_\lambda, v) d\xi_d d\xi_\lambda = B(0,v). \tag{8.44}$$

Matching terms at successive levels of approximation we find at $\mathcal{O}(\epsilon)$ that $\tilde{\lambda}_1(\cdot)$ must satisfy

$$\int_0^v (\overline{\lambda}(t_1) - \tilde{\lambda}_1(t_1) e^{-B^*_d(t_1,v)\Sigma_{\lambda d}(0,t_1)}) dt_1 = 0, \tag{8.45}$$

whence, upon differentiation w.r.t. v

$$\tilde{\lambda}_1(t) = \overline{\lambda}(t) + \int_0^t \tilde{\lambda}_1(t_1) \phi_d(t_1,t) \Sigma_{d\lambda}(0,t_1) e^{-B^*_d(t_1,t)\Sigma_{d\lambda}(0,t_1)} dt_1, \tag{8.46}$$

the latter expression lending itself better to iterative approximation for small $\Sigma_{d\lambda}(\cdot)$. Likewise, making use of (8.45) and noting that

$$\Lambda_j\left(x_\lambda + \frac{\Sigma_{\lambda\lambda}(t,t_1)}{\phi_\lambda(t,t_1)}, t, t_2\right) = \Lambda_j(x_\lambda, t, t_2) e^{\phi_\lambda(t_1,t_2)\Sigma_{\lambda\lambda}(t,t_1)},$$

we have at $\mathcal{O}(\epsilon^2)$ that $\tilde{\lambda}_2(\cdot)$ must satisfy

$$\int_0^v \tilde{\lambda}_1(t_2)e^{-B_d^*(t_2,v)\Sigma_{\lambda d}(0,t_2)} \int_0^{t_2} \tilde{\lambda}_1(t_1)e^{-B_d^*(t_1,v)\Sigma_{\lambda d}(0,t_1)} \left(e^{\phi_\lambda(t_1,t_2)\Sigma_{\lambda\lambda}(0,t_1)} - 1\right) dt_1 dt_2 \\ - \int_0^v \tilde{\lambda}_2(t_1)e^{-B_d^*(t_1,v)\Sigma_{\lambda d}(0,t_1)} dt_1 = 0,$$

whence, upon differentiation w.r.t. v

$$\begin{aligned}\tilde{\lambda}_2(t) &= \tilde{\lambda}_1(t)\int_0^t \tilde{\lambda}_1(t_1)e^{-B_d^*(t_1,t)\Sigma_{d\lambda}(0,t_1)} \left(e^{\phi_\lambda(t_1,t)\Sigma_{\lambda\lambda}(0,t_1)} - 1\right) dt_1 \\ &- \int_0^t \tilde{\lambda}_1(t_2)e^{-B_d^*(t_2,t)\Sigma_{\lambda d}(0,t_2)} \int_0^{t_2} \tilde{\lambda}_1(t_1)e^{-B_d^*(t_1,t)\Sigma_{\lambda d}(0,t_1)} \left(e^{\phi_\lambda(t_1,t_2)\Sigma_{\lambda\lambda}(0,t_1)} - 1\right) \\ &\qquad (\phi_d(t_2,t)\Sigma_{\lambda d}(0,t_2) + \phi_d(t_1,t)\Sigma_{\lambda d}(0,t_1))dt_1 dt_2 \\ &+ \int_0^t \tilde{\lambda}_2(t_1)\phi_d(t_1,t)\Sigma_{d\lambda}(0,t_1)e^{-B_d^*(t_1,t)\Sigma_{d\lambda}(0,t_1)} dt_1. \end{aligned} \tag{8.47}$$

This expression, although complex, does lend itself like the first-order expression to iterative solution. This completes the proof.

8.3 CDS PRICING

We illustrate the use of our pricing kernel (8.14) by applying it in its first-order representation to credit default swap (CDS) pricing. This requires us to be able to price risky coupon payments, which are essentially zero coupon bonds, and loss-at-default payments on a protection leg. We also consider credit-risky LIBOR payments, which are often specified in association with credit-linked notes and interest rate swap extinguishers.

8.3.1 Risky Cash Flow Pricing

Consider a unit payoff at time v. Denote the value at time t as

$$V_F^v(x_d, x_\lambda, t) = f^v(x_d, t) \sum_{j=0}^{\infty} \iint_{\mathbb{R}^2} G_j(x_d, x_\lambda, t; \xi_d, \xi_\lambda, v) d\xi_d d\xi_\lambda \tag{8.48}$$

We obtain by straightforward integration

$$V_F^v(x_d, x_\lambda, t) \sim B(t,v)f^v(x_d,t)\Big(1 - \Delta F_1^*(x_\lambda,t,v) + \tfrac{1}{2}\Delta F_1^{*2}(x_\lambda,t,v) - \Delta F_2(x_\lambda,t,v) \\ + \int_t^v \Lambda_1(x_\lambda,t,t_2)\int_t^{t_2} \Lambda_1(x_\lambda,t,t_1)\left(e^{\phi_\lambda(t_1,t_2)\Sigma_{\lambda\lambda}(t,t_1)} - 1\right) dt_1 dt_2\Big) \tag{8.49}$$

accurate to second order in ϵ,[5] where

$$\Delta F_i(x_\lambda, t, v) = \int_t^v \Lambda_i(x_\lambda, t, t_1) e^{-B_d^*(t_1,v)\Sigma_{d\lambda}(t,t_1)} dt_1, \quad i > 0$$

$$= \int_t^v \tilde{\lambda}_i(t_1) e^{-B_d^*(t_1,v)\Sigma_{d\lambda}(t,t_1)+\theta_\lambda(x_\lambda,t,t_1)} dt_1, \tag{8.50}$$

$$\Delta F_1^*(x_\lambda, t, v) = \Delta F_1(x_\lambda, t, v) - \int_t^v \overline{\lambda}(t_1) dt_1. \tag{8.51}$$

It is a straightforward matter to ascertain that, setting $x_d = x_\lambda = t = 0$ gives rise to a PV for the cash flow of $V_F^v(0,0,0) \sim B(0,v)$, as expected, based on the asymptotic satisfaction of the calibration condition (8.44).

Tower Property. From the tower property of conditional expectations, we can equate the PV of a cash flow at future time $T > 0$ with the expectation (under the risk-neutral measure) of the time-v value of the same cash flow, for any $v \in (0, T)$. Thus we have the identity

$$\iint_{\mathbb{R}^2} V_F^T(\xi_d, \xi_\lambda, v) G(0,0,0; \xi_d, \xi_\lambda, v) d\xi_d d\xi_\lambda = B(0,T), \tag{8.52}$$

independently of v. We look to verify that this is satisfied asymptotically when we substitute the asymptotic expressions (8.48) and (8.14) into (8.52). At zeroth order the l.h.s. gives rise to $B(v,T)B(0,v)$ which can be trivially equated to the r.h.s. At first order we obtain, applying Theorem 3.3

$$B(v,T) \iint_{\mathbb{R}^2} f^T(\xi_d, v)(G_1(0,0,0;\xi_d,\xi_\lambda,v) + \Delta F_1^*(\xi_\lambda, v, T) G_0(0,0,0;\xi_d,\xi_\lambda,v)) d\xi_d d\xi_\lambda$$

$$= \int_0^v \left(\tilde{\lambda}_1(t_1) e^{F_1(v,t_1,T)} - \overline{\lambda}(t_1)\right) dt_1 + \int_v^T \left(\tilde{\lambda}_1(t_1) e^{F_2(v,t_1,T)} - \overline{\lambda}(t_1)\right) dt_1,$$

where, making use of the definition (4.14) of $r_d^*(t)$ and of (4.42),

$$\begin{aligned} F_1(v,t_1,T) &= -B_d^*(v,T)\phi_d(0,v)\frac{\Sigma_{d\lambda}(0,t_1)}{\phi_d(0,t_1)} - \tfrac{1}{2}B_d^{*2}(v,T)\Sigma_{dd}(0,v) - B_d^*(t_1,v)\Sigma_{d\lambda}(0,t_1) \\ &\quad + \tfrac{1}{2}B_d^{*2}(v,T)\Sigma_{dd}(0,v) \\ &= -(\phi_d(t_1,v)B_d^*(v,T) + B_d^*(t_1,v))\Sigma_{d\lambda}(0,t_1) \\ &= -B_d^*(t_1,T)\Sigma_{d\lambda}(0,t_1). \end{aligned}$$

[5]The first three terms in brackets in (8.49) of course constitute a leading order representation of an exponential, which it may be considered desirable to complete, as was done in (5.54) above. Note that doing so conveniently preserves the calibration condition (8.44), since we observe that $\Delta F_1^*(0,0,v) = 0$.

and, making use also of (8.36)

$$
\begin{aligned}
F_2(v,t_1,T) &= -\tfrac{1}{2}B_d^{*2}(v,T)\Sigma_{dd}(0,v) + \phi_\lambda(v,t_1)B_d^*(v,t_1)\Sigma_{d\lambda}(0,v) \\
&\quad - \tfrac{1}{2}\phi_\lambda^2(v,t_1)\Sigma_{\lambda\lambda}(0,v) - B_d^*(t_1,T)\Sigma_{d\lambda}(v,t_1) \\
&\quad + \tfrac{1}{2}B_d^{*2}(v,T)\Sigma_{dd}(0,v) - B_d^*(v,T)\phi_\lambda(v,t_1)\Sigma_{d\lambda}(0,v) + \tfrac{1}{2}\phi_\lambda^2(v,t_1)\Sigma_{\lambda\lambda}(0,v) \\
&= -\phi_\lambda(v,t_1)\phi_d(v,t_1)B_d^*(t_1,T)\Sigma_{d\lambda}(0,v) - B_d^*(t_1,T)\Sigma_{d\lambda}(v,t_1) \\
&= -B_d^*(t_1,T)\Sigma_{d\lambda}(0,t_1).
\end{aligned}
$$

Notably the v-dependence drops out in each case, as is required. Combining both terms we obtain

$$
\int_0^T \left(\tilde{\lambda}_1(t_1)e^{-B_d^*(t_1,T)\Sigma_{d\lambda}(0,t_1)} - \overline{\lambda}(t_1)\right) dt_1,
$$

which is of course zero by the definition of $\tilde{\lambda}_1(\cdot)$. The second order term in the representation of (8.52) can be shown by a similar process also to be zero.

8.3.2 Protection Leg Pricing

For the protection leg we have a unit payoff[6] at default time $\tau > 0$ driven by a default intensity process λ_τ. Consequently the value of protection up to time $T > t$ is

$$
\begin{aligned}
V_P(x_d,x_\lambda,t) &= \int_t^T \iint_{\mathbb{R}^2} \lambda(\xi_\lambda,v)G(x_d,x_\lambda,t;\xi_d,\xi_\lambda,v)d\xi_d d\xi_\lambda dv \\
&\sim \int_t^T f^v(x_d,t)(\tilde{\lambda}_1(v)+\tilde{\lambda}_2(v))e^{I^*_{\lambda d}(0,v)-\frac{1}{2}\Sigma_{\lambda\lambda}(0,v)} \\
&\quad \times \iint_{\mathbb{R}^2} e^{\xi_\lambda}G_0(x_d,x_\lambda,t;\xi_d,\xi_\lambda,v)d\xi_d d\xi_\lambda dv \\
&\quad + \int_t^T f^v(x_d,t)\tilde{\lambda}_1(v)e^{I^*_{\lambda d}(0,v)-\frac{1}{2}\Sigma_{\lambda\lambda}(0,v)} \iint_{\mathbb{R}^2} e^{\xi_\lambda}G_1(x_d,x_\lambda,t;\xi_d,\xi_\lambda,v)d\xi_d d\xi_\lambda dv \\
&\sim \int_t^T B(t,v)f^v(x_d,t)e^{\theta_\lambda(x_\lambda,t,v)}\Big(\tilde{\lambda}_1(v)+\tilde{\lambda}_2(v) \\
&\quad - \tilde{\lambda}_1(v)\int_t^v \tilde{\lambda}_1(u)e^{-B_d^*(u,v)\Sigma_{d\lambda}(t,u)}\left(e^{\phi_\lambda(u,v)\Sigma_{\lambda\lambda}(t,u)+\theta_\lambda(x_\lambda,t,u)}-1\right)du\Big)dv,
\end{aligned}
\tag{8.53}
$$

[6]In practice, the payoff in the event that there is a recovery rate $R < 1$ on the defaulting debt is typically $N(1-R)$, where N is the notional of the CDS. It is a straightforward matter to multiply the PV associated with a unit notional by this amount to obtain the PV of the actual protection leg.

where in the final expression we have made use of (8.36), (8.37) and (8.45). Setting $x_d = x_\lambda = t = 0$, we obtain the following second-order accurate expression for the protection leg PV

$$V_P(0,0,0) \sim \int_0^T B(0,v) \times \left(\tilde{\lambda}_1(v) + \tilde{\lambda}_2(v) - \tilde{\lambda}_1(v) \int_0^v \tilde{\lambda}_1(u) e^{-B_d^*(u,v)\Sigma_{d\lambda}(0,u)} \left(e^{\phi_\lambda(u,v)\Sigma_{\lambda\lambda}(0,u)} - 1 \right) du \right) dv. \tag{8.54}$$

From the definition of $\tilde{\lambda}_1(\cdot)$ in (8.46) above, we infer that the PV of protection will increase roughly linearly with the rates-credit correlation; likewise for the CDS fair premium. Also, from (8.47), we see that the contribution of the second and third terms in brackets in (8.54) is $\mathcal{O}(\rho_{d\lambda}^2)$; furthermore, provided $\phi_\lambda(0,t) \to 0$ as $t \to \infty$, the asymptoticness will be uniform, in the sense that the contribution will remain asymptotically small even in the limit as $T \to \infty$, which is a potentially important consideration in pricing long-term trades. However, we would emphasise that in most practical circumstances the contribution of these terms will be negligible; they are recorded here mainly for completeness.

An illustrative example is presented in Fig. 8.1 comparing the price of a 10y CDS whose protection leg is valued using our first-order asymptotic representation with the results of a Monte Carlo calculation for various assumed rates-credit correlation levels. The default intensity is chosen to be 8%, so not particularly small, the credit volatility to be 60% with a mean reversion rate of 0.3, and the notional to be 100. As can be seen, the agreement is excellent, the small discrepancy (1bp of notional) clearly being essentially second order with parabolic dependence on the correlation, as our asymptotic expansion would suggest.

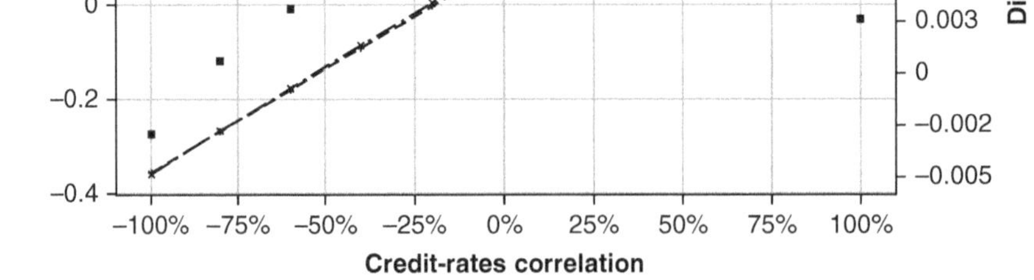

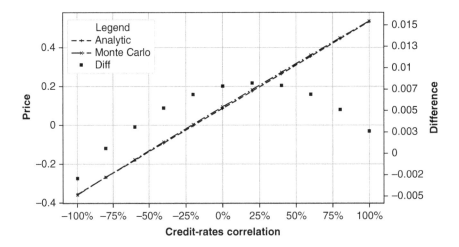

FIGURE 8.1 Prices for 10y maturity CDS

8.3.3 Defaultable LIBOR Pricing

We consider next the pricing of floating rate payments, as is often required when credit protection is purchased through the writing of a credit-linked note. We consider a (defaultable) payment at T_2 of tenor-τ LIBOR, fixed at $T_1 = T_2 - \tau$. We will look to calculate this correct to first order in ϵ. The payoff in this case is

$$P_L(x_d) = \frac{1}{D(T_1, T_2) f^{T_2}(x_d, T_1)} - 1, \tag{8.55}$$

where we have used $D(\cdot, \cdot)$ as a short-hand for the discount factor $D_d(\cdot, \cdot)$ defined in (4.7) whence the denominator in (8.55) is the risk-free zero coupon bond price. We seek the value of this payoff in the first instance as of the fixing time T_1

$$V_L(x_d, x_\lambda, T_1) \sim B(T_1, T_2)(D^{-1}(T_1, T_2) - f^{T_2}(x_d, T_1))(1 - \Delta F_1^*(x_\lambda, T_1, T_2)) \tag{8.56}$$

where we ignore in this instance the second order term in (8.49). We next use (8.56) as a payoff at time T_1 to be priced as of time $t < T_1$, again to first-order accuracy in ϵ. Applying (8.14) and ignoring second order terms arising, we obtain

$$\begin{aligned}
V_L(x_d, x_\lambda, t) \sim\ & \frac{B(T_1, T_2)}{D(T_1, T_2)} \iint_{\mathbb{R}^2} (1 - \Delta F_1^*(\xi_\lambda, T_1, T_2)) G_0(x_d, x_\lambda, t; \xi_d, \xi_\lambda, T_1) d\xi_d d\xi_\lambda \\
& + \frac{B(T_1, T_2)}{D(T_1, T_2)} \iint_{\mathbb{R}^2} G_1(x_d, x_\lambda, t; \xi_d, \xi_\lambda, T_1) d\xi_d d\xi_\lambda \\
& - B(t, T_2) f^{T_2}(x_d, t)(1 - \Delta F_1^*(x_\lambda, t, T_2)) \\
\sim\ & \frac{B(t, T_2) f^{T_1}(x_d, t)}{D(T_1, T_2)} (1 - \Delta F_1^*(x_\lambda, t, T_1)) \\
& - B(t, T_2) f^{T_2}(x_d, t)(1 - \Delta F_1^*(x_\lambda, t, T_2)) \\
& - \frac{B(t, T_2) f^{T_1}(x_d, t)}{D(T_1, T_2)} \int_{T_1}^{T_2} \Big(\Lambda_1(\phi_\lambda(t, t_1) x_\lambda - I_{\lambda d}^*(t, T_1), T_1, t_1) \\
& e^{-B_d^*(t_1, T_2)\Sigma_{d\lambda}(T_1, t_1) + \frac{1}{2}\Sigma_{\lambda\lambda}(t, t_1)} - \overline{\lambda}(t_1) \Big) dt_1.
\end{aligned} \tag{8.57}$$

Unpacking the final integral yields

$$\int_{T_1}^{T_2} \left(\tilde{\lambda}_1(t_1) e^{-B_d^*(t_1, T_2)\Sigma_{d\lambda}(T_1, t_1) + \theta_\lambda(x_\lambda, t, t_1)} - \overline{\lambda}(t_1) \right) dt_1.$$

Noting that $\theta_\lambda(x_\lambda = 0, t = 0, t_1) = 0$ and $\Delta F_1{}^*(0,0,.)) = 0$, we see the PV is given to first order by

$$V_L(0, 0, 0) \sim B(0, T_2)(D^{-1}(T_1, T_2)(1 - \phi_L(T_1, T_2)) - 1), \tag{8.58}$$

$$\phi_L(T_1, T_2) := \int_{T_1}^{T_2} \left(\tilde{\lambda}_1(t_1) e^{-B_d^*(t_1, T_2)\Sigma_{d\lambda}(T_1, t_1)} - \overline{\lambda}(t_1) \right) dt_1, \tag{8.59}$$

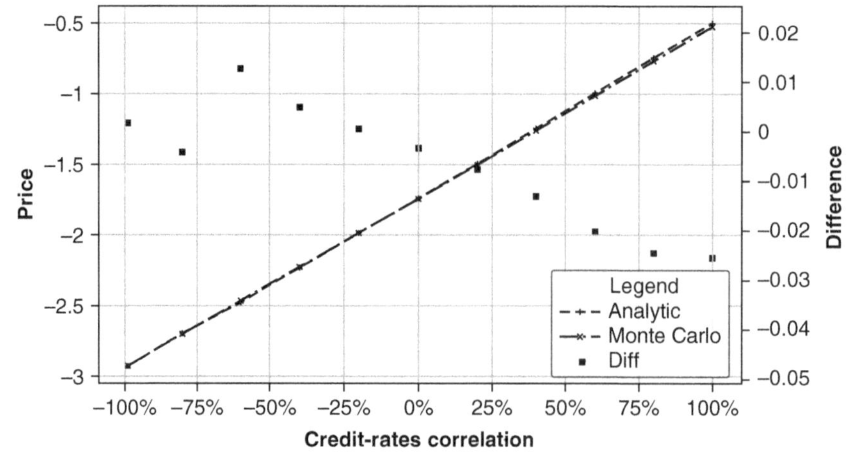

FIGURE 8.2 Correlation impact on prices for 10y maturity IR swap extinguisher

Here the factor $\phi_L(\cdot) \geq 0$ expresses the small *reduction* in the value of LIBOR payments associated with positive rates-credit correlation. In the event of zero correlation, clearly $\phi_L(\cdot) \to 0$ and the well known deterministic rates result is recovered as expected; likewise when $T_1 = 0$, in which case of course LIBOR is already fixed.

An illustrative example is presented in Fig. 8.2 comparing the price of a 10y extinguishing swap[7] with a notional of 100 whose float leg is valued using (8.58) with the results of a Monte Carlo calculation for various assumed credit-rates correlation levels. The swap was assumed to pay LIBOR with a 6m tenor, so its value increases with correlation; other trade and market details are as for Fig. 8.1. As can be seen, the agreement is excellent, the correlation impact being priced with a relative error of less than 2%.

Accrual Adjustment. If, upon default, accrued LIBOR remains due (for example, if the payment is in the context of an extinguishing swap), the value of this should be calculated and added to the value of the defaultable LIBOR payment. Since the original LIBOR payment was calculated only correct to $O(\epsilon)$, we do the same for the accrual. The accrual payoff associated with a default time $v \in (T_1, T_2)$ and $x_{dT_1} = x_d$ is

$$P_A(x_d, v) = \Delta_A(v) P_L(x_d),$$
$$\Delta_A(v) := \frac{\delta_L(T_1, v)}{\delta_L(T_1, T_2)} \tag{8.60}$$

[7]By this is meant a fixed-floating swap whose cash flows expire if a named debt issuer defaults.

with $\delta_L(\cdot)$ the relevant day count fraction for the LIBOR. We must evaluate this in the first instance as of time T_1

$$\Delta V_L(x_d, x_\lambda, T_1) = \int_{T_1}^{T_2} \iint_{\mathbb{R}^2} P_A(x_d, v)\lambda(\xi_\lambda, v)G(x_d, x_\lambda, T_1; \xi_d, \xi_\lambda, v)d\xi_d d\xi_\lambda dv$$

$$\sim P_L(x_d) \int_{T_1}^{T_2} \Delta_A(v)B(T_1, v)f^v(x_d, T_1)\Lambda_1(x_\lambda, T_1, v)dv, \qquad (8.61)$$

where we have considered only leading order contributions. Further evaluating as of time $t = 0$, we find the defaultable LIBOR PV adjustment associated with accrual can be written

$$\Delta V_L(0,0,0) \sim \int_{T_1}^{T_2} \int_{\mathbb{R}^2} B(0,v)\Delta_A(v)f^v(\xi_d, T_1)P_L(\xi_d)\Lambda_1(\xi_\lambda, T_1, v)$$

$$\times\, G(0,0,0; \xi_d, \xi_\lambda, T_1)d\xi_d d\xi_\lambda dv$$

$$\sim \int_{T_1}^{T_2} \int_{\mathbb{R}^2} B(0,v)\left(\frac{e^{\phi_d(T_1,v)B_d^*(v,T_2)\left(\xi_d + r^*(T_1) + \frac{1}{2}(B_d^*(T_1,T_2)+B_d^*(T_1,v))\Sigma_{dd}(0,T_1)\right)}}{D(T_1,T_2)}\right.$$

$$\left. - f^v(\xi_d, T_1)\right)$$

$$\Delta_A(v)\Lambda_1(\xi_\lambda, T_1, v)G(0,0,0; \xi_d, \xi_\lambda, T_1)d\xi_d d\xi_\lambda dv$$

$$\sim \int_{T_1}^{T_2} B(0,v)\tilde{\lambda}_1(v)\Delta_A(v)\left(\frac{F_{\text{convexity}}(T_1, T_2, v)}{D(T_1, T_2)} - 1\right)dv, \qquad (8.62)$$

where $F_{\text{convexity}}(\cdot)$ is defined by (4.22). The convexity impact here is likely to be small as the value of accrual is already only first order, so assumed small compared with the main (zeroth order) LIBOR payment. We include it here mainly for completeness.

Adjusted Payment Date. We consider next the case where the LIBOR payment date is adjusted to be not T_2, the end of the payment period, but $T_2 + \Delta T$, with ΔT allowed to be positive or negative. Thus, the payoff (8.55) is made at time $T_2 + \Delta T$. We value this as of time T_1 as follows

$$V_L(x_d, x_\lambda, T_1) \sim B(T_1, T_2 + \Delta T)f^{T_2+\Delta T}(x_d, T_1)\left(\frac{1}{D(T_1, T_2)f^{T_2}(x_d, T_1)} - 1\right)$$

$$(1 - \Delta F_1^*(x_\lambda, T_1, T_2 + \Delta T)). \qquad (8.63)$$

We define for convenience the $\mathcal{O}(1)$ function

$$P_0(x_d) := B(T_1, T_2 + \Delta T)f^{T_2+\Delta T}(x_d, T_1)\left(\frac{1}{D(T_1, T_2)f^{T_2}(x_d, T_1)} - 1\right).$$

Evaluating the effective T_1-payoff as of $t = 0$, we have

$$\begin{aligned} V_L(0,0,0) &\sim \iint_{\mathbb{R}^2} V_L(\xi_d, \xi_\lambda, T_1) G(0,0,0; \xi_d, \xi_\lambda, T_1) d\xi_d d\xi_\lambda \\ &\sim V_L^{(0)} + V_L^{(1)} \end{aligned}$$

with

$$\begin{aligned} V_L^{(0)} &:= \iint_{\mathbb{R}^2} P_0(\xi_d, \xi_\lambda, T_1) G_0(0,0,0; \xi_d, \xi_\lambda, T_1) d\xi_d d\xi_\lambda, \\ V_L^{(1)} &:= \iint_{\mathbb{R}^2} P_0(\xi_d, \xi_\lambda, T_1)(G_1(0,0,0; \xi_d, \xi_\lambda, T_1) \\ &\quad - \Delta F_1^*(\xi_\lambda, T_1, T_2 + \Delta T) G_0(0,0,0; \xi_d, \xi_\lambda, T_1)) d\xi_d d\xi_\lambda \end{aligned}$$

at zeroth and first order, respectively. Applying Theorem 3.3 yields in turn

$$V_L^{(0)} = B(0, T_2 + \Delta T) \left(\frac{F_{\text{convexity}}(T_1, T_2, T_2 + \Delta T)}{D(T_1, T_2)} - 1 \right) \tag{8.64}$$

and

$$V_L^{(1)} = -B(0, T_2 + \Delta T) \frac{F_{\text{convexity}}(T_1, T_2, T_2 + \Delta T) \phi_C(T_1, T_2, T_2 + \Delta T)}{D(T_1, T_2)}, \tag{8.65}$$

where

$$\begin{aligned} \phi_C(T_1, T_2, v) := &\int_0^{T_1} \left(\tilde{\lambda}_1(t_1) e^{-B_d^*(t_1, T_1)\Sigma_{d\lambda}(0, t_1) - \phi_d(t_1, T_1)(B_d^*(T_1, v) - B_d^*(T_1, T_2))\Sigma_{d\lambda}(0, t_1)} - \overline{\lambda}(t_1) \right) dt_1 \\ &+ \int_{T_1}^{v} \left(\tilde{\lambda}_1(t_1) e^{-B_d^*(t_1, v)\Sigma_{d\lambda}(T_1, t_1) - \phi_\lambda(T_1, t_1)(B_d^*(T_1, v) - B_d^*(T_1, T_2))\Sigma_{d\lambda}(0, T_1)} - \overline{\lambda}(t_1) \right) dt_1. \end{aligned} \tag{8.66}$$

Combining contributions, we see the PV for the adjusted LIBOR is given asymptotically by

$$\begin{aligned} &V_L(0,0,0) \\ &= B(0, T_2 + \Delta T) \left(\frac{F_{\text{convexity}}(T_1, T_2, T_2 + \Delta T)(1 - \phi_C(T_1, T_2, T_2 + \Delta T))}{D(T_1, T_2)} - 1 \right) + \mathcal{O}(\epsilon^2). \end{aligned} \tag{8.67}$$

We observe that, since $\phi_C(T_1, T_2, T_2) = \phi_L(T_1, T_2)$ and $F_{\text{convexity}}(T_1, T_2, T_2) = 1$, the result (8.58) is recovered as expected in the event that $\Delta T = 0$. We conclude from (8.67) that, aside from the obvious (negative) impact of delayed payment, positive ΔT

results in a *negative* convexity impact on the LIBOR value, which effect is mitigated slightly by positive rates-credit correlation but exacerbated by negative correlation, the converse being true for $\Delta T < 0$.

Comparisons were made of (8.67) against Monte Carlo simulations for a 10y IR swap extinguisher with quarterly LIBOR payments delayed by a month. Results showing the impact of rates-credit correlation and of interest rate volatility are displayed in Figs. 8.3 and 8.4, respectively. As can be seen, the comparisons are in all cases favourable. Note also that, when the IR volatility is increased by a factor of three

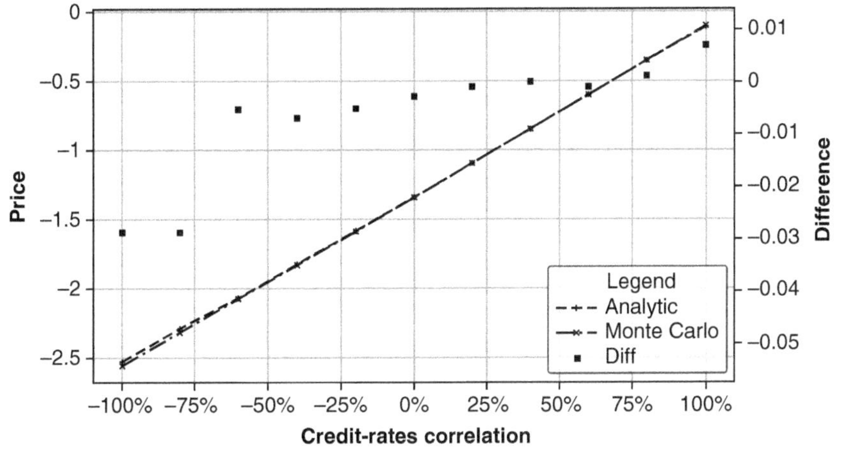

FIGURE 8.3 Correlation impact on prices for IR swap extinguisher with delayed LIBOR payment

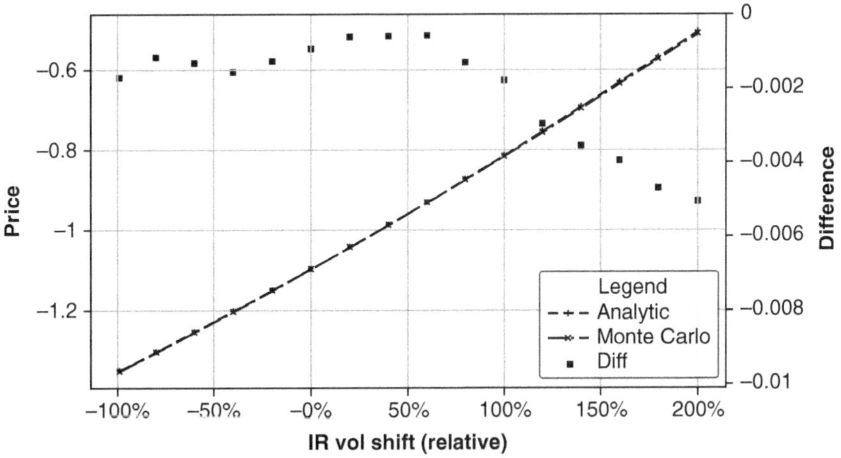

FIGURE 8.4 IR volatility impact on prices for IR swap extinguisher with delayed LIBOR payment

(200% bump) from its market-observed level, a clear departure can be seen from linear dependence, which departure is captured accurately even with just a first-order approximation. This is because Hull–White interest rate volatility is handled exactly in our methodology.

8.3.4 Defaultable Capped LIBOR Pricing

We consider also the impact of imposing a cap on the LIBOR payments. This can be taken into account by subtracting off the value of a caplet from the LIBOR PV. We therefore consider the following caplet payoff at time T_2

$$\begin{aligned} P_K(x_d) &= [P_L(x_d) - K\delta(T_1, T_2)]^+ \\ &= [D^{-1}(T_1, T_2) f^{T_2}(x_d, T_1)^{-1} - \kappa^{-1}]^+ \end{aligned} \tag{8.68}$$

where κ is given as previously by (4.24). We value this as of $t = T_1$ as before to obtain

$$V_K(x_d, x_\lambda, T_1) \sim \left(D^{-1}(T_1, T_2) - \kappa^{-1} f^{T_2}(x_d, T_1)\right) \mathbb{1}_{x_d > \xi^*} B(T_1, T_2)(1 - \Delta F_1^*(x_\lambda, T_1, T_2)), \tag{8.69}$$

where ξ^* is the highest value of x satisfying $P_K(x) = 0$. Applying again (8.14) and making use of Theorem 3.5, we obtain the caplet price

$$\begin{aligned} V_K(x_d, x_\lambda, t) \sim\ & \frac{B(t, T_2)}{D(T_1, T_2)} f^{T_1}(x_d, t) \left(\left(1 + \int_t^{T_2} \bar{\lambda}(t_1) dt_1 \right) \Phi(-d_2(\xi^* - \phi_d(t, T_1) x_d, t)) \right. \\ & - \left(\Delta F_1(x_\lambda, t, T_1) \right. \\ & \left. + \int_{T_1}^{T_2} \tilde{\lambda}_1(t_1) e^{-B_d^*(t_1, T_2)\Sigma_{d\lambda}(T_1, t_1) + \theta_\lambda(x_\lambda, t, t_1)} \right) \\ & \left. \Phi(-d_2(\xi^* - \Sigma_{d\lambda}(t, T_1) - \phi_d(t, T_1) x_d, t)) \right) \\ & - \frac{B(t, T_2)}{\kappa} f^{T_2}(x_d, t) \left(\left(1 + \int_t^{T_2} \bar{\lambda}(t_1) dt_1 \right) \Phi(-d_1(\xi^* - \phi_d(t, T_1) x_d, t)) \right. \\ & - \Delta F_1(x_\lambda, t, T_2) \Phi(-d_1(\xi^* - \Sigma_{d\lambda}(t, T_1) \\ & \left. - \phi_d(t, T_1) x_d, t)) \right) \end{aligned} \tag{8.70}$$

with $\Phi(\cdot)$ a cumulative Gaussian distribution function and

$$\begin{aligned} d_2(\xi, t) &:= \frac{\xi + I_{dd}^*(t, T_1)}{\sqrt{\Sigma_{dd}(t, T_1)}}, \\ d_1(\xi, t) &:= d_2(\xi + B_d^*(T_1, T_2)\Sigma_{dd}(t, T_1)) \end{aligned} \tag{8.71}$$

In particular, we find the caplet PV is given to first order by

$$
\begin{aligned}
V_K(0,0,0) \sim{}& \frac{B(0,T_2)}{D(T_1,T_2)}(\Phi(-d_2(\xi^*,0)) - \phi_L(T_1,T_2)\Phi(-d_2(\xi^* - \Sigma_{d\lambda}(0,T_1),0)))\\
&- \frac{B(0,T_2)}{\kappa}\Phi(-d_1(\xi^*,0))\\
&+ \frac{B(0,T_2)}{D(T_1,T_2)}\int_0^{T_2}\overline{\lambda}(t_1)dt_1(\Phi(-d_2(\xi^*,0)) - \Phi(-d_2(\xi^* - \Sigma_{d\lambda}(0,T_1),0)))\\
&- \frac{B(0,T_2)}{\kappa}\int_0^{T_2}\overline{\lambda}(t_1)dt_1(\Phi(-d_1(\xi^*,0)) - \Phi(-d_1(\xi^* - \Sigma_{d\lambda}(0,T_1),0))),
\end{aligned}
\tag{8.72}
$$

We see here, letting $\overline{\lambda}(\cdot) \to 0$, that $B(0,T_2) \to D(0,T_2)$ while $\phi_L(T_1,T_2) \to 0$, leading to recovery of the well known Hull–White caplet formula. Finally, combining this result with (8.58), we find the value of a defaultable capped LIBOR payment will be given by the difference

$$V_{L,K}(0,0,0) = V_L(0,0,0) - V_K(0,0,0) \tag{8.73}$$

8.3.5 Contingent CDS with IR Swap Underlying

We consider next the pricing of contingent credit default swaps (CCDS) with interest rate swap underlyings. We consider only the leading order impact of credit effects, ignoring terms arising from the use of $G_i(\cdot)$ for $i \geq 1$. It is necessary to be able to calculate the value of future fixed and floating rate LIBOR payments in the event of default, contingent on the value of the swap exceeding some threshold. Under the assumption of a Hull–White interest rate model, the exposure value of the swap underlying will be determined at any stopping time τ by knowledge of the short rate x_τ; for LIBOR payments which have already fixed, there will be an additional dependence on the value of $x_{T^*(\tau)}$ where

$$T^*(\tau) = \max_i \{T_i \mid T_i < \tau\} \tag{8.74}$$

and $T_i, i = 0, \ldots, M-1$ are the fixing times of the M swap payments, with T_M the swap maturity.

The value of the LIBOR payment made at time T_i is given from (8.55) by

$$L_i(T_i) = \frac{1}{D(T_{i-1},T_i)f^{T_i}(x_{dT_{i-1}},T_{i-1})} - 1. \tag{8.75}$$

In valuing this payment for general t, we must consider three possible cases:

1. If $t > T_i$, the payment has already been made so the value is zero;
2. If $t \in (T_{i-1}, T_i]$, the LIBOR rate will have been fixed at time T_{i-1}, based on the value of $x_{T_{i-1}}$ so we have

$$L_i(t) = D(t,T_i)f^{T_i}(x_{dt},t)\left(\frac{1}{D(T_{i-1},T_i)f^{T_i}(x_{dT_{i-1}},T_{i-1})} - 1\right); \tag{8.76}$$

3. If $t \leq T_{i-1}$, we have more straightforwardly

$$L_i(t) = D(t, T_{i-1}) f^{T_{i-1}}(x_{dt}, t) - D(t, T_i) f^{T_i}(x_{dt}, t). \tag{8.77}$$

We can on this basis write the value of a (payer) swap with coupon rate K as $V_{\text{swap}}(x_{dt}, t)$, where

$$V_{\text{swap}}(x_d, t) = \sum_{k=1}^{M} \left(L_i(t) - K\delta(T_{i-1}, T_i) D(t, T_i) f^{T_i}(x_{dt}, t) \right) \mathbb{1}_{t<T_i}. \tag{8.78}$$

We are interested, for a default at time $\tau \in (0, T_M]$, in whether $V_{\text{swap}}(x_{d\tau}, \tau)$ exceeds some critical value. For a naked swap exposure the critical value will be zero. For a predetermined collateral schedule $C(t)$ it will be the collateral amount $C(\tau)$. For a dynamic collateral schedule adjusted so as to eliminate the exposure at each payment date T_i it will be $V_{\text{swap}}(T^*(\tau))$. The expression is of course identical for a receiver swap.

Let us denote by $\xi^*(\tau)$ the critical value of $x_{d\tau}$ for which $V_{\text{swap}}(\tau) = C(\tau)$ or $V_{\text{swap}}(T^*(\tau))$.[8] Now suppose without loss of generality that the contingent CDS offers protection only over some interval $(T_{i-1}, T_i]$; the value of protection over $(T_0, T_M]$ will be a sum of such contributions, their mutual influence captured through knowledge of $\xi^*(\tau)$.

Defining

$$\kappa_i := \frac{1}{1 + K\delta(T_{i-1}, T_i)}, \tag{8.79}$$

the value of the payoff at time T_i as of default time $\tau < T_{i-1}$ contingent on $x_{d\tau} = x_d$ will, using (8.77), be

$$P_i(x_d, \tau) = D(\tau, T_i)(D^{-1}(T_{i-1}, T_i) f^{T_{i-1}}(x_d, \tau) - \kappa_i^{-1} f^{T_i}(x_d, \tau)) \mathbb{1}_{x_d > \xi^*(\tau)}, \tag{8.80}$$

if the protection is on a payer swap and

$$P_i(x_d, \tau) = D(\tau, T_i)(\kappa_i^{-1} f^{T_i}(x_d, \tau) - D^{-1}(T_{i-1}, T_i) f^{T_{i-1}}(x_d, \tau)) \mathbb{1}_{x_d < \xi^*(\tau)}, \tag{8.81}$$

[8] In the event that the collateral is updated to reflect the new fixing at $T^*(\tau)$ the problematic dependence on $x_{dT^*(\tau)}$ should cancel between the exposure and the collateral. Otherwise, we can make the approximation $x_{dT_{i-1}} \approx x_{d\tau}$ in (8.76) to allow $\xi^*(\tau)$ to be calculated to a good approximation. If wished, this can be corrected for with a linear adjustment, replacing $\xi^*(\tau) \to \xi^*(\tau) + \delta\xi^*(\tau)(\xi^*(\tau) - x_{dT_{i-1}})$. This slightly complicates our task, requiring the protection value to be calculated first as of time T_{i-1}, then as of the earlier time t. The only difference in the end result will be that $\xi^*(u) \to \xi^*(u)(1 + \delta\xi^*(u))$ and $x_d \to x_d(1 + \delta\xi^*(u)/\phi_d(T_{i-1}, u))$ in the expressions for $V_{\text{protection}}(x_d, t)$.

in the case of a receiver swap. We consider only the first of these, the second being a straightforward extension. The corresponding payer swap expression for $\tau \in [T_{i-1}, T_i]$ is, using (8.76)

$$P_i(x_d, \tau) = D(\tau, T_i)(D^{-1}(T_{i-1}, T_i)\frac{f^{T_i}(x_d, \tau)}{f^{T_i}(x_{dT_{i-1}}, T_{i-1})} - \kappa_i^{-1} f^{T_i}(x_d, \tau))\mathbb{1}_{x_d > \xi^*(\tau)}, \quad (8.82)$$

We consider separately contributions from the first and second terms in each of (8.80) and (8.82), writing the protection value of the swap payments at T_i as $V_i = V_i^{(1)} - V_i^{(2)}$, with (1) referring to the contribution from the first terms and (2) that from the second terms. The first will have a contribution which we denote $V_{i,1}^{(1)}$ associated with $[t, T_{i-1}]$ from (8.80) and one of $V_{i,2}^{(1)}$ associated with $[T_{i-1}, T_i]$ from (8.82), which contributions must be calculated separately. However, since the form of the second term is identical between the two equations, a single calculation can be carried out for $V_i^{(2)}$ over $[t, T_i]$. As it is the simpler, we start with this latter case

$$\begin{aligned}
V_i^{(2)}(x_d, x_\lambda, t) &= \kappa_i^{-1} \int_t^{T_i} \tilde{\lambda}(v) D(v, T_i) \iint_{\mathbb{R}^2} e^{\xi_\lambda} f^{T_i}(\xi_d, v) \mathbb{1}_{\xi_d < \xi^*(v)} \\
&\quad \times G(x_d, x_\lambda, t; \xi_d, \xi_\lambda, v) d\xi_d d\xi_\lambda dv \\
&\sim \kappa_i^{-1} \int_t^{T_i} f^v(x_d, t) D(v, T_i) \tilde{\lambda}_1(v) e^{I^*_{\lambda d}(0,v) - \frac{1}{2}\Sigma_{\lambda\lambda}(0,v)} \\
&\qquad \iint_{\mathbb{R}^2} e^{\xi_\lambda} f^{T_i}(\xi_d, v) \mathbb{1}_{\xi_d < \xi^*(v)} G_0(x_d, x_\lambda, t; \xi_d, \xi_\lambda, v) d\xi_d d\xi_\lambda dv \\
&\sim \kappa_i^{-1} f^{T_i}(x_d, t) \int_t^{T_i} B(t, v) \tilde{\lambda}_1(v) D(v, T_i) N(-\hat{d}(x_d, t, v, T_i)) \\
&\quad \times e^{-B_d^*(v, T_i)\Sigma_{d\lambda}(t,v) + \theta_\lambda(x_\lambda, t, v)} dv,
\end{aligned} \quad (8.83)$$

where

$$\hat{d}(x_d, t, v, T) = \frac{\xi^*(v) - \phi_d(t, v)x_d + I^*_{dd}(t, v) + B_d^*(v, T)\Sigma_{dd}(t, v) - \Sigma_{d\lambda}(t, v)}{\sqrt{\Sigma_{dd}(t, v)}}. \quad (8.84)$$

Considering next the two contributions to $V_i^{(1)}$, the contribution from $[t, T_{i-1}]$ valued as of time t is seen by a similar calculation to be

$$\begin{aligned}
V_{i,1}^{(1)}(x_d, x_\lambda, t) &\sim \int_t^{T_{i-1}} f^v(x_d, t) D(v, T_{i-1}) \tilde{\lambda}_1(v) e^{I^*_{\lambda d}(0,v) - \frac{1}{2}\Sigma_{\lambda\lambda}(0,v)} \\
&\qquad \iint_{\mathbb{R}^2} f^{T_{i-1}}(\xi_d, v) \mathbb{1}_{\xi_d < \xi^*(v)} e^{x_\lambda} G_0(x_d, x_\lambda, t; \xi_d, \xi_\lambda, v) d\xi_d d\xi_\lambda dv \\
&\sim f^{T_{i-1}}(x_d, t) \int_t^{T_{i-1}} B(t, v) \tilde{\lambda}_1(v) D(v, T_{i-1}) \Phi(-\hat{d}(x_d, t, v, T_{i-1})) \\
&\qquad e^{-B_d^*(v, T_{i-1})\Sigma_{d\lambda}(t,v) + \theta_\lambda(x_\lambda, t, v)} dv.
\end{aligned} \quad (8.85)$$

The corresponding contribution from $(T_{i-1}, T_i]$ priced in the first instance as of T_{i-1} will be

$$V_{i,2}^{(1)}(x_d, x_\lambda, T_{i-1}) = \int_{T_{i-1}}^{T_i} f^v(x_d, T_{i-1}) D(v, T_{i-1}) \tilde{\lambda}_1(v) e^{I^*_{\lambda d}(0,v) - \frac{1}{2}\Sigma_{\lambda\lambda}(0,v)}$$

$$\iint_{\mathbb{R}^2} \frac{f^{T_i}(\xi_d, v)}{f^{T_i}(x_d, T_{i-1})} \mathbb{1}_{\xi_d < \xi^*(v)} \, e^{\xi_\lambda} G(x_d, x_\lambda, T_{i-1}; \xi_d, \xi_\lambda, v) d\xi_d d\xi_\lambda dv$$

$$\sim \int_{T_{i-1}}^{T_i} f^v(x_d, T_{i-1}) B(T_{i-1}, v) \tilde{\lambda}_1(v) D(v, T_{i-1}) \Phi(-\hat{d}(x_d, T_{i-1}, v, v))$$

$$e^{-B_d^*(v,T_i)\Sigma_{d\lambda}(T_{i-1},v) + \theta_\lambda(x_\lambda, T_{i-1}, v)} dv. \tag{8.86}$$

Valuing this as of time $t \le T_{i-1}$

$$V_{i,2}^{(1)}(x_d, x_\lambda, t) \sim \int_{T_{i-1}}^{T_i} f^v(x_d, t) B(t, v) \tilde{\lambda}_1(v) D(v, T_{i-1}) \Phi(-\hat{d}(x_d, t, v, v))$$

$$e^{-B_d^*(v,T_i)\Sigma_{d\lambda}(T_{i-1},v) + \theta_\lambda(x_\lambda, t, v)} dv. \tag{8.87}$$

Combining all three contributions from (8.83), (8.85) and (8.87) we obtain

$$V_i(x_d, x_\lambda, t) \sim V_{i,1}^{(1)}(x_d, x_\lambda, t) + V_{i,2}^{(1)}(x_d, x_\lambda, t) - V_i^{(2)}(x_d, x_\lambda, t) \tag{8.88}$$

Setting $x_d = x_\lambda = t = 0$ and further combining contributions from *all* swap payments, we obtain the following easily calculated formula for the PV of protection

$$V_{\text{CCDS}} = \sum_{i=1}^{M} V_i, \tag{8.89}$$

$$V_i \sim \int_0^{T_i} B(0, v) \tilde{\lambda}_1(v) D(v, T_i) \Big(D(T_{i-1}, T_i)^{-1} \Phi(-\hat{d}_0(v, v \vee T_{i-1})) e^{-\Gamma^*(v, T_{i-1}, T_i)}$$

$$- \kappa_i^{-1} \Phi(-\hat{d}_0(v, T_i)) e^{-B_d^*(v,T_i)\Sigma_{d\lambda}(0,v)} \Big) dv, \tag{8.90}$$

where we define $\hat{d}_0(v, w) := \hat{d}(0, 0, v, w)$ and

$$\Gamma^*(v, T_1, T_2) := \begin{cases} B_d^*(v, T_1)\Sigma_{d\lambda}(0, v), & 0 \le v \le T_1, \\ B_d^*(v, T_2)\Sigma_{d\lambda}(T_1, v), & T_1 < v \le T_2. \end{cases} \tag{8.91}$$

As can be seen, positive correlation increases the value of protection mainly through increasing the effective default intensity from $\overline{\lambda}(t)$ to $\tilde{\lambda}_1(t)$. There will also be a small impact of correlation on the discounting with the value of both terms in brackets

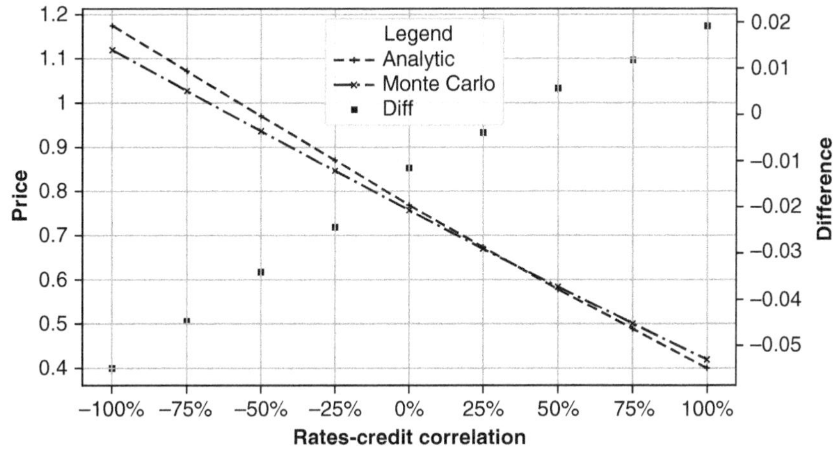

FIGURE 8.5 Prices for a CCDS on a 10y IR swap underlying

in (8.90) being reduced for positive correlation. This will further increase the cost of protection. Similar considerations apply for receiver swaps.

An example calculation is shown in Fig. 8.5, in which our leading order asymptotic approximation is compared with a Monte Carlo simulation. The notional in this case was set to be 100. The comparison looks less favourable than the IR swap extinguisher we considered above, but the magnitude of discrepancies is in fact larger only by about a factor of two. The differences may in part be a consequence of the difficulty in the Monte Carlo computation where default events could necessarily be observed only at discrete times, not continuously.

We consider next the effect of introducing a deterministic collateral schedule $C(t)$. The associated payoff is simply $C(\tau)\mathbb{1}_{\xi_d<\xi^*(\tau)}$ at a default time $\tau \in [0, T_M]$, which has to be subtracted away from the payoff associated with the swap flows. This leads to a time-t value of

$$V_C(x_d, x_y, t) \sim \int_t^{T_M} B(t,v) f^v(x_d,t)\tilde{\lambda}_1(v)C(v)\Phi(-\hat{d}(x_d,t,v,v))e^{\theta_\lambda(x_\lambda,t,v)}dv \tag{8.92}$$

and a PV given by

$$V_C \sim \int_0^{T_M} B(0,v)\tilde{\lambda}_1(v)C(v)\Phi(-\hat{d}_0(v,v))dv. \tag{8.93}$$

The impact of the collateral is, other than the redefinition of $\xi^*(\tau)$ as specified above, to cause an adjustment $V_{\text{CCDS}} \to V_{\text{CCDS}} - V_C$, which is guaranteed by the definition of $\xi^*(\tau)$ to remain positive.

CHAPTER 9

Credit-Equity Hybrid Modelling

9.1 BACKGROUND

We look to deal in this chapter with the problem of modelling equity derivatives in a context where credit risk is considered to impact on the pricing. We will, as in the previous chapter, make use of the reduced-form approach pioneered in the classic paper of Merton [1976], wherein a diffusive process for equity price is supplemented by a jump process, driven by an intensity λ_t. Although it is not often recognised, Merton [1976] did not in this paper equate the jump process with default but (as its title suggests) with the arrival of a jump whose size (positive or negative) was governed by some assumed probability distribution. It was only in subsequent extensions that the jump was considered to be of size –1, taking the equity price to a terminal state of zero value; at the same time the default model was separated off from the equity model for the purpose of pricing credit derivatives whose payoff(s) do not depend on the equity price. In this chapter, as stated, we will be interested in the case where payoffs *do* depend on equity prices.

There is quite an extensive literature on different models of the joint credit-equity process, although no clear consensus has arisen as to which approach is to be preferred. Based on the observation that, as the equity price decreases, the credit default intensity tends to increase, the credit default intensity is commonly taken to be a decreasing function of the equity price. Andersen and Buffum [2003] mention three formulations which have been employed based on power law, logarithmic and exponential relationships, preferring the first of these in practice. Other authors, such as Carr and Wu [2010] have, citing empirical evidence, allowed the credit intensity to depend on the equity *volatility* level, assuming this to be stochastic.

Another approach is that adopted by Chung and Kwok [2014]. They assumed a framework within which the credit intensity process and the equity process were both affine diffusions, the latter with a jump at default, but with a negative correlation posed between them to replicate the observed behaviour. Ehlers and Schönbucher [2004] take an analogous approach for joint FX-credit modelling, the main difference being that, while the FX rate is assumed to jump at default, it is not in their case assumed to jump to zero.

However, there are well-documented problems with affine diffusions as credit models. In the case of normal volatility (Hull–White), credit intensities can become negative which potentially violates the condition of no arbitrage, while in the other commonly considered case of square-root volatility (Cox–Ingersoll–Ross) there arise in practice restrictive upper limits on the implied (lognormal) credit volatility which can be produced, which mitigate against the model's use (Brigo and Mercurio, 2006). For this reason authors have in recent times tended to prefer a lognormal credit volatility model (Black–Karasinski), as was discussed in the previous chapter in relation to rates-credit hybrid modelling. For example Brigo et al. [2019], Chung and Gregory [2019] and Itkin et al. [2019] all adapt the model of Ehlers and Schönbucher [2004] in this way for joint FX-credit modelling in a quanto CDS context.

Thus we consider below a Black–Karasinski credit model with equity modelled by a (negatively correlated) jump-diffusion process, where the jump occurs at default. In most cases we shall consider the jump in the equity price to be to zero. However, we will have reason to consider the case when the jump has a smaller magnitude; in particular it may be zero.

We shall consider in the first instance convertible bonds, which typically have an embedded European-style option[1] for the holder to receive at maturity a predetermined number of shares in the issuing corporation in lieu of receiving the notional repayment. Effectively this is a vanilla European option, except in that the payoff is made contingent on survival of the issuer and therefore needs to be discounted at the credit-risky rate, not the risk-free rate as is usually done. Provided that the bond is not callable by the issuer, its value can be obtained through separate calculations for a vanilla bond and the embedded equity option. For that reason we deal here only with the latter.

The other case we shall consider is where an equity-dependent payoff is made contingent on the survival of a debt issuer other than the issuer of the referenced equity. This is typically the case when we consider the counterparty risk associated with the writer of an equity option. We shall consider specifically the calculation for the counterparty valuation adjustment (CVA), or rather, equivalently, the fair price of buying default protection, on the mark-to-market of a vanilla European-style equity option. We shall assume that the option contract is partially collateralised, giving the payment upon default the character of a compound option (call option on a put/call option). As we shall see, fairly accurate closed-form representations of the PV of such protection can be obtained, making use of the compound option pricing formulae of Geske [1979].

9.2 DERIVATION OF CREDIT-EQUITY PRICING KERNEL

9.2.1 Pricing Equation

Consider the credit intensity λ_t to be governed by a Black–Karasinski model as set out in §8.1.3 above and denoted for $x_{\lambda t} = x_\lambda$ by

$$\lambda(x_\lambda, t) :- \bar{\lambda}(t) e^{x_\lambda - \frac{1}{2}\Sigma_{\lambda\lambda}(0,t)} \tag{9.1}$$

[1]The option may in the alternative be Bermudan with multiple exercise dates. However, this situation is not amenable to the type of analytic approximation we are looking to use here, so we do not consider it further.

Further let the equity price S_t be given by a jump-diffusion process with (lognormal) volatility $\sigma_z(t)$, undergoing a jump of relative size $k \in [-1, 0]$ in the event of a credit default event. We expect in practice $k = -1$ but, in §9.4 below, we shall be interested in situations where other values of k become relevant so we choose to keep the value of k open in our derivation. Under these assumptions we can write

$$\frac{dS_t}{S_t} = (\bar{r}_d(t) - q(t) - k\lambda_t)dt + kdn_t + \sigma_z(t)dW_t^z, \tag{9.2}$$

with $\bar{r}_d(t)$ and $q(t)$ the (instantaneous) risk-free interest rate and dividend rate, respectively, and n_t a Cox process with intensity λ_t functioning as an indicator of a default event. Further, let us introduce an auxiliary process z_t defined implicitly by

$$S_t = F(t)e^{z_t - \frac{1}{2}\Sigma_{zz}(0,t) - k\Lambda_0(0,t)}, \tag{9.3}$$

with

$$\Sigma_{zz}(t, v) = \int_t^v \sigma_z^2(u)du, \tag{9.4}$$

$$\Lambda_0(t, v) = \int_t^v \bar{\lambda}(u)du, \tag{9.5}$$

and $F(t)$ the forward rate given by

$$F(t) = S_0 e^{\int_0^t (\bar{r}_d(u) - q(u))du}, \tag{9.6}$$

Applying Itô's lemma to (9.3) we find z_t satisfies

$$dz_t = -k(\lambda_t - \bar{\lambda}(t))dt + \ln(1 + k)dn_t + \sigma_z(t)dW_t^z. \tag{9.7}$$

Further suppose that W_t^z is correlated with W_t^2 in (8.2) as follows

$$\text{corr}(W_t^2, W_t^z) = \rho_{\lambda z}. \tag{9.8}$$

Let us denote the time of default by $\tau > 0$. The value at time t of a survival-contingent payoff at time $T > t$ of $P(z_T)$ based on an equity underlying will, from Ehlers and Schönbucher [2004], be

$$\begin{aligned} V_t &= E\left[e^{-\int_t^T (\bar{r}_d(u)} \mathbb{1}_{\tau > T} P(z_T) \middle| \mathcal{F}_t \right] \\ &= \mathbb{1}_{\tau > t} E\left[e^{-\int_t^T (\bar{r}_d(u) + \lambda_u)du} P(z_T) \middle| \mathcal{F}_t \right], \end{aligned} \tag{9.9}$$

where $\mathcal{F}_t$ represents the filtration associated with the Brownian motions W_t^z and W_t^2. From the Feynman–Kac theorem $V_t = f(x_{\lambda t}, z_t, t)$ emerges as the solution $f(x_\lambda, z, t)$ to the following Kolmogorov backward diffusion equation

$$\begin{aligned}
&\frac{\partial f}{\partial t} - \alpha_\lambda(t) x_\lambda \frac{\partial f}{\partial x_\lambda} - k(\lambda(x_\lambda, t) - \overline{\lambda}(t)) \frac{\partial f}{\partial z} \\
&\quad + \frac{1}{2}\left(\sigma_\lambda^2(t)\frac{\partial^2 f}{\partial x_\lambda^2} + 2\rho_{\lambda z}\sigma_\lambda(t)\sigma_z(t)\frac{\partial^2 f}{\partial x_\lambda \partial z} + \sigma_z^2(t)\frac{\partial^2 f}{\partial z^2}\right) \\
&\qquad - (\overline{r}_d(t) + \lambda(x_\lambda, t))f = 0. \qquad (9.10)
\end{aligned}$$

The jump in the value of S_τ has no direct impact on $f(x_\lambda, z, t)$ since, by assumption, its value is based only on contributions for which $\tau > T$.

9.2.2 Pricing Kernel

We reuse the notation introduced in §8.2 above. In addition we define

$$\Sigma_{\lambda z}(t, v) = \rho_{\lambda z} \int_t^v \phi_\lambda(u, v)\sigma_\lambda(u)\sigma_z(u)du. \qquad (9.11)$$

and let $\Sigma_{zz}(t, v)$ be defined by (7.12), redefining in this context:

$$\boldsymbol{\Sigma}(t, v) = \begin{pmatrix} \Sigma_{\lambda\lambda}(t, v) & \Sigma_{\lambda z}(t, v) \\ \Sigma_{\lambda z}(t, v) & \Sigma_{zz}(t, v) \end{pmatrix}, \qquad (9.12)$$

We seek an evolution operator $\mathcal{U}(t, T)$ satisfying

$$\begin{aligned}
\left(\frac{\partial}{\partial t} + \mathcal{L}_1(t) + \mathcal{L}_2(t) + \mathcal{V}_1(t)\right)\mathcal{U}(t, T) &= 0, \\
\mathcal{U}(T, T) &= I,
\end{aligned} \qquad (9.13)$$

with

$$\mathcal{L}_1(t) = \frac{1}{2}\left(\sigma_\lambda^2(t)\frac{\partial^2}{\partial x_\lambda^2} + 2\rho_{\lambda z}\sigma_\lambda(t)\sigma_z(t)\frac{\partial^2}{\partial x_\lambda \partial z} + \sigma_z^2(t)\frac{\partial^2}{\partial z^2}\right) - (\overline{r}_d(t) + \overline{\lambda}(t)), \qquad (9.14)$$

$$\mathcal{L}_2(t) = -\alpha_\lambda(t) x_\lambda \frac{\partial}{\partial x_\lambda}, \qquad (9.15)$$

$$\mathcal{V}_1(t) = -(\lambda(x_\lambda, t) - \overline{\lambda}(t))\left(1 + k\frac{\partial}{\partial z}\right). \qquad (9.16)$$

Solving for $\mathcal{U}(t,T)$ and handling the mean reversion factor as previously, we obtain

$$\mathcal{U}(t,T) = \mathcal{E}_t^T(\mathcal{L}(t,\cdot) + \mathcal{V}(t,\cdot))\mathcal{E}_t^T(\mathcal{L}_2(\cdot)), \tag{9.17}$$

$$\mathcal{L}(t,u) = \frac{1}{2}\left(\frac{\sigma_\lambda^2(u)}{\phi_\lambda^2(t,u)}\frac{\partial^2}{\partial x_\lambda^2} + 2\rho_{\lambda z}\frac{\sigma_\lambda(t)\sigma_z(t)}{\phi_\lambda(t,u)}\frac{\partial^2}{\partial x_\lambda \partial z} + \sigma_z^2(t)\frac{\partial^2}{\partial z^2}\right) - (\overline{r}_d(t) + \overline{\lambda}(t)) \tag{9.18}$$

$$\mathcal{V}(t,u) = -\left(\tilde{\lambda}(u)e^{\phi_\lambda(t,u)x_\lambda - \frac{1}{2}\Sigma_{\lambda\lambda}(0,t)} - \overline{\lambda}(u)\right)\left(1 + k\frac{\partial}{\partial z}\right). \tag{9.19}$$

Applying Theorem 3.2 in the standard manner, we obtain

$$\mathcal{E}_t^T(\mathcal{L}(t,\cdot) + \mathcal{V}(t,\cdot)) = \mathcal{E}_t^T(\mathcal{W}(t,\cdot))\mathcal{E}_t^T(\mathcal{L}(t,\cdot)), \tag{9.20}$$

$$\mathcal{W}(t,u) = \mathcal{E}_t^u(\mathrm{ad}_{\mathcal{L}(t,\cdot)})(\mathcal{V}(t,u)). \tag{9.21}$$

The calculation for $\mathcal{W}(t,u)$ can be considered as analogous to that in Chapter 8. The only significant difference is the inclusion of the jump. But, considering the pricing equation (9.10), we see the only impact of this is that the risky discounting term $\lambda(x_\lambda, t)$ must be replaced effectively by $\lambda(x_\lambda, t)\left(1 + k\frac{\partial}{\partial z}\right)$. Since the z-derivative commutes with all other terms in the equation it can be treated in the analysis as if it were a function rather than an operator. In this way we obtain

$$\mathcal{W}(t,u) = \left(\overline{\lambda}(u) - \tilde{\lambda}(u)e^{\phi_\lambda(t,u)x_\lambda - \frac{1}{2}\phi_\lambda^2(t,u)\Sigma_{\lambda\lambda}(0,t)}e^{\frac{\Sigma_{\lambda\lambda}(t,u)}{\phi_\lambda(t,u)}\frac{\partial}{\partial x_\lambda} + \Sigma_{\lambda z}(t,u)\frac{\partial}{\partial z}}\right)\left(1 + k\frac{\partial}{\partial z}\right). \tag{9.22}$$

In a similar vein, noting that the integral kernel associated with $\mathcal{E}_t^T(\mathcal{L}(\cdot))\mathcal{E}_t^T(\mathcal{L}_2(\cdot))$ is

$$G_0(x_\lambda, z, t; \xi_\lambda, \zeta, v) = B(t,v)N_2(\xi_\lambda - \phi_\lambda(t,v)x_\lambda, \zeta - z; \mathbf{\Sigma}(t,v)), \tag{9.23}$$

we conclude that the kernel we seek for $\mathcal{U}(t,T)$ is

$$G(x_\lambda, z, t; \xi_\lambda, \zeta, v) = \mathcal{E}_t^T(\mathcal{W}(t,\cdot))G_0(x_\lambda, z, t; \xi_\lambda, \zeta, v). \tag{9.24}$$

It remains to expand the operator $\mathcal{E}_t^T(\mathcal{W}(t,\cdot))$ and apply it term-by-term to the Gaussian $G_0(\cdot;\cdot)$.

9.2.3 Asymptotic Expansion

Supposing as in Chapter 8 that $\| \overline{\lambda}(\cdot) \| = \mathcal{O}(\epsilon)$, we look to construct a representation of the Green's function (9.24) as a power series in ϵ. Following the same process as previously, calibration to the credit curve requires a representation of $\tilde{\lambda}(t)$ of the form

$$\tilde{\lambda}(t) = \sum_{j=1}^{\infty} \tilde{\lambda}_j(t) \tag{9.25}$$

with $\| \tilde{\lambda}_j(\cdot) \| = \mathcal{O}(\epsilon^j)$ and, in particular

$$\tilde{\lambda}_1(t) = \overline{\lambda}(t), \tag{9.26}$$

$$\tilde{\lambda}_2(t) = \overline{\lambda}(t) \int_0^t \overline{\lambda}(t_1)(e^{\phi_\lambda(t_1,t)\Sigma_{\lambda\lambda}(0,t_1)} - 1)dt_1, \tag{9.27}$$

analogous to (5.12) and (5.13) above. Calibration of the equity model to the forward curve has already been guaranteed by construction. We further pose

$$G(x_\lambda, z, t; \xi_\lambda, \zeta, v) = \sum_{j=0}^{\infty} G_j(x_\lambda, z, t; \xi_\lambda, \zeta, v), \tag{9.28}$$

with $\| G_j(\cdot;\cdot) \| = \mathcal{O}(\epsilon^j)$ and $G_0(\cdot;\cdot)$, given in particular by (9.23). Matching terms at successive powers between (9.28) and (9.24) and making use of (3.39) gives rise to

$$\begin{aligned} G_1(x_\lambda, z, t; \xi_\lambda, \zeta, v) &= \Lambda_0(t, v)(1 + k\partial_z)G_0(x_\lambda, z, t; \xi_\lambda, \zeta, v) \\ &\quad - \int_t^v \overline{\lambda}(t_1)e^{\theta_\lambda(x_\lambda,t,t_1)}(1 + k\partial_z) \\ &\quad \times G_0\left(x_\lambda + \frac{\Sigma_{\lambda\lambda}(t,t_1)}{\phi_\lambda(t,t_1)}, z + \Sigma_{\lambda z}(t,t_1), t; \xi_\lambda, \zeta, v\right) dt_1 \end{aligned} \tag{9.29}$$

where we define, analogous to (8.35),

$$\theta_\lambda(x_\lambda, t, t_1) = \phi_\lambda(t, t_1)x_\lambda - \frac{1}{2}\phi_\lambda^2(t, t_1)\Sigma_{\lambda\lambda}(0, t), \tag{9.30}$$

so that $\theta_\lambda(0, 0, t_1) = 0$, and

$$\begin{aligned} G_2(x_\lambda, z, t; \xi_\lambda, \zeta, v) &= \frac{1}{2}\Lambda_0^2(t, v)(1 + k\partial_z)^2 G_0(x_\lambda, z, t; \xi_\lambda, \zeta, v) \\ &\quad - \int_t^v \left(\Lambda_0(t, v)\overline{\lambda}(t_1)(1 + k\partial_z) + \tilde{\lambda}_2(t_1)\right) e^{\theta_\lambda(x_\lambda,t,t_1)}(1 + k\partial_z) \\ &\quad\quad G_0\left(x_\lambda + \frac{\Sigma_{\lambda\lambda}(t,t_1)}{\phi_\lambda(t,t_1)}, z + \Sigma_{\lambda z}(t,t_1), t; \xi_\lambda, \zeta, v\right) dt_1 \\ &\quad + \int_t^v \overline{\lambda}(t_2)e^{\theta_\lambda(x_\lambda,t,t_2)} \int_t^{t_2} \overline{\lambda}(t_1)e^{\theta_\lambda(x_\lambda,t,t_1)+\phi_\lambda(t_1,t_2)\Sigma_{\lambda\lambda}(t,t_1)}(1 + k\partial_z)^2 \\ &\quad\quad G_0\left(x_\lambda + \sum_{i=1}^{2} \frac{\Sigma_{\lambda\lambda}(t,t_i)}{\phi_\lambda(t,t_i)}, z + \sum_{i=1}^{2} \Sigma_{\lambda z}(t,t_i), t; \xi_\lambda, \zeta, v\right) dt_1 dt_2. \end{aligned} \tag{9.31}$$

9.3 CONVERTIBLE BONDS

Let us consider pricing a convertible bond which has an option to convert into K stocks per unit notional at maturity T. We suppose that the bond is not callable by the issuer, so the pricing of the coupon and notional repayment are standard (independent of the stochastic credit model) so need not concern us here. To price the option to convert, we must use the above pricing kernel. The payoff per unit notional is given by

$$P(\zeta) = \left[KF(T)e^{\zeta-\frac{1}{2}\Sigma_{zz}(0,T)+\Lambda_0(0,T)} - 1\right]^+ \tag{9.32}$$

where we have in this instance set $k = -1$. Let us denote the root of the expression in brackets, considered as a function of ζ by

$$\zeta^* = \frac{1}{2}\Sigma_{zz}(0,T) - \Lambda_0(0,T) - \ln(KF(T)). \tag{9.33}$$

Considering first the leading order representation of the price obtained by using $G_0(x_\lambda, z, t; \xi_\lambda, \zeta, v)$ as given by (9.23), we find

$$\begin{aligned} V_0(z,t) &= \int_{\zeta^*}^{\infty}\int_{\mathbb{R}} G_0(x_\lambda, z, t; \xi_\lambda, \zeta, T)P(\zeta)d\xi_\lambda d\zeta \\ &= B(t,T)\left(KF(T)e^{z-\frac{1}{2}\Sigma_{zz}(0,t)+\Lambda_0(0,T)}\int_{\zeta^*}^{\infty} e^{\zeta-z-\frac{1}{2}\Sigma_{zz}(t,T)}N\left(\frac{\zeta-z}{\sqrt{\Sigma_{zz}(t,T)}}\right)d\zeta\right. \\ &\qquad \left. - \int_{\zeta^*}^{\infty} N\left(\frac{\zeta-z}{\sqrt{\Sigma_{zz}(t,T)}}\right)d\zeta\right) \\ &= B(t,T)\left(KF(T)e^{z-\frac{1}{2}\Sigma_{zz}(0,t)+\Lambda_0(0,T)}\Phi(d_1(z-\zeta^*,t,T)) - \Phi(d_2(z-\zeta^*,t,T))\right), \end{aligned} \tag{9.34}$$

where

$$d_2(z,t,T) = \frac{z}{\sqrt{\Sigma_{zz}(t,T)}} \tag{9.35}$$

$$d_1(z,t,T) = d_2(z,t,T) + \sqrt{\Sigma_{zz}(t,T)}. \tag{9.36}$$

This gives rise to

$$V_0(0,0) = B(t,T)\left(KF(T)e^{\Lambda_0(0,T)}\Phi(d_1(-\zeta^*,0,T)) - \Phi(d_2(-\zeta^*,0,T))\right). \tag{9.37}$$

To leading order this is just the Black–Scholes formula except in that a) the relevant discount factor $B(t,T)$ incorporates credit risk and b) the jump-compensating drift adjustment $\Lambda_0(0,T)$ elevates the (survival-contingent) stock price. The impact of the credit-equity correlation $\rho_{\lambda z}$, the other main factor, is not felt until first-order contributions are considered. Applying $G_1(x_\lambda, z, t; \xi_\lambda, \zeta, v)$ yields a contribution[2]

$$V_1(x_\lambda, z, t) = (1 - \partial_z) \int_t^T \overline{\lambda}(t_1)(V_0(z,t) - e^{\theta_\lambda(x_\lambda,t,t_1)} V_0(z + \Sigma_{\lambda z}(t,t_1), t))dt_1.$$

Similarly, applying $G_2(x_\lambda, z, t; \xi_\lambda, \zeta, v)$ yields

$$\begin{aligned} V_2(x_\lambda, z, t) = (1 - \partial_z)^2 \int_t^T \overline{\lambda}(t_2) \int_t^{t_2} \overline{\lambda}(t_1) \big(V_0(z,t) - e^{\theta_\lambda(x_\lambda,t,t_1)} V_0(z + \Sigma_{\lambda z}(t,t_1), t)) \\ + e^{\theta_\lambda(x_\lambda,t,t_1)+\theta_\lambda(x_\lambda,t,t_2)+\phi_\lambda(t_1,t_2)\Sigma_{\lambda\lambda}(t,t_1)} V_0(z + \Sigma_{\lambda z}(t,t_1) + \Sigma_{\lambda z}(t,t_2), t)\big) \, dt_1 dt_2 \\ - (1 - \partial_z) \int_t^T \tilde{\lambda}_2(t_1) e^{\theta_\lambda(x_\lambda,t,t_1)} V_0(z + \Sigma_{\lambda z}(t,t_1), t) dt_1. \end{aligned}$$

Notice that only at this level of approximation does the stochastic credit model impact on the price other than indirectly through correlation. Combining the above results we deduce the following expression for the PV of the equity conversion option

$$\begin{aligned} PV &= V_0(0,0) + V_1(0,0,0) + V_2(0,0,0) + \mathcal{O}(\epsilon^3) \\ &= \Bigg[\left(1 + \Lambda_0(0,T)(1 - \partial_z) + \frac{1}{2}\Lambda_0^2(0,T)(1 - \partial_z)^2\right) V_0(z,0) \\ &\quad - \int_0^T \left(\left(\overline{\lambda}(t_1) + \tilde{\lambda}_2(t_1)\right)(1 - \partial_z) - \Lambda_0(0,T)\overline{\lambda}(t_1)(1 - \partial_z)^2\right) V_0(z + \Sigma_{\lambda z}(0,t_1), 0) dt_1 \\ &\quad + \int_0^T \overline{\lambda}(t_2) \int_0^{t_2} \overline{\lambda}(t_1) e^{\phi_\lambda(t_1,t_2)\Sigma_{\lambda\lambda}(0,t_1)} (1 - \partial_z)^2 V_0(z + \Sigma_{\lambda z}(0,t_1) + \Sigma_{\lambda z}(0,t_2)) dt_1 dt_2 \Bigg]_{z=0} + \mathcal{O}(\epsilon^3). \end{aligned} \tag{9.38}$$

The resulting expression can be computed straightforwardly using quadrature, the integrands consisting of nothing more than Gaussian and cumulative Gaussian functions. The corresponding first-order approximation is given straightforwardly by omitting the terms associated with $V_2(0,0,0)$. We have not sought to carry out explicit comparisons with full solutions computed by numerical means. However, the approximation made here is very similar to that made by Turfus and Shubert [2017] in the related problem of pricing contingent convertible (CoCo) bonds. They use a Hull–White representation for the credit model and report favourable comparison with finite difference calculations, typically within 2% relative (35bp of notional) for bonds with a maturity of up to 35y, making use only of a first-order expansion. On this basis we would suggest that our second-order accurate expression (9.38) ought to be more than adequate for most practical purposes.

[2]In fact the most efficient way of generating these results is not to apply the $G_i(\cdot;\cdot)$ directly to the payoff but rather to apply the expansion capturing $\mathcal{E}_t^T(\mathcal{W}(t,\cdot))$ to $V_0(z,t)$ instead, so avoiding complicated integrations over the multivariate Gaussian distribution function.

9.4 CONTINGENT CDS ON EQUITY OPTION

We consider next an extension of the calculation in §8.3.5 above where we valued the protection provided by a contingent CDS on an interest rate swap underlying. We shall look to consider here the protection on an equity option underlying. This problem was considered by Turfus [2016] as part of a wider investigation. In this instance the issuer of the equity is different from the debt issuer against whom protection is being bought. We shall suppose that there may be a correlation between the equity process and the credit intensity of the debt issuer. But, since it is typically not feasible to infer a jump in equity value at default of the debt issuer, we shall assume here that $k = 0$. This has the added advantage that we can assume the same equity process, and therefore volatility level, before and after the default. The calculation of Turfus [2016] shows how a non-zero value of k can if wished be incorporated.

We consider a vanilla call option with strike K and maturity T. The call option price will be given under the previously defined notation by the standard Black formula

$$C^{K,T}(z,t) = D(t,T)\left(F(T)e^{z-\frac{1}{2}\Sigma_{zz}(0,t)}N(d_1(z-z^*,t,T)) - KN(d_2(z-z^*,t,T))\right), \quad (9.39)$$

where $D(t,T)$ is given by (3.49) and

$$z^* := \tfrac{1}{2}\Sigma_{zz}(0,T) + \ln K - \ln F(T). \quad (9.40)$$

We further suppose that, if default occurs at some time $v \in (0,T)$, the payoff of the contingent CDS is given by

$$P(\zeta,v) = [C^{K,T}(\zeta,v) - C(v)]^+, \quad (9.41)$$

where $C(v)$ represents a collateral schedule, i.e. the value at time v (assumed known deterministically at $t = 0$) of any collateral against which the value of the option can be offset. Turfus [2016] shows how the calculation can be extended if the collateral schedule is not deterministic. Let us define the critical point at which the protection amount comes into the money as

$$\zeta^*(v) := \sup\{\zeta \mid P(\zeta,v) = 0\}. \quad (9.42)$$

By the same arguments as used in Chapter 8, we infer that the value of protection over the period $(0,T)$ is given by

$$\begin{aligned} PV &= \int_0^T \iint_{\mathbb{R}^2} \lambda(\xi_\lambda,v)P(\zeta,v)G(0,0,0;\xi_\lambda,\zeta,v)\,d\xi_\lambda\,d\zeta\,dv \\ &= PV_1 + PV_2 + \mathcal{O}(\epsilon^3), \end{aligned} \quad (9.43)$$

with, at first order

$$\begin{aligned} PV_1 &= \int_0^T \iint_{\mathbb{R}^2} \bar{\lambda}(v)e^{\xi_\lambda-\frac{1}{2}\Sigma_{\lambda\lambda}(0,v)}P(\zeta,v)G_0(0,0,0;\xi_\lambda,\zeta,v)\,d\xi_\lambda\,d\zeta\,dv \\ &= \int_0^T \frac{B(0,v)\bar{\lambda}(v)}{\sqrt{\Sigma_{zz}(0,v)}}\int_{\zeta^*(v)}^\infty P(\zeta,v)N\left(\frac{\zeta-\Sigma_{\lambda z}(0,v)}{\sqrt{\Sigma_{zz}(0,v)}}\right)d\zeta\,dv \end{aligned} \quad (9.44)$$

and, at second order

$$
\begin{aligned}
PV_2 &= \int_0^T \iint_{\mathbb{R}^2} e^{\xi_\lambda - \frac{1}{2}\Sigma_{\lambda\lambda}(0,t_2)} P(\zeta, t_2)\left(\tilde{\lambda}_2(t_2) G_0(0,0,0;\xi_\lambda,\zeta,t_2)\right. \\
&\quad \left. + \overline{\lambda}(t_2) G_1(0,0,0;\xi_\lambda,\zeta,t_2)\right) d\xi_\lambda d\zeta dt_2 \\
&= \int_0^T \frac{B(0,t_2)(\Lambda_0(0,t_2)\overline{\lambda}(t_2) + \tilde{\lambda}_2(t_2))}{\sqrt{\Sigma_{zz}(0,t_2)}} \int_{\zeta^*(t_2)}^{\infty} P(\zeta,t_2) N\left(\frac{\zeta - \Sigma_{\lambda z}(0,t_2)}{\sqrt{\Sigma_{zz}(0,t_2)}}\right) d\zeta dt_2 \\
&\quad - \int_0^T \frac{B(0,t_2)\overline{\lambda}(t_2)}{\sqrt{\Sigma_{zz}(0,t_2)}} \int_0^{t_2} \overline{\lambda}(t_1) e^{\phi_\lambda(t_1,t_2)\Sigma_{\lambda\lambda}(0,t_1)} \\
&\quad \times \int_{\zeta^*(t_2)}^{\infty} P(\zeta,t_2) N\left(\frac{\zeta - F_{\lambda z}(t_1,t_2)}{\sqrt{\Sigma_{zz}(0,t_2)}}\right) d\zeta dt_1 dt_2, \qquad (9.45)
\end{aligned}
$$

where we define

$$
F_{\lambda z}(t_1,t_2) := \sum_{i=1}^{2} \Sigma_{\lambda z}(0,t_i). \qquad (9.46)
$$

The integrals over ζ in the above expressions are precisely the price of a compound option (call option on a call option) considered by Geske [1979] and can be evaluated as such using the formulae set out in that paper. We deduce

$$
\begin{aligned}
PV_1 = \int_0^T \frac{B(0,v)\overline{\lambda}(v)}{\sqrt{\Sigma_{zz}(0,v)}} &\left(F(T)e^{\Sigma_{\lambda z}(0,v)}\psi_1^+(\Sigma_{\lambda z}(0,v),v,T) - K\psi_2^+(\Sigma_{\lambda z}(0,v),v,T)\right. \\
&\left. - C(v)\Phi(d_2(\Sigma_{\lambda z}(0,v) - \zeta^*(v),0,v))\right) dv \qquad (9.47)
\end{aligned}
$$

where

$$
\psi_i^{\pm}(z,v,w) := D(v,w)\Phi_2(\pm d_i(z - \zeta^*(v),0,v), \pm d_i(z - z^*,0,w); R(v,w)), \quad i = 1,2, \qquad (9.48)
$$

$$
R(v,w) := \sqrt{\frac{\Sigma_{zz}(0,v)}{\Sigma_{zz}(0,w)}}, \quad v \le w, \qquad (9.49)
$$

and $\Phi_2(\cdot,\cdot;R)$ denotes a standard bivariate cumulative Gaussian distribution with correlation R. An analogous calculation for the second order contribution yields

$$
\begin{aligned}
PV_2 = \int_0^T \frac{B(0,t_2)\left(\Lambda_0(0,t_2)\overline{\lambda}(t_2) + \tilde{\lambda}_2(t_2)\right)}{\sqrt{\Sigma_{zz}(0,t_2)}} &\left(F(T)e^{\Sigma_{\lambda z}(0,t_2)}\psi_1^+(\Sigma_{\lambda z}(0,t_2),t_2,T)\right. \\
&- K\psi_2^+(\Sigma_{\lambda z}(0,t_2),t_2,T) \\
&\left. - C(t_2)\Phi(d_2(\Sigma_{\lambda z}(0,t_2) - \zeta^*(t_2),0,t_2))\right) dt_2
\end{aligned}
$$

$$
\begin{aligned}
&- \int_0^T \frac{B(0,t_2)\bar{\lambda}(t_2)}{\sqrt{\Sigma_{zz}(0,t_2)}} \int_0^{t_2} \bar{\lambda}(t_1) e^{\phi_\lambda(t_1,t_2)\Sigma_{\lambda\lambda}(0,t_1)} \left(F(T) e^{F_{\lambda z}(t_1,t_2)} \psi_1^+(F_{\lambda z}(t_1,t_2), t_2, T) \right. \\
&\quad \left. - K\psi_2^+(F_{\lambda z}(t_1,t_2), t_2, T) - C(t_2)\Phi(d_2(F_{\lambda z}(t_1,t_2) - \zeta^*(t_2), 0, t_2)) \right) dt_1 dt_2.
\end{aligned} \tag{9.50}
$$

We observe here that, once again, the influence of the stochastic credit model is first felt at second order, although in this case the leading order term is first order, rather than zeroth order as in the previous calculation for the option embedded in a convertible bond, since the payoff is default- rather than survival-driven. Analogous expressions are easily deduced for the case of a put option underlying, making use of $\psi_i^-(z,v,w)$ rather than $\psi_i^+(z,v,w)$, in the manner illustrated by Turfus [2016].

CHAPTER 10

Credit-FX Hybrid Modelling

10.1 BACKGROUND

In this chapter we shall look to deal with the problem of pricing multi-currency derivative products depending on (stochastic) FX rates in a context where credit risk is considered to impact on the pricing. The model we shall choose for the FX process will be mathematically identical to that chosen for the equity process in the previous chapter. For that reason, the pricing kernel will have an identical structure and need not be re-calculated for the new context.

We consider an economy with two currencies, foreign and domestic, and a credit default intensity process associated either with a corporation based in the foreign economy or with a foreign sovereign debt issuer, the CDS market for which operates in the *domestic* currency. We suppose, in the interests of tractability, that the foreign and domestic interest rates are deterministic, but that there is a stochastic exchange rate between the two currencies and further that upon default of the named issuer there is a *decrease* in the value of the foreign currency giving rise to a proportional downward jump in the exchange rate from foreign to domestic currency.

In particular we look in §10.3 to price quanto CDS, for which the debt against which default protection is bought is denominated in a different currency from that for which the default curve is inferred, in particular capturing the difference in the CDS spreads associated with the two currencies. The calculation presented below is similar to that of Turfus [2018d], although in the latter case the foreign interest rate is allowed to be stochastic (Hull–White); also the situation is there considered when a cap is placed on the protection payment, denominated in a currency other than that of the debt protected. We also consider in §10.4 the problem of a contingent CDS on a cross-currency swap, where wrong-way risk between the credit default intensity and the FX rate can likewise be of importance.

A similar model was considered in a seminal paper by Ehlers and Schönbucher [2004], who took the interest rate and credit intensity models to be affine, viz. in practice either of Hull and White [1990] or of Cox et al. [1991] (CIR) type. They did not solve directly the equations they derived but inferred jump levels from market data in the light of their modelling approach.

The model we propose with a Black–Karasinski credit process appears to have been first considered in this context by EL-Mohammadi [2009] who used it to price defaultable FX options and quanto CDS. Brigo et al. [2019] also used this model in their work reviewing the evidence from the comparative USD and EUR CDS rates for Italian sovereign debt of an implied FX jump in the wake of the euro crisis. Both the previous authors calculated prices using finite difference approaches. The same modelling assumptions were made in the work performed recently by Chung and Gregory [2019] to illustrate the calculation of wrong-way risk in a CVA context. A similar approach was taken by Fenger [2016] but without mean reversion in the credit intensity, which he took to be governed by a Ho–Lee model; solutions were found by Monte Carlo simulation. In more recent work by Itkin et al. [2019], both the interest rates were taken to be stochastic, governed by a CIR model, the foreign rate allowing of a jump at default as with the FX rate; the credit model was again taken to be Black–Karasinski. We will consider in more detail in Chapter 12 the impact of incorporating (Hull–White) stochastic rates into the calculation.

10.2 CREDIT-FX PRICING KERNEL

We look to derive a pricing kernel for a joint credit-FX-hybrid model with interest rates (domestic and foreign) assumed deterministic. Consider the credit model to be identical to that assumed in the previous chapter. Let the FX rate Z_t be given by a jump-diffusion process with (lognormal) volatility $\sigma_z(t)$, undergoing a jump of relative size $k < 0$ in the event of a credit default event. This model is typically used when a credit name which is systemically important in a foreign economy is priced using a default curve specified for debt denominated in the *domestic* currency. Under these assumptions we can write

$$\frac{dZ_t}{Z_t} = (\overline{r}_d(t) - \overline{r}_f(t) - k\lambda_t)dt + k\,dn_t + \sigma_z(t)dW_t^z, \tag{10.1}$$

with $\overline{r}_d(t)$ and $\overline{r}_f(t)$ the (instantaneous) domestic and foreign risk-free interest rates, respectively, and n_t a Cox process with intensity λ_t functioning as an indicator of a default event. Further, let us introduce an auxiliary process z_t defined implicitly by

$$Z_t = F(t)e^{z_t - \frac{1}{2}\Sigma_{zz}(0,t) - k\Lambda_0(0,t)}, \tag{10.2}$$

with $\Lambda_0(t, v)$ defined by (9.5) and $F(t)$ the forward rate given by

$$F(t) = e^{\int_0^t (\overline{r}_d(u) - \overline{r}_f(u))du}. \tag{10.3}$$

By an application of Itô's lemma, z_t is seen to be governed by

$$dz_t = -k(\lambda_t - \overline{\lambda}(t))dt + \ln(1 + k)dn_t + \sigma_z(t)dW_t^z. \tag{10.4}$$

The value V_t at time t of a survival-contingent payoff at time $T > t$ of $P(z_T)$ based on an FX rate underlying will be given by (9.9). From the Feynman–Kac theorem $V_t = f(x_{\lambda t}, z_t, t)$ emerges as the solution $f(x_\lambda, z, t)$ to the Kolmogorov backward equation (9.10). The pricing kernel $G(x_\lambda, z, t; \xi_\lambda, \zeta, v)$ for this equation will be given as previously by the perturbation expansion (9.28). This completes our model analysis.

10.3 QUANTO CDS

We will be interested in pricing analytically quanto CDS where in particular the protection is on debt denominated in a currency other than that with reference to which the default curve has been calibrated. In addition to pricing protection, we need to be able to price coupon flows in both domestic and foreign currency. We consider these first before going on to consider the valuation of the protection leg.

10.3.1 Domestic Currency Fixed Flow

Consider first a risky domestic currency flow (notional or coupon) of N_d at time T. This is straightforwardly priced using our second order Green's function to obtain

$$\begin{aligned}V_d^T(x_\lambda, z, t) &\sim N_d B(t,T)\\ &\times\left(1 - \int_t^T \bar{\lambda}(t_1)\left(e^{\theta_\lambda(x_\lambda,t,t_1)} - 1\right)dt_1 + \frac{1}{2}\left(\int_t^T \bar{\lambda}(t_1)\left(e^{\theta_\lambda(x_\lambda,t,t_1)} - 1\right)dt_1\right)^2\right.\\ &+ \int_t^T \bar{\lambda}(t_2)e^{\theta_\lambda(x_\lambda,t,t_2)}\int_t^{t_2}\bar{\lambda}(t_1)e^{\theta_\lambda(x_\lambda,t,t_1)}(e^{\phi_\lambda(t_1,t_2)\Sigma_{\lambda\lambda}(t,t_1)} - 1)dt_1 dt_2\\ &\left. - \int_t^T \tilde{\lambda}_2(t_1)e^{\theta_\lambda(x_\lambda,t,t_1)}dt_1\right)\end{aligned} \tag{10.5}$$

correct to second order, where we have made use of the definition (9.27) of $\tilde{\lambda}_2(t)$. The corresponding PV is

$$PV_d^T = N_d B(t,T), \tag{10.6}$$

the result in this case being exact.

10.3.2 Foreign Currency Fixed Flow

Consider next a risky foreign currency flow (notional or coupon) of N_f at time T. This will have from (10.2) a *domestic* currency value of

$$P_f^T(z_T) = N_f F(T)e^{z_T - \frac{1}{2}\Sigma_{zz}(0,T) - k\Lambda_0(0,T)}$$

and a corresponding value at time t of

$$V_f^T(x_\lambda, z, t) \sim N_f B(t,T)F(T)e^{z_t - \frac{1}{2}\Sigma_{zz}(0,t) - k\Lambda_0(0,T)}$$
$$\Bigg(1 - (1+k)\int_t^T \bar{\lambda}(t_1)\left(e^{\theta_\lambda(x_\lambda,t,t_1)+\Sigma_{\lambda z}(t,t_1)} - 1\right)dt_1$$
$$+ \frac{1}{2}(1+k)^2\left(\int_t^T \bar{\lambda}(t_1)\left(e^{\theta_\lambda(x_\lambda,t,t_1)+\Sigma_{\lambda z}(t,t_1)} - 1\right)dt_1\right)^2$$
$$+ (1+k)\int_t^T \bar{\lambda}(t_2)e^{\theta_\lambda(x_\lambda,t,t_2)+\Sigma_{\lambda z}(t,t_2)}\int_t^{t_2}\bar{\lambda}(t_1)(1+k)e^{\theta_\lambda(x_\lambda,t,t_1)+\Sigma_{\lambda z}(t,t_1)}$$
$$\left(e^{\phi_\lambda(t_1,t_2)\Sigma_{\lambda\lambda}(t,t_1)} - 1\right)dt_1 dt_2 - (1+k)\int_t^T \tilde{\lambda}_2(t_1)e^{\theta_\lambda(x_\lambda,t,t_1)+\Sigma_{\lambda z}(t,t_1)}dt_1\Bigg) \tag{10.7}$$

correct to second order. The corresponding PV is

$$PV_f^T \sim N_f B(0,T)F(T)e^{-k\Lambda_0(0,T)}$$
$$\Bigg(1 - (1+k)\int_0^T \bar{\lambda}(t_1)\left(e^{\Sigma_{\lambda z}(0,t_1)} - 1\right)dt_1 + \frac{1}{2}(1+k)^2\left(\int_0^T \bar{\lambda}(t_1)\left(e^{\Sigma_{\lambda z}(0,t_1)} - 1\right)dt_1\right)^2$$
$$+ (1+k)\int_0^T \bar{\lambda}(t_2)e^{\Sigma_{\lambda z}(0,t_2)}\int_0^{t_2}\bar{\lambda}(t_1)\left((1+k)e^{\Sigma_{\lambda z}(0,t_1)} - 1\right)$$
$$\times \left(e^{\phi_\lambda(t_1,t_2)\Sigma_{\lambda\lambda}(0,t_1)} - 1\right)dt_1 dt_2\Bigg). \tag{10.8}$$

The term involving $-k\Lambda_0(\cdot)$ gives the leading order impact of the jump at default while the first-order correction in brackets shows the corresponding impact of the correlation on the result: as can be seen, a negative jump and a negative correlation both result in an enhanced PV. Notice that, in the absence of correlation, the term in brackets becomes

$$1 + k(1+k)\int_0^T \tilde{\lambda}_2(t_1)dt_1,$$

so there remains a small second order correction resulting from the stochastic credit intensity unless the jump is set to zero.

It might be observed that the first line of (10.8) contains the opening terms of the power series representation of an exponential. Completing the series we obtain

$$PV_f^T = N_f D(0,T)F(T)e^{-\int_0^T (1+k)\bar{\lambda}(t_1)e^{\Sigma_{\lambda z}(0,t_1)}dt_1} + \dots.$$

So to leading order the behaviour is as if an effective default intensity of

$$\lambda_{\text{eff}}(t) = (1 + k)\overline{\lambda}(t)e^{\Sigma_{\lambda z}(0,t)} \tag{10.9}$$

were applied, although convexity effects at higher order complicate the situation. Such complication is a consequence of the fact that the Black–Karasinski model is not affine like the Hull–White model.

10.3.3 Foreign Currency LIBOR Flow

It is a straightforward matter from the above to price a foreign currency LIBOR payment made at T_2 for a payment period $[T_1, T_2]$. Using the usual replication arguments, this is seen to be given for $t \leq T_2$ by

$$V_L(x_\lambda, z, t) = (D_f(T_1, T_2)^{-1} - 1)V_f^{T_2}(x_\lambda, z, t). \tag{10.10}$$

With this we can price also cross-currency IR swap extinguishers involving a float leg potentially in a different currency from the fix leg.

10.3.4 Foreign Currency Notional Protection

Next consider a payoff of N_f at time τ^+, just after default, so that the jump in the FX rate has occurred. This will have from (10.2) a *domestic* currency value of $P_{\text{prot}}(\lim_{t\to\tau^-} z_t, \tau)$ with

$$P_{\text{prot}}(z, \tau) := N_f(1 + k)F(\tau)e^{z - \frac{1}{2}\Sigma_{zz}(0,\tau) - k\Lambda_0(0,\tau)},$$

where the factor $1 + k$ captures the impact of the jump at default. The cost of protection on this notional amount up to time T from an observation time of t will be

$$V_{\text{prot}}(x_\lambda, z, t) = \int_t^T \iint_{\mathbb{R}^2} \lambda(\xi_\lambda, v)P_{\text{prot}}(\zeta, v)G(x_\lambda, z, t; \xi_\lambda, \zeta, v)d\xi_\lambda d\zeta dv. \tag{10.11}$$

We write this as

$$V_{\text{prot}}(x_\lambda, z, t) = V_1(x_\lambda, z, t) + V_2(x_\lambda, z, t) + \mathcal{O}(\epsilon^3) \tag{10.12}$$

where at first order, making use of our leading order Green's function,

$$V_1(x_\lambda, z, t) = N_f e^{z - \frac{1}{2}\Sigma_{zz}(0,t)}(1 + k)\int_t^T B(t, v)\overline{\lambda}(v)e^{\Sigma_{\lambda z}(t,v) + \theta_\lambda(x_\lambda, t, v)}F(v)e^{-k\Lambda_0(0,v)}dv, \tag{10.13}$$

while at second order

$$
\begin{aligned}
V_2(x_\lambda, z, t) &= \int_t^T \iint_{\mathbb{R}^2} \tilde{\lambda}_2(v) e^{\xi_\lambda - \frac{1}{2}\Sigma_{\lambda\lambda}(0,v) +} P_{prot}(\zeta, v) G_0(x_\lambda, z, t; \xi_\lambda, \zeta, v) d\xi_\lambda d\zeta dv \\
&+ \int_t^T \iint_{\mathbb{R}^2} \overline{\lambda}(v) e^{\xi_\lambda - \frac{1}{2}\Sigma_{\lambda\lambda}(0,t) +} P_{prot}(\zeta, v) G_1(x_\lambda, z, t; \xi_\lambda, \zeta, v) d\xi_\lambda d\zeta dv \\
&= N_f e^{z - \frac{1}{2}\Sigma_{zz}(0,t)} (1+k) \int_t^T B(t,v) e^{\Sigma_{\lambda z}(t,v) + \theta_\lambda(x_\lambda, t, v)} F(v) e^{-k\Lambda_0(0,v)} \\
&\left(\tilde{\lambda}_2(v) + (1+k)\overline{\lambda}(v) \int_t^v \overline{\lambda}(u) \left(e^{\phi_\lambda(u,v)\Sigma_{\lambda\lambda}(t,u) + \Sigma_{\lambda z}(t,u) + \theta_\lambda(x_\lambda,t,u)} - 1 \right) du \right) dv.
\end{aligned}
\tag{10.14}
$$

Combining both terms and setting $t = 0$, the resultant PV is, to second order

$$
PV_{\text{prot}} \sim N_f(1+k) \int_0^T B(0,v) e^{\Sigma_{\lambda z}(0,v)} F(v) e^{-k\Lambda_0(0,v)} (\overline{\lambda}(v) + \tilde{\lambda}_2(v) - (1+k)\tilde{\lambda}_2^*(v)) dv,
\tag{10.15}
$$

where

$$
\tilde{\lambda}_2^*(t) := \overline{\lambda}(t) \int_0^t \overline{\lambda}(t_1) \left(e^{\phi_\lambda(t_1,t)\Sigma_{\lambda\lambda}(0,t_1) + \Sigma_{\lambda z}(0,t_1))} - 1 \right) dt_1. \tag{10.16}
$$

As can be seen, unlike for the fixed foreign currency payment, a negative correlation here results in a *diminished* PV. Note also the close similarity between the first-order terms in (10.15) and those in (10.8): essentially the correlation adjustment to the price of a fixed payment at T is specified by its impact on the default protection cost of a payment at maturity (rather than at default, as with (10.15)). We see that the effect of stochastic credit and credit-FX correlation on the credit default risk is captured by replacing $\overline{\lambda}(t)$ with an effective credit default intensity of

$$
\lambda_{\text{eff}}(t) = (1+k) \left(\overline{\lambda}(t) + \tilde{\lambda}_2(t) - (1+k)\tilde{\lambda}_2^*(t) \right) e^{\Sigma_{\lambda z}(0,t)}. \tag{10.17}
$$

Note also how the second order correction disappears even for $k \neq 0$ in the limit of zero credit volatility but *not* in the limit of zero correlation, wherein $\tilde{\lambda}_2^*(t) \to \tilde{\lambda}_2(t)$: a residual effect remains from the combination of credit volatility and jump at default, specifically

$$
PV_{\text{prot}} \to N_f(1+k) \int_0^T B(0,v) F(v) e^{-k\Lambda_0(0,v)} \left(\overline{\lambda}(v) - k\tilde{\lambda}_2(v) \right) dv. \tag{10.18}
$$

We infer from the fact that $\tilde{\lambda}_2(v) > 0$ that the impact of credit volatility in the event of a negative jump at default is to *increase* slightly the effective credit default risk, although the main impact from the jump will be directly on the FX rate.

With the above formulae at our disposal it is possible to price quanto CDS with any combination of fixed and floating payment legs in either domestic or foreign currency. Calculations by Turfus [2018d] comparing results obtained using only the first-order versions of these formulae with Monte Carlo simulations show the approximations to be highly accurate; essentially the graphs are indistinguishable to visual accuracy for any correlation level, for jump magnitudes between 0 and –0.6 and for credit default intensities of up to 1000bp, which is by no means a "small" number.

10.4 CONTINGENT CDS ON CROSS-CURRENCY SWAPS

We consider next a contingent CDS wherein the buyer pays a regular coupon, either in foreign or domestic currency, and receives protection on the loss at default of a named credit issuer on a cross-currency receiver swap, say, with fixed coupon payments at a rate c_d on a domestic currency notional of N_d, fixed coupon receipts at a rate c_f on a foreign currency notional of N_f and notional exchange at maturity. The coupon leg pricing is exactly analogous to that for a quanto CDS so we focus here only on the protection leg.

Let the payments be synchronised at payment dates T_i, $i = 1, 2, \dots, M$. We wish to know the value of the swap immediately after default of a referenced credit at time τ. In this case the FX rate will have incurred a jump such that $Z_{\tau^+} = (1+k)Z_\tau$. The value of the swap at time τ^+ can for the purposes of determining the protection payment thus be written $V_{\text{ccs}}(\lim_{t\to\tau^-} z_t, \tau)$, where

$$\begin{aligned} V_{\text{ccs}}(z,\tau) = &\sum_{i=1}^{M}(c_f N_f(1+k)Z(z,\tau) - c_d N_d)\Delta T_i D(\tau, T_i)\mathbb{1}_{\tau<T_i} \\ &+ (N_f(1+k)Z(z,\tau) - N_d)D(\tau, T_M)\mathbb{1}_{\tau<T_M}, \end{aligned} \tag{10.19}$$

with

$$Z(z,t) := F(t)e^{z-\frac{1}{2}\Sigma_{zz}(0,t)-k\Lambda_0(0,t)}. \tag{10.20}$$

Choose $z^*(\tau)$ to satisfy $V_{\text{ccs}}(z^*(\tau),\tau) = 0$. Alternatively, if we are interested in the situation where the losses are considered to be collateralised by an amount $C(t)$ denominated in domestic currency (for example if the collateral were a domestic currency bond), we can consider instead $V_{\text{ccs}}(z^*(\tau),\tau) = C(\tau)$. The amount of the loss payment due in the event of default will be $\lim_{t\to\tau^-}(V_{\text{ccs}}(z_t,\tau) - C(\tau))\mathbb{1}_{z_t>z^*(\tau)}$.

To ascertain the fair price of the protection leg, we must calculate the expected value at time τ of each of the individual payments contingent on $z_\tau > z^*(\tau)$. It suffices to consider w.l.o.g. a fixed unit payment and a fixed foreign currency payment at time $T_i \le T_M$. Considering first the former, making use of our leading order pricing kernel, this will be given asymptotically from Theorem 3.5 by

$$\begin{aligned} V^{(i)}_{\text{prot,d}}(x_\lambda, z, t) &\sim \int_t^{t\vee T_i} \bar{\lambda}(v)D(v,T_i)e^{-\frac{1}{2}\Sigma_{\lambda\lambda}(0,v)} \int_{z^*(v)}^{\infty}\int_{\mathbb{R}} e^{\xi_\lambda} G_0(x_\lambda, z, t; \xi_\lambda, \zeta, v)d\xi_\lambda d\zeta dv \\ &\sim \int_t^{t\vee T_i} e^{\theta_\lambda(x_\lambda,t,v)}B(t,v)\bar{\lambda}(v)D(v,T_i)\Phi(d_2(z,t,v))dv, \end{aligned} \tag{10.21}$$

with $\Phi(\cdot)$ a cumulative normal distribution and

$$d_2(z,t,v) = \frac{z - z^*(v) + \Sigma_{\lambda z}(t,v)}{\sqrt{\Sigma_{zz}(t,v)}} \tag{10.22}$$

and corresponding PV

$$PV^{(i)}_{\text{prot,d}} \sim \int_0^{T_i} B(0,v)\bar{\lambda}(v)D(v,T_i)\Phi(d_2(0,0,v))dv. \tag{10.23}$$

Considering next a foreign currency payment we obtain by similar means

$$\begin{aligned} V^{(i)}_{\text{prot,f}}(x_\lambda, z, t) &\sim (1+k)\int_t^{t\vee T_i} \bar{\lambda}(v)D(v,T_i)F(v)e^{-\frac{1}{2}\Sigma_{\lambda\lambda}(0,v)-\frac{1}{2}\Sigma_{zz}(0,v)-k\Lambda_0(v)} \\ &\qquad \int_{z^*(v)}^{\infty}\int_{\mathbb{R}} e^{\xi_\lambda+\zeta}G_0(x_\lambda,z,t;\xi_\lambda,\zeta,v)d\xi_\lambda d\zeta dv \\ &\sim (1+k)\int_t^{t\vee T_i} e^{\theta_\lambda(x_\lambda,t,v)+z_t-\frac{1}{2}\Sigma_{zz}(0,t)+\Sigma_{\lambda z}(t,v)-k\Lambda_0(v)}F(v)B(t,v)\bar{\lambda}(v)D(v,T_i) \\ &\qquad \Phi(d_1(z,t,v))dv, \end{aligned} \tag{10.24}$$

with

$$d_1(z,t,v) = d_2(z+\Sigma_{zz}(t,v),t,v) \tag{10.25}$$

and corresponding PV

$$PV^{(i)}_{\text{prot,f}} \sim (1+k)\int_0^{T_i} F(v)e^{\Sigma_{\lambda z}(0,v)-k\Lambda_0(v)}B(0,v)\bar{\lambda}(v)D(v,T_i)\Phi(d_1(0,0,v))dv. \tag{10.26}$$

Combining terms we see the PV of the entire protection leg is

$$PV_{\text{prot}} \sim \sum_{i=1}^{M}\left(c_f N_f PV^{(i)}_{prot,f} - c_d N_d PV^{(i)}_{prot,d}\right)\Delta T_i + N_f PV^{(M)}_{prot,f} - N_d PV^{(M)}_{prot,d}. \tag{10.27}$$

Higher-order terms can also be calculated as with the standard CDS protection calculation above. The expression for the domestic notional payment becomes

$$\begin{aligned} PV^{(i)}_{\text{prot,d}} \sim \int_0^{T_i} B(0,v)D(v,T_i)\Bigg(&\left(\bar{\lambda}(v)(1-\Lambda_0(0,v))+\tilde{\lambda}_2(v)\right)\Phi(d_2(0,0,v)) \\ &- \bar{\lambda}(v)\int_0^v \bar{\lambda}(u)e^{\phi_\lambda(u,v)\Sigma_{\lambda\lambda}(0,u)}\Phi(d_2(\Sigma_{\lambda z}(0,u),0,v))du\Bigg)dv, \end{aligned} \tag{10.28}$$

while for the foreign notional payment the result is

$$PV^{(i)}_{\text{prot,f}} \sim (1+k)\int_0^{T_i} F(v)e^{\Sigma_{\lambda z}(0,v)-k\Lambda_0(v)}B(0,v)D(v,T_i)$$
$$\left(\left(\overline{\lambda}(v)(1-(1+k)\Lambda_0(0,v))+\tilde{\lambda}_2(v)\right)\Phi(d_1(0,0,v))\right.$$
$$-\overline{\lambda}(v)\int_0^v \overline{\lambda}(u)e^{\phi_\lambda(u,v)\Sigma_{\lambda\lambda}(0,u)+\Sigma_{\lambda z}(0,u)}$$
$$\left.\left((1+k)\Phi(d_1(\Sigma_{\lambda z}(0,u),0,v))-k\frac{N(d_1(\Sigma_{\lambda z}(0,u),0,v))}{\sqrt{\Sigma_{zz(0,v)}}}\right)du\right)dv. \tag{10.29}$$

We observe that on this occasion the replacement of $\overline{\lambda}(t)$ with the effective default intensity of (10.17) does not quite work because of the term proportional to k (rather than $1+k$) on the second line. Nonetheless, in the absence of jumps, we conclude it is still possible to price contingent CDS protection using an effective default intensity, which device could prove a useful one to save computational effort in practice.

Finally, in the event that a collateral schedule of $C(t)$ is imposed, (10.27) must be augmented by an additional contribution of

$$-\int_0^{T_M} B(0,v)C(v)\left(\left(\overline{\lambda}(v)(1-\Lambda_0(0,v))+\tilde{\lambda}_2(v)\right)\Phi(d_2(0,0,v))\right.$$
$$\left.-\overline{\lambda}(v)\int_0^v \overline{\lambda}(u)e^{\phi_\lambda(u,v)\Sigma_{\lambda\lambda}(0,u)}\Phi(d_2(\Sigma_{\lambda z}(0,u),0,v))du\right)dv,$$

with of course $z^*(v)$ redefined in accordance, as indicated above. Similar expressions can be obtained for a payer swap underlying wherein the foreign currency payments are considered to be paid by the protection buyer, making use of the above results and the principle of put–call parity.

Note also from (10.10) that, under our assumption of deterministic rates, LIBOR flows can be considered mathematically equivalent to fixed flows. This means that the pricing of CCDS on cross-currency IR swaps is intrinsically no more complex than the above: effectively the foreign currency fixed coupon payment $c_f\Delta T_i$ at T_i must be replaced by the foreign LIBOR payment amount, namely $D_f(T_{i-1},T_i)^{-1}-1$.

Results obtained with a first-order version of our analytic formula for the protection value on a seven-year cross-currency swap are compared with those obtained from Monte Carlo simulation for various values of the credit-FX correlation in Fig. 10.1.

A number of observations can be made. In the first instance, the impact of the correlation is substantial, potentially doubling or halving the value of protection. Secondly, the analytic approximation appears to perform well other than for strongly negative values of the correlation (which are unlikely to be encountered in practice). As expected the error appears to be second order (quadratic), although a small first-order

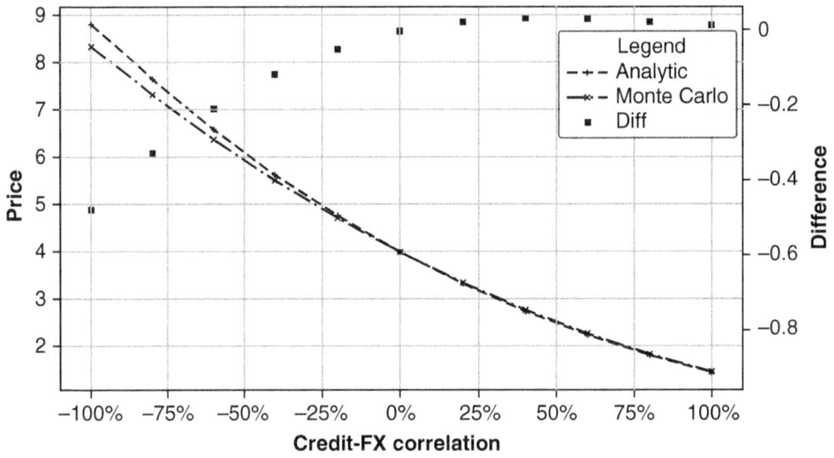

FIGURE 10.1 Pricing of counterparty risk protection on a cross-currency swap

discrepancy is also evident with the slope of the Monte Carlo graph slightly less steep than that of the analytic result. (We would tend to attribute the latter discrepancy to computational issues rather than to any intrinsic limitation in accuracy in the asymptotic formula, which is virtually exact at zero correlation.) If greater accuracy is sought, the second order expansion could of course be used. However, we would suggest that the uncertainty around forward credit volatility levels is likely to be far greater than any discrepancies arising from use of the analytic approximation.

CHAPTER 11

Multi-Currency Modelling

Having looked at all models of interest based on two stochastic underlyings in Chapters 7 to 10, we move on in our investigation to consider pricing problems with three or more underlyings, starting with the simplest case where we have two interest rates and a spot underlying.[1] Specifically, we consider stochastic interest rates for foreign and domestic currencies and a stochastic exchange rate between these two currencies.

11.1 PREVIOUS WORK

The problem of finding analytic pricing kernels and/or option pricing formulae in the case of two stochastic interest rates with a stochastic FX rate appears to have received less attention than the rather simpler problem in relation to a hybrid equity-rates model which we visited in Chapter 7. We follow closely the method of derivation used there based on the ideas expounded in Chapter 6.

A model closely related to the one we consider here was proposed by Jarrow and Yildirim [2003], albeit in the context of inflation derivatives pricing, rather than FX options. In their case the "nominal" interest rate is simply the domestic interest rate, while the "real" interest rate corresponds to the foreign interest rate and the consumer price index (CPI) to the FX rate. Jarrow and Yildirim [2003] produced exact closed-form pricing formulae for vanilla options on the inflation index under the assumption of an HJM framework for the interest rates (Heath et al., 1992). An extensive discussion of the model and related work is provided in Part VI of Brigo and Mercurio [2006].

A more general discussion of FX derivatives pricing in the context of assumed lognormal LIBOR rates (the so-called LIBOR market model or LMM) is provided in Chapter 14 of Part V of Brigo and Mercurio [2006]. Unlike in the present work, interest rates are supposed by them *not* to be mean-reverting. While many exact analytic

[1]We are of course ignoring the trivial cases involving extension from one to two spot underlyings, since the second spot underlying makes little difference to the essential dynamics.

formulae are available for option pricing under the LMM, it would appear no attempt has been made to find a pricing kernel for a rates-FX hybrid model. We present here an exact closed-form expression for the pricing kernel in the case where the two interest rates are governed by Hull–White models and the FX rate is assumed to be lognormal, noting that through the Jarrow–Yildirim analogy this result is equally applicable to inflation-related derivative products. The result is identical to that derived by Turfus [2018c] directly from the pricing equation (11.13) below rather than, as here, making use of the general multi-factor formulae derived in Chapter 6. We use the result in §11.4 to derive an exact Black-type expression for the price of an FX option.

11.2 STATEMENT OF PROBLEM

We consider the joint distribution of interest rates r_{dt} and r_{ft} for domestic and foreign currencies respectively and the FX rate Z_t between the two currencies with a view to calculating a pricing kernel for multi-currency rates derivatives. For rates we assume the short-rate model of Hull and White [1990]. Rather than the short rates themselves, we shall find it convenient to work with auxiliary processes x_{dt} and x_{ft} satisfying the following canonical Ornstein–Uhlenbeck processes

$$dx_{dt} = -\alpha_d(t)x_{dt}dt + \sigma_d(t)dW_t^1, \tag{11.1}$$

$$dx_{ft} = -\alpha_f(t)x_{ft}dt + \sigma_f(t)d\tilde{W}_t^2, \tag{11.2}$$

where $\alpha_d, \alpha_f, \sigma_d, \sigma_f : \mathbb{R}^+ \to \mathbb{R}^+$ are piecewise continuous functions, the first two L_1- and the second two L_2-integrable, and W_t^1 and $\tilde{W}_t^2$ are Brownian motions under their respective equivalent martingale measures for $t \geq 0$, with

$$\text{corr}(W_t^1, \tilde{W}_t^2) = \rho_{df} \tag{11.3}$$

assumed and $x_{d0} = x_{f0} = 0$.

Under the Hull–White model, these auxiliary processes are related to their instantaneous short rates r_{dt} and r_{ft} by

$$r_{dt} = \bar{r}_d(t) + r_d^*(t) + x_{dt}, \tag{11.4}$$

$$r_{ft} = \bar{r}_f(t) + r_f^*(t) + x_{ft}, \tag{11.5}$$

where $r_d^*, r_f^* : \mathbb{R}^+ \to \mathbb{R}^+$ are L_1-integrable functions to be determined by calibration to fit the (L_1-integrable) instantaneous forward curves given by $\bar{r}_d, \bar{r}_f : \mathbb{R}^+ \to \mathbb{R}$.

Next, we suppose the FX process Z_t specifying the instantaneous exchange rate from foreign to domestic currency to be given by

$$\frac{dZ_t}{Z_t} = (r_{dt} - r_{ft})dt + \sigma_z(t)dW_t^3, \tag{11.6}$$

under the domestic currency equivalent martingale measure, with

$$\mathrm{corr}(W_t^1, W_t^3) = \rho_{dz} \tag{11.7}$$

$$\mathrm{corr}(\tilde{W}_t^2, W_t^3) = \rho_{fz}. \tag{11.8}$$

Define a new stochastic variable z_t such that

$$Z_t = F(t)e^{z_t - \frac{1}{2}\Sigma_{zz}(0,t)},$$

$$F(t) = Z_0 e^{\int_0^t (\bar{r}_d(u) - \bar{r}_f(u))du}. \tag{11.9}$$

It follows from Itô lemma that

$$dz_t = (r_d^*(t) - r_f^*(t) + x_{dt} - x_{ft})dt + \sigma_z(t)dW_t^3. \tag{11.10}$$

11.3 THE PRICING KERNEL

11.3.1 Main Result

To proceed we must find representations of all processes defined above under the *domestic* currency numéraire. Specifically we must modify (11.2). We see that, by application of the Girsanov theorem, this can be written equivalently as

$$dx_{ft} = -\alpha_f(t)\, x_{ft}dt - \rho_{fz}\sigma_f(t)\sigma_z(t)dt + \sigma_f(t)\, dW_t^2, \tag{11.11}$$

with W_t^2 a Brownian motion under the domestic currency equivalent martingale measure (see for example Santean [2020]). This has a solution subject to $x_{f0} = 0$ given by

$$x_{ft} = -\Sigma_{fz}(0,t) + \int_0^t \phi_f(s,t)\sigma_f(s)dW_s^2 \tag{11.12}$$

where $\phi_f(\cdot,\cdot)$ and $\Sigma_{fz}(\cdot,\cdot)$ are defined in (11.18) and (11.21) below, respectively.

If the price of a European-type security depending for its payout amount on the spot FX rate and/or instantaneous short rate values (or, equivalently, zero coupon bond prices or LIBOR rates) is expressed as $f(x_d, x_f, z, t)$, this price is governed under the rates-FX hybrid model specified above for $t \geq 0$ by the following Kolmogorov backward diffusion equation

$$\begin{aligned}
&\frac{\partial f}{\partial t} - \alpha_d(t)x_d\frac{\partial f}{\partial x_d} - (\alpha_f(t)x_f + \rho_{fz}\sigma_f(t)\sigma_z(t))\frac{\partial f}{\partial x_f} + (r_d^*(t) - r_f^*(t) + x_d - x_f)\frac{\partial f}{\partial z}\\
&+\frac{1}{2}\left(\sigma_d^2(t)\frac{\partial^2 f}{\partial x_d^2} + \sigma_f^2(t)\frac{\partial^2 f}{\partial x_f^2} + \sigma_z^2(t)\frac{\partial^2 f}{\partial z^2}\right) + \rho_{df}\sigma_d(t)\sigma_f(t)\frac{\partial^2 f}{\partial x_d \partial x_f} + \rho_{dz}\sigma_d(t)\sigma_z(t)\frac{\partial^2 f}{\partial x_d \partial z}\\
&+\rho_{fz}\sigma_f(t)\sigma_z(t)\frac{\partial^2 f}{\partial x_f \partial z} - (\bar{r}_d(t) + r_d^*(t) + x_d)f = 0,
\end{aligned} \tag{11.13}$$

subject to the final condition $\lim_{t\to v^-} f(x_d, x_f, z, t) = P(x_d, x_f, z)$ for some payoff function $P(\cdot,\cdot,\cdot)$. This is of the form of (6.2). Here we look to derive in closed form an exact Green's function solution for this pricing equation. In terms of the notation introduced in the previous chapter, we have $\boldsymbol{x} \equiv (x_d, x_f, z)^T$, $\boldsymbol{\beta}(t) \equiv (0, -\rho_{fz}\sigma_f(t)\sigma_z(t), r_d^*(t) - r_f^*(t))^T$ and

$$\boldsymbol{\kappa}(t) = \begin{pmatrix} \alpha_d(t) & 0 & 0 \\ 0 & \alpha_f(t) & 0 \\ -1 & 1 & 0 \end{pmatrix}. \tag{11.14}$$

Using the method set out in §6.1, we obtain

$$\boldsymbol{\Phi}(t) = \begin{pmatrix} \phi_d(0,t) & 0 & 0 \\ 0 & \phi_f(0,t) & 0 \\ B_d^*(0,t) & -B_f^*(0,t) & 1 \end{pmatrix}; \boldsymbol{\Phi}^{-1}(t) = \begin{pmatrix} \phi_d(0,t)^{-1} & 0 & 0 \\ 0 & \phi_f(0,t)^{-1} & 0 \\ -\phi_d(0,t)^{-1}B_d^*(0,t) & \phi_f(0,t)^{-1}B_f^*(0,t) & 1 \end{pmatrix} \tag{11.15}$$

and

$$\boldsymbol{\Psi}(t,v) = \begin{pmatrix} \phi_d(0,t)B_d^*(t,v) & 0 & 0 \\ 0 & \phi_f(0,t)B_f^*(t,v) & 0 \\ \int_t^v B_d^*(0,u)du & -\int_t^v B_f^*(0,u)du & v-t \end{pmatrix}, \tag{11.16}$$

in terms of which we define $\boldsymbol{y} = \boldsymbol{\Phi}^{-1}(t)\boldsymbol{x}$. The required pricing kernel can then be derived using the results of Chapter 6.

Theorem 11.1 *(Multi-Currency Pricing Kernel): The pricing kernel for* (11.13) *is seen to consist of the zero coupon bond formula multiplied by a trivariate Gaussian distribution function* $N_3(\cdot,\cdot,\cdot;\boldsymbol{\Sigma})$ *with term covariance* $\boldsymbol{\Sigma}$*, as follows*

$$\begin{aligned} G(x_d, x_f, z, t; \xi_d, \xi_f, \zeta, v) = D_d(t,v)e^{-\mu_d^*(x_d,t,v)} N_3(&\xi_d + I_{dd}^*(t,v) - x_d\phi_d(t,v), \\ &\xi_f + \Sigma_{fz}(t,v) + I_{fd}^*(t,v) - x_f\phi_f(t,v), \zeta + \Delta_{zz}(x_d,x_f,t,v) \\ &- z; \boldsymbol{\Sigma}^+(t,v)), \end{aligned} \tag{11.17}$$

with

$$\phi_{[d,f]}(t,v) = e^{-\int_t^v \alpha_{[d,f]}(u)du}, \tag{11.18}$$

$$\Sigma_{\alpha\alpha}(t,v) = \int_t^v \phi_\alpha^2(u,v)\sigma_\alpha^2(u)du, \quad \alpha \in \{d,f\}, \tag{11.19}$$

$$\Sigma_{zz}(t,v) = \int_t^v \sigma_z^2(u)du, \tag{11.20}$$

$$\Sigma_{\alpha z}(t,v) = \rho_{\alpha z}\int_t^v \phi_\alpha(u,v)\sigma_\alpha(u)\sigma_z(u)du, \quad \alpha \in \{d,f\}, \tag{11.21}$$

$$\Sigma_{df}(t,v) = \rho_{df}\int_t^v \phi_d(u,v)\phi_f(u,v)\sigma_d(u)\sigma_f(u)du, \tag{11.22}$$

$$I^*_{\alpha\beta}(t,v) = \int_t^v \phi_\alpha(u,v)\Sigma_{\alpha\beta}(t,u)du, \quad \alpha,\beta \in \{d,f\}, \tag{11.23}$$

$$I^*_{z\alpha}(t,v) = \int_t^v \Sigma_{\alpha z}(t,u)du, \quad \alpha \in \{d,f\}, \tag{11.24}$$

$$K^*_{\alpha\beta}(t,v) = \int_t^v I^*_{\alpha\beta}(t,u)du, \quad \alpha\beta \in \{d,f\}, \tag{11.25}$$

$$\mathbf{\Sigma}(t,v) = \begin{pmatrix} \Sigma_{dd}(t,v) & \Sigma_{df}(t,v) & \Sigma_{dz}(t,v) \\ \Sigma_{df}(t,v) & \Sigma_{ff}(t,v) & \Sigma_{fz}(t,v) \\ \Sigma_{dz}(t,v) & \Sigma_{fz}(t,v) & \Sigma_{zz}(t,v) \end{pmatrix}, \tag{11.26}$$

$$\mathbf{\Sigma}^+(t,v) = \mathbf{\Sigma}(t,v) + \begin{pmatrix} 0 & 0 & I^*_{dd}(t,v) - I^*_{df}(t,v) \\ 0 & 0 & I^*_{fd}(t,v) - I^*_{ff}(t,v) \\ I^*_{dd}(t,v) - I^*_{df}(t,v) & I^*_{fd}(t,v) - I^*_{ff}(t,v) & 2K^*(t,v) \end{pmatrix}, \tag{11.27}$$

$$K^*(t,v) = K^*_{dd}(t,v) + K^*_{ff}(t,v) - K^*_{df}(t,v) - K^*_{fd}(t,v) + I^*_{zd}(t,v) - I^*_{zf}(t,v), \tag{11.28}$$

$$D_{[d,f]}(t,v) = e^{-\int_t^v \bar{r}_{[d,f]}(s)ds}, \tag{11.29}$$

$$B^*_{[d,f]}(t,v) = \int_t^v \phi_{[d,f]}(t,u)du, \tag{11.30}$$

$$\Delta_{zz}(x_d,x_f,t,v) = K^*(t,v) - \mu^*_d(x_d,t,v) + \mu^*_f(x_f,t,v), \tag{11.31}$$

$$\begin{aligned} \mu^*_{[d,f]}(x,t,v) &= \int_t^v (x\phi_{[d,f]}(t,u) + r^*_{[d,f]}(u) - I^*_{[dd,ff]}(t,u))du \\ &= B^*_{[d,f]}(t,v)(x_{[d,f]} + r^*_{[d,f]}(t)) + \tfrac{1}{2}B^{*2}_{[d,f]}(t,v)\Sigma_{[dd,ff]}(0,t). \end{aligned} \tag{11.32}$$

Further, to fit the instantaneous forward curves, we must choose

$$r^*_{[d,f]}(t) = I^*_{[dd,ff]}(0,t), \tag{11.33}$$

Proof: The proof of these results is provided in the following subsection.

In essence, the solution (11.17) consists of the zero coupon bond formula multiplied by the joint distribution function of x_d, x_f and z with the mean and covariance parameters shifted by given time-dependent amounts. It is consequently very easy to apply to option pricing problems. More specifically, the shifted covariance $\boldsymbol{\Sigma}^{+}(t,v)$ can be interpreted as the covariance of the rates processes and the FX forward price. We also observe that, in the case where the payoff considered has no dependence on foreign rates, (11.17) can be straightforwardly integrated over x_f to obtain the requisite two-factor marginal transition density. This differs from the two-factor expression deduced in Chapter 7, on account of the residual impact on the mean and covariance mainly from correlations involving foreign rates, but also from convexity effects through $K^*_{ff}(t,v)$.

11.3.2 Derivation of Multi-Currency Pricing Kernel

We now provide a derivation of the results presented in Theorem 11.1. We observe from (6.8) and (6.9) that

$$\boldsymbol{\sigma}^*(t) = \begin{pmatrix} \frac{\sigma_d^2(t)}{\phi_d^2(0,t)} & \rho_{df}\frac{\sigma_d(t)\sigma_f(t)}{\phi_d(0,t)\phi_f(0,t)} & \sigma^*_{dz}(t) \\ \rho_{df}\frac{\sigma_d(t)\sigma_f(t)}{\phi_d(0,t)\phi_f(0,t)} & \frac{\sigma_f^2(t)}{\phi_f^2(0,t)} & \sigma^*_{fz}(t) \\ \sigma^*_{dz}(t) & \sigma^*_{fz}(t) & \sigma^*_{zz}(t), \end{pmatrix}, \tag{11.34}$$

$$\boldsymbol{\beta}^*(t) = \begin{pmatrix} 0 \\ -\rho_{fz}\frac{\sigma_f(t)\sigma_z(t)}{\phi_f(0,t)} \\ -\rho_{fz}\frac{B_f^*(0,t)\sigma_f(t)\sigma_z(t)}{\phi_f(0,t)} + r_d^*(t) - r_f^*(t) \end{pmatrix}, \tag{11.35}$$

where

$$\sigma^*_{dz}(t) = \rho_{dz}\frac{\sigma_d(t)\sigma_z(t)}{\phi_d(0,t)} - \frac{B_d^*(0,t)\sigma_d^2(t)}{\phi_d^2(0,t)} + \rho_{df}\frac{B_f^*(0,t)\sigma_d(t)\sigma_f(t)}{\phi_d(0,t)\phi_f(0,t)}, \tag{11.36}$$

$$\sigma^*_{fz}(t) = \rho_{fz}\frac{\sigma_f(t)\sigma_z(t)}{\phi_f(0,t)} - \rho_{df}\frac{B_d^*(0,t)\sigma_d(t)\sigma_f(t)}{\phi_d(0,t)\phi_f(0,t)} + \frac{B_f^*(0,t)\sigma_f^2(t)}{\phi_f^2(0,t)}, \tag{11.37}$$

$$\begin{aligned}\sigma^*_{zz}(t) = \sigma_z^2(t) &- 2\rho_{dz}\frac{B_d^*(0,t)\sigma_d(t)\sigma_z(t)}{\phi_d(0,t)} + 2\rho_{fz}\frac{B_f^*(0,t)\sigma_f(t)\sigma_z(t)}{\phi_f(0,t)} \\ &+ \frac{B_d^{*2}(0,t)\sigma_d^2(0,t)}{\phi_d^2(0,t)} - 2\rho_{df}\frac{B_d^*(0,t)B_f^*(0,t)\sigma_d(t)\sigma_f(t)}{\phi_d(0,t)\phi_f(0,t)} + \frac{B_f^{*2}(0,t)\sigma_f^2(0,t)}{\phi_f^2(0,t)}.\end{aligned} \tag{11.38}$$

Integrating these expressions (by parts where necessary) yields, respectively

$$\boldsymbol{\Sigma}^*(t,v) = \begin{pmatrix} \frac{\Sigma_{dd}(t,v)}{\phi_d^2(0,v)} & \frac{\Sigma_{df}(t,v)}{\phi_d(0,v)\phi_f(0,v)} & \Sigma^*_{dz}(t,v) \\ \frac{\Sigma_{df}(t,v)}{\phi_d(0,v)\phi_f(0,v)} & \frac{\Sigma_{ff}(t,v)}{\phi_f^2(0,v)} & \Sigma^*_{fz}(t,v) \\ \Sigma^*_{dz}(t,v) & \Sigma^*_{fz}(t,v) & \Sigma^*_{zz}(t,v) \end{pmatrix}, \tag{11.39}$$

$$\gamma^*(t,v) = \begin{pmatrix} 0 \\ -\frac{\Sigma_{fz}(t,v)}{\phi_f(0,v)} \\ I^*_{zf}(t,v) - \frac{B^*_f(0,v)\Sigma_{fz}(t,v)}{\phi_f(0,v)} + \int_t^v \left(r^*_d(u) - r^*_f(u)\right) du \end{pmatrix}, \tag{11.40}$$

with

$$\begin{aligned} \Sigma^*_{dz}(t,v) &:= \frac{1}{\phi_d(0,v)}\left(\Sigma_{dz}(t,v) + I^*_{dd}(t,v) - I^*_{df}(t,v)\right) \\ &\quad - \frac{B^*_d(0,v)\Sigma_{dd}(t,v)}{\phi_d^2(0,v)} + \frac{B^*_f(0,v)\Sigma_{df}(t,v)}{\phi_d(0,v)\phi_f(0,v)}, \\ \Sigma^*_{fz}(t,v) &:= \frac{1}{\phi_f(0,v)}\left(\Sigma_{fz}(t,v) + I^*_{fd}(t,v) - I^*_{ff}(t,v)\right) \\ &\quad - \frac{B^*_d(0,v)\Sigma_{df}(t,v)}{\phi_d(0,v)\phi_f(0,v)} + \frac{B^*_f(0,v)\Sigma_{ff}(t,v)}{\phi_f^2(0,v)}, \\ \Sigma^*_{zz}(t,v) &:= \Sigma_{zz}(t,v) + 2K^*(t,v) - 2B^*_d(0,v)\Sigma^*_{dz}(t,v) + 2B^*_f(0,v)\Sigma^*_{fz}(t,v), \end{aligned}$$

with $K^*(t,v)$ given by (11.28), from which we infer by construction that

$$\boldsymbol{\Phi}(v)\boldsymbol{\Sigma}^*(t,v)\boldsymbol{\Phi}^T(v) = \boldsymbol{\Sigma}^+(t,v),$$

$$\int_t^T \left[\boldsymbol{\Phi}(u)\boldsymbol{\Sigma}^*(0,t)\boldsymbol{\Psi}^T(t,u)\right]_{11} du = \tfrac{1}{2}B^{*2}_d(t,T)\Sigma_{dd}(0,t)$$

The derivation of the pricing kernel proceeds along the lines of that in §6.3. Using (6.30), (11.39) and (11.40) we infer

$$\Delta y_1(t,v) = \frac{I^*_{dd}(t,v)}{\phi_d(0,v)}$$

$$\Delta y_2(t,v) = \frac{\Sigma_{fz}(t,v) + I^*_{fd}(t,v)}{\phi_f(0,v)}$$

$$\begin{aligned}
\Delta y_3(t,v) &= I^*_{zd}(t,v) + K^*_{dd}(t,v) - \int_t^v I^*_{df}(t,u)du - \int_t^v \frac{B^*_d(0,u)\Sigma_{dd}(t,u)}{\phi_d(0,u)}du \\
&\quad + \int_t^v \frac{B^*_f(0,u)\Sigma_{df}(t,u)}{\phi_f(0,u)}du - \int_t^v \left(r^*_d(u) - r^*_f(u)\right)du \\
&= K^*(t,v) - \frac{B^*_d(0,v)I^*_{dd}(t,v)}{\phi_d(0,v)} + \frac{B^*_f(0,v)\left(\Sigma_{fz}(t,v) + I^*_{fd}(t,v) - I^*_{zf}(t,v)\right)}{\phi_f(0,v)} \\
&\quad - B^*_d(t,v)r^*_d(t) - \tfrac{1}{2}B^{*2}_d(t,v)\Sigma_{dd}(0,t) + B^*_f(t,v)r^*_f(t)) + \tfrac{1}{2}B^{*2}_f(t,v)\Sigma_{ff}(0,t),
\end{aligned}$$

where in the final line we have employed integration by parts and made use of (4.45) and the equivalent result for $K^*_{ff}(t,v)$. Making use also of (11.33), we infer

$$[\boldsymbol{\Psi}(t,v)\Delta y(0,t)]_1 = B^*_d(t,v)r^*_d(t).$$

We deduce that the pricing kernel in transformed coordinates has the form

$$G_{\text{M-C}}(y,t;\boldsymbol{\eta},v) = F^v(y,t)N(y - \Delta y(t,v) - \boldsymbol{\eta};\boldsymbol{\Sigma}^*(t,v)), \tag{11.41}$$

with $F^v(y,t)$ given by (6.36). Substituting using the expressions set out above and reverting to the original variable $\boldsymbol{x}$, we obtain

$$G(\boldsymbol{x},t;\boldsymbol{\xi},v) = D(t,v)e^{-\mu^*_d(x_d,t,v)}N\left(\boldsymbol{\xi} + \Delta\boldsymbol{\xi}(t,v) - \boldsymbol{\Phi}(v)\boldsymbol{\Phi}^{-1}(t)\boldsymbol{x};\boldsymbol{\Sigma}^+(t,v)\right), \tag{11.42}$$

where

$$\begin{aligned}
\Delta\boldsymbol{\xi}(t,v) &:= \boldsymbol{\Phi}(v)\Delta y(t,v) \\
&= \begin{pmatrix} I^*_{dd}(t,v) \\ \Sigma_{fz}(t,v) + I^*_{fd}(t,v) \\ K^*(t,v) - B^*_d(t,v)r^*_d(t) - \frac{1}{2}B^{*2}_d(t,v)\Sigma_{dd}(0,t) + B^*_f(t,v)r^*_f(t) + \frac{1}{2}B^{*2}_f(t,v)\Sigma_{ff}(0,t) \end{pmatrix}.
\end{aligned}$$

Rewriting (11.42) in component notation, we arrive at (11.17). This completes the proof.

11.4 INFLATION AND FX OPTIONS

It is now a straightforward matter using (11.17) to calculate the price of European-style FX or inflation options. For example, a call option with strike K and maturity T is seen using Theorem 3.5 to have time-t price given by

$$\begin{aligned}
V^{K,T}_{\text{Call}}(x_d,x_f,z,t) &= \iiint_{\mathbb{R}^3} G(x_d,x_f,z,t;\xi_d,\xi_f,\zeta,T)[F(T)e^{\zeta} - K]^+ d\xi_d d\xi_f d\zeta \\
&= D_d(t,T)e^{-\mu^*_d(x_d,t,T)}\left(F(T)\Phi(d^{K,T}_1(x_d,x_f,z,t)) - K\Phi(d^{K,T}_2(x_d,x_f,z,t))\right),
\end{aligned} \tag{11.43}$$

with $\Phi(\cdot)$ a unit normal cumulative distribution function and

$$d_1^{K,T}(x_d, x_f, z, t) = \frac{\ln \frac{F(T)}{K} + z - \frac{1}{2}\Sigma_{zz}(0,t) + \mu_d^*(x_d, t, T) - \mu_f^*(x_f, t, T) + \frac{1}{2}\Sigma_{zz}^+(t,T)}{\sqrt{\Sigma_{zz}^+(t,T)}}, \tag{11.44}$$

$$d_2^{K,T}(x_d, x_f, z, t) = d_1^{K,T}(x_d, x_f, z, t) - \sqrt{\Sigma_{zz}^+(t,T)}, \tag{11.45}$$

$$\Sigma_{zz}^+(t,v) = \Sigma_{zz}(t,v) + 2K^*(t,v)). \tag{11.46}$$

This can be seen to be equivalent to the inflation option price derived by Jarrow and Yildirim [2003] with real and nominal rates modelled by constant-coefficients Vasicek models, which can be interpreted as a special case of the HJM model. Essentially, the impact of the stochastic rates here is that the volatility appearing in the standard Black–Scholes formula is the term volatility not of the FX rate but of the FX forward price. The small adjustment terms which arise in (11.44) vanish at $t = 0$ and as $t \to T$. Also, we see that the pricing kernel in (11.17) specifies modifications to the covariance terms in (11.27) which may impact the pricing of other multi-currency rates derivatives.

CHAPTER 12

Rates-Credit-FX Hybrid Modelling

12.1 PREVIOUS WORK

We now seek to extend the pricing kernel derived in the previous chapter to incorporate credit risk. In other words we wish to consider multi-currency cash flows which are either contingent on survival of a given debt issuer (or counterparty) or else are default contingent (protection or loss payment). To this end we will consider a multi-factor model with four underlying assets. Essentially we shall be extending the three-factor modelling of Chapter 11 with two interest rates and an FX rate to include credit risk in the manner set out in Chapters 8 and 10, allowing the FX rate to jump at default.

Our model is closely related to that considered by Itkin et al. [2019] except in that they take the interest rates to be governed by CIR square-root volatility processes rather than Hull–White and they also allow of a jump in the foreign interest rate at default. They consider the basis spread between CDS spreads in the two currencies and find a significant near-linear dependence on the FX jump but a much weaker non-linear dependence (a few bps) on the interest rate jump, which furthermore diminishes as the FX jump size increases. The credit-FX correlation is found to have a strong linear impact and the others very little.

On that basis we expect, for such "linear" products as quanto CDS, that the difference in prices compared with the use of the simpler model presented in Chapter 10 will not be great. We none the less consider this impact in §12.3, going on to revisit also in §12.4 the problem of pricing a contingent CDS on an underlying cross-currency swap, or equivalently of calculating the CVA on such a swap underlying.

12.2 DERIVATION OF RATES-CREDIT-FX PRICING KERNEL

12.2.1 Pricing Equation

We shall take the domestic and foreign interest rates to be as defined as in (11.1)–(11.5). For the credit intensity we specify

$$dx_{\lambda t} = -\alpha_{\lambda}(t)x_{\lambda t}dt + \sigma_{\lambda}(t)dW_t^3 \tag{12.1}$$

under the domestic currency measure with $\lambda_t = \lambda(x_{\lambda t}, t)$ where

$$\lambda(x_\lambda, t) := \lambda^*(t)e^{x_\lambda} \tag{12.2}$$

in line with our rates-credit kernel of Chapter 8. Let us denote the time of default as usual by τ.

For the FX rate we consider an auxiliary process z_t defined for $t < \tau$ by

$$dz_t = -k(\lambda_t - \overline{\lambda}(t))dt + \ln(1+k)dn_t + \sigma_z(t)dW_t^4, \tag{12.3}$$

where n_t is a Cox process with intensity λ_t functioning as an indicator of a default event. The FX rate is then taken to be

$$Z_t = Z(z_t, t) \tag{12.4}$$

with $Z(z,t)$ given by (10.20). Here and subsequently we reuse freely the notation of Theorem 11.1 (with the exception of the matrix expressions (11.26) and (11.27) which we shall extend to four dimensions). The FX rate is assumed to jump at default by a relative amount $k > -1$ (usually taking $k < 0$), whence the FX rate immediately after default is given by $Z_\tau = (1+k)\lim_{t\to\tau^-} Z_t$. Let us further define correlations $\rho_{\alpha\beta}$ in the usual manner for $\alpha, \beta \in \{d, f, \lambda, z\}$, $\alpha \neq \beta$.

If the price of a European-type security depending for its payout amount on the spot FX rate and/or instantaneous values (or, equivalently, zero coupon bond prices or LIBOR rates) is expressed as $f(x_d, x_\lambda, x_f, z, t)$, this price is governed under the hybrid model specified above for $t \in [0, \tau)$ by the following Kolmogorov backward diffusion equation

$$\begin{aligned}
&\frac{\partial f}{\partial t} - \alpha_d(t)x_d\frac{\partial f}{\partial x_d} - (\alpha_f(t)x_f + \rho_{fz}\sigma_f(t)\sigma_z(t))\frac{\partial f}{\partial x_f} - \alpha_\lambda(t)x_\lambda\frac{\partial f}{\partial x_\lambda}\\
&\quad + \left(r_d^*(t) - r_f^*(t) + x_d - x_f - k(\lambda(x_\lambda, t) - \overline{\lambda}(t)\right)\frac{\partial f}{\partial z}\\
&\quad + \frac{1}{2}\left(\sigma_d^2(t)\frac{\partial^2 f}{\partial x_d^2} + \sigma_f^2(t)\frac{\partial^2 f}{\partial x_f^2} + \sigma_\lambda^2(t)\frac{\partial^2 f}{\partial x_\lambda^2} + \sigma_z^2(t)\frac{\partial^2 f}{\partial z^2}\right)\\
&\quad + \rho_{df}\sigma_d(t)\sigma_f(t)\frac{\partial^2 f}{\partial x_d \partial x_f} + \rho_{d\lambda}\sigma_d(t)\sigma_\lambda(t)\frac{\partial^2 f}{\partial x_d \partial x_\lambda} + \rho_{f\lambda}\sigma_f(t)\sigma_\lambda(t)\frac{\partial^2 f}{\partial x_f \partial x_\lambda}\\
&\quad + \rho_{dz}\sigma_d(t)\sigma_z(t)\frac{\partial^2 f}{\partial x_d \partial z} + \rho_{fz}\sigma_f(t)\sigma_z(t)\frac{\partial^2 f}{\partial x_f \partial z} + \rho_{\lambda z}\sigma_\lambda(t)\sigma_z(t)\frac{\partial^2 f}{\partial x_\lambda \partial z}\\
&\quad - (r_d(x_d, t) + \lambda(x_\lambda, t))\, f = 0,
\end{aligned} \tag{12.5}$$

subject to the final condition $\lim_{t\to v^-} f(x_d, x_\lambda, x_f, z, t) = P(x_d, x_f, z)$ for some payoff function $P(\cdot,\cdot,\cdot)$, with $r_d(\cdot)$ given by (4.3). In the event that there is a payoff

$P_{def}(x_{d\tau}, x_{f\tau}, z_\tau)$ at default time τ, at which time the FX rate will be assumed to have jumped, we note that this can be represented as $P_{def}(x_{d\tau}, x_{f\tau}, \ln(1+k)\lim_{t\to\tau^-} z_t)$. So we take the default payoff associated with (12.5) to be given by $P_{def}(x_d, x_f, \ln(1+k)z)$.

12.2.2 Pricing Kernel

As in Chapter 8, we shall make use of the general result derived in §6.5 for a hybrid rates-credit kernel, augmented to take account of a jump in the FX rate at default. Our main result can be stated as follows:

Theorem 12.1 *(Rates-Credit-FX Hybrid Pricing Kernel): Taking $\boldsymbol{x} = (x_d, x_\lambda, x_f, z)$ and $\boldsymbol{\xi} = (\xi_d, \xi_\lambda, \xi_f, \zeta)$, the required pricing kernel for* (12.5) *can be expressed asymptotically for some parameter ϵ representing the smallness of the credit default intensity by*

$$G(\boldsymbol{x}, t; \boldsymbol{\xi}, v) = f^v(x_d, t) \sum_{j=0}^{\infty} G_j(\boldsymbol{x}, t; \boldsymbol{\xi}, v), \tag{12.6}$$

where $f^v(x_d, t)$ is given by (8.15), *the $G_j(\cdot)$ are $\mathcal{O}(\epsilon^j)$ and the first three terms in the series are given by* (12.29)–(12.31) *below.*

Furthermore, to fit the risk-free forward curve, we must choose $r_d^*(t)$ to be given by (4.14) and, to fit the risky curve, $\lambda^*(t)$ in (12.2) *to be given by* (8.16).

Proof: The proof here is in essence an extension and consolidation of previous results. The starting point in our calculation is the knowledge based on (6.78) that the Green's function is given by

$$\begin{aligned} G(x, t; \boldsymbol{\xi}, v) &= |\boldsymbol{\Phi}^{-1}(v)| G_{\text{R-C}}(\boldsymbol{\Phi}^{-1}(t)\boldsymbol{x}, t; \boldsymbol{\Phi}^{-1}(v)\boldsymbol{\xi}, v) \\ &= B(t, v)\mathcal{E}_t^v(\mathcal{G}_3(t, \cdot))\mathcal{E}_t^v(\mathcal{G}_1(t, \cdot))\mathcal{E}_t^v(-\mathcal{L}_1(t, \cdot)) \\ &\qquad N\left(\boldsymbol{\Phi}(v)\left(\boldsymbol{\Phi}^{-1}(t)\boldsymbol{x} + \boldsymbol{\gamma}^*(t, v)\right) - \boldsymbol{\xi}; \boldsymbol{\Sigma}^+(t, v)\right), \end{aligned} \tag{12.7}$$

where $\boldsymbol{\Sigma}^+(t, v) := \boldsymbol{\Phi}(v)\boldsymbol{\Sigma}^*(t, v)\boldsymbol{\Phi}^T(v)$. As with our analysis in Chapter 10, we note that the impact of the FX jump at default can be incorporated by considering the stochastic discounting to be given not by $\lambda(x_\lambda, t) - \overline{\lambda}(t)$ but by $\left(\lambda(x_\lambda, t) - \overline{\lambda}(t)\right)\left(1 + k\frac{\partial}{\partial z}\right)$. Correspondingly we must interpret $\mathcal{G}_3(t, u)$ not through (6.77) but through the modified expression

$$\mathcal{G}_3(t, u) = \left(\overline{\lambda}(u) - \lambda^*(u)e^{[\boldsymbol{\Phi}(u)\boldsymbol{y}]_2 - \int_t^u [\boldsymbol{\Theta}(t,t_1)\boldsymbol{\Phi}^T(u)]_{12}dt_1} e^{\mathcal{L}_2(t,u) + \int_t^u [\boldsymbol{\Theta}(t,u)\boldsymbol{\Phi}^T(t_1)]_{21}dt_1}\right)\left(1 + k\frac{\partial}{\partial z}\right). \tag{12.8}$$

In addition we must redefine the functional expressions appearing in the operators appropriately. To that end we note that in the present context we have

$$\boldsymbol{\kappa}(t) = \begin{pmatrix} \alpha_d(t) & 0 & 0 & 0 \\ 0 & \alpha_\lambda(t) & 0 & 0 \\ 0 & 0 & \alpha_f(t) & 0 \\ -1 & 0 & 1 & 0 \end{pmatrix}, \tag{12.9}$$

whence

$$\mathbf{\Phi}(t) = \begin{pmatrix} \phi_d(0,t) & 0 & 0 & 0 \\ 0 & \phi_\lambda(0,t) & 0 & 0 \\ 0 & 0 & \phi_f(0,t) & 0 \\ B_d^*(0,t) & 0 & -B_f^*(0,t) & 1 \end{pmatrix}, \tag{12.10}$$

$$\mathbf{\Phi}^{-1}(t) = \begin{pmatrix} \phi_d(0,t)^{-1} & 0 & 0 & 0 \\ 0 & \phi_\lambda(0,t)^{-1} & 0 & 0 \\ 0 & 0 & \phi_f(0,t)^{-1} & 0 \\ -\phi_d(0,t)^{-1}B_d^*(0,t) & 0 & \phi_f(0,t)^{-1}B_f^*(0,t) & 1 \end{pmatrix}, \tag{12.11}$$

We infer from (6.8) that

$$\boldsymbol{\sigma}^*(t) = \begin{pmatrix} \frac{\sigma_d^2(t)}{\phi_d^2(0,t)} & \rho_{d\lambda}\frac{\sigma_d(t)\sigma_\lambda(t)}{\phi_d(0,t)\phi_\lambda(0,t)} & \rho_{df}\frac{\sigma_d(t)\sigma_f(t)}{\phi_d(0,t)\phi_f(0,t)} & \sigma_{dz}^*(t) \\ \rho_{d\lambda}\frac{\sigma_d(t)\sigma_\lambda(t)}{\phi_d(0,t)\phi_\lambda(0,t)} & \frac{\sigma_\lambda^2(t)}{\phi_\lambda^2(0,t)} & \rho_{\lambda f}\frac{\sigma_\lambda(t)\sigma_f(t)}{\phi_\lambda(0,t)\phi_f(0,t)} & \sigma_{\lambda z}^*(t) \\ \rho_{df}\frac{\sigma_d(t)\sigma_f(t)}{\phi_d(0,t)\phi_f(0,t)} & \rho_{\lambda f}\frac{\sigma_\lambda(t)\sigma_f(t)}{\phi_\lambda(0,t)\phi_f(0,t)} & \frac{\sigma_f^2(t)}{\phi_f^2(0,t)} & \sigma_{fz}^*(t) \\ \sigma_{dz}^*(t) & \sigma_{\lambda z}^*(t) & \sigma_{fz}^*(t) & \sigma_{zz}^*(t), \end{pmatrix}, \tag{12.12}$$

where we define, analogous to Chapter 11

$$\sigma_{dz}^*(t) = \rho_{dz}\frac{\sigma_d(t)\sigma_z(t)}{\phi_d(0,t)} - \frac{B_d^*(0,t)\sigma_d^2(t)}{\phi_d^2(0,t)} + \rho_{df}\frac{B_f^*(0,t)\sigma_d(t)\sigma_f(t)}{\phi_d(0,t)\phi_f(0,t)}, \tag{12.13}$$

$$\sigma_{\lambda z}^*(t) = \rho_{\lambda z}\frac{\sigma_\lambda(t)\sigma_z(t)}{\phi_\lambda(0,t)} - \rho_{d\lambda}\frac{B_d^*(0,t)\sigma_d(t)\sigma_\lambda(t)}{\phi_d(0,t)\phi_\lambda(0,t)} + \rho_{\lambda f}\frac{B_f^*(0,t)\sigma_\lambda(t)\sigma_f(t)}{\phi_\lambda(0,t)\phi_f(0,t)} \tag{12.14}$$

$$\sigma_{fz}^*(t) = \rho_{fz}\frac{\sigma_f(t)\sigma_z(t)}{\phi_f(0,t)} - \rho_{df}\frac{B_d^*(0,t)\sigma_d(t)\sigma_f(t)}{\phi_d(0,t)\phi_f(0,t)} + \frac{B_f^*(0,t)\sigma_f^2(t)}{\phi_f^2(0,t)}, \tag{12.15}$$

$$\begin{aligned}\sigma_{zz}^*(t) = \sigma_z^2(t) - 2\rho_{dz}\frac{B_d^*(0,t)\sigma_d(t)\sigma_z(t)}{\phi_d(0,t)} + 2\rho_{fz}\frac{B_f^*(0,t)\sigma_f(t)\sigma_z(t)}{\phi_f(0,t)} \\ + \frac{B_d^{*2}(0,t)\sigma_d^2(0,t)}{\phi_d^2(0,t)} - 2\rho_{df}\frac{B_d^*(0,t)B_f^*(0,t)\sigma_d(t)\sigma_f(t)}{\phi_d(0,t)\phi_f(0,t)} + \frac{B_f^{*2}(0,t)\sigma_f^2(0,t)}{\phi_f^2(0,t)}.\end{aligned} \tag{12.16}$$

We further infer from (6.9) and the fact $\boldsymbol{\beta}(t) = \left(0, 0, -\rho_{fz}\sigma_f(t)\sigma_z(t), r_d^*(t) - r_f^*(t)\right)^T$ that

$$\boldsymbol{\beta}^*(t) = \begin{pmatrix} 0 \\ 0 \\ -\rho_{fz}\frac{\sigma_f(t)\sigma_z(t)}{\phi_f(0,t)} \\ -\rho_{fz}\frac{B_f^*(0,t)\sigma_f(t)\sigma_z(t)}{\phi_f(0,t)} + r_d^*(t) - r_f^*(t) \end{pmatrix}, \tag{12.17}$$

Integrating (12.12) and (12.17) (by parts where necessary) yields, respectively:

$$\boldsymbol{\Sigma}^*(t,v) = \begin{pmatrix} \frac{\Sigma_{dd}(t,v)}{\phi_d^2(0,v)} & \frac{\Sigma_{d\lambda}(t,v)}{\phi_d(0,v)\phi_\lambda(0,v)} & \frac{\Sigma_{df}(t,v)}{\phi_d(0,v)\phi_f(0,v)} & \Sigma_{dz}^*(t,v) \\ \frac{\Sigma_{d\lambda}(t,v)}{\phi_d(0,v)\phi_\lambda(0,v)} & \frac{\Sigma_{\lambda\lambda}(t,v)}{\phi_\lambda^2(0,v)} & \frac{\Sigma_{\lambda f}(t,v)}{\phi_\lambda(0,v)\phi_f(0,v)} & \Sigma_{\lambda z}^*(t,v) \\ \frac{\Sigma_{df}(t,v)}{\phi_d(0,v)\phi_f(0,v)} & \frac{\Sigma_{\lambda f}(t,v)}{\phi_\lambda(0,v)\phi_f(0,v)} & \frac{\Sigma_{ff}(t,v)}{\phi_f^2(0,v)} & \Sigma_{fz}^*(t,v) \\ \Sigma_{dz}^*(t,v) & \Sigma_{\lambda z}^*(t,v) & \Sigma_{fz}^*(t,v) & \Sigma_{zz}^*(t,v) \end{pmatrix}, \tag{12.18}$$

$$\boldsymbol{\gamma}^*(t,v) = \begin{pmatrix} 0 \\ 0 \\ -\frac{\Sigma_{fz}(t,v)}{\phi_f(0,v)} \\ I_{zf}^*(t,v) - \frac{B_f^*(0,v)\Sigma_{fz}(t,v)}{\phi_f(0,v)} + \int_t^v (r_d^*(u) - r_f^*(u))du \end{pmatrix}, \tag{12.19}$$

with $I_{zf}^*(t,v)$ given by (11.24),

$$\Sigma_{dz}^*(t,v) := \frac{1}{\phi_d(0,v)}\left(\Sigma_{dz}(t,v) + I_{dd}^*(t,v) - I_{df}^*(t,v)\right) - \frac{B_d^*(0,v)\Sigma_{dd}(t,v)}{\phi_d^2(0,v)} + \frac{B_f^*(0,v)\Sigma_{df}(t,v)}{\phi_d(0,v)\phi_f(0,v)},$$

$$\Sigma_{\lambda z}^*(t,v) := \frac{1}{\phi_\lambda(0,v)}\left(\Sigma_{\lambda z}(t,v) + I_{\lambda d}^*(t,v) - I_{\lambda f}^*(t,v)\right) - \frac{B_d^*(0,v)\Sigma_{d\lambda}(t,v)}{\phi_d(0,v)\phi_\lambda(0,v)} + \frac{B_f^*(0,v)\Sigma_{\lambda f}(t,v)}{\phi_\lambda(0,v)\phi_f(0,v)},$$

$$\Sigma_{fz}^*(t,v) := \frac{1}{\phi_f(0,v)}\left(\Sigma_{fz}(t,v) + I_{fd}^*(t,v) - I_{ff}^*(t,v)\right) - \frac{B_d^*(0,v)\Sigma_{df}(t,v)}{\phi_d(0,v)\phi_f(0,v)} + \frac{B_f^*(0,v)\Sigma_{ff}(t,v)}{\phi_f^2(0,v)},$$

$$\Sigma_{zz}^*(t,v) := \Sigma_{zz}(t,v) + 2K^*(t,v) - 2B_d^*(0,v)\Sigma_{dz}^*(t,v) + 2B_f^*(0,v)\Sigma_{fz}^*(t,v),$$

and $K^*(t,v)$ given by (11.28). We infer by construction that

$$\boldsymbol{\Theta}(t,v) = \begin{pmatrix} \frac{\Sigma_{dd}(t,v)}{\phi_d(0,v)} & \frac{\Sigma_{d\lambda}(t,v)}{\phi_\lambda(0,v)} & \frac{\Sigma_{df}(t,v)}{\phi_f(0,v)} & \phi_d(0,v)\Sigma^*_{dz}(t,v) \\ \frac{\Sigma_{d\lambda}(t,v)}{\phi_d(0,v)} & \frac{\Sigma_{\lambda\lambda}(t,v)}{\phi_\lambda(0,v)} & \frac{\Sigma_{\lambda f}(t,v)}{\phi_f(0,v)} & \phi_\lambda(0,v)\Sigma^*_{\lambda z}(t,v) \\ \frac{\Sigma_{df}(t,v)}{\phi_d(0,v)} & \frac{\Sigma_{\lambda f}(t,v)}{\phi_\lambda(0,v)} & \frac{\Sigma_{ff}(t,v)}{\phi_f(0,v)} & \phi_f(0,v)\Sigma^*_{fz}(t,v) \\ \Theta_{41}(t,v) & \Theta_{42}(t,v) & \Theta_{43}(t,v) & \Theta_{44}(t,v) \end{pmatrix}, \tag{12.20}$$

where

$$\begin{aligned}
\Theta_{41}(t,v) &:= \Sigma^*_{dz}(t,v) + \frac{B^*_d(0,v)\Sigma_{dd}(t,v)}{\phi^2_d(0,v)} - \frac{B^*_f(0,v)\Sigma_{df}(t,v)}{\phi_d(0,v)\phi_f(0,v)}, \\
\Theta_{42}(t,v) &:= \Sigma^*_{\lambda z}(t,v) + \frac{B^*_d(0,v)\Sigma_{d\lambda}(t,v)}{\phi_d(0,v)\phi_\lambda(0,v)} - \frac{B^*_f(0,v)\Sigma_{\lambda f}(t,v)}{\phi_\lambda(0,v)\phi_f(0,v)}, \\
\Theta_{43}(t,v) &:= \Sigma^*_{fz}(t,v) + \frac{B^*_d(0,v)\Sigma_{df}(t,v)}{\phi_d(0,v)\phi_f(0,v)} - \frac{B^*_f(0,v)\Sigma_{ff}(t,v)}{\phi^2_f(0,v)}, \\
\Theta_{44}(t,v) &:= \Sigma^*_{zz}(t,v) + B^*_d(0,v)\Sigma^*_{dz}(t,v) - B^*_f(0,v)\Sigma^*_{fz}(t,v).
\end{aligned}$$

The covariance matrix required for the pricing kernel expression in (12.7) is then seen, after some simplification, to be

$$\begin{aligned}
\boldsymbol{\Sigma}^+(t,v) &= \boldsymbol{\Theta}(t,v)\boldsymbol{\Phi}^T(v) \\
&= \boldsymbol{\Sigma}(t,v) + \begin{pmatrix} 0 & 0 & 0 & I^*_{dd}(t,v) - I^*_{df}(t,v) \\ 0 & 0 & 0 & I^*_{\lambda d}(t,v) - I^*_{\lambda f}(t,v) \\ 0 & 0 & 0 & I^*_{fd}(t,v) - I^*_{ff}(t,v) \\ I^*_{dd}(t,v) - I^*_{df}(t,v) & I^*_{\lambda d}(t,v) - I^*_{\lambda f}(t,v) & I^*_{fd}(t,v) - I^*_{ff}(t,v) & 2K^*(t,v) \end{pmatrix}
\end{aligned} \tag{12.21}$$

where

$$\boldsymbol{\Sigma}(t,v) = \begin{pmatrix} \Sigma_{dd}(t,v) & \Sigma_{d\lambda}(t,v) & \Sigma_{df}(t,v) & \Sigma_{dz}(t,v) \\ \Sigma_{d\lambda}(t,v) & \Sigma_{\lambda\lambda}(t,v) & \Sigma_{\lambda f}(t,v) & \Sigma_{\lambda z}(t,v) \\ \Sigma_{df}(t,v) & \Sigma_{\lambda f}(t,v) & \Sigma_{ff}(t,v) & \Sigma_{fz}(t,v) \\ \Sigma_{dz}(t,v) & \Sigma_{\lambda z}(t,v) & \Sigma_{fz}(t,v) & \Sigma_{zz}(t,v) \end{pmatrix}. \tag{12.22}$$

In addition we find that (8.23)–(8.26) remain true in this case, while

$$\sum_{j=1}^{n} \Theta_{1j}(t,u)\frac{\partial}{\partial y_j} = \sum_{k=1}^{n} [\boldsymbol{\Theta}(t,u)\boldsymbol{\Phi}^T(t)]_{1k}\frac{\partial}{\partial x_k}$$
$$= \frac{\Sigma_{dd}(t,v)}{\phi_d(t,v)}\frac{\partial}{\partial x_d} + \frac{\Sigma_{d\lambda}(t,v)}{\phi_\lambda(t,v)}\frac{\partial}{\partial x_\lambda} + \frac{\Sigma_{df}(t,v)}{\phi_f(t,v)}\frac{\partial}{\partial x_f} + \phi_d(0,v)\Sigma^*_{dz}(t,v)\frac{\partial}{\partial z}, \tag{12.23}$$

$$\sum_{j=1}^{n} \Theta_{2j}(t,u)\frac{\partial}{\partial y_j} = \sum_{k=1}^{n} \left[\boldsymbol{\Theta}(t,u)\boldsymbol{\Phi}^T(t)\right]_{2k}\frac{\partial}{\partial x_k}$$
$$= \frac{\Sigma_{d\lambda}(t,v)}{\phi_d(t,v)}\frac{\partial}{\partial x_d} + \frac{\Sigma_{\lambda\lambda}(t,v)}{\phi_\lambda(t,v)}\frac{\partial}{\partial x_\lambda} + \frac{\Sigma_{\lambda f}(t,v)}{\phi_f(t,v)}\frac{\partial}{\partial x_f} + \phi_d(0,v)\Sigma^*_{\lambda z}(t,v)\frac{\partial}{\partial z}. \tag{12.24}$$

We now seek to evaluate (12.7). We note in this regard that since $[\boldsymbol{\Phi}(u)\boldsymbol{\gamma}^*(t,u)]_k = 0$ for $k = 1, 2$, the leading terms in (6.65) and (6.66) make no contribution. From (6.65) we therefore have

$$\int_t^v \mathcal{L}_1(t,u)du = \frac{I^*_{dd}(t,v)}{\phi_d(t,v)}\frac{\partial}{\partial x_d} + \frac{I^*_{\lambda d}(t,v)}{\phi_\lambda(t,v)}\frac{\partial}{\partial x_\lambda} + \frac{I^*_{fd}(t,v)}{\phi_f(t,v)}\frac{\partial}{\partial x_f} + K^*(t,v)\frac{\partial}{\partial z}.$$

Because all the terms in this expression commute with each other, it is possible to replace the time-ordered exponential of $\mathcal{L}_1(t,u)$ by a simple exponential of the integral. Likewise for $\mathcal{G}_1(t,u)$ and, repeating the calculation performed in Chapter 8, we see

$$\int_t^v \mathcal{G}_1(t,u)du = \mu^*_d(x_d,t,v).$$

We conclude that (12.7) can, making use of the shift operator property (3.39), be expressed as

$$G(x,t;\xi,v) = B(t,v)\mathcal{E}_t^v(\mathcal{G}_3(t,\cdot))e^{-\mu^*_d(x_d,t,v)}N_4(\phi_d(t,v)x_d - I^*_{dd}(t,v) - \xi_d,$$
$$\phi_\lambda(t,v)x_\lambda - I^*_{\lambda d}(t,v) - \xi_\lambda, \phi_f(t,v)x_f - \Sigma_{fz}(t,v) - I^*_{df}(t,v) - \xi_f,$$
$$z - \Delta_{zz}(x_d,x_f,t,v) - \zeta; \boldsymbol{\Sigma}^+(t,v)), \tag{12.25}$$

where $N_4(\cdot;\boldsymbol{\Sigma})$ is a four-dimensional Gaussian distribution function with variance $\boldsymbol{\Sigma}$, $\boldsymbol{\Sigma}^+(\cdot)$ is given by (12.21) and $\Delta_{zz}(x_d,x_f,t,v)$ is given as before by (11.31). It remains to explicate $\mathcal{E}_t^v(\mathcal{G}_3(t,\cdot))$, to which end we must first consider $\mathcal{L}_2(t,u)$. From (6.66), using (12.24), we have

$$\mathcal{L}_2(t,u) = \frac{1}{2}\Sigma_{\lambda\lambda}(t,u) + \frac{\Sigma_{d\lambda}(t,u)}{\phi_d(t,u)}\frac{\partial}{\partial x_d} + \frac{\Sigma_{\lambda\lambda}(t,u)}{\phi_\lambda(t,u)}\frac{\partial}{\partial x_\lambda} + \frac{\Sigma_{\lambda f}(t,u)}{\phi_f(t,u)}\frac{\partial}{\partial x_f} + \Delta_{z\lambda}(t,u)\frac{\partial}{\partial z},$$

where we define

$$\Delta_{z\lambda}(t,u) := \Sigma_{\lambda z}(t,u) + I^*_{\lambda d}(t,u) - I^*_{\lambda f}(t,u). \tag{12.26}$$

From (12.8) we then have

$$\mathcal{G}_3(t,u) = \left(\overline{\lambda}(u) - \lambda^*(u)e^{\phi_\lambda(t,u)x_\lambda - I^*_{\lambda d}(t,u)+\frac{1}{2}\Sigma_{\lambda\lambda}(t,u)}e^{B^*_d(t,u)\frac{\Sigma_{d\lambda}(t,u)}{\phi_d(t,u)}+\mathcal{L}_2(t,u)}\right)\left(1 + k\frac{\partial}{\partial z}\right).$$

Performing a manipulation analogous to that in Chapter 8, using the notation there introduced, and inverting the order of the time-ordered exponential and the plain exponential, we obtain

$$\mathcal{E}_t^v(\mathcal{G}_3(t,\cdot))e^{-\mu^*_d(x_d,t,v)} = e^{-\mu^*_d(x_d,t,v)}\mathcal{E}_t^v\left(\left(\overline{\lambda}(u) - \mathcal{M}(t,\cdot)\right)\left(1 + k\frac{\partial}{\partial z}\right)\right),$$

where we define in this instance

$$\mathcal{M}(t,t_1) = \Lambda(x_\lambda,t,t_1)e^{\frac{\Sigma_{d\lambda}(t,t_1)}{\phi_d(t,t_1)}\frac{\partial}{\partial x_d}+\frac{\Sigma_{\lambda\lambda}(t,t_1)}{\phi_\lambda(t,t_1)}\frac{\partial}{\partial x_\lambda}+\frac{\Sigma_{\lambda f}(t,t_1)}{\phi_f(t,t_1)}\frac{\partial}{\partial x_f}+\Delta_{z\lambda}(t,t_1)\frac{\partial}{\partial z}}, \tag{12.27}$$

with $\Lambda(x_\lambda,t,t_1)$ defined by (8.34) and $\Delta_{z\lambda}(t,t_1)$ by (12.26). Substitution into (12.25) gives the required result

$$G(\boldsymbol{x},t;\boldsymbol{\xi},v) = f^v(x_d,t)\mathcal{E}_t^v\left(\left(\overline{\lambda}(u) - e^{-B^*_d(t_1,v)\Sigma_{d\lambda}(t,t_1)}\mathcal{M}(t,\cdot)\right)\left(1 + k\frac{\partial}{\partial z}\right)\right)G_0(\boldsymbol{x},t;\boldsymbol{\xi},v), \tag{12.28}$$

where we define

$$\begin{aligned}G_0(\boldsymbol{x},t;\boldsymbol{\xi},v) :=\ & B(t,v)N_4(\phi_d(t,v)x_d - I^*_{dd}(t,v) - \xi_d, \phi_\lambda(t,v)x_\lambda - I^*_{\lambda d}(t,v) - \xi_\lambda,\\ & \phi_f(t,v)x_f - \Sigma_{fz}(t,v) - I^*_{df}(t,v) - \xi_f, z - \Delta_{zz}(x_d,x_f,t,v) - \zeta;\boldsymbol{\Sigma}^+(t,v)).\end{aligned} \tag{12.29}$$

The asymptotic expansion of this expression is likewise analogous to the exercise performed in Chapter 8 and the calibration identical. In particular the form of $\tilde{\lambda}(\cdot)$ and $\Lambda(\cdot)$ and their asymptotic representations in (8.17), (8.46), (8.47), (8.38) and (8.39) are unchanged. We therefore propose that the solution can be written asymptotically in the form (12.6). We again suppose a corresponding series representation of $\mathcal{M}(t,u)$, introducing $\mathcal{O}(\epsilon^j)$ operators $\mathcal{M}_j(t,u)$, $j = 1,2,\ldots$ obtained by replacing

$\Lambda(x_\lambda, t, t_1)$ in (12.27) with $\Lambda_j(x_\lambda, t, t_1)$. Considering terms in turn at $\mathcal{O}(\epsilon)$ and at $\mathcal{O}(\epsilon^2)$ we find

$$G_1(x, t; \xi, v) = \left(1 + k\frac{\partial}{\partial z}\right) \int_t^v \left(\overline{\lambda}(t_1) - e^{-B_d^*(t_1,v)\Sigma_{d\lambda}(t,t_1)}\mathcal{M}_1(t, t_1)\right) G_0(x, t; \xi, v)dt_1, \tag{12.30}$$

$$\begin{aligned} G_2(x, t; \xi, v) = {} & \left(1 + k\frac{\partial}{\partial z}\right)^2 \int_t^v \left(\overline{\lambda}(t_2) - e^{-B_d^*(t_2,v)\Sigma_{d\lambda}(t,t_2)}\mathcal{M}_1(t, t_2)\right) \\ & \int_t^{t_2} \left(\overline{\lambda}(t_1) - e^{-B_d^*(t_1,v)\Sigma_{d\lambda}(t,t_1)}\mathcal{M}_1(t, t_1)\right) G_0(x, t; \xi, v)dt_1 dt_2 \\ & - \left(1 + k\frac{\partial}{\partial z}\right) \int_t^v e^{-B_d^*(t_1,v)\Sigma_{d\lambda}(t,t_1)}\mathcal{M}_2(t, t_1)G_0(x, t; \xi, v)dt_1. \end{aligned} \tag{12.31}$$

Notice that the fact the $\mathcal{M}_j(\cdot)$ operators have no functional dependence on z allows us to move the $\left(1 + k\frac{\partial}{\partial z}\right)$ terms outside of the integral. Higher-order terms can be derived in a similar manner but are likely to be of limited use in practice. We make the further observation that the impact of the operator $\mathcal{M}_j(t, t_1)$ is to pre-multiply by $\Lambda_j(x_\lambda, t, t_1)$ and to shift

$$x_d \to x_d + \frac{\Sigma_{d\lambda}(t, t_1)}{\phi_d(t, t_1)}; \; x_\lambda \to x_\lambda + \frac{\Sigma_{\lambda\lambda}(t, t_1)}{\phi_\lambda(t, t_1)}; \; x_f \to x_f + \frac{\Sigma_{\lambda f}(t, t_1)}{\phi_f(t, t_1)}; \; z \to z + \Delta_{z\lambda}(t, t_1),$$

with $\Delta_{z\lambda}(\cdot)$ given by (12.26). This completes the proof.

It is worth commenting on the characteristics of the solution derived above. We observe first that the form of the covariance matrix $\mathbf{\Sigma}^+(t, v)$ in (12.21) is such that the submatrix generated by ignoring the third and fourth indices is identical to that derived in Chapter 8 for the hybrid rates-credit kernel, while that obtained by ignoring the second index is identical to that derived in Chapter 11 for the rates-FX kernel. The only non-trivial cross-linkage which occurs is in the credit-FX covariance where a term $I_{\lambda d}^*(t, v) - I_{\lambda f}^*(t, v)$ arises. This represents the (indirect) impact of stochastic credit intensity on the FX rate through the stochastic drift of the latter. In particular we see that the FX variance is influenced by the two interest rates which contribute to the FX drift, but not by the credit intensity which has no direct impact.

Considering the shifts which are applied to the variables in the Gaussian distribution function through $\mathcal{L}_1(t, u)$ and $\mathcal{L}_2(t, u)$, these can be interpreted as a combination of the impacts observed in Chapters 8, 10 and 11. However there is again an adjustment of $I_{\lambda d}^*(t, t_1) - I_{\lambda f}^*(t, t_1)$ arising in addition to the direct impact of stochastic credit intensity on the FX rate through $\Sigma_{\lambda z}(t, t_1)$.

12.3 QUANTO CDS REVISITED

In §10.3 we considered the pricing of quanto CDS under the assumption that interest rates were deterministic. We consider here how the PV results there derived are affected by stochastic interest rates. We will be particularly interested in flows associated with foreign currency notionals since any cash flows, fixed or floating, which are made in domestic currency (with reference to which the credit calibration is carried out) can be priced under the model specified in Chapter 8 without reference to the foreign economy, so the pricing formulae listed there can be reused for this purpose. We focus here on foreign currency protection payments and foreign currency fixed flows. As we saw in Chapters 8 and 10, the former are expected to depend for their PV on both the rates-credit and the credit-FX correlations, while the latter are expected to depend for their PV on at least the credit-FX correlation. Of course, we would in general expect other correlations to impact also, if taken properly into account.

12.3.1 Domestic Currency Fixed Flow

Based on our observation that the marginal model for pricing in the absence of foreign currency (FX or rates) effects is precisely that considered in Chapter 8, we infer that the pricing of domestic currency risky cash flows is as described in §8.3.1. We therefore make no further comment here.

12.3.2 Foreign Currency Fixed Flow

Consider then a risky foreign currency flow (notional or coupon) of N_f at time T. This will have from (12.4) a *domestic* currency payoff value of

$$P_f(z_T) = N_f Z(z_T, T),$$

conditional on survival with $Z(z, t)$ given by (10.20). Let us denote the time-t value by

$$V_f^T(\mathbf{x}, t) = e^{-\mu_f^*(x_f,t,T)} \sum_{j=0}^{\infty} V_f^{(j)}(\mathbf{x}, t, T), \tag{12.32}$$

with the (j) superscript indicating an $\mathcal{O}(\epsilon^j)$ contribution. The leading order contribution is given from our pricing kernel in Theorem 12.1 by

$$\begin{aligned}
e^{-\mu_f^*(x_f,t,T)} V_f^{(0)}(\mathbf{x}, t, T) &= f^T(\mathbf{x}, t) \int_{\mathbb{R}^4} P_f(\zeta) G_0(\mathbf{x}, t; \boldsymbol{\xi}, T) d\boldsymbol{\xi} \\
&= N_f B(t, T) F(T) f^T(\mathbf{x}, t) e^{-k\Lambda_0(0,T)} \int_{\mathbb{R}} \frac{e^{\zeta - \frac{1}{2}\Sigma_{zz}(0,T)}}{\sqrt{\Sigma_{zz}(t, T) + 2K^*(t, T)}} \\
&\qquad N\left(\frac{\zeta + \Delta_{zz}(x_d, x_f, t, T) - z}{\sqrt{\Sigma_{zz}(t, T) + 2K^*(t, T)}} \right) d\zeta \\
&= N_f B(t, T) F(T) e^{z - \frac{1}{2}\Sigma_{zz}(0,t) - k\Lambda_0(0,T) - \mu_f^*(x_f,t,T)}.
\end{aligned} \tag{12.33}$$

The first and second order contributions are obtained by applying the required operators to $V_f^{(0)}(x,t)$

$$V_f^{(1)}(x,t,T) = \left(1 + k\frac{\partial}{\partial z}\right)\int_t^T \left(\overline{\lambda}(t_1) - e^{-B_d^*(t_1,v)\Sigma_{d\lambda}(t,t_1)}\mathcal{M}_1(t,t_1)\right) V_f^{(0)}(x,t)dt_1$$

$$= -V_f^{(0)}(x,t,T)(1+k)\int_t^T \left(e^{-B_d^*(t_1,v)\Sigma_{d\lambda}(t,t_1)+\Delta_{z\lambda}(t,t_1)}\Lambda_1(x_\lambda,t,t_1) - \overline{\lambda}(t_1)\right)dt_1, \tag{12.34}$$

$$V_f^{(2)}(x,t,T) = \left(1 + k\frac{\partial}{\partial z}\right)^2\int_t^T \left(\overline{\lambda}(t_2) - e^{-B_d^*(t_2,v)\Sigma_{d\lambda}(t,t_2)}\mathcal{M}_1(t,t_2)\right)$$

$$\int_t^{t_2} \left(\overline{\lambda}(t_1) - e^{-B_d^*(t_1,v)\Sigma_{d\lambda}(t,t_1)}\mathcal{M}_1(t,t_1)\right) V_f^{(0)}(x,t,T)dt_1 dt_2$$

$$-\left(1 + k\frac{\partial}{\partial z}\right)\int_t^T e^{-B_d^*(t_1,v)\Sigma_{d\lambda}(t,t_1)}\mathcal{M}_2(t,t_1)V_f^{(0)}(x,t,T)dt_1$$

$$= V_f^{(0)}(x,t,T)(1+k)^2\int_t^T \left(e^{-B_d^*(t_2,v)\Sigma_{d\lambda}(t,t_2)+\Delta_{z\lambda}(t,t_2)}\Lambda_1(x_\lambda,t,t_2) - \overline{\lambda}(t_2)\right)$$

$$\int_t^{t_2} \left(e^{-B_d^*(t_1,v)\Sigma_{d\lambda}(t,t_1)+\Delta_{z\lambda}(t,t_1)}\Lambda_1(x_\lambda,t,t_1) - \overline{\lambda}(t_1)\right)dt_1 dt_2$$

$$+ V_f^{(0)}(x,t,T)(1+k)^2\int_t^T e^{-B_d^*(t_2,v)\Sigma_{d\lambda}(t,t_2)+\Delta_{z\lambda}(t,t_2)}\Lambda_1(x_\lambda,t,t_2)$$

$$\int_t^{t_2} e^{-B_d^*(t_1,v)\Sigma_{d\lambda}(t,t_1)+\Delta_{z\lambda}(t,t_1)}\Lambda_1(x_\lambda,t,t_1)\left(e^{\phi_\lambda(t_1,t_2)\Sigma_{\lambda\lambda}(0,t_1)} - 1\right)dt_1 dt_2$$

$$- V_f^{(0)}(x,t,T)(1+k)\int_t^T e^{-B_d^*(t_1,v)\Sigma_{d\lambda}(t,t_1)+\Delta_{z\lambda}(t,t_1)}\Lambda_2(x_\lambda,t,t_1)dt_1. \tag{12.35}$$

We deduce a second order PV representation of

$$PV_f^T \sim N_f B(0,T)F(T)e^{-k\Lambda_0(0,T)}\Bigg(1-(1+k)\int_0^T e^{-B_d^*(t_1,T)\Sigma_{d\lambda}(0,t_1)}\tilde{\lambda}_1(t_1)\left(e^{\Delta_{z\lambda}(0,t_1)}-1\right)dt_1$$

$$+\frac{1}{2}(1+k)^2\left(\int_0^T e^{-B_d^*(t_1,T)\Sigma_{d\lambda}(0,t_1)}\tilde{\lambda}_1(t_1)\left(e^{\Delta_{z\lambda}(0,t_1)}-1\right)dt_1\right)^2$$

$$+(1+k)\int_0^T e^{-B_d^*(t_1,T)\Sigma_{d\lambda}(0,t_1)+\Delta_{z\lambda}(0,t_1)}\left((1+k)\tilde{\lambda}_{2f}(t_1) - \tilde{\lambda}_2(t_1)\right)dt_1\Bigg), \tag{12.36}$$

where we define

$$\tilde{\lambda}_{2f}(t) = \tilde{\lambda}_1(t) \int_0^t e^{-B_d^*(t_1,t)\Sigma_{d\lambda}(0,t_1)+\Delta_{z\lambda}(0,t_1)} \tilde{\lambda}_1(t_1) \left(e^{\phi_\lambda(t_1,t)\Sigma_{\lambda\lambda}(0,t_1)} - 1 \right) dt_1. \tag{12.37}$$

Comparing (12.36) with the corresponding result (10.8) obtained for deterministic rates, it can be seen that the latter result is recovered when all rates correlations are set to zero in the former. It is of interest that all λ-related terms in the covariance matrix $\mathbf{\Sigma}(t, v)$ contribute to this result, although overwhelmingly the most important is $\Sigma_{\lambda z}(t, v)$. Noting as we did in Chapter 10 that the first two lines in brackets in (12.36) can be interpreted as the start of an exponential expansion, we can complete the exponential and infer that, in modulo convexity correction terms, the pricing of the cash flow is as if it were controlled by an effective default intensity $\lambda_{\text{eff}}(t)$ satisfying

$$\int_0^T \lambda_{\text{eff}}(t_1)dt_1 = (1+k) \int_0^T e^{-B_d^*(t_1,T)\Sigma_{d\lambda}(0,t_1)+\Delta_{z\lambda}(0,t_1)} \tilde{\lambda}_1(t_1)dt_1 + \mathcal{O}(\epsilon^2).$$

Differentiating this expression and setting $T = t$ we obtain that

$$\lambda_{\text{eff}}(t) = (1+k) \left(e^{\Delta_{z\lambda}(0,t)} \tilde{\lambda}_1(t) - \int_0^t \phi_d(t_1,t)\Sigma_{d\lambda}(0,t_1) e^{-B_d^*(t_1,t)\Sigma_{d\lambda}(0,t_1)+\Delta_{z\lambda}(0,t_1)} \tilde{\lambda}_1(t_1)dt_1 \right) + \mathcal{O}(\epsilon^2). \tag{12.38}$$

This can be compared with the equivalent, and much simpler, result of $(1+k)e^{\Sigma_{\lambda z}(0,t)} \overline{\lambda}(t)$ obtained in the absence of stochastic rates. As is evident, the way in which the three covariances interact in influencing the effective rate of default is quite intricate, bearing in mind that $\tilde{\lambda}_1(t)$ itself has a non-trivial implicit dependence on $\Sigma_{d\lambda}(0, t)$. Although it would appear that the dependence on the jump k is simpler, this is of course only the case at leading order: consideration of the additional convexity correction term in (12.36) brings in more subtle effects at second order. In particular we note that, in the absence of credit-FX correlation, $\tilde{\lambda}_{2f}(t) \to \tilde{\lambda}_2(t)$ so the term in brackets in (12.36) can be simplified to

$$1 + k(1+k) \int_0^T e^{-B_d^*(t_1,T)\Sigma_{d\lambda}(0,t_1)} \tilde{\lambda}_2(t_1)dt_1,$$

which is notably not monotonic in k.

Foreign Currency Float Leg. It is a straightforward matter to extend the above calculation to provide the price of a risky foreign currency LIBOR float leg. Suppose that this is being priced at a time t_0 which is the start of a payment period. Then we can express the value of the upcoming LIBOR payment as

$$P_1(x, t_0) = 1 - V_f^{t_1}(x, t_0),$$

where the superscript t_1 indicates that the payment is being made at the period end date t_1. Likewise the value of a Libor payment for a future payment period $[t_{i-1}, t_i]$ is given by

$$P_i(\boldsymbol{x}, t_0) = V_f^{t_{i-1}}(\boldsymbol{x}, t_0) - V_f^{t_i}(\boldsymbol{x}, t_0).$$

Summing the value of all such payments up to the nth yields

$$V_{\text{float leg}} = 1 - V_f^{t_n}(\boldsymbol{x}, t_0). \tag{12.39}$$

For pricing as of times t which are in the middle of a payment period, there may be an adjustment required to take account of the accrued LIBOR. The required addition can be viewed as equivalent to an immediate fixed payment of the accrued amount and calculated accordingly, since the LIBOR fixing will already have taken place.

12.3.3 Foreign Currency Notional Protection

Next consider a payoff of N_f at time τ, so that the jump in the FX rate has occurred. This will have from (12.4) a *domestic* currency value of $P_{\text{prot}}(\lim_{t\to\tau^-} z_t, \tau)$ with

$$P_{\text{prot}}(z, \tau) := N_f(1+k)Z(z, \tau),$$

where the factor $1 + k$ captures the impact of the jump at default. The cost of protection on this notional amount up to time T from an observation time of t will be

$$V_{\text{prot}}(\boldsymbol{x}, t) = \int_t^T \int_{\mathbb{R}^4} \lambda(\xi_\lambda, v) P_{\text{prot}}(\zeta, v) G(\boldsymbol{x}, t; \boldsymbol{\xi}, v) d\boldsymbol{\xi} dv. \tag{12.40}$$

Posing

$$V_{\text{prot}}(\boldsymbol{x}, t) \sim V_{\text{prot}}^{(1)}(\boldsymbol{x}, t) + V_{\text{prot}}^{(2)}(\boldsymbol{x}, t) + \mathcal{O}(\epsilon^3) \tag{12.41}$$

and making use of our pricing kernel in Theorem 12.1 and Theorem 3.3, we obtain at first order

$$\begin{aligned} V_{\text{prot}}^{(1)}(\boldsymbol{x}, t) &= \int_t^T \int_{\mathbb{R}^4} \Lambda_1(\xi_\lambda, v, v) P_{\text{prot}}(\zeta, v) f^v(x_d, t) G_0(\boldsymbol{x}, t; \boldsymbol{\xi}, v) d\boldsymbol{\xi} dv \\ &= N_f e^{z - \frac{1}{2}\Sigma_{zz}(0,t)}(1+k) \int_t^T B(t, v) F(v) e^{-k\Lambda_0(0,v) - \mu_f^*(x_f,t,v)} e^{\Sigma_{\lambda z}(t,v) + \theta_\lambda(x_\lambda,t,v)} \tilde{\lambda}_1(v) dv, \end{aligned} \tag{12.42}$$

while at second order

$$\begin{aligned} V_{\text{prot}}^{(2)}(\boldsymbol{x}, t) &= \int_t^T \int_{\mathbb{R}^4} P_{\text{prot}}(\zeta, v) f^v(x_d, t)(\Lambda_2(\xi_\lambda, v, v) G_0(\boldsymbol{x}, t; \boldsymbol{\xi}, v) + \Lambda_1(\xi_\lambda, v, v) G_1(\boldsymbol{x}, t; \boldsymbol{\xi}, v)) d\boldsymbol{\xi} dv \\ &= N_f e^{z - \frac{1}{2}\Sigma_{zz}(0,t)}(1+k) \int_t^T B(t, v) F(v) e^{-k\Lambda_0(0,v)} e^{\Delta_{z\lambda}(t,v) + \theta_\lambda(x_\lambda,t,v)} \left(\tilde{\lambda}_2(v) - (1+k)\tilde{\lambda}_1(v)\right. \\ &\qquad \left. \int_t^v \left(e^{-B_d^*(u,v)\Sigma_{d\lambda}(0,u) + \phi_\lambda(u,v)\Sigma_{\lambda\lambda}(t,u) + \Delta_{z\lambda}(t,u) + \theta_\lambda(x_\lambda,t,u)} \tilde{\lambda}_1(u) - \overline{\lambda}(u)\right) du\right) dv. \end{aligned} \tag{12.43}$$

Setting $t = 0$ and $x = 0$, the resultant PV is, to second order

$$PV_{\text{prot}} \sim N_f(1+k)\int_0^T B(0,v)e^{\Delta_{z\lambda}(0,v)}F(v)e^{-k\Lambda_0(0,v)}\left(\tilde{\lambda}_1(v)+\tilde{\lambda}_2(v)-(1+k)\tilde{\lambda}_{2p}(v)\right)dv, \tag{12.44}$$

where we define

$$\tilde{\lambda}_{2p}(t) := \tilde{\lambda}_1(t)\int_0^t e^{-B_d^*(t_1,t)\Sigma_{d\lambda}(0,t_1)}\tilde{\lambda}_1(t_1)\left(e^{\phi_\lambda(t_1,t)\Sigma_{\lambda\lambda}(0,t_1)+\Delta_{z\lambda}(0,t_1))}-1\right)dt_1. \tag{12.45}$$

We see that the effect of stochastic credit intensity and associated correlations on the credit default risk is captured by replacing $(1+k)\overline{\lambda}(t)$ with an effective credit default intensity of

$$\lambda_{\text{eff}}(t) = (1+k)\left(\tilde{\lambda}_1(t)+\tilde{\lambda}_2(t)-(1+k)\tilde{\lambda}_{2p}(t)\right)e^{\Delta_{z\lambda}(0,t)} + \mathcal{O}(\epsilon^3), \tag{12.46}$$

which is of course different, even at first order in ϵ, from the effective credit default intensity inferred at (12.38) above from considering a risky foreign currency fixed flow. Again the interaction among the correlations is seen to be quite intricate. We suggest that these expressions for effective credit default intensity could be useful in assessing, or making adjustments for, so-called wrong-way risk in counterparty risk calculations without having to resort to time-consuming numerical calculation.

12.4 CCDS ON CROSS-CURRENCY SWAPS REVISITED

We next reconsider the contingent CDS examined in Chapter 10 wherein the buyer pays a regular coupon, either in foreign or domestic currency, and receives protection on the loss at default of a named credit issuer on a cross-currency swap, with fixed coupon payments of c_d on a domestic currency notional of N_d, fixed coupon receipts of c_f on a foreign currency notional of N_f and notional exchange at maturity. The coupon leg pricing for the contingent CDS is exactly analogous to that for a quanto CDS so we focus here only on the protection leg.

Let the payments be synchronised at payment dates T_i, $i = 1, 2, \ldots, M$. We wish to know the value of the swap immediately after default of a referenced credit at time τ. In this case the FX rate will have incurred a jump such that $Z_{\tau^+} = (1+k)Z_\tau$. The value of the swap at time τ^+ can for the purposes of determining the protection payment thus be written $\lim_{t\to\tau^-} V_{\text{ccs}}(x_{d\tau}, z_t, \tau)$, with

$$V_{\text{ccs}}(x_d, z, \tau) = \sum_{i=1}^{M}(c_fN_f(1+k)Z(z,\tau) - c_dN_d)\Delta T_i D(\tau, T_i)f^{T_i}(x_d,\tau)\mathbb{1}_{\tau<T_i}$$
$$+ (N_f(1+k)Z(z,\tau) - N_d)D(\tau, T_M)f^{T_M}(x_d,\tau)\mathbb{1}_{\tau<T_M}. \tag{12.47}$$

Choose $z^*(x_d, \tau)$ to satisfy $V_{ccs}(x_d, z^*(x_d, \tau), \tau) = 0$. Alternatively, if we are interested in the situation where the losses are considered to be collateralised by an amount $C(t)$ denominated in domestic currency, we can consider instead $V_{ccs}(x_d, z^*(x_d, \tau), \tau) = C(\tau)$. The amount of the loss payment due in the event of default will be $\lim_{t\to\tau^-}(V_{ccs}(x_{d\tau}, z_t, \tau) - C(\tau))\mathbb{1}_{z_t>z^*(\tau)}$.

To ascertain the fair price of the protection leg, we must calculate the expected value at time τ of each of the individual payments contingent on the payoff being in the money. It suffices to consider w.l.o.g. fixed domestic and foreign currency payments at time $T_i \leq T_M$. Considering first the former, making use of our leading order pricing kernel, this will be given asymptotically to leading order by

$$V^{(i)}_{prot,d}(x, t) \sim \int_t^{t\vee T_i} f^v(x_d, t)D(v, T_i)\int_{\mathbb{R}^4} \Lambda_1(\xi_\lambda, v, v)\mathbb{1}_{\zeta>z^*(\xi_d,v)}G_0(x, t; \xi, v)d\xi dv. \tag{12.48}$$

The integrations over ξ_λ and ξ_f here are straightforward. The residual double integral over ξ_d and ζ cannot however be carried out analytically. To proceed further we make the assumption that $\| \sigma_d(\cdot) \| = \mathcal{O}(\epsilon_d)$ is small and look to perform an asymptotic expansion of (12.48) in powers of ϵ_d. We expect, as with the asymptotic credit expansion, a first-order approximation should prove adequate for practical purposes. To that end let us perform a Taylor expansion of $z^*(\xi_d, v)$ about $\xi_d = 0$, writing

$$z^*(\xi_d, v) = z_0^*(v) + \xi_d z_1^*(v) + \mathcal{O}(\epsilon_d^2), \tag{12.49}$$

$$z_0^*(v) := z^*(0, v), \tag{12.50}$$

$$z_1^*(v) := \left.\frac{\partial z^*(\xi_d, v)}{\partial \xi_d}\right|_{\xi_d=0}. \tag{12.51}$$

On that basis we can write

$$\begin{aligned}\mathbb{1}_{\zeta>z^*(\xi_d,v)} &\equiv H(\zeta - z^*(\xi_d, v))\\ &\sim H(\zeta - z_0^*(v)) - \xi_d z_1^*(v)\delta(\zeta - z_0^*(v)),\end{aligned} \tag{12.52}$$

with $H(\cdot)$ the Heaviside step function and $\delta(\cdot)$ the Dirac delta function. Substituting back, we conclude

$$\begin{aligned}\int_{\mathbb{R}^4} \Lambda_1(\xi_\lambda, v, v)\mathbb{1}_{\zeta>z^*(\xi_d,v)}G_0(x, t; \xi, v)d\xi &\sim \int_{\mathbb{R}^4} \Lambda_1(\xi_\lambda, v, v)\mathbb{1}_{\zeta>z_0^*(v)}G_0(x, t; \xi, v)d\xi\\ &- z_1^*(v)\iiint_{\mathbb{R}^3} \xi_d\Lambda_1(\xi_\lambda, v, v)G_0(x, t; \xi, v)|_{\zeta=z_0^*(v)}d\xi_d d\xi_\lambda d\xi_f.\end{aligned}$$

The first (quadruple) integral here can be calculated using Theorem 3.5 as

$$B(t, v)\Lambda_1(x_\lambda, t, v)\Phi(d_2(z, t, v))$$

with

$$d_2(z, t, v) := \frac{z - z_0^*(v) + \Delta_{z\lambda}(t, v)}{\sqrt{\Sigma_{zz}(t, v) + 2K^*(t, v)}} \tag{12.53}$$

while the triple integral can be calculated using Theorem 3.4 as

$$B(t,v)\left(x_d + \frac{\Sigma_{d\lambda}(t,v)}{\phi_\lambda(t,v)}\frac{\partial}{\partial x_\lambda}\right)\frac{\Lambda_1(x_\lambda,t,v)N(d_2(z,t,v))}{\sqrt{\Sigma_{zz}(t,v)+2K^*(t,v)}},$$

whence

$$V^{(i)}_{prot,d}(\mathbf{x},t) \sim \int_t^{t\vee T_i} B(t,v)f^v(x_d,t)\Lambda_1(x_\lambda,t,v)D(v,T_i)(\Phi(d_2(z,t,v)) - z_1^*(v)\Psi_2(x_d,z,t,v))dv, \tag{12.54}$$

with $\Phi(\cdot)$ a cumulative Gaussian distribution and

$$\Psi_2(x_d,z,t,v) := (x_d + \Sigma_{d\lambda}(t,v))\frac{N(d_2(z,t,v))}{\sqrt{\Sigma_{zz}(t,v)+2K^*(t,v)}}. \tag{12.55}$$

The corresponding PV is

$$PV^{(i)}_{prot,d} \sim \int_0^{T_i} B(0,v)\tilde{\lambda}_1(v)D(v,T_i)(\Phi(d_2(0,0,v)) - z_1^*(v)\Psi_2(0,0,0,v))dv. \tag{12.56}$$

Considering next a foreign currency payment we obtain

$$V^{(i)}_{prot,f}(\mathbf{x},t) \sim (1+k)\int_t^{t\vee T_i} f^v(x_d,t)D(v,T_i)F(v)e^{-k\Lambda_0(v)} \int_{\mathbb{R}^4}\Lambda_1(\xi_\lambda,v,v)e^{\zeta-\frac{1}{2}\Sigma_{zz}(0,v)}G_0(\mathbf{x},t;\boldsymbol{\xi},v)d\boldsymbol{\xi}dv. \tag{12.57}$$

Continuing as previously we deduce that the quadruple integral in (12.57) can be expressed asymptotically as

$$\int_{\mathbb{R}^4}\Lambda_1(\xi_\lambda,v,v)e^{\zeta-\frac{1}{2}\Sigma_{zz}(0,v)}\mathbb{1}_{\zeta>z_0^*(v)}G_0(\mathbf{x},t;\boldsymbol{\xi},v)d\boldsymbol{\xi} - z_1^*(v)\iiint_{\mathbb{R}^3}\xi_d\Lambda_1(\xi_\lambda,v,v)e^{\zeta-\frac{1}{2}\Sigma_{zz}(0,v)}G_0(\mathbf{x},t;\boldsymbol{\xi},v)|_{\zeta=z_0^*(v)}d\xi_d d\xi_\lambda d\xi_f.$$

The first integral here can be calculated using Theorem 3.5 as

$$B(t,v)\Lambda_1(x_\lambda,t,v)e^{z-\frac{1}{2}\Sigma_{zz}(0,t)+K^*(t,v)-\Delta_{zz}(t,v)+\Delta_{z\lambda}(t,v)}\Phi(d_1(z,t,v))$$

with

$$d_1(z,t,v) = d_2(z+\Sigma_{zz}(t,v)+2K^*(t,v),t,v), \tag{12.58}$$

while the triple integral in the second line can be calculated using Theorem 3.4 as

$$B(t,v)\Lambda_1(x_\lambda,t,v)e^{z-\frac{1}{2}\Sigma_{zz}(0,t)+K^*(t,v)-\Delta_{zz}(t,v)+\Delta_{z\lambda}(t,v)}$$
$$\left(x_d+\Sigma_{d\lambda}(t,v)+\Sigma_{dz}(t,v)\frac{\partial}{\partial z}\right)\frac{N(d_1(z,t,v))}{\sqrt{\Sigma_{zz}(t,v)+2K^*(t,v)}}.$$

We conclude, making use of (11.31) for $\Delta_{zz}(t,v)$, that

$$V^{(i)}_{prot,f}(\boldsymbol{x},t)\sim(1+k)e^{z_t-\frac{1}{2}\Sigma_{zz}(0,t)}\int_t^{t\vee T_i}B(t,v)e^{-\mu_f^*(x_f,t,v)}\Lambda_1(x_\lambda,t,v)$$
$$D(v,T_i)F(v)e^{-k\Lambda_0(v)+\Delta_{z\lambda}(t,v)}$$
$$(\Phi(d_1(z,t,v))-z_1^*(v)\Psi_1(x_d,z,t,v))dv, \quad (12.59)$$

where

$$\Psi_1(x_d,x_\lambda,z,t,v):=\left(x_d+\Sigma_{d\lambda}(t,v)-\frac{d_1(z,t,v)\Sigma_{dz}(t,v)}{\sqrt{\Sigma_{zz}(t,v)+2K^*(t,v)}}\right)\frac{N(d_1(z,t,v))}{\sqrt{\Sigma_{zz}(t,v)+2K^*(t,v)}}. \quad (12.60)$$

The corresponding PV is

$$PV^{(i)}_{prot,f}\sim(1+k)\int_0^{T_i}B(0,v)\tilde{\lambda}_1(v)D(v,T_i)F(v)e^{-k\Lambda_0(v)+\Delta_{z\lambda}(0,v)}$$
$$\times(\Phi(d_1(0,0,v))-z_1^*(v)\Psi_1(0,0,0,v))dv. \quad (12.61)$$

Combining terms we see the PV of the entire protection leg is

$$PV_{prot}\sim\sum_{i=1}^{M}(c_fN_fPV^{(i)}_{prot,f}-c_dN_dPV^{(i)}_{prot,d})\Delta T_i+N_fPV^{(M)}_{prot,f}-N_dPV^{(M)}_{prot,d}. \quad (12.62)$$

Finally, in the event that a (domestic currency) collateral schedule of $C(t)$ is imposed, (12.62) must be augmented by an additional contribution of

$$-\int_0^{T_M}B(0,v)C(v)\tilde{\lambda}_1(v)(\Phi(d_2(0,0,v))-z_1^*(v)\Psi_2(0,0,0,v))dv,$$

with of course $z^*(x_d,t)$ redefined in accordance, as indicated above. Similar expressions can also be obtained for the opposite swap underlying wherein the foreign currency payments are considered to be paid by the protection buyer, making use of the above results and the principle of put–call parity.

CHAPTER 13

Risk-Free Rates

13.1 BACKGROUND

In our discussion hitherto we have assumed that interest rate payments are always based on LIBOR rates, or else swap rates which are derived from forward LIBOR rates and are essentially weighted averages thereof. However, it is by now well known that, in the wake of a number of scandals which came to light in 2012 involving illicit manipulation of LIBOR interest rates, the financial world is in the throes of a major transition away from such term rates, set in advance of the period for which they are applicable, in favour of backward-looking rates which are set daily, with the rates compounded over the period for which interest is to be paid. This helps avoid the possibility that particular LIBOR term rates can be manipulated on a particular day to the advantage of one or more financial institutions.

It also addresses the problem which arose in the wake of the 2007 credit crunch that different tenors of LIBOR had different spread levels reflecting the fact greater counterparty default risk was embedded in loans of longer tenors. We will return to this problem and the strategies which have been proposed to address it in Chapter 14. As explained by Lyashenko and Mercurio [2019]:

> In 2013–2014, the Financial Stability Board (FSB) conducted fundamental reviews of major interest rate benchmarks and recommended developing alternative nearly risk-free rates (RFRs) that are better suited as the reference rates for certain financial transactions. By now, RFRs have been selected in all major economies: The US selected a new Treasuries repo financing rate called SOFR (Secured Overnight Funding Rate); the UK selected the reformed SONIA (Sterling Overnight Index Average); Switzerland selected SARON (Swiss Average Rate Overnight); Japan selected TONA (Tokyo Overnight Average Rate); and the eurozone selected a new unsecured overnight rate called ESTER (Euro Short-Term Rate).

However, the changes proposed have resulted in great disruption across the financial industry as institutions of all types have struggled, in general reluctantly, to make the necessary changes to allow them to trade and manage the risk on financial instruments citing the new compounded rates rather than LIBOR. Henrard [2019] presents a critical perspective, pointing out that there have been problems with a lack of precision in the proposals being put forward resulting in difficulty in progressing discussions; and a lack of measurability resulting in impediments to implementation in practice. A particular headache has been what to do about legacy LIBOR-based trades, some of which have many decades to run. This is as much a legal problem as it is a financial engineering issue. Another challenge has been the need to build discounting curves and forward curves based on the new rates. One advantage of the proposed change is that it dispenses (at least in principle) with the aforementioned problem of multiple, mutually incompatible, forward curves incorporating different tenor-dependent LIBOR spreads over the risk-free rate. The complexity of calculating backward-looking compounded rates and the fact that the payment amount is not known until the end of the compounding period has led to pressure to publish term rates alongside the daily rates, something which looks certain to happen, but without the mechanism having yet been clearly defined. Whether the advantages will outweigh the costs remains to be seen, but the perceived scale of the latter continues for the moment to increase.

We will not discuss here the business of building the new curves, which has been much deliberated on elsewhere. See for example Mercurio [2018] and references therein. Suffice it to say that, once that job has been done, we have essentially risk-free discount factors $D_d(t_1, t_2)$ exactly analogous to those we have used hitherto. The important difference we face is that interest rate derivatives such as caps and swaptions which might be used for hedging financial products mandating payments based on the new compounded rates cannot in some cases be priced using the LIBOR-based formulae we derived above. To address this limitation, it is necessary to extend the models to allow compounded rates to be produced, rather than just the short rate and term rates.

Lyashenko and Mercurio [2019] went on in their seminal paper to set out how the LIBOR market model can be extended to allow it to be used for the pricing of interest rate derivative products where the referenced underlyings may be compounded rates instead of or in addition to term rates. This they do by extending the T_{i-1}-bond numéraire for an extra tenor period up to T_i by investing the proceeds of the bond maturing at T_{i-1} at the daily compounding rate until T_i. Under this extended numéraire, options on compounded rates payments become tractable. They apply their extended model to the pricing of interest rate futures contracts, caps and swaptions.

We look here to perform a similar task, illustrating the analytic pricing of caplets on compounded rates under both the Hull–White short-rate model of Chapter 4 and the Black–Karasinski model of Chapter 5. To this end we must extend the kernels there introduced to provide not just the short rate but also its integral, which is needed in the calculation of compounded rates. Such an extension was first performed for the Hull–White case by Van Steenkiste and Foresi [1999]. A similar extension was carried out by Cuchiero et al. [2019] in their analysis of the Hull–White model in a multi-curve model context. The kernel extension for the Black–Karasinski case, on the other hand, is presented here for the first time.

13.2 HULL–WHITE KERNEL EXTENSION

For our calculations, we make essentially the same modelling assumptions as in Chapter 4 and reuse the notation there introduced. The novel feature here is that, since a daily compounded rate payoff is used, we will look to represent this (to a good approximation) through continuous compounding, whence the payoff for a payment period $[T_1, T_2]$ is

$$e^{\int_{T_1}^{T_2} r_d(x_{dt},t)dt} - 1.$$

Our problem here is that the payoff is not a function of the stochastic variable x_{dt} but of its integral over the payment period. In other words, it is a path-dependent Asian option rather than a European one. To address this we introduce a new integrated variable z_{dt} defined by

$$z_{dt} = \int_0^t (r_d^*(s) + x_{ds})ds, \tag{13.1}$$

in terms of which we can write the payoff using (4.2) as

$$P(z_{dT_1}, z_{dT_2}) = D_d(T_1, T_2)^{-1} e^{z_{dT_2} - z_{dT_1}} - 1. \tag{13.2}$$

We are thus led to consider derivative contracts whose payoff at time T has the general form $P(x_{dT}, z_{dT})$, i.e. may depend on the variable z_d as well as x_d.[1] We write the associated derivative price on this basis as $f(x_d, z_d, t)$. Of course, to address a payoff of the particular form of (13.2), we will need to calculate the derivative price in two stages, in the first instance pricing the payoff as of time T_1, then treating the result as the payoff at time T_1 for a derivative contract priced as of time $t < T_1$, as is standard practice with payoffs involving term rates.

Noting (4.1) and the fact that (13.1) gives rise to $dz_{dt} = (r_d^*(t) + x_{dt})dt$, we infer from the Feynman–Kac theorem that the function $f(x_d, z_d, t)$ emerges as the solution to the following Kolmogorov backward diffusion equation

$$\frac{\partial f}{\partial t} - \alpha_d(t)x_d\frac{\partial f}{\partial x_d} + (r_d^*(t) + x_d)\frac{\partial f}{\partial z_d} + \frac{1}{2}\sigma_d^2(t)\frac{\partial^2 f}{\partial x_d^2} - r_d(x_d, t)f = 0, \quad t \geq 0, \tag{13.3}$$

subject to the final condition $\lim_{t\to T^-} f(x_d, z_d, t) = P(x_d, z_d)$, with $r_d(x_d, t)$ given by (4.3). As can be seen, this equation is a special case of the Hull–White rates-equity pricing equation (7.4), with $\sigma_z(t) \equiv 0$. It follows straightforwardly that the pricing kernel is given, making use of (7.17), by the following:

[1] In fact it is adequate for our purposes to be able to price payoffs of the form $P(x_{dT})$ or $P(z_{dT})$, a fact we shall take advantage of in §13.4 below.

Theorem 13.1 *The pricing kernel for the extended Hull–White pricing equation* (13.3) *is*

$$G(x_d, z_d, t; \xi_d, \zeta_d, v) = D_d(t, v) e^{-\mu_d^*(x_d, t, v)} N_2(\xi_d + I_{dd}^*(t, v) - x_d \phi_d(t, v),$$
$$\zeta + K_{dd}^*(t, v) - \mu_d^*(x_d, t, v) - z; \mathbf{\Sigma}^+(t, v)), \tag{13.4}$$

where we define

$$\mathbf{\Sigma}^+(t, v) := \begin{pmatrix} \Sigma_{dd}(t, v) & I_{dd}^*(t, v) \\ I_{dd}^*(t, v) & 2K_{dd}^*(t, v) \end{pmatrix} \tag{13.5}$$

and other notations are as set out in Chapter 4.

13.3 APPLICATIONS

13.3.1 Compounded Rates Payment

Let us consider the valuation of the payoff (13.2) as of some time $t \in [0, T_1]$. As indicated above, we must first carry out the valuation as of T_1. Applying (13.4), we obtain

$$\begin{aligned} V(x_d, T_1) &= \iint_{\mathbb{R}^2} P(z_d, \zeta_d) G(x_d, z_d, T_1; \xi_d, \zeta_d, T_2) d\xi_d d\zeta_d \\ &= \frac{e^{-\mu_d^*(x_d, T_1, T_2)}}{\sqrt{2K_{dd}^*(T_1, T_2)}} \int_{\mathbb{R}} (e^{\zeta_d - z_d} - D_d(T_1, T_2)) N \left(\frac{\zeta_d + K_{dd}^*(T_1, T_2) - \mu_d^*(x_d, T_1, T_2) - z_d}{\sqrt{2K_{dd}^*(T_1, T_2)}} \right) d\zeta_d \\ &= 1 - F^{T_2}(x_d, T_1). \end{aligned} \tag{13.6}$$

Applying (13.4) again to price (13.6) as of some prior time $t \geq 0$, we obtain straightforwardly

$$V(x_d, t) = F^{T_1}(x_d, t) - F^{T_2}(x_d, t). \tag{13.7}$$

In other words, the value of a backward-looking compounded-rate payment is identical to that of a forward-looking LIBOR-rate payment, as must be the case from the constraint of absence of arbitrage.

13.3.2 Caplet Pricing

Consider next a caplet based on the compounded risk-free rate over a payment period $[T_1, T_2]$ and a payoff with strike K at time T_2 of

$$\begin{aligned} P_{\text{caplet}}(z_1, z_2) &= \left[e^{\int_{T_1}^{T_2} r_d(x_{dt}, t) dt} - 1 - K\delta(T_1, T_2) \right]^+ \\ &= [D_d(T_1, T_2)^{-1} e^{z_2 - z_1} - \kappa^{-1}]^+ \end{aligned} \tag{13.8}$$

where we take $z_1 = z_{dT_1}$, $z_2 = z_{dT_2}$ and $\kappa = (1 + K\delta(T_1, T_2))^{-1}$. Defining the critical value of $z_2 - z_1$ as

$$\Delta z_d^* = \ln(\kappa^{-1} D_d(T_1, T_2)), \tag{13.9}$$

introducing the notation that, for $t \le T_1$

$$\hat{d}_2(x_d, t) := \frac{\Delta z_d^* - \mu_d^*(x_d, t, T_2) + \mu_d^*(x_d, t, T_1) - \frac{1}{2}(B_d^{*2}(T_1, T_2)\Sigma_{dd}(t, T_1) + 2K_{dd}^*(T_1, T_2))}{\sqrt{B_d^{*2}(T_1, T_2)\Sigma_{dd}(t, T_1) + 2K_{dd}^*(T_1, T_2)}}, \tag{13.10}$$

$$\hat{d}_1(x_d, t) := \hat{d}_2(x_d, t) + \sqrt{B_d^{*2}(T_1, T_2)\Sigma_{dd}(t, T_1) + 2K_{dd}^*(T_1, T_2)}, \tag{13.11}$$

and making use of (13.4), the caplet value as of time T_1 will be

$$\begin{aligned} V_{\text{caplet}}(x_d, T_1) &= \iint_{\mathbb{R}^2} P_{\text{caplet}}(z_d, \zeta_d) G(x_d, z_d, T_1; \xi_d, \zeta_d, T_2) d\xi_d d\zeta_d \\ &= \frac{e^{-\mu_d^*(x_d, T_1, T_2)}}{\sqrt{2K_{dd}^*(T_1, T_2)}} \int_{z_d + \Delta z_d^*}^{\infty} (e^{\zeta_d - z_d} - \kappa^{-1} D_d(T_1, T_2)) \\ &\qquad N\left(\frac{\zeta_d + K_{dd}^*(T_1, T_2) - \mu_d^*(x_d, T_1, T_2) - z_d}{\sqrt{2K_{dd}^*(T_1, T_2)}} \right) d\zeta_d \\ &= \Phi(-\hat{d}_2(x_d, T_1)) - \kappa^{-1} F^{T_2}(x_d, T_1) \Phi(-\hat{d}_1(x_d, T_1)), \end{aligned} \tag{13.12}$$

with $F^T(x_d, t)$ the T-maturity Hull–White zero coupon bond price given by (4.15). Taking this price as the payoff at T_1 and valuing as of time t, we obtain, by a process of manipulation similar to that employed in §4.3.3, but using Theorem 3.6 rather than Theorem 3.5

$$\begin{aligned} V_{\text{caplet}}(x_d, t) &= \iint_{\mathbb{R}^2} V_{\text{caplet}}(\xi_d, T_1) G(x_d, z_d, t; \xi_d, \zeta_d, T_1) d\xi_d d\zeta_d \\ &= \frac{F^{T_1}(x_d, t)}{B_d^*(T_1, T_2)\sqrt{\Sigma_{dd}(t, T_1)}} \int_{\mathbb{R}} V_{\text{caplet}}(\xi_d, T_1) N \\ &\quad \left(\frac{\xi_d + I_{dd}^*(t, T_1) - x_d \phi_d(t, T_1)}{B_d^*(T_1, T_2)\sqrt{\Sigma_{dd}(t, T_1)}} \right) d\xi_d \\ &= F^{T_1}(x_d, t)\Phi(-\hat{d}_2(x_d, t)) - \kappa^{-1} F^{T_2}(x_d, t) \Phi(-\hat{d}_1(x_d, t)). \end{aligned} \tag{13.13}$$

Letting $t \to 0$ in (13.13), the resultant expression for the PV is

$$PV_{\text{caplet}} = D_d(0, T_1)\Phi(-d_2) - \kappa^{-1} D_d(0, T_2)\Phi(-d_1), \tag{13.14}$$

where

$$d_2 = \frac{\Delta z_d^* - \frac{1}{2}(B_d^{*2}(T_1, T_2)\Sigma_{dd}(0, T_1) + 2K_{dd}^*(T_1, T_2))}{\sqrt{B_d^{*2}(T_1, T_2)\Sigma_{dd}(0, T_1) + 2K_{dd}^*(T_1, T_2)}}, \tag{13.15}$$

$$d_1 = d_2 + \sqrt{B_d^{*2}(T_1, T_2)\Sigma_{dd}(0, T_1) + 2K_{dd}^*(T_1, T_2)}. \tag{13.16}$$

Comparing the above with the well known Hull–White result derived in §4.3.3, we see the difference resulting from using compounded rates is only in the appearance of the variance adjustment $2K_{dd}^*(T_1, T_2)$, and the consequent adjustment to x_d^* which is required. Indeed it can be seen that, letting $K_{dd}^*(T_1, T_2) \to 0$ (for example by specifying $\sigma_d(t) = 0$ for $t \in [T_1, T_2]$), the standard result of (4.30) is recovered. The main impact of the adjustment is to increase the caplet value by a small proportionate amount, as can be straightforwardly seen by differentiating the result with respect to $K_{dd}^*(T_1, T_2)$.

Similarly we find the floorlet price to be

$$V_{\text{floorlet}}(x_d, t) = \kappa^{-1} F^{T_2}(x_d, t)\Phi(\hat{d}_1(x_d, t)) - F^{T_1}(x_d, t)\Phi(\hat{d}_2(x_d, t)). \tag{13.17}$$

By put–call parity, this will be slightly higher than the standard Hull–White result of (4.31).

The result (13.12) was previously presented as Theorem 4 of Henrard [2004] for the special case when $x_d = 0$ and $\sigma_d(t) = \sigma$ (constant), whereupon we have $K_{dd}^*(t, T) = \frac{1}{2}\sigma^2 \int_t^T B_d^{*2}(t, u)du$. Note that our $B_d^*(t, u)$ is $v(t, u)$ in his notation.

Daily Compounding. A word should also be said about the adequacy of our approximate representation of the daily compounding conventions of SONIA, SOFR, etc. by continuous compounding. Effectively, the use of daily compounding means that the rate for each day is set at the beginning of that day rather than at the end, based on rates putatively realised during the day. This may sound like a trivial distinction and the difference would not be be expected to be too great. In fact, it is not difficult to calculate by iterative application of the Hull–White pricing kernel of Chapter 4 the exact value for daily compounding rates. This problem was previously considered by Henrard [2007] from within a HJM framework, the result for PV being presented as his Theorem 1.

Suppose then that the daily compounding dates are $t_0, t_1, \ldots, t_{n-1}$, with $t_0 = T_1$ and $t_n = T_2$. Recursive application of (4.6) reveals that the caplet price is given again by (13.13), but with $K_{dd}^*(T_1, T_2)$ replaced by

$$K_{dd}^*(T_1, T_2) \to \frac{1}{2}\sum_{i=0}^{n-1}(B_d^{*2}(t_i, t_n) - B_d^{*2}(t_i, t_{n-1}))\Sigma_{dd}(t_{i-1}, t_i). \tag{13.18}$$

The above daily compounding result is a close approximation to $K_{dd}^*(T_1, T_2)$ and is effectively a (zero order) numerical quadrature formula for this quantity. The differences between the two formulae will be $= \mathcal{O}((T_2 - T_1)/n)$ as $n \to \infty$. Since $K_{dd}^*(T_1, T_2)$

is in any event expected to be small, the two approaches can for practical purposes be treated as interchangeable.

13.3.3 European Swaption Pricing

The calculation for European swaption prices for compounded rates likewise follows closely the derivation in §4.3.4. We reuse the notation there introduced. The exercise value of the swaption will then be the positive part of the time-t_0 value of the swap underlying, with $t_0 < T_0$. For a payer swaption, making use of (13.7), this will be

$$P_{\text{payer}}(x_d) = \sum_{i=1}^{n} [F^{T_{i-1}}(x_d, t_0) - \kappa^{-1} F^{T_i}(x_d, t_0)] \mathbb{1}_{x_d > x_d^*}, \tag{13.19}$$

with x_d^* now denoting the value of x_d at which the swap underlying comes into the money. But this is identical to the expression appearing in the Hull–White derivation in §4.3.4. Consequently the results for European swaption prices are identical to those there derived, namely (4.33) and (4.34). The same point was made in relation to the LIBOR market model by Lyashenko and Mercurio [2019].

13.3.4 Average Rate Options

It has been proposed that, as well as options on compounded rates, there may also be interest following the LIBOR transition in trading swaps based on average daily rates; in other words, where the payoff rather than (13.2) is effectively given under the same approximation as previously by

$$P_{\text{ave}}(z_{dT_1}, z_{dT_2}) = -\ln D_d(T_1, T_2) + z_{dT_2} - z_{dT_1}. \tag{13.20}$$

In particular, bank interest on loan and deposit accounts is often calculated in this way. The corresponding caplet payoff at T_2 is therefore

$$P_{\text{caplet}}(z_{dT_1}, z_{dT_2}) = \left[z_{dT_2} - z_{dT_1} + \int_{T_1}^{T_2} \bar{r}(t_1) dt_1 - K\delta(T_1, T_2) \right]^+, \tag{13.21}$$

whence the critical value of $z_{dT_2} - z_{dT_1}$ is instead given by

$$\Delta z_d^* = K\delta(T_1, T_2) - \int_{T_1}^{T_2} \bar{r}(t_1) dt_1. \tag{13.22}$$

Applying our pricing kernel (13.4) to price this payoff as of time T_1 yields, via a calculation analogous to that for the Bachelier option pricing formula

$$V_{\text{caplet}}(x_d, T_1) = D_d(T_1, T_2) e^{-\mu_d^*(x_d, T_1, T_2)} \sqrt{2K_{dd}^*(T_1, T_2)}$$
$$(N(-\tilde{d}(x_d, T_1)) - \tilde{d}(x_d, T_1)\Phi(-\tilde{d}(x_d, T_1)))$$

where, for $t \leq T_1$, we define

$$\tilde{d}(x_d, t) := \frac{\Delta z_d^* - \mu_d^*(x_d, t, T_2) + \mu_d^*(x_d, t, T_1) - K_{dd}^*(T_1, T_2)}{\sqrt{B_d^{*2}(T_1, T_2)\Sigma_{dd}(t, T_1) + 2K_{dd}^*(T_1, T_2)}}. \tag{13.23}$$

Further pricing as of $t < T_1$, we obtain

$$V_{\text{caplet}}(x_d, t) = D_d(t, T_2)e^{-\mu_d^*(x_d, t, T_2)}\sqrt{B_d^{*2}(T_1, T_2)\Sigma_{dd}(t, T_1) + 2K_{dd}^*(T_1, T_2)}$$
$$(N(-\tilde{d}(x_d, t)) - \tilde{d}(x_d, t)\Phi(-\tilde{d}(x_d, t))), \tag{13.24}$$

with consequent PV

$$PV_{\text{caplet}} = D_d(0, T_2)\sqrt{B_d^{*2}(T_1, T_2)\Sigma_{dd}(0, T_1) + 2K_{dd}^*(T_1, T_2)}(N(-d_0) - d_0\Phi(-d_0)), \tag{13.25}$$

where

$$d_0 := \frac{\Delta z_d^* - K_{dd}^*(T_1, T_2)}{\sqrt{B_d^{*2}(T_1, T_2)\Sigma_{dd}(0, T_1) + 2K_{dd}^*(T_1, T_2)}}.$$

The quantity $2K_{dd}^*(T_1, T_2)$ clearly plays an analogous role here as in the compounded interest rate case.

13.4 BLACK–KARASINSKI KERNEL EXTENSION

The corresponding calculation for the Black–Karasinski short-rate model is similar. Our starting point and notations are as given in Chapter 5. In this case we define the auxiliary co-ordinate to be

$$z_{dt} = \int_0^t \left(\tilde{r}(s)e^{x_{ds} - \frac{1}{2}\Sigma_{dd}(0,s)} - \overline{r}_d(s)\right) ds. \tag{13.26}$$

The corresponding pricing equation for a derivative contract with price $f(x_d, z_d, t)$ is

$$\frac{\partial f}{\partial t} - \alpha_d(t)x_d\frac{\partial f}{\partial x_d} + \left(\tilde{r}(t)e^{x_{dt} - \frac{1}{2}\Sigma_{dd}(0,t)} - \overline{r}_d(t)\right)\frac{\partial f}{\partial z_d}$$
$$+ \frac{1}{2}\sigma_d^2(t)\frac{\partial^2 f}{\partial x_d^2} - \tilde{r}(t)e^{x_{dt} - \frac{1}{2}\Sigma_{dd}(0,t)}f = 0, \quad t \geq 0. \tag{13.27}$$

As can be seen this equation is a special case of the Black–Karasinski credit-equity pricing equation (9.10), with $\sigma_z(\cdot) \equiv \overline{r}_d(\cdot) \equiv 0$, $k = -1$ and the credit intensity being interpreted as an instantaneous interest rate. It follows straightforwardly that the pricing kernel is given by the following:

Theorem 13.2 *The pricing kernel for the extended Black–Karasinski pricing equation (13.27) can be written asymptotically for* $\| \bar{r}_d(\cdot) \| = \mathcal{O}(\epsilon)$ *as*

$$G(x_d, z_d, t; \xi_d, \zeta_d, v) = D_d(t, v) \sum_{j=0}^{\infty} G_j(x_d, z_d, t; \xi_d, \zeta_d, v), \tag{13.28}$$

with $\| G_j(\cdot; \cdot) \| = \mathcal{O}(\epsilon^j)$

$$G_0(x_d, z_d, t; \xi_d, \zeta_d, v) = \frac{1}{\sqrt{\Sigma_{dd}(t, v)}} N\left(\frac{\xi_d - \phi_d(t, v) x_d}{\sqrt{\Sigma_{dd}(t, v)}} \right) \delta(\zeta_d - z_d), \tag{13.29}$$

$$\begin{aligned} G_1(x_d, z_d, t; \xi_d, \zeta_d, v) &= Z_0(t, v)(1 - \partial_z) G_0(x_d, z_d, t; \xi_d, \zeta_d, v) \\ &\quad - \int_t^v \bar{r}_d(t_1) e^{\theta_d(x_d, t, t_1)} (1 - \partial_z) G_0(x_d, z_d, t; \xi_d - \Sigma_{dd}(t, t_1), \zeta_d, v) dt_1, \end{aligned} \tag{13.30}$$

and

$$\begin{aligned} G_2(x_d, z_d, t; \xi_d, \zeta_d, v) &= \frac{1}{2} Z_0^2(t, v)(1 - \partial_z)^2 G_0(x_d, z_d, t; \xi_d, \zeta_d, v) \\ &\quad - \int_t^v (Z_0(t, v) \bar{r}_d(t_1)(1 - \partial_z) + \bar{r}_2(t_1)) e^{\theta_d(x_d, t, t_1)} (1 - \partial_z) \\ &\qquad G_0(x_d, z_d, t; \xi_d - \Sigma_{dd}(t, t_1), \zeta_d, v) dt_1 \\ &\quad + \int_t^v \bar{r}_d(t_2) e^{\theta_d(x_d, t, t_2)} \int_t^{t_2} \bar{r}_d(t_1) e^{\theta_d(x_d, t, t_1) + \phi_d(t_1, t_2) \Sigma_{dd}(t, t_1)} (1 - \partial_z)^2 \\ &\qquad G_0\left(x_d, z_d, t; \xi_d - \sum_{i=1}^{2} \Sigma_{dd}(t, t_i), \zeta_d, v \right) dt_1 dt_2, \end{aligned} \tag{13.31}$$

where $\delta(\cdot)$ *is the Dirac delta function, we define*

$$Z_0(t, v) = \int_t^v \bar{r}_d(s) ds \tag{13.32}$$

and other notations are as set out in Chapter 5.

13.5 APPLICATIONS

13.5.1 Compounded Rates Payment

As a consistency check we consider, as for the Hull–White case, the valuation of the payoff (13.2) as of some time $t \in [0, T_1]$. As indicated above, we must first carry out the valuation as of T_1. We obtain, making use of our second-order accurate representation of $G(\cdot)$ from Theorem 13.2 and integration by parts

$$\begin{aligned} V(x_d, T_1) &= \iint_{\mathbb{R}^2} P(z_d, \zeta_d) G(x_d, z_d, T_1; \xi_d, \zeta_d, T_2) d\xi_d d\zeta_d \\ &\sim 1 - D_d(T_1, T_2) - F_1^{T_2}(x_d, T_1) - F_2^{T_2}(x_d, T_1). \end{aligned} \tag{13.33}$$

This is equivalent to a second order representation of (13.6). Applying our pricing kernel once more to value this as of time $t < T_1$, we obtain, exactly as in Chapter 5

$$V(x_d, t) \sim D_d(t, T_1) + F_1^{T_1}(x_d, t) + F_2^{T_1}(x_d, t) - D_d(t, T_2) - F_1^{T_2}(x_d, t) - F_2^{T_2}(x_d, t), \tag{13.34}$$

which is equivalent to a second order representation of (13.7). So in the Black–Karasinski case too, compounded-rate and LIBOR-rate payments have identical expected values.

13.5.2 Caplet Pricing

We consider next the pricing of a caplet with payoff given by (13.8). We will look to price this to second order accuracy. In the first instance we value the payoff as of time T_1, making use of a second-order accurate representation of the pricing kernel. The calculation is a little intricate but results in the following.

Theorem 13.3 *For a Black–Karasinski short rate process governed by* (5.1), *the PV of a caplet with a compounded rate underlying, strike K and payment period* $[T_1, T_2]$ *is given to a good approximation by*

$$PV_{caplet} \sim PV^{(0)}_{caplet} + \Delta PV_{caplet}, \tag{13.35}$$

where

$$\begin{aligned} PV^{(0)}_{caplet} &= (D_d(0, T_1) - \kappa^{-1} D_d(0, T_2)) \Phi(-d_1(x_d^*, 0, T_1)) \\ &\quad - D_d(0, T_1) \int_0^{T_1} \bar{r}_d(t_1)(\Phi(-d_2(x_d^*, 0, T_1, t_1)) - \Phi(-d_1(x_d^*, 0, T_1))) dt_1 \\ &\quad + \kappa^{-1} D_d(0, T_2) \int_0^{T_2} \bar{r}_d(t_1)(\Phi(-d_2(x_d^*, 0, T_1, t_1)) - \Phi(-d_1(x_d^*, 0, T_1))) dt_1 \\ &\quad - \kappa^{-1} D_d(0, T_2) \int_{T_1}^{T_2} \bar{r}_d(t_2) \int_0^{t_2} \bar{r}_d(t_1) e^{\phi_d(t_1, t_2)\Sigma_{dd}(0, t_1)} (\Phi(-d_2^*(x_d^*, 0, T_1, t_1, t_2)) \\ &\quad - \Phi(-d_2(x_d^*, 0, T_1, t_1))) dt_1 dt_2 \\ &\quad + \kappa^{-1} D_d(0, T_2) \int_{T_1}^{T_2} \bar{r}_d(t_2) \int_0^{t_2} \bar{r}_d(t_1)(\Phi(-d_1^*(x_d^*, 0, T_1, t_1, t_2)) \end{aligned}$$

$$- \Phi(-d_2(x_d^*, 0, T_1, t_2)) + \Phi(-d_2(x_d^*, 0, T_1, t_1)) - \Phi(-d_1(x_d^*, 0, T_1)))dt_1 dt_2. \tag{13.36}$$

with x_d^* defined as in §5.3.2, the $d_i(\cdot,\cdot,\cdot)$ redefined from §5.3.2 as

$$d_1(\xi_d, t, T_1) := \frac{\xi_d + K^*(T_1, T_2)}{\sqrt{\Sigma_{dd}(t, T_1) + 2K^*(T_1, T_2)}}, \tag{13.37}$$

$$d_2(\xi_d, t, T_1, w) := d_1(\xi_d - \phi_d(T_1 \wedge w, T_1 \vee w)\Sigma_{dd}(t, T_1 \wedge w) - 2K^*(T_1, T_2), t, T_1) \tag{13.38}$$

$$K^*(T_1, T_2) := \int_{T_1}^{T_2} \bar{r}_d(t_2) \int_{T_1}^{t_2} \bar{r}_d(t_1) e^{\Delta x_d^*(T_1, t_1, t_2)} (e^{\phi_d(t_1, t_2)\Sigma_{dd}(T_1, t_1)} - 1) dt_1 dt_2, \tag{13.39}$$

$$\Delta x_d^*(T_1, t_1, t_2) := \phi_d(T_1, t_1)\phi_d(T_1, t_2)\Sigma_{dd}(0, T_1), \tag{13.40}$$

and ΔPV_{caplet} given by (13.54) below. The errors in the first term of (13.35) are $\mathcal{O}(\epsilon^2)$ with $\epsilon = \| \tilde{r}(\cdot) \|$ and those in the second term are $\mathcal{O}(\Sigma_{dd}^2(T_1, T_2))$.

Proof: As in the Hull–White case above we have

$$V_{\text{caplet}}(x_d, T_1) = \int_{z_d + \Delta z_d^*}^{\infty} \int_{\infty}^{\infty} P_{\text{caplet}}(z_d, \zeta_d) G(x_d, z_d, T_1; \xi_d, \zeta_d, T_2) d\xi_d d\zeta_d \tag{13.41}$$

with Δz_d^* satisfying (13.9). Rather than working with the form of $G(\cdot)$ derived above, it turns out that a more convenient way of deriving the caplet result is to work with an exact expression analogous to that presented in §5.6. A calculation similar to the one presented there leads to

$$\begin{aligned} G(x_d, z_d, t; \xi_d, \zeta_d, v) &= D_d(t, v) e^{-F_1(x_d, t, v)(1 - \partial_{z_d})} G_0(x_d, z_d, t; \xi_d, \zeta_d, v) \\ &+ D_d(t, v) \sum_{n=1}^{\infty} (-1)^n (1 - \partial_{z_d})^n \int_t^v \int_t^{t_n} \cdots \int_t^{t_2} \\ &\left(\prod_{i=1}^{n} (R(x_d, t, t_i)\mathcal{M}(t, t_i) - \bar{r}_d(t_i)) \right. \\ &\left. - \prod_{i=1}^{n} (R(x_d, t, t_i) - \bar{r}_d(t_i)) \right) dt_1 \ldots dt_{n-1} dt_n G_0(x_d, z_d, t; \xi_d, \zeta_d, v), \end{aligned} \tag{13.42}$$

where the operator $\mathcal{M}(t, t_1)$ is interpreted as in (5.10) and we define, in the above and for later use

$$F_1(x_d, T_1, T_2) := \int_{T_1}^{T_2} (R(x_d, T_1, t_1) - \bar{r}_d(t_1)) dt_1, \tag{13.43}$$

$$F_2(x_d, T_1, T_2) := \int_{T_1}^{T_2} R(x_d, T_1, t_2) \int_{T_1}^{t_2} R(x_d, T_1, t_1)(e^{\phi_d(t_1,t_2)\Sigma_{dd}(T_1,t_1)} - 1)dt_1 dt_2. \tag{13.44}$$

In applying (13.42) to calculate the T_1-price of the payoff at T_2, since the payoff is independent of x_d, we require only the marginal distribution w.r.t. z_d. To that end we observe

$$\begin{aligned}
&\int_{\mathbb{R}} G(x_d, z_d, T_1; \xi_d, \zeta_d, T_2) d\xi_d \\
&\quad = D_d(T_1, T_2)(e^{-F_1(x_d,T_1,T_2)(1-\partial_{z_d})} + F_2(x_d, T_1, T_2)(1 - \partial_{z_d})^2 + \mathcal{O}(\epsilon^3)) \\
&\qquad \int_{\mathbb{R}} G_0(x_d, z_d, T_1; \xi_d, \zeta_d, T_2) d\xi_d \\
&\quad = D_d(T_1, T_2) e^{-F_1(x_d,T_1,T_2)(1-\partial_{z_d}) + F_2(x_d,T_1,T_2)(1-\partial_{z_d})^2} \\
&\qquad \int_{\mathbb{R}} G_0(x_d, z_d, T_1; \xi_d, \zeta_d, T_2) d\xi_d + \mathcal{O}(\epsilon^3) \\
&\quad = F^{T_2}(x_d, T_1) e^{F_2(x_d,T_1,T_2)\partial^2_{z_d}} \\
&\qquad \int_{\mathbb{R}} G_0(x_d, z_d + F_1(x_d, T_1, T_2) - 2F_2(x_d, T_1, T_2), T_1; \xi_d, \zeta_d, T_2) d\xi_d + \mathcal{O}(\epsilon^3).
\end{aligned} \tag{13.45}$$

to obtain

$$V_{\text{caplet}}(x_d, T_1) = \Phi(-\tilde{d}_2(x_d, T_1, T_2)) - \kappa^{-1} F^{T_2}(x_d, T_1) \Phi(-\tilde{d}_1(x_d, T_1, T_2)), \tag{13.46}$$

where we have made use as previously of the fact that exponentials of first and second derivatives acting on a Gaussian distribution function serve to shift the first and second moments respectively and we define

$$\tilde{d}_1(x_d, T_1, T_2) := \frac{x_d^* - x_d - F_2(x_d, T_1, T_2)}{\sqrt{2F_2(x_d, T_1, T_2)}}, \tag{13.47}$$

$$\tilde{d}_2(x_d, T_1, T_2) := \tilde{d}_1(x_d, T_1, T_2) + \sqrt{2F_2(x_d, T_1, T_2)}, \tag{13.48}$$

with x_d^* defined as in §5.3.2. Note that we can, if wished, replace $R(\cdot)$ with $R_1(\cdot)$ in the expression for $F_2(x_d, T_1, T_2)$ while retaining second order accuracy, and will indeed do so below.

Our work is complicated at this point compared to the corresponding Hull–White calculation by the fact that the convexity adjustment factor $F_2(\cdot)$ associated with the compounding period is not constant but depends on x_d. We seek to render the situation analytically tractable by freezing this in (13.47) and (13.48) at the representative value $K^*(T_1, T_2)$ defined in (13.39) above, denoting the resulting expressions

$$\bar{d}_1(x_d, T_1, T_2) := \frac{x_d^* - x_d - K^*(T_1, T_2)}{\sqrt{2K^*(T_1, T_2)}}, \tag{13.49}$$

$$\bar{d}_2(x_d, T_1, T_2) := \bar{d}_1(x_d, T_1, T_2) + \sqrt{2K^*(T_1, T_2)}, \tag{13.50}$$

respectively. We then seek to correct for the replacement via a Taylor expansion w.r.t. the z-variance. We find

$$\begin{aligned} V_{\text{caplet}}(x_d, T_1) \sim\ & \Phi(-\bar{d}_2(x_d, T_1, T_2)) - \kappa^{-1} F^{T_2}(x_d, T_1)\Phi(-\bar{d}_1(x_d, T_1, T_2)) \\ & - \frac{F_2(x_d, T_1, T_2) - K^*(T_1, T_2)}{2K^*(T_1, T_2)} (\bar{d}_1(x_d, T_1, T_2) N(-\bar{d}_2(x_d, T_1, T_2)) \\ & + \kappa^{-1} D_d(T_1, T_2)\bar{d}_2(x_d, T_1, T_2) N(-\bar{d}_1(x_d, T_1, T_2))) \\ \sim\ & \Phi(-\bar{d}_2(x_d, T_1, T_2)) - \kappa^{-1} F^{T_2}(x_d, T_1)\Phi(-\bar{d}_1(x_d, T_1, T_2)) \\ & + \frac{F_2(x_d, T_1, T_2) - K^*(T_1, T_2)}{K^*(T_1, T_2)} \frac{x_d - x_d^*}{\sqrt{2K^*(T_1, T_2)}} N(-\bar{d}_2(x_d, T_1, T_2)), \end{aligned} \tag{13.51}$$

where we have used the fact that $N(-\bar{d}_2) = \kappa^{-1} D_d(T_1, T_2) N(-\bar{d}_1)$ and taken the opportunity to replace $F^{T_2}(x_d, T_1)$ consistently with its leading order approximation in the final line.[2]

The further calculation necessary to obtain the time-t value is analogous to that set out in §5.3.2. Indeed, the first line of (13.51) gives a result which is essentially identical. Specifically, we obtain

$$\begin{aligned} V^{(0)}_{\text{caplet}}(x_d, t) =\ & (D_d(t, T_1) - \kappa^{-1} D_d(t, T_2))\Phi(-d_1(x_d^* - \phi_d(t, T_1)x_d, t, T_1)) \\ & - D_d(t, T_1) \int_t^{T_1} (R_1(x_d, t, t_1)\Phi(-d_2(x_d^* - \phi_d(t, T_1)x_d, t, T_1, t_1)) \\ & \qquad - \bar{r}_d(t_1)\Phi(-d(x_d^* - \phi_d(t, T_1)x_d, t, T_1)))dt_1 \\ & + \kappa^{-1} D_d(t, T_2) \int_t^{T_2} (R_1(x_d, t, t_1)\Phi(-d_2(x_d^* - \phi_d(t, T_1)x_d, t, T_1, t_1)) \\ & \qquad - \bar{r}_d(t_1)\Phi(-d_1(x_d^* - \phi_d(t, T_1)x_d, t, T_1)))dt_1 \end{aligned}$$

---

[2]The appropriateness of using a first-order Taylor expansion here relies effectively on an assumption that $\Sigma^2_{dd}(T_1, T_2) \ll 1$. We estimate this is likely to be satisfied in most cases of practical interest to within a relative error margin of less than 1%.

$$
\begin{aligned}
&- \kappa^{-1} D_d(t, T_2) \int_{T_1}^{T_2} R_1(x_d, t, t_2) \int_t^{t_2} \\
&\qquad (e^{\phi_d(t_1,t_2)\Sigma_{dd}(t,t_1)} R_1(x_d, t, t_1)\Phi(-d_2^*(x_d^* - \phi_d(t, T_1)x_d, t, T_1, t_1, t_2)) \\
&\qquad\qquad - \bar{r}_d(t_1)\Phi(-d_1^*(x_d^* - \phi_d(t, T_1)x_d, t, T_1, t_1, t_2)))dt_1 dt_2 \\
&+ \kappa^{-1} D_d(t, T_2) \int_{T_1}^{T_2} R_1(x_d, t, t_2) \int_t^{t_2} \\
&\qquad (R_1(x_d, t, t_1)\Phi(-d_2(x_d^* - \phi_d(t, T_1)x_d, t, T_1, t_1)) \\
&\qquad\qquad - \bar{r}_d(t_1)\Phi(-d_1(x_d^* - \phi_d(t, T_1)x_d, t, T_1)))dt_1 dt_2 \\
&+ \kappa^{-1} D_d(t, T_2) \int_{T_1}^{T_2} R_2(x_d, t, t_1)\Phi(-d_2(x_d^* - \phi_d(t, T_1)x_d, t, T_1, t_1))dt_1.
\end{aligned} \tag{13.52}
$$

Note that the definitions (5.25) and (5.26) of $d_1^*(\cdot)$ and $d_2^*(\cdot)$ need to be reinterpreted as referring to the new definitions of $d_1(\cdot)$ and $d_2(\cdot)$ above. Setting $x_d = t = 0$ in this expression gives rise to (13.36). Denoting the remaining term in (13.51)

$$
\Delta V_{\text{caplet}}(x_d, T_1) := \left(\frac{F_2(x_d, T_1, T_2)}{K^*(T_1, T_2)} - 1 \right) \frac{x_d - x_d^*}{\sqrt{2K^*(T_1, T_2)}} N(-\bar{d}_2(x_d, T_1, T_2)) \tag{13.53}
$$

and carrying out the required calculation, making use of (4.39), we obtain for the value at $t = 0$

$$
\begin{aligned}
\Delta PV_{\text{caplet}} &= D_d(0, T_1) \iint_{\mathbb{R}^2} G_0(0, 0, 0; \xi_d, \zeta_d, T_1)\Delta V_{\text{caplet}}(\xi_d, T_1) d\zeta_d d\xi_d \\
&= \frac{D_d(0, T_1)}{\sqrt{\Sigma_{dd}(0, T_1)}} \int_{\mathbb{R}} N\left(\frac{\xi_d}{\sqrt{\Sigma_{dd}(0, T_1)}} \right) \left(\frac{F_2(\xi_d, T_1, T_2)}{K^*(T_1, T_2)} - 1 \right) \frac{\xi_d - x_d^*}{\sqrt{2K^*(T_1, T_2)}} \\
&\qquad N(-\bar{d}_2(\xi_d, T_1, T_2)) d\xi_d \\
&= \frac{D_d(0, T_1)}{K^*(T_1, T_2)} \int_{T_1}^{T_2} \bar{r}_d(t_2) \int_{T_1}^{t_2} \bar{r}_d(t_1) e^{\Delta x_d^*(T_1, t_1, t_2)} (e^{\phi_d(t_1, t_2)\Sigma_{dd}(T_1, t_1)} - 1) \\
&\qquad (N(-d_2(x_d^* - \Delta x_d^*(T_1, t_1, t_2), 0, T_1)) - N(-d_2(x_d^*, 0, T_1)))dt_1 dt_2.
\end{aligned} \tag{13.54}
$$

This completes the proof.

Note the close relationship between the role played by our $K^*(T_1, T_2)$ and that of the analogous quantity $K_{dd}^*(T_1, T_2)$ which arose in the Hull–White case, specifying the additional variance which arises through the impact of stochastic effects during the compounding period. Unlike in that case, however, there is a further contribution

$\Delta PV_{\text{caplet}}$ to the caplet PV. This is a consequence of the fact that the Black–Karasinski short rate volatility scales in proportion to the stochastic rate, rendering the volatility impact occurring during the compounding period dependent on the evolution of the rate in the prior period. We infer from the form of (13.54) that this will be such as to increase the option value when x_d^* is large and positive (out-of-the money caplets and in-the-money floorlets) since the rate will be high when x_d is close to x_d^*, and *vice versa* when x_d^* is large and negative.

13.6 A NOTE ON TERM RATES

It has been suggested that, in addition to compounded risk-free rates, there will be a need, when LIBOR rates are deprecated, for a "term rate" whose value is fixed at the start of the compounding period at the implied forward value observed in the market. Since this term rate behaves by assumption exactly like a LIBOR rate, caplets can be priced, like European swaptions on compounded rates, using the standard formulae for LIBOR underlyings, both for the Hull–White and for the Black–Karasinski cases. So the above formulae should be considered applicable only for cases where the payoff is explicitly on a compounded rate underlying, not a term rate based thereon.

CHAPTER 14

Multi-Curve Framework

14.1 BACKGROUND

In our discussion hitherto we have based our calculations on the assumption that, for any given currency there is a single yield curve which can be used for the purpose both of calculating discount factors (the discounting curve) and of fixing LIBOR rates (the forward curve). As is well known, this is only true to a first approximation in current markets: since the credit crunch which began in 2007, longer-term LIBOR rates have been trading at a premium over shorter-term rates, reflecting the credit risk associated with the term of the loan/investment with which the LIBOR payment is associated. As observed by Mercurio [2010]:

> When August 2007 arrived, the market had to face an unprecedented scenario. Interest rates that until then had been almost equivalent, suddenly became unrelated, with the degree of incompatibility that worsened as time passed by. For instance, the forward rate implied by two deposits, the corresponding FRA rate and the forward rate implied by the corresponding OIS rates became substantially different, and started to be quoted with large, non-negligible spreads.

Consequently, practitioners typically build a "risk-free" discounting curve from OIS (daily compounded overnight) rates, or swaps based thereon. For each LIBOR tenor for which forward rates need to be produced in the course of a calculation, a separate curve is built with reference to market instruments (swaps, futures and/or forward rate agreements) citing LIBOR rates of that tenor. A spread can then be defined for each LIBOR tenor as the difference between the short rate inferred from the LIBOR curve of that tenor and the corresponding value inferred from the risk-free (OIS) curve. For more details on the process of building multiple, mutually consistent LIBOR curves, the reader is referred to the excellent review by Fernando and Bianchetti [2013]. We will assume here that Libor and risk-free curves are known for a given date and on that basis the spread of forward Libor rates over their risk-free alternatives. We will be interested in modelling the co-evolution of a single LIBOR rate and its spread under the assumption that both are stochastic and potentially correlated. Let us denote the risk-free short rate by r_{dt}, and the value per unit notional of a tenor-τ LIBOR payment for the period $[T_1, T_2]$ at time T_2 by $L^{\tau}(T_1, T_2)$. Then, approximating the daily compounding by continuous compounding as in the previous chapter, we have that the value of an OIS compounded risk-free rate payment will be given by

$$L^0(T_1, T_2) = e^{\int_{T_1}^{T_2} r_{du} du} - 1. \tag{14.1}$$

The forward value of this payment will be given by

$$\begin{aligned} F^0(t, T_1, T_2) &= E\left[e^{-\int_t^{T_2} r_{du} du} L^0(T_1, T_2) \middle| \mathcal{F}_t \right] \\ &= F^{T_1}(x_d, t) - F^{T_2}(x_d, t), \end{aligned} \tag{14.2}$$

with $F^T(x_d, t)$ the T-maturity risk-free zero coupon bond price, obtainable from the risk-free pricing kernel.

We now define the tenor-τ LIBOR spread s_t^τ over the risk-free rate implicitly by

$$L^\tau(T_1, T_2) = e^{\int_{T_1}^{T_2} (r_{du} + s_u^\tau) du} - 1, \tag{14.3}$$

with $L^\tau(t, T_1, T_2)$ representing the value per unit notional of a tenor-τ LIBOR payment. (We will typically have $\tau \equiv T_2 - T_1$.) This spread is expected to be a non-decreasing function of τ. The issue we face is the choice of the discount factor for calculating forward values for LIBOR payments with $\tau > 0$. The appropriate value should reflect the credit risk of the payment. In general, therefore, there is no single right answer. If we are considering uncollateralised payments on a loan, LIBOR discounting, rather than risk-free, may be appropriate. Then we would have

$$\begin{aligned} F^\tau(t, T_1, T_2) &= E\left[e^{-\int_t^{T_2} (r_{du} + s_u^\tau) du} L^\tau(T_1, T_2) \middle| \mathcal{F}_t \right] \\ &= F^{T_1,\tau}(x_d, t) - F^{T_2,\tau}(x_d, t), \end{aligned} \tag{14.4}$$

where $F^{T,\tau}(x_d, t)$ denotes the tenor-τ LIBOR-based T-maturity zero coupon bond price. Alternatively, if the borrowing counterparty were riskier, we would seek to use a larger spread value in the discounting which more faithfully reflected the default risk. However, if the loan were perfectly collateralised or were guaranteed by a third party, there would be *no* credit risk and risk-free discounting would again be appropriate, leading to

$$F^\tau(t, T_1, T_2) = E\left[e^{-\int_t^{T_2} r_{du} du} L^\tau(T_1, T_2) \middle| \mathcal{F}_t \right]. \tag{14.5}$$

It is this latter case we shall mainly be interested in. In particular, it is the relevant situation when pricing exchange-traded swaps, the main data used for calibrating yield curves in practice. Setting $t = 0$ in (14.5) we find the PV of a LIBOR payment is in this view

$$\begin{aligned} F^\tau(0, T_1, T_2) &= E\left[e^{-\int_0^{T_2} r_{du} du} L^\tau(T_1, T_2) \right] \\ &= E\left[e^{-\int_0^{T_2} r_{du} du} \left(e^{\int_{T_1}^{T_2} (r_{du} + s_u^\tau) du} - 1 \right) \right]. \end{aligned} \tag{14.6}$$

Swaps can then be priced using $F^{T_2}(0,0)$ times the payment amount for fixed coupon payments and $F^{\tau}(0,T_1,T_2)$ for tenor-τ LIBOR payments. The calibration condition for an appropriate modelling choice for s_t^{τ} is that the values of $F^{\tau}(0,T_1,T_2)$ it gives rise to are commensurate with market prices of swaps (and other instruments). This calibration condition is usually specified in terms of a mean spread $\bar{s}^{\tau}(t)$ over the risk-free rate defined such that

$$F^{\tau}(0,T_1,T_2) = e^{\int_{T_1}^{T_2} \bar{s}^{\tau}(u)du} F^0(0,T_1,T_2). \tag{14.7}$$

Mercurio [2010] has shown how the LIBOR market model can be extended to incorporate such a spread over LIBOR for a specified tenor τ, defined in such a way as to be commensurate with (14.7). In his model he allows the spreads associated with different tenors to be potentially correlated with each other but not with the risk-free rate r_{dt}. He derives expressions for caplets, European swaptions and basis swaps in terms of the distribution functions for the risk-free rate and for the spread(s). Explicit formulae are produced for an extended LIBOR market model wherein the spreads are assumed to follow SABR dynamics.

More recently Cuchiero et al. [2019] presented an extension to this framework addressing affine interest rate models more generally. Their framework thus encompassed short rate and HJM models in addition to the LIBOR market model considered above. As with Mercurio [2010], they assume no correlation between the spreads and the risk-free rate. They provide in their §3.4 a convenient résumé of various related approaches which have been taken to date, to which summary the interested reader is referred. They go on to illustrate how analytic formulae for caplets and European swaptions can be derived as inverse Fourier transform integrals.

We consider below a similar extension to the Hull–White short-rate model, where the stochastic spreads are taken to be governed by a Black–Karasinski model. In our case we suppose that the spreads *can* potentially be correlated with the risk-free rate: this gives rise to a contribution at higher order than that considered by Mercurio [2010] and Cuchiero et al. [2019], which contribution is potentially of greater importance. Like Cuchiero et al. [2019], we derive analytic pricing formulae for caplets and European swaptions. However, rather than using Fourier analysis we employ our perturbation approach which gives rise to approximate (but nonetheless very accurate) closed form solutions, rather than the more opaque inverse transform integral expressions which arise from Fourier analysis.

14.2 STOCHASTIC SPREADS

Suppose as previously that there exists a risk-free interest rate expressed in terms of an instantaneous forward rate $\bar{r}_d(t)$. This gives rise to the discount factors $D_d(0,t)$ defined by (4.7). We further suppose that this forward rate can be equated with the overnight (OIS) interest rate, the forward curve for which can be inferred from the market so considered known.

We take as the starting point of our LIBOR model the view that the risk-free rate r_{dt} can be modelled as in Chapter 4 by a Hull–White short-rate model, whereas the short rate associated with the LIBOR forward for a given tenor τ will be given by adding a stochastic spread λ_t, i.e. will be given by $r_{dt} + \lambda_t$. Since λ_t here represents credit risk (associated with the LIBOR payment period) we shall require that it be positive and elect to model it in the same way as in Chapter 8 with a Black–Karasinski model potentially correlated with the (risk-free) short rate. In other words, we shall assume r_{dt} and λ_t are governed by (4.3) and (8.1)–(8.4), respectively.

The complication which arises here is the asymmetry in the modelling assumptions which are required before and after the LIBOR fixing time. If we wish to model the LIBOR rate consistently in the latter case, we must make the same risky discounting assumption as in Chapter 8. Consider then a LIBOR payment fixed at time T_1 for a payment period $[T_1, T_2]$ with $T_2 = T_1 + \tau$. The relevant risky zero coupon bond price is under our assumptions given by $V_F^{T_2}(x_d, x_\lambda, T_1)$, using the notation introduced in (8.49). The LIBOR payment at T_2 will thus be given by

$$P_{\text{LIBOR}}(x_d, x_\lambda) = V_F^{T_2}(x_d, x_\lambda, T_1)^{-1} - 1. \tag{14.8}$$

Application of our second order Green's function (8.14) gives rise to a valuation as of time T_1 of

$$V_{\text{LIBOR}}(x_d, x_\lambda, T_1) \sim 1 - V_F^{T_2}(x_d, x_\lambda, T_1). \tag{14.9}$$

Calculation of the PV of derivatives which reference the LIBOR rate requires greater care since the credit risk associated with the LIBOR rate does not apply to the derivative. In general there may be credit risk associated with the derivative counterparty which needs to be taken account of. However, as is often the case, if the derivative is collateralised (or can be considered so), it can be taken to be free of credit risk and priced using risk-free discounting. Thus we have that the derivative price $f(x_d, x_\lambda, t)$ is governed for $t \in [0, T_1]$ by

$$\begin{aligned}\frac{\partial f}{\partial t} &- \alpha_d(t)x_d\frac{\partial f}{\partial x_d} - \alpha_\lambda(t)x_\lambda\frac{\partial f}{\partial x_\lambda} + \frac{1}{2}\left(\sigma_d^2(t)\frac{\partial^2 f}{\partial x_d^2} + 2\rho_{d\lambda}\sigma_d(t)\sigma_\lambda(t)\frac{\partial^2 f}{\partial x_d \partial x_\lambda} + \sigma_\lambda^2(t)\frac{\partial^2 f}{\partial x_\lambda^2}\right)\\ &- \bar{r}_d(t)f = 0,\end{aligned} \tag{14.10}$$

rather than by (8.7), the important difference being that the last (risky discounting) term is now omitted. We consider next the pricing kernel associated with (14.10).

Hull–White Kernel Extension. The calculation of the pricing kernel associated with (14.10) is closely related to, but simpler than, that presented in Theorem 8.1. We omit the details, noting only that the (exact) result obtained is, in the notation there introduced

$$\begin{aligned}G(x_d, x_\lambda, t; \xi_d, \xi_\lambda, v) &= D(t, T)f^v(x_d, t)\\ &N_2(\phi_d(t, v)x_d - I^*_{dd}(t, v) - \xi_d, \phi_\lambda(t, v)x_\lambda - I^*_{\lambda d}(t, v) - \xi_\lambda; \boldsymbol{\Sigma}(t, v)),\end{aligned} \tag{14.11}$$

with in particular $f^v(x_d.t)$ given by (8.15). The correct calibration is automatically obtained by the choice of $r^*_d(t)$ made in (4.14).

14.3 APPLICATIONS

14.3.1 LIBOR Pricing

We look to apply the above pricing kernel to the LIBOR payoff (14.9). Since the values of x_d and x_λ are those observed at time T_1 they can be considered fixed for valuing the payoff as of time T_1. We obtain straightforwardly

$$V_{\text{LIBOR}}(x_d, x_\lambda, T_1) = D(T_1, T_2) f^{T_2}(x_d, T_1) P_{\text{LIBOR}}(x_d, x_\lambda). \tag{14.12}$$

The time-t price can now be calculated using (14.11) as an asymptotic expansion in $\epsilon = \|\tilde{\lambda}(\cdot)\|$

$$\begin{aligned} V_{\text{LIBOR}}(x_d, x_\lambda, t) &= \iint_{\mathbb{R}^2} V_{\text{LIBOR}}(\xi_d, \xi_\lambda, T_1) G(x_d, x_\lambda, t; \xi_d, \xi_\lambda, T_1) d\xi_d d\xi_\lambda \\ &\sim V^{(0)}_{\text{LIBOR}}(x_d, t) + V^{(1)}_{\text{LIBOR}}(x_d, x_\lambda, t) \end{aligned} \tag{14.13}$$

with $V^{(j)}_{\text{LIBOR}}(\cdot) = \mathcal{O}(\epsilon^j)$. Making use of the tower property of §4.3.1, we find straightforwardly at leading order

$$\begin{aligned} V^{(0)}_{\text{LIBOR}}(x_d, t) &= D(t, T_2) f^{T_1}(x_d, t) \iint_{\mathbb{R}^2} \left(B^{-1}(T_1, T_2) - f^{T_2}(\xi_d, T_1)\right) \\ &N_2(\phi_d(t, T_1)x_d - I^*_{dd}(t, T_1) - \xi_d, \phi_\lambda(t, T_1)x_\lambda - I^*_{\lambda d}(t, T_1) - \xi_\lambda; \mathbf{\Sigma}(t, T_1)) d\xi_\lambda d\xi_d \\ &= D(t, T_2)\left(B^{-1}(T_1, T_2) f^{T_1}(x_d, t) - f^{T_2}(x_d, t)\right). \end{aligned} \tag{14.14}$$

Similarly at first order, making use of Theorem 3.3, we have

$$\begin{aligned} V^{(1)}_{\text{LIBOR}}(x_d, x_\lambda, t) &= -D(t, T_2) f^{T_1}(x_d, t) \iint_{\mathbb{R}^2} \left(B^{-1}(T_1, T_2) - f^{T_2}(\xi_d, T_1)\right) \Delta F^*_1(\xi_\lambda, T_1, T_2) \\ &N_2(\phi_d(t, T_1)x_d - I^*_{dd}(t, T_1) - \xi_d, \phi_\lambda(t, T_1)x_\lambda - I^*_{\lambda d}(t, T_1) - \xi_\lambda; \mathbf{\Sigma}(t, T_1)) d\xi_\lambda d\xi_d \\ &= D(t, T_2) B^{-1}(T_1, T_2) f^{T_1}(x_d, t) \int_{T_1}^{T_2} \left(\overline{\lambda}(t_1) - \tilde{\lambda}_1(t_1) e^{-B^*_d(t_1, T_2)\Sigma_{d\lambda}(T_1, t_1) + \theta_\lambda(x_\lambda, t, t_1)}\right) dt_1 \\ &- D(t, T_2) f^{T_2}(x_d, t) \\ &\int_{T_1}^{T_2} \left(\overline{\lambda}(t_1) - \tilde{\lambda}_1(t_1) e^{-B^*_d(t_1, T_2)\Sigma_{d\lambda}(T_1, t_1) - B^*_d(T_1, T_2)\phi_\lambda(T_1, t_1)\Sigma_{d\lambda}(t, T_1) + \theta_\lambda(x_\lambda, t, t_1)}\right) dt_1. \end{aligned}$$

Combining terms gives rise to a PV of

$$PV_{\text{LIBOR}} = D(0, T_2) B^{-1}(T_1, T_2) \left(1 + \int_{T_1}^{T_2} \left(\overline{\lambda}(t_1) - \tilde{\lambda}_1(t_1) e^{-B^*_d(t_1, T_2)\Sigma_{d\lambda}(T_1, t_1)}\right) dt_1\right)$$

$$- D(0,T_2)\left(1+\int_{T_1}^{T_2}\left(\overline{\lambda}(t_1)-\tilde{\lambda}_1(t_1)e^{-B_d^*(t_1,T_2)\Sigma_{d\lambda}(T_1,t_1)-B_d^*(T_1,T_2)\phi_\lambda(T_1,t_1)\Sigma_{d\lambda}(0,T_1)}\right)dt_1\right)$$
$$+\mathcal{O}(\epsilon^2). \tag{14.15}$$

14.3.2 LIBOR Caplet Pricing

We consider the caplet payoff for the LIBOR payment for a period $[T_1, T_2]$ fixed at time T_1 and paid at time T_2 with strike K. This payoff can be written

$$\begin{aligned} P_{\text{caplet}}(x_d, x_\lambda) &= [P_{\text{LIBOR}}(x_d, x_\lambda) - K\delta(T_1,T_2)]^+ \\ &= [V_F^{T_2}(x_d, x_\lambda, T_1)^{-1} - \kappa^{-1}]^+, \end{aligned} \tag{14.16}$$

with κ given by (4.24). We look to calculate the caplet price to first order in ϵ. Since the values of x_d and x_λ are those observed at time T_1 they can be considered fixed for valuing the payoff as of time T_1. We obtain straightforwardly

$$V_{\text{caplet}}(x_d, x_\lambda, T_1) = D(T_1,T_2)f^{T_2}(x_d, T_1)P_{\text{caplet}}(x_d, x_\lambda). \tag{14.17}$$

To proceed, let us define a critical value $x_d^*(x_\lambda)$ as the highest value of x_d for which the LIBOR caplet payoff is zero for a given value of x_λ. Making use of this, we can write

$$V_{\text{caplet}}(x_d, x_\lambda, T_1) = D(T_1,T_2)f^{T_2}(x_d, T_1)\left(V_F^{T_2}(x_d, x_\lambda, T_1)^{-1} - \kappa^{-1}\right)\mathbb{1}_{x_d > x_d^*(x_\lambda)}. \tag{14.18}$$

To render the calculation more analytically tractable, we will make the further assumption that the stochastic variation of the spreads is small compared to that of the associated LIBOR rate, specifically that $\|\overline{\lambda}(\cdot)\sigma_\lambda(\cdot)\|^2 \ll \|\sigma_d(\cdot)\|^2$. This is consistent with our considering the limit as $\epsilon \to 0$ in the process of deriving (14.9); it is also invariably the case in practice. On that basis, we propose that $x_d^*(x_\lambda)$ can usefully be expanded as a Taylor series about $x_\lambda = -I_{\lambda d}^*(0, T_1)$, viz.

$$x_d^*(x_\lambda) \sim \xi_0^* + \xi_1^*(x_\lambda + I_{\lambda d}^*(0, T_1)) \tag{14.19}$$

where $\xi_0^* := x_d^*(-I_{\lambda d}^*(0,T_1))$ and $\xi_1^* := x_d^{*\prime}(-I_{\lambda d}^*(0,T_1))$ and furthermore $\xi_j^* = \mathcal{O}(\epsilon^j)$. We infer

$$\mathbb{1}_{x_d > x_d^*(x_\lambda)} = H(x_d - \xi_0^*) + \xi_1^*(x_\lambda + I_{\lambda d}^*(0,T_1))\delta(x_d - \xi_0^*) + \mathcal{O}(\epsilon^j),$$

with $H(\cdot)$ the Heaviside step function and $\delta(\cdot)$ the Dirac delta function. The time-t price can now be calculated using (14.11) as an asymptotic expansion

$$\begin{aligned} V_{\text{caplet}}(x_d, x_\lambda, t) &= \iint_{\mathbb{R}^2} V_{\text{caplet}}(\xi_d, \xi_\lambda, T_1)G(x_d, x_\lambda, t; \xi_d, \xi_\lambda, T_1)d\xi_d d\xi_\lambda \\ &\sim V_{\text{caplet}}^{(0)}(x_d, t) + V_{\text{caplet}}^{(1)}(x_d, x_\lambda, t), \end{aligned} \tag{14.20}$$

with $V^{(j)}_{\text{caplet}}(\cdot) = \mathcal{O}(\epsilon^j)$. Making use of the tower property of §4.3.1, we find straightforwardly at leading order

$$
\begin{aligned}
V^{(0)}_{\text{caplet}}(x_d, t) &= D(t, T_2) f^{T_1}(x_d, t) \int_{\xi_0^*}^{\infty} \int_{-\infty}^{\infty} \left(B^{-1}(T_1, T_2) - \kappa^{-1} f^{T_2}(\xi_d, T_1)\right) \\
&\quad N_2(\phi_d(t, T_1)x_d - I^*_{dd}(t, T_1) - \xi_d, \\
&\quad \phi_\lambda(t, T_1)x_\lambda - I^*_{\lambda d}(t, T_1) - \xi_\lambda; \mathbf{\Sigma}(t, T_1)) d\xi_\lambda d\xi_d \\
&= D(t, T_2) f^{T_1}(x_d, t) \int_{\xi_0^*}^{\infty} \left(B^{-1}(T_1, T_2) - \kappa^{-1} f^{T_2}(\xi_d, T_1)\right) \\
&\quad N\left(\frac{\phi_d(t, T_1)x_d - I^*_{dd}(t, T_1) - \xi_d}{\sqrt{\Sigma_{dd}(t, T_1)}}\right) d\xi_d \\
&= D(t, T_2) \left(B^{-1}(T_1, T_2) f^{T_1}(x_d, t) \Phi(d_2(\xi_0^* - \phi_d(t, T_1)x_d, t))\right. \\
&\quad \left. - \kappa^{-1} f^{T_2}(x_d, t) \Phi(d_1(\xi_0^* - \phi_d(t, T_1)x_d, t))\right) \qquad (14.21)
\end{aligned}
$$

where $\Phi(\cdot)$ is a cumulative Gaussian distribution function and the $d_i(\cdot)$ are as given by (8.71).

At first order, we consider contributions both from the first-order term in $V_F^{T_2}(x_d, x_\lambda, T_1)$ and from that in $x_d^*(x_\lambda)$, which contributions we denote $V_1^{(1)}(x_d, x_\lambda, t)$ and $V_2^{(1)}(x_d, x_\lambda, t)$, respectively. Making use of the definition (8.51) of $\Delta F_1^*(\cdot)$ and Theorem 3.5, we have

$$
\begin{aligned}
V_1^{(1)}(x_d, x_\lambda, t) &= -D(t, T_2) f^{T_1}(x_d, t) \int_{\xi_0^*}^{\infty} \int_{-\infty}^{\infty} \left(B^{-1}(T_1, T_2) - \kappa^{-1} f^{T_2}(\xi_d, T_1)\right) \Delta F_1^*(\xi_\lambda, T_1, T_2) \\
&\quad N_2(\phi_d(t, T_1)x_d - I^*_{dd}(t, T_1) - \xi_d, \phi_\lambda(t, T_1)x_\lambda - I^*_{\lambda d}(t, T_1) - \xi_\lambda; \mathbf{\Sigma}(t, T_1)) d\xi_\lambda d\xi_d \\
&= D(t, T_2) \int_{T_1}^{T_2} \int_{-\infty}^{\infty} \left(B^{-1}(T_1, T_2) - \kappa^{-1} f^{T_2}(\xi_d, T_1)\right) \\
&\quad \left(\overline{\lambda}(t_1) - \tilde{\lambda}_1(t_1) e^{-B_d^*(t_1, T_2)\Sigma_{d\lambda}(T_1, t_1) + \theta_\lambda(x_\lambda, t, t_1)}\right) \\
&\quad N\left(\frac{\phi_d(t, T_1)x_d - I^*_{dd}(t, T_1) - \xi_d + \Sigma_{d\lambda}(t, T_1)}{\sqrt{\Sigma_{dd}(t, T_1)}}\right) d\xi_d dt_1 \\
&= D(t, T_2) B^{-1}(T_1, T_2) f^{T_1}(x_d, t) \Phi(-d_2(\xi_0^* - \Sigma_{d\lambda}(t, T_1) - \phi_d(t, T_1)x_d, t)) \\
&\quad \int_{T_1}^{T_2} (\overline{\lambda}(t_1) - \tilde{\lambda}_1(t_1) e^{-B_d^*(t_1, T_2)\Sigma_{d\lambda}(T_1, t_1) + \theta_\lambda(x_\lambda, t, t_1)}) dt_1 \\
&\quad - D(t, T_2) \kappa^{-1} f^{T_2}(x_d, t) \Phi(-d_1(\xi_0^* - \Sigma_{d\lambda}(t, T_1) - \phi_d(t, T_1)x_d, t)) \\
&\quad \int_{T_1}^{T_2} \left(\overline{\lambda}(t_1) - \tilde{\lambda}_1(t_1) e^{-B_d^*(t_1, T_2)\Sigma_{d\lambda}(T_1, t_1) - B_d^*(T_1, T_2)\phi_\lambda(T_1, t_1)\Sigma_{d\lambda}(t, T_1) + \theta_\lambda(x_\lambda, t, t_1)}\right) dt_1
\end{aligned}
$$

Correspondingly, we have

$$V_2^{(1)}(x_d, x_\lambda, t) = D(t, T_2) f^{T_1}(x_d, t)\xi_1^* \iint_{\mathbb{R}^2} \left(B^{-1}(T_1, T_2) - \kappa^{-1} f^{T_2}(\xi_d, T_1)\right)$$
$$\delta(\xi_d - \xi_0^*)(\xi_\lambda + I_{\lambda d}^*(0, T_1))$$
$$N_2(\phi_d(t, T_1)x_d - I_{dd}^*(t, T_1) - \xi_d, \phi_\lambda(t, T_1)x_\lambda - I_{\lambda d}^*(t, T_1)$$
$$- \xi_\lambda; \mathbf{\Sigma}(t, T_1)) d\xi_\lambda d\xi_d$$
$$= D(t, T_2) f^{T_1}(x_d, t)\xi_1^* \left(B^{-1}(T_1, T_2) - \kappa^{-1} f^{T_2}(\xi_0^*, T_1)\right)$$
$$\left(x_\lambda + \phi_\lambda(t, T_1)(I_{\lambda d}^*(0, t) + B_d^*(t, T_1)\Sigma_{d\lambda}(0, t)) + \frac{\Sigma_{d\lambda}(t, T_1)}{\phi_d(t, T_1)} \frac{\partial}{\partial x_d}\right)$$
$$N(-d_2(\xi_0^* - \phi_d(t, T_1)x_d, t)),$$

where in the last line we have made use of Theorem 3.4 and (8.37). We conclude that

$$V_{\text{caplet}}(x_d, x_\lambda, t) = V_{\text{caplet}}^{(0)}(x_d, t) + V_1^{(1)}(x_d, x_\lambda, t) + V_2^{(1)}(x_d, x_\lambda, t) + \mathcal{O}(\epsilon^2),$$

whence substituting back into (14.20) yields the required result for the LIBOR caplet price to the required accuracy. Setting $x_d = x_\lambda = t = 0$ and simplifying, we obtain the PV as

$$\begin{aligned} PV_{\text{caplet}} &= D(0, T_2) B^{-1}(T_1, T_2) \\ &\left(\Phi(-d_2(\xi_0^*, 0)) + \Phi(-d_2(\xi_0^* - \Sigma_{d\lambda}(0, T_1), 0))\right. \\ &\left.\times \int_{T_1}^{T_2} \left(\overline{\lambda}(t_1) - \tilde{\lambda}_1(t_1) e^{-B_d^*(t_1, T_2)\Sigma_{d\lambda}(T_1, t_1)}\right) dt_1\right) \\ &- D(0, T_2)\kappa^{-1} \\ &\left(\Phi(-d_1(\xi_0^*, 0)) + \Phi(-d_1(\xi_0^* - \Sigma_{d\lambda}(0, T_1), 0))\right. \\ &\left.\times \int_{T_1}^{T_2} \left(\overline{\lambda}(t_1) - \tilde{\lambda}_1(t_1) e^{-B_d^*(t_1, T_2)\Sigma_{d\lambda}(T_1, t_1) - B_d^*(T_1, T_2)\phi_\lambda(T_1, t_1)\Sigma_{d\lambda}(0, T_1)}\right) dt_1\right) \\ &+ D(0, T_2)\left(B^{-1}(T_1, T_2) - \kappa^{-1} f^{T_2}(\xi_0^*, T_1)\right) \frac{\Sigma_{d\lambda}(0, T_1)}{\sqrt{\Sigma_{dd}(0, T_1)}} \xi_1^* d_2(\xi_0^*, 0) N(-d_2(\xi_0^*, 0)) \\ &+ \mathcal{O}(\epsilon^2). \end{aligned} \tag{14.22}$$

As can be seen, correlation has a significantly greater impact on the contribution from the fixed payment (second term) than that from the floating rate payment (first term). The floorlet price is obtained similarly as

$$\begin{aligned} PV_{\text{floorlet}} &= D(0, T_2)\kappa^{-1} \\ &\left(\Phi(d_1(\xi_0^*, 0)) + \Phi(d_1(\xi_0^* - \Sigma_{d\lambda}(0, T_1), 0))\right. \end{aligned}$$

$$
\begin{aligned}
&\times \int_{T_1}^{T_2} \left(\overline{\lambda}(t_1) - \tilde{\lambda}_1(t_1) e^{-B_d^*(t_1,T_2)\Sigma_{d\lambda}(T_1,t_1) - B_d^*(T_1,T_2)\phi_\lambda(T_1,t_1)\Sigma_{d\lambda}(0,T_1)}\right) dt_1 \Bigg) \\
&- D(0,T_2)B^{-1}(T_1,T_2) \\
&\Bigg(\Phi(d_2(\xi_0^*,0)) + \Phi(d_2(\xi_0^* - \Sigma_{d\lambda}(0,T_1),0)) \\
&\times \int_{T_1}^{T_2} (\overline{\lambda}(t_1) - \tilde{\lambda}_1(t_1) e^{-B_d^*(t_1,T_2)\Sigma_{d\lambda}(T_1,t_1)}) dt_1 \Bigg) \\
&+ D(0,T_2)(B^{-1}(T_1,T_2) - \kappa^{-1} f^{T_2}(\xi_0^*,T_1)) \frac{\Sigma_{d\lambda}(0,T_1)}{\sqrt{\Sigma_{dd}(0,T_1)}} \xi_1^* d_2(\xi_0^*,0) N(d_2(\xi_0^*,0)) \\
&+ \mathcal{O}(\epsilon^2). \qquad (14.23)
\end{aligned}
$$

Observe that, in the absence of correlation between the spread and the risk-free rate, the correction terms all disappear and the formula reverts to that associated with deterministic spreads. The $\mathcal{O}(\epsilon^2)$ approximation error in this case will be that due purely to spread volatility. This suggests that the modelling approaches of Mercurio [2010] and Cuchiero et al. [2019] considered above may be considered deficient insofar as they ignore the potentially lower order effect of correlation with stochastic spreads in favour of the higher-order convexity effect due to spread volatility.

14.3.3 European Swaption Pricing

A similar calculation to the above should be possible for European swaption prices. We outline here the details of how this could be achieved. Consider again the swap defined in 4.3.4, but where the LIBOR incorporates a stochastic spread as detailed above. Its value as of (swaption) exercise time $t_0 > 0$ can be written as

$$V_{\text{swap}}(x_d, x_\lambda, t_0) = \sum_{i=1}^{n} V_{\text{fwd}}^{(i)}(x_d, x_\lambda, t_0), \qquad (14.24)$$

where $V_{\text{fwd}}^{(i)}(x_d, x_\lambda, t)$ represents the value at $t \le T_{i-1}$ of a forward contract based on LIBOR fixed at time T_{i-1} for payment at T_i. This forward contract has a value at T_{i-1} (subject to risk-free discounting) of

$$V_{\text{fwd}}^{(i)}(x_d, x_\lambda, T_{i-1}) = D(T_{i-1}, T_i) f^{T_i}(x_d, T_{i-1}) \left(V_F^{T_i}(x_d, x_\lambda, T_{i-1})^{-1} - \kappa_i^{-1} \right) \qquad (14.25)$$

in the notation of §8.3.1, with κ_i given by (8.79). This can be valued as of time t_0 as follows:

$$V_{\text{fwd}}^{(i)}(x_d, x_\lambda, t_0) = \iint_{\mathbb{R}^2} P_{\text{fwd}}^{(i)}(\xi_d, \xi_\lambda) G(x_d, x_\lambda, t_0; \xi_d, \xi_\lambda, T_{i-1}) d\xi_d d\xi_\lambda. \qquad (14.26)$$

The payoff (14.24) can then in principle be priced as of time $t < t_0$ conditional on the (swap) moneyness condition being satisfied. The optimal exercise boundary will again have to be represented approximately as an expansion in powers of ϵ.

CHAPTER 15

Scenario Generation

15.1 OVERVIEW

It is a common requirement in risk management that models, as well as being used for generating end-of-day prices, are required to produce hypothetical prices under a range of future possible market scenarios. The calculations that we have provided in the preceding, insofar as they have been provided not only as PV at $t = 0$, but as prices of the form $f(\boldsymbol{x}_t, t)$, $t > 0$, can be used in this way. In other cases, some extra work allows formulae for conditional prices of this kind to be produced.

In addition to calculating the prices under hypothetical scenarios, there is also often a need to generate the scenarios themselves under the assumption that they arise from an evolution of the market underlyings in the pricing model from time 0 to time t. Typically, we make use of the joint distribution of the (usually Gaussian) variables in the vector $\boldsymbol{x}_t$ to produce scenarios through random number generation and obtain the distribution of prices by applying $f(\boldsymbol{x}_t, t)$. In this way we can simulate, for example, expected loss distributions such as are required for the purpose of calculating the credit risk component of risk capital requirements under Basel III and under the Fundamental Review of the Trading Book [Bank for International Settlements, 2014].

However, in many cases evolution of the market data under the pricing model is inadequate for capturing the possible distributions of future prices which might be observed and a different model is needed for this purpose. For example, if we want to capture the counterparty credit exposure of a (collateralised) vanilla equity option at some future time, we can use a Black–Scholes formula in the form $f_{BS}(z_t, t)$, where, say, $S_t = F(t)e^{z_t - \frac{1}{2}\int_0^t \sigma_z^2(s)ds}$ is the equity price at time t and z_t a normally distributed variable. The forward distribution of prices at t can be simulated by generating realisations of z_t in the manner discussed. But this is not the whole story. If rates are stochastic (say, Hull–White), there will be variation in price consequent upon variations in *rates* across scenarios. In the notation of Chapter 4, we need to include in the Black–Scholes price an additional factor $e^{-\mu^*(x_{dt}, t, T)}$ where x_{dt} is governed by the

(Gaussian) law $G(0, 0; x_d, t)$ for the Hull–White model.[1] In addition, there may be correlation between rates and equity processes which needs to be captured.

More generally, in order to specify the scenario which is to be priced we will typically need to calculate not only the values of spot variables at the exposure time t, but also *the shapes* of rates curves and, in the case of credit derivatives or CVA calculations, of credit curves. Particularly when dealing with more exotic rates derivatives, it may be necessary to do better than generating curve scenarios based on just a single stochastic factor. The possible changes in the shape of the curve may have a significant impact on the distribution of prices, whence a multi-factor rates (and/or credit) model may be called for. Specifically, we may want stochastic fluctuations with fast and slow decay times to drive different behaviour at the short and long ends of the curve(s), respectively.

Because of the difficulty of evolving a curve in its entirety, a strategy often adopted in practice is to evolve a number of forward rates on the curve and rebuild the curve at the future scenario times of interest. In addition, to reduce the number of factors in the simulation, principal components analysis (PCA) is often used with a smaller number of factors capturing the most important types of variation. An example of such a strategy for interest rate curves is provided by Redfern and McLean [2014]. We propose instead that rates and credit curves can be evolved *in their entirety* respecting typical modelling assumptions, in our case Hull–White and/or Black–Karasinski, by making use of the multi-factor framework we set out in Chapter 6 to provide convenient analytic formulae.

15.2 PREVIOUS WORK

Multi-factor modelling of yield curves has long been of interest for macroeconomic analysis aimed at matching yield curve evolution to past behaviour. We review briefly some of the strategies which have been proposed previously. A simple approach is provided by the well known Nelson-Siegel model [Nelson and Siegel, 1987], which provides a parametric representation of the shape of the yield curve. Donati and Donati [2008], writing for the European Central Bank, proposed a variant more closely related to what we propose below. It is essentially a three-factor version of the multi-factor Hull–White model defined by (6.2) in Chapter 6, but with zero volatility and the matrix $\boldsymbol{\kappa}(t)$ governing mean reversion to be of the form

$$\boldsymbol{\kappa}(t) = \begin{pmatrix} 0 & 0 & 0 \\ a & -a & 0 \\ 0 & b & -b \end{pmatrix}. \tag{15.1}$$

Also, rather than (6.21), they take the short rate to be given, in our notation, by

$$r(\boldsymbol{x}, t) = \tilde{r}(t) + x_3. \tag{15.2}$$

[1] More accurately we ought to allow for a joint distribution of x_{dt} and z_t as propounded in Chapter 7.

Since their model is a deterministic representation of the yield curve evolution, they seek to minimise fitting errors to past data rather than generating future scenarios.

Of more interest for us is the work done with stochastic models. A good summary of this approach is provided by Dempster et al. [2012] although, as they point out, the literature on this subject is vast and so difficult to do justice to. Their literature survey is focussed on the most popular class of short-rate models, namely affine models in which the drift and diffusion terms in the pricing equation are affine functions of the short rate. These can be further categorised between those of Hull–White type where the diffusion coefficient is independent of the short rate and those of CIR type [Cox et al., 1991] where it is taken to be proportional to the short rate (resulting in a square-root volatility).

Dempster et al. [2012], guided by the seminal investigative work of Dai and Singleton [2000], consider models of both types. They also consider hybrid models where different factors are of different types. They find that, although it is attractive to use CIR processes since these can be configured to guarantee positive rates, any advantage that might accrue through better fitting to the in-sample data is outweighed by the disadvantage of unrealistic out-of-sample behaviour and the fact that such models are in general more cumbersome to work with. So they focus on pricing equations of the form of (6.2) with the short rate an affine function of x, taking advantage of its greater analytic tractability.

In their specification they assume that the matrix $\boldsymbol{\kappa}(t)$ is lower triangular and $\boldsymbol{\sigma}(t)$ diagonal. However, subject to the further reasonable assumption that $\boldsymbol{\kappa}(t)$ has only non-negative real eigenvalues, a linear change of co-ordinates renders their pricing equation equivalent to (6.2). Furthermore, re-scaling and re-ordering of factors allows their expression for the short rate to be expressed in the form (6.21). We set out in §15.4 below explicit formulae for the yield curve specification in this case, which should prove useful for scenario generation purposes.

Dempster et al. [2012] find they are able to obtain a better fit to data under these modelling assumptions. However, the main drawback is that under long evolution times there is a non-negligible probability of unrealistically negative rates. They sought to address this problem by using the modification proposed by Black [1995], effectively putting a floor of zero under the instantaneous forward rates. This method proved to be effective but quite computationally demanding on account of the lack of availability of analytic pricing formulae for forward rates.

We propose as another prospective alternative the two-factor Black–Karasinski model set out in §15.5 below, which avoids the above-mentioned drawbacks of a Hull–White model, but whose analytic tractability is, as we shall see, not in practical terms a great deal less when use is made of the (asymptotic) formulae set out below. This model is closely related to that proposed by Peterson et al. [1999]. They sought to model the 3m LIBOR spot rate (rather than the short rate), taking it to be proportional to the exponential of the first stochastic factor, viewing the second stochastic factor as providing a drift of the mean reversion level associated with the first. They built a bivariate binomial lattice which provided an efficient numerical scheme for pricing European and Bermudan options on bonds.

Also worthy of consideration in this context is the recent work of Keller-Ressel [2019] on the two-factor Vasicek model. He finds that, whereas the greatest variability obtainable with a one-factor Vasicek model is a single local maximum, a two-factor Vasicek model with essentially the same five-parameter combination as we use below (but with constant mean reversion levels) is capable of having up to two local maxima and two local minima. So, if our concern is to enable a richer variety of curve shapes, the proposed two-factor model offers significant advantages in return for the one additional factor.

We observe that, interpreting the short rate as a credit default intensity, our Black–Karasinski model can be equally viewed as describing the evolution of a credit default intensity curve. The inferred zero coupon bond prices should in this case be interpreted as survival probabilities. This model has the desirable property that it allows the requirement for default intensities to be strictly non-negative to be respected. A similar model was indeed proposed by Realdon [2007] for sovereign credit default swap pricing, except in that he proposed a credit default intensity based on the sum, rather than the product, of two lognormal contributions. He finds that his model, based on maximum likelihood inference of the parameters associated with the two factors, is able to explain 90% of the variation of sovereign CDS rates observed in the market. Notably, however, he does not allow for correlation between the two factors as we do here.

A word should also be said about multi-rate simulation. This is in the main a fairly straightforward extension of the above: correlations between rates can be incorporated straightforwardly by randomly generating a vector of (Ornstein–Uhlenbeck) state variables $\boldsymbol{x}_t$ with the requisite correlations. In the event that we jointly simulate a credit curve and a rates curve for the associated currency, the same applies, provided the forward credit curves are interpreted as default rates, rather than credit spreads. If we wish to make the latter interpretation, say in order that risky discount factors can be conveniently produced, we must make use instead of the joint rates-credit approach set out in §8 above. We present in §15.6 below the further analysis that needs to be done to derive forward credit curves in this case.

15.3 PRICING EQUATION

We consider the following generic two-factor short-rate model, defining the short rate $r_t = r(x_t, y_t, t)$ for some function $r(\cdot)$ through auxiliary processes x_t and y_t satisfying the following for $t \geq 0$

$$dx_t = -\alpha_x(t)x_t dt + \sigma_x(t)\, dW_t^1, \tag{15.3}$$

$$dy_t = -\alpha_y(t)y_t dt + \sigma_y(t)\, dW_t^2, \tag{15.4}$$

with $x_0 = y_0 = 0$, where $t = 0$ is the "as of" date for which the model is calibrated, W_t^1 and W_t^2 are Wiener processes under the standard martingale measure Q with

$$\mathrm{cov}(dW_t^1, dW_t^2) = \rho(t)dt, \tag{15.5}$$

$\alpha_{[x,y]} : \mathbb{R}^+ \to \mathbb{R}^+$ are mean reversion rates and $\sigma_{[x,y]} : \mathbb{R}^+ \to \mathbb{R}^+$ local volatility functions, the former assumed L^1-integrable and the latter L^2-integrable.

We would typically operate the model with relatively large values for $\sigma_x(\cdot)$ and $\alpha_x(\cdot)$ capturing fluctuations at the short end of the curve, while smaller values for $\sigma_y(\cdot)$ and $\alpha_y(\cdot)$ (possibly even zero in the latter case) allow smaller movements at the long end of the curve to build up over time and eventually become significant.

Consider, therefore, the (stochastic) time-t price of a European-style security which pays a cash amount $P(x_T, y_T)$ at maturity T, denoting this by

$$f(x_t, y_t, t) = \mathbb{E}^{\mathbb{Q}}\left[e^{-\int_t^T r_s ds} P(x_T, y_T) \middle| \mathcal{F}_t \right], \tag{15.6}$$

with $\mathcal{F}_t$ the filtration of $\{x_t, y_t\}$ under the martingale measure $\mathbb{Q}$. We note in particular that the price of a T-maturity zero coupon bond is obtained by taking $P(x, y) = 1$. We infer as a consequence of the Feynman–Kac theorem that $f(x, y, t)$ emerges as the solution of the following Kolmogorov backward diffusion equation

$$\begin{aligned}\frac{\partial f}{\partial t} - \alpha_x(t)x\frac{\partial f}{\partial x} - \alpha_y(t)y\frac{\partial f}{\partial y} + \frac{1}{2}\sigma_x^2(t)\frac{\partial^2 f}{\partial x^2} + \rho(t)\sigma_x(t)\sigma_y(t)\frac{\partial^2 f}{\partial x\partial y} \\ + \frac{1}{2}\sigma_y^2(t)\frac{\partial^2 f}{\partial y^2} - r(x, y, t)f = 0,\end{aligned} \tag{15.7}$$

subject to the final condition $f(x, y, T) = P(x, y)$. We look to establish a pricing kernel for (15.7) under the assumption of low rates as a perturbation expansion in powers of the assumed small parameter. We will make use throughout this chapter of the following notation

$$D(t, v) = e^{-\int_t^v \bar{r}(t_1)dt_1} \tag{15.8}$$

$$\phi_{[x,y]}(u, v) = e^{-\int_u^v \alpha_{[x,y]}(s)ds}, \tag{15.9}$$

$$\Sigma_{\alpha\alpha}(t, v) = \int_t^v \phi_\alpha^2(u, v)\sigma_\alpha^2(u)du, \quad \alpha \in \{x, y\}, \tag{15.10}$$

$$\Sigma_{xy}(t, v) = \int_t^v \rho(u)\phi_x(u, v)\phi_y(u, v)\sigma_x(u)\sigma_y(u)du, \tag{15.11}$$

$$I_{\alpha\beta}^*(t, v) = \int_t^v \phi_\alpha(u, v)\Sigma_{\alpha\beta}(t, u)du, \quad \alpha, \beta \in \{x, y\} \tag{15.12}$$

$$\mathbf{\Sigma}(t, v) = \begin{pmatrix} \Sigma_{xx}(t, v) & \Sigma_{xy}(t, v) \\ \Sigma_{xy}(t, v) & \Sigma_{yy}(t, v) \end{pmatrix}, \tag{15.13}$$

$$\Sigma(t, v) = \Sigma_{xx}(t, v) + 2\Sigma_{xy}(t, v) + \Sigma_{yy}(t, v), \tag{15.14}$$

$$G_0(x, y, t; \xi, \eta, v) = D(t, T)N_2(\phi_x(t, v)x - \xi, \phi_y(t, v)y - \eta; \mathbf{\Sigma}(t, v)), \tag{15.15}$$

where $N_2(\cdot, \cdot; \mathbf{\Sigma})$ is a bivariate Gaussian probability density function with covariance matrix $\mathbf{\Sigma}$. Note that in particular $\Sigma(0, t)$ is the variance of $x_t + y_t$.

15.4 HULL–WHITE RATES

15.4.1 Two-Factor Pricing Kernel

For the Hull–White case, we make the choice[2]

$$r(x, y, t) = \overline{r}(t) + r_2^*(t) + x + y \tag{15.16}$$

with $r_2^*(t)$ to be determined by calibration to the forward curve $\overline{r}(t)$. We note that the result we seek is a special case of Theorem 6.2 with $m' = m = 2$. We thus need only to compute the particular form of the coefficient functions appearing in (6.38). In terms of the notation introduced in Chapter 6, we have $\boldsymbol{x} = (x, y)^T$, $\boldsymbol{\beta}(t) = (0, 0)^T$ and

$$\boldsymbol{\kappa}(t) = \begin{pmatrix} \alpha_x(t) & 0 \\ 0 & \alpha_y(t) \end{pmatrix}, \tag{15.17}$$

whence we obtain

$$\boldsymbol{\Phi}(t) = \begin{pmatrix} \phi_x(0,t) & 0 \\ 0 & \phi_y(0,t) \end{pmatrix}; \qquad \boldsymbol{\Phi}^{-1}(t) = \begin{pmatrix} \phi_x(0,t)^{-1} & 0 \\ 0 & \phi_y(0,t)^{-1} \end{pmatrix} \tag{15.18}$$

and

$$\boldsymbol{\Psi}(t, v) = \begin{pmatrix} \phi_x(0,t)B_x^*(t,v) & 0 \\ 0 & \phi_y(0,t)B_y^*(t,v) \end{pmatrix}, \tag{15.19}$$

with

$$B_\alpha^*(t, v) = \int_t^v \phi_\alpha(t, u)du, \quad \alpha \in \{x, y\}. \tag{15.20}$$

We can now define the new co-ordinates

$$\begin{aligned} \boldsymbol{y} &= \boldsymbol{\Phi}^{-1}(t)\boldsymbol{x} \\ &= \left(\frac{x}{\phi_x(0,t)}, \frac{y}{\phi_y(0,t)} \right)^T \end{aligned}$$

Our result for the pricing kernel can be stated in the following theorem. Note the symmetry w.r.t. the role of x and y in this and the corresponding Black–Karasinski result in Theorem (15.2) below.

---

[2]We recall the observation made in §6.2.2 that the use of a rate specification depending on more than one factor renders the resultant pricing kernel less amenable for use in pricing interest rate derivatives. Since our interest here is more in curve evolution than options pricing, we see the advantage of maintaining a diagonal $\boldsymbol{\kappa}(t)$ as outweighing the loss of amenity resulting from the interest rate depending on two factors.

Theorem 15.1 *(Two-Factor Hull–White Pricing Kernel): The pricing kernel for (15.7) with $r(x,y,t)$ given by (15.16) can be written*

$$G(x,y,t;\xi,\eta,v) = e^{-\mu^*(x,y,t,v)} G_0(x,y,t;\xi + \Delta_x^*(t,v), \eta + \Delta_y^*(t,v), v), \tag{15.21}$$

where

$$\mu^*(x,y,t,v) = B_x^*(t,v)(x + r_x^*(t)) + B_y^*(t,v)(y + r_y^*(t)) + \tfrac{1}{2}\Sigma_{HW}(t,v), \tag{15.22}$$

$$r_x^*(t) = I_{xx}^*(0,t) + I_{xy}^*(0,t), \tag{15.23}$$

$$r_y^*(t) = I_{yx}^*(0,t) + I_{yy}^*(0,t), \tag{15.24}$$

$$\Delta_x^*(t,v) = I_{xx}^*(t,v) + I_{xy}^*(t,v), \tag{15.25}$$

$$\Delta_y^*(t,v) = I_{yx}^*(t,v) + I_{yy}^*(t,v), \tag{15.26}$$

$$\Sigma_{HW}(t,v) = B_x^{*2}(t,v)\Sigma_{xx}(0,t) + 2B_x^*(t,v)B_y^*(t,v)\Sigma_{xy}(0,t) + B_y^{*2}(t,v)\Sigma_{yy}(0,t). \tag{15.27}$$

The necessary calibration condition is that

$$r_2^*(t) = r_x^*(t) + r_y^*(t). \tag{15.28}$$

Proof: We observe from (6.13) that $\boldsymbol{\gamma}^*(t,v) = 0$, and from (6.8) that

$$\boldsymbol{\sigma}^*(t) = \begin{pmatrix} \frac{\sigma_x^2(t)}{\phi_x^2(0,t)} & \frac{\rho(t)\sigma_x(t)\sigma_y(t)}{\phi_x(0,t)\phi_y(0,t)} \\ \frac{\rho(t)\sigma_x(t)\sigma_y(t)}{\phi_x(0,t)\phi_y(0,t)} & \frac{\sigma_y^2(t)}{\phi_y^2(0,t)}, \end{pmatrix}. \tag{15.29}$$

Integrating this expression yields

$$\boldsymbol{\Sigma}^*(t,v) = \begin{pmatrix} \frac{\Sigma_{xx}(t,v)}{\phi_x^2(0,v)} & \frac{\Sigma_{xy}(t,v)}{\phi_x(0,v)\phi_y(0,v)} \\ \frac{\Sigma_{xy}(t,v)}{\phi_x(0,v)\phi_y(0,v)} & \frac{\Sigma_{yy}(t,v)}{\phi_y^2(0,v)} \end{pmatrix}.$$

from which we infer, using (6.27) and (6.30), that

$$\boldsymbol{\Phi}(v)\boldsymbol{\Sigma}^*(t,v)\boldsymbol{\Phi}^T(v) = \boldsymbol{\Sigma}(t,v),$$

$$\boldsymbol{\Theta}(t,u) = \begin{pmatrix} \frac{\Sigma_{xx}(t,u)}{\phi_x(0,u)} & \frac{\Sigma_{xy}(t,u)}{\phi_y(0,u)} \\ \frac{\Sigma_{xy}(t,u)}{\phi_x(0,u)} & \frac{\Sigma_{yy}(t,u)}{\phi_y(0,u)} \end{pmatrix}$$

$$\Delta y_j(t,v) = \sum_{i=1}^{2} \int_t^v \Theta_{ij}(t,u)\,du$$

$$= \left(\frac{I^*_{xx}(t,v) + I^*_{xy}(t,v)}{\phi_x(0,v)}, \frac{I^*_{yx}(t,v) + I^*_{yy}(t,v)}{\phi_y(0,v)} \right)_j$$

$$\sum_{k=1}^{2} [\mathbf{\Psi}(t,v)\Delta\mathbf{y}(0,t)]_k = B^*_x(t,v)(I^*_{xx}(0,t) + I^*_{xy}(0,t)) + B^*_y(t,v)(I^*_{yx}(0,t) + I^*_{yy}(0,t)),$$

$$\begin{aligned}\frac{1}{2}\sum_{k=1}^{2}\sum_{i=1}^{2} \left[\mathbf{\Psi}(t,v)\mathbf{\Sigma}^*(0,t)\mathbf{\Psi}^T(t,v)\right]_{ki} du &= \tfrac{1}{2}B^{*2}_x(t,v)\Sigma_{xx}(0,t) + B^*_x(t,v)B^*_y(t,v)\Sigma_{xy}(0,t) \\ &\quad + \tfrac{1}{2}B^{*2}_y(t,v)\Sigma_{yy}(0,t) \\ &= \tfrac{1}{2}\Sigma_{HW}(t,v).\end{aligned}$$

From Theorem 6.2, making the necessary substitutions, we obtain (15.21) and (15.28). This completes the proof.

It is straightforwardly inferred that the zero coupon bond price is given by

$$F^T(x,y,t) = D(t,T)e^{-\mu^*(x,y,t,T)}, \qquad (15.30)$$

from which the instantaneous T-forward rate $f^T(x,y,t)$ is easily inferred using the well-known result that

$$\begin{aligned} f^T(x,y,t) &= -\frac{\partial}{\partial T} \ln F^T(x,y,t) \\ &= \bar{r}(T) + \frac{\partial \mu^*(x,y,t,T)}{\partial T}. \end{aligned} \qquad (15.31)$$

15.4.2 m-Factor Extension

It is not difficult to obtain analogous results for the more general m-factor case. Suppose that we start with (6.21) and $m' = m$, rather than (15.16). The zero coupon bond price will then be given in terms of the transformed co-ordinate vector $\mathbf{y}$ by (6.36) and the instantaneous forward rate by (6.37). In the case that the mean reversion matrix $\boldsymbol{\kappa}(t)$ is assumed diagonal as above, the transformation matrix $\mathbf{\Phi}(t)$ is likewise diagonal and the change of co-ordinates trivial. However, it is probably more convenient to maintain the $\mathbf{y}$ co-ordinates since they are by assumption not mean-reverting so easier to roll out successively in a Monte Carlo simulation.

Notice also that if, rather than assuming $\boldsymbol{\kappa}(t)$ diagonal as in (15.17), a more general choice is made with a lower triangular form, the analysis in Chapter 6 goes through identically. Some additional work will be necessary to ascertain the form of the required auxiliary functions $\Phi(t)$, $\Psi(t,v)$ and $\Delta y(t,v)$. However, the zero coupon bond formula will be precisely as given by (6.36).

15.5 BLACK–KARASINSKI RATES

15.5.1 Two-Factor Pricing Kernel

We now consider the corresponding calculation for the Black–Karasinski case. The short rate, which we can think of in this case as representing either an interest rate or an instantaneous credit intensity, we take to be given by

$$r(x, y, t) := \tilde{r}(t)e^{x+y-\frac{1}{2}\Sigma(0,t)} + s(t), \quad t \geq 0, \tag{15.32}$$

with $s(t)$ a displacement factor which would typically be chosen to be zero in a credit context but negative in an interest rate context to allow of the possibility of the short rate becoming negative, as may be required to calibrate to the forward curve. The following results were previously published by Turfus and Shubert [2020]. Our result for the pricing kernel is stated in the following theorem.

Theorem 15.2 *(Two-Factor Black–Karasinski Pricing Kernel): The pricing kernel for* (15.7) *with $r(x, y, t)$ given by* (15.32) *can be written*

$$G(x, y, t; \xi, \eta, T) = \mathcal{E}_t^T(\mathcal{W}(t, \cdot))G_0(x, y, t; \xi, \eta, T), \tag{15.33}$$

where

$$\mathcal{W}(t, u) = \bar{r}(u) - s(u) - \tilde{r}(u)e^{\phi_x(t,u)x+\phi_y(t,u)y-\frac{1}{2}\Sigma^*_{BK}(t,u)}e^{\Delta_x(t,u)\frac{\partial}{\partial x}}e^{\Delta_y(t,u)\frac{\partial}{\partial y}}, \tag{15.34}$$

$$\Sigma^*_{BK}(t, u) = \phi_x^2(t, u)\Sigma_{xx}(0, t) + 2\phi_x(t, u)\phi_y(t, u)\Sigma_{xy}(0, t) + \phi_y^2(t, u)\Sigma_{yy}(0, t), \tag{15.35}$$

$$\Delta_x(t, u) = \frac{\Sigma_{xx}(t, u) + \Sigma_{xy}(t, u)}{\phi_x(t, u)}, \tag{15.36}$$

$$\Delta_y(t, u) = \frac{\Sigma_{xy}(t, u) + \Sigma_{yy}(t, u)}{\phi_y(t, u)}. \tag{15.37}$$

$$\tag{15.38}$$

Proof: The above result is a special case of (6.53) so can be inferred therefrom. However, a proof of this specific result from first principles can be found in Turfus and Shubert [2020], to which the reader is referred for details. The satisfaction of the calibration condition is considered in the following subsection.

15.5.2 Asymptotic Expansion

Suppose now that $\| r(x, y, t) \| = \mathcal{O}(\epsilon)$ is measured under some suitable norm and consider the limit as $\epsilon \to 0$. We pose the following perturbation expansion representation of our solution

$$G(x, y, t; \xi, \eta, T) = D(t, T) \sum_{n=0}^{\infty} G_n(x, y, t; \xi, \eta, T), \tag{15.39}$$

with $G_n(\cdot) = \mathcal{O}(\epsilon^n)$. We pose also

$$\tilde{r}(t) = \sum_{n=1}^{\infty} \tilde{r}_n(t), \tag{15.40}$$

with $\tilde{r}_n(\cdot) = \mathcal{O}(\epsilon^n)$. Further define

$$R_n(x, y, t, t_1) = \tilde{r}_n(t_1) e^{\phi_x(t,t_1)x + \phi_y(t,t_1)y - \frac{1}{2}\Sigma^*_{BK}(t,t_1)}, \tag{15.41}$$

noting that $R_n(0, 0, 0, t_1) = \tilde{r}_n(t_1)$.

Substituting into (15.33), we see at $\mathcal{O}(1)$ that the implicit choice of $G_0(\cdot)$ being given by (15.15) is a consistent one. At $\mathcal{O}(\epsilon)$ we obtain, making use again of (3.39)

$$\begin{aligned} G_1(x, y, t; \xi, \eta, T) &= \Delta(t, v) G_0(x, y, t; \xi, \eta, v) \\ &\quad - \int_t^T R_1(x, y, t, t_1) G_0(x + \Delta_x(t, t_1), y + \Delta_y(t, t_1), t; \xi, \eta, T) dt_1, \end{aligned} \tag{15.42}$$

$$\Delta(t, v) := \int_t^v (\overline{r}(t_1) - s(t_1)) dt_1 \tag{15.43}$$

and at $\mathcal{O}(\epsilon^2)$

$$\begin{aligned} G_2(x, y, t; \xi, \eta, T) &= \frac{1}{2}\Delta^2(t, v) G_0(x, y, t; \xi, \eta, v) - \int_t^T (\Delta(t, v) R_1(x, y, t, t_1) + R_2(x, y, t, t_1)) \\ &\qquad G_0(x + \Delta_x(t, t_1), y + \Delta_y(t, t_1), t; \xi, \eta, T) dt_1 \\ &\quad + \int_t^T R_1(x, y, t, t_1) \int_{t_1}^T R_1(x, y, t, t_2) e^{F_\phi(t, t_1, t_2)} \\ &\qquad G_0(x + \sum_{i=1}^{2} \Delta_x(t, t_i), y + \sum_{i=1}^{2} \Delta_y(t, t_i), t; \xi, \eta, T) dt_2 dt_1, \end{aligned} \tag{15.44}$$

$$F_\phi(t, t_1, t_2) := \phi_x(t_1, t_2)\Sigma_{xx}(t, t_1) + (\phi_x(t_1, t_2) + \phi_y(t_1, t_2))\Sigma_{xy}(t, t_1) + \phi_y(t_1, t_2)\Sigma_{yy}(t, t_1). \tag{15.45}$$

Finally, matching the T-maturity zero coupon bond price requires

$$\iint_{\mathbb{R}^2} G(0, 0, 0; \xi, \eta, T) d\xi d\eta = D(0, T)$$

for any $T > 0$. This is satisfied to $\mathcal{O}(\epsilon^2)$ by the choice

$$\begin{aligned} \tilde{r}_1(t) &= \bar{r}(t) - s(t), \\ \tilde{r}_2(t) &= \tilde{r}_1(t) \int_0^t \tilde{r}_1(t_1) \left(e^{F_\phi(0,t_1,t)} - 1 \right) dt_1, \end{aligned} \tag{15.46}$$

where, in deriving the second of these expressions, we have applied Fubini's theorem to the double integrals in (15.44). This leads to the following result:

Theorem 15.3 ***(Zero Coupon Bond Price):*** *The T-maturity zero coupon bond price satisfying* (15.7) *with* $P(x, y) \equiv 1$ *is given asymptotically in the limit as* $\epsilon \to 0$ *by*

$$\begin{aligned} F^T(x, y, t) = D(t, T) \Bigg(1 &- \int_t^T (R_1(x, y, t, t_1) + s(t_1) - \bar{r}(t_1)) dt_1 \\ &+ \frac{1}{2} \left(\int_t^T (R_1(x, y, t, t_1) + s(t_1) - \bar{r}(t_1)) dt_1 \right)^2 \\ &+ \int_t^T \Bigg(R_1(x, y, t, t_2) \\ &\int_t^{t_2} R_1(x, y, t, t_1) \left(e^{F_\phi(t,t_1,t_2)} - 1 \right) dt_1 - R_2(x, y, t, t_2) \Bigg) dt_2 \Bigg) \\ &+ \mathcal{O}(\epsilon^3). \end{aligned} \tag{15.47}$$

As in Chapter 6, the first three terms in brackets can be interpreted as the commencement of a power series representation of an exponential, which can be completed. The following representation is asymptotically equivalent.

$$F^T(x, y, t) e^{-\int_t^T (R_1(x,y,t,t_1) + s(t_1) + \Delta R_2(x,y,t_1)) dt_1} + \mathcal{O}(\epsilon^3). \tag{15.48}$$

with

$$\Delta R_2(x, y, t, T) := R_2(x, y, t, T) - R_1(x, y, t, T) \int_t^T R_1(x, y, t, t_1) \left(e^{F_\phi(t,t_1,T)} - 1 \right) dt_1. \tag{15.49}$$

Notably the calibration condition at $t = 0$ is preserved in this representation. This result can be given the following alternative interpretation.

Proposition 15.5.1 *(Survival Probability):* If $r(x, y, t)$ in (15.32) is taken instead to be the instantaneous default intensity of a named debt issuer, (15.47) and (15.48) can, in the absence of correlation between interest rates and credit intensities, be taken as giving the survival probability of this issuer from t to T.

As in the Hull–White case, we can easily infer the instantaneous T-forward rate $f^T(x, y, t)$ using (15.31). Following straightforward differentiation of (15.48) we obtain

$$f^T(x, y, t) = R_1(x, y, t, T) + s(T) + \Delta R_2(x, y, t, T) + \mathcal{O}(\epsilon^3). \tag{15.50}$$

This expression can equally be considered to describe the instantaneous forward default intensity for a credit default process, which result should prove useful in CVA calculations.

15.5.3 m-Factor Extension

As with the Hull–White case, it is not difficult to obtain analogous results for the more general m-factor case. Suppose that we start with (6.22) and $m' = m$ rather than (15.32). The zero coupon bond price will then be given in terms of the transformed co-ordinate vector $\mathbf{y}$ by (6.54) or (6.55) and the instantaneous forward rate by (6.57).

15.5.4 Representative Calculations

We consider for illustrative purposes the evolution of a USD forward rate curve from January 2018 under our two-factor Black–Karasinski model. For simplicity of calculation, we take all model parameters to be constant, as specified in Table 15.1.

The initial curve is evolved for fifteen years, the curve shape being captured after evolution times of 1y, 5y, 10y and 15y. The results based on (15.50) for three different scenarios are illustrated in Figs. 15.1–15.3.

As can be seen, there are considerable differences in the phenomenology. In Fig. 15.1 the typical one-factor model situation is seen for the first 10y of evolution whereby the short end of the curve undergoes significant movements but the long end changes little by comparison. However, between 10y and 15y, the situation changes

TABLE 15.1 Model parameters used in USD rates evolution

Parameter	Value
σ_x	0.20
σ_y	0.10
α_x	0.15
α_y	0.02
ρ	−0.30

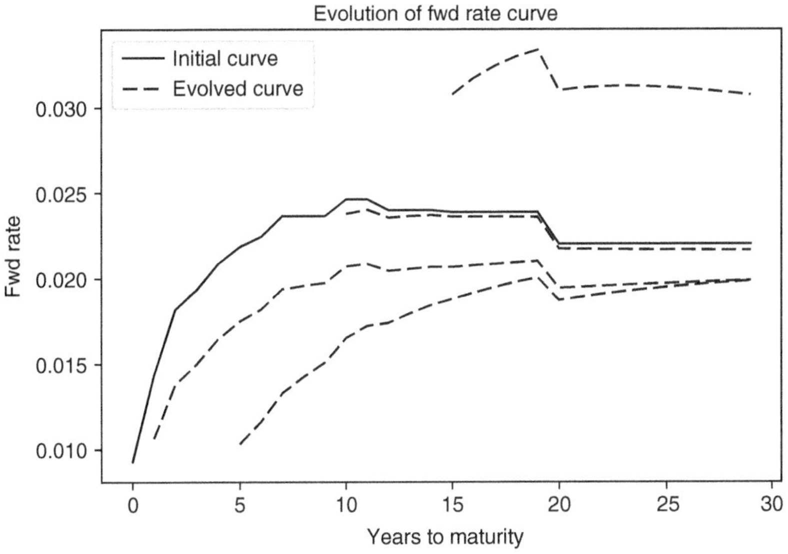

FIGURE 15.1 USD rates evolution: Scenario 1

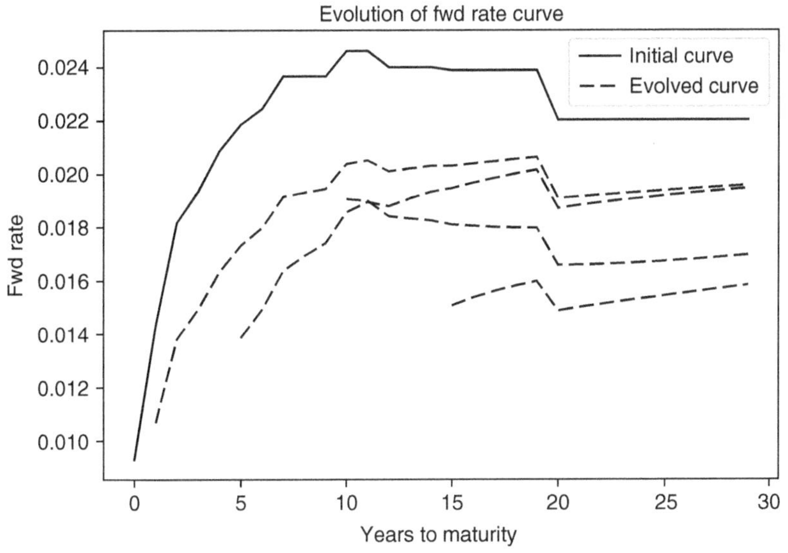

FIGURE 15.2 USD rates evolution: Scenario 2

with a significant contribution building up from σ_y (with slow mean reversion), which causes the whole curve from the 15y point to the 30y to rise by more than 100bp. In Fig. 15.2 the whole curve moves down for the first 1y; after a subsequent 4y period during which the short end moves down slightly, the long end moves down for 5y, after which time the whole curve starts to move down again, the short end by slightly

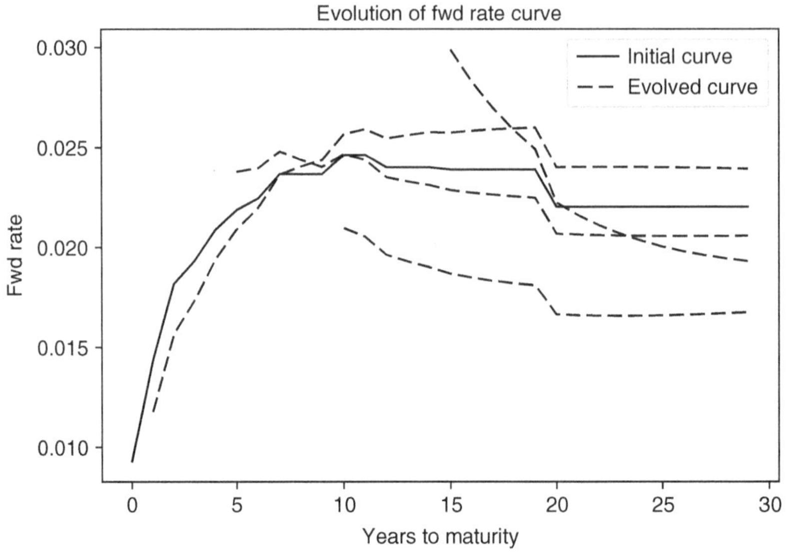

FIGURE 15.3 USD rates evolution: Scenario 3

less than the long end. In Fig. 15.3, we see that, interestingly, between the 10y and the 15y point, the short end of the curve rises considerably more than the long end, resulting in an inversion with the short end 100bp higher than the long end.

We also illustrate the dependence of $F^T(x, y, t)$ on x and y using (15.47). Parameter values are again as in Table 15.1, except that in this case we set $\bar{r}(t) = 0.02$ (constant), so the curves depend only on $T - t$, not on t and T separately. Formulae were coded up in Python and took on average about 30 ms to calculate a first-order approximation and about 700 ms for second order. Results for the first and second order approximations are shown together in Fig. 15.4 for comparison. As can be seen, with values of $|x|, |y| \leq 1$ the difference between the first and second order results remains small in relative terms, suggesting the second order expansion remains accurate in such cases.

We will of course encounter significant divergence in the case of extremely large values of x and y. But, since extreme values occur with a correspondingly small probability, this should not be too much of an obstacle to the use of our expansion for simulation purposes. In any event, the model itself is not expected *a priori* to be a good representation in the event of very large deviations. The condition of rates being strictly positive when $s(t) \geq 0$ should be satisfied even with truncated expansions, particularly if (15.48) is used rather than (15.47), although this may not be true in the event that ϵ is so large as to compromise the accuracy of a truncated version of (15.40). Such problems can be easily addressed by the exigency of flooring rates at zero.

Similar calculations using (15.48) rather than (15.47) were found to give results visually indistinguishable from each other, suggesting that third order terms can indeed be neglected, as proposed.

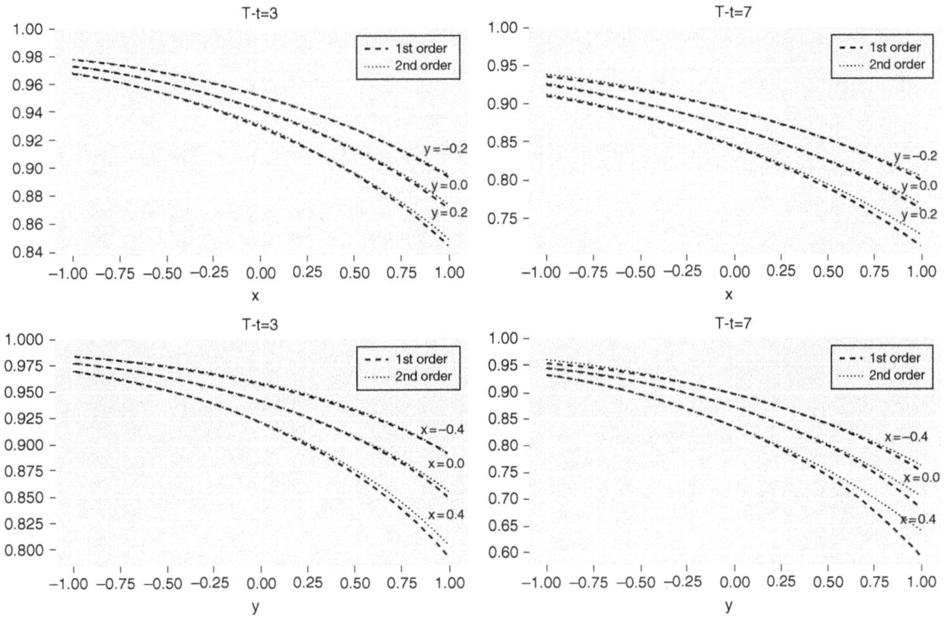

FIGURE 15.4 Comparison of 1st and 2nd order results for $F^T(x, y, t)$

15.6 JOINT RATES-CREDIT SCENARIOS

Suppose now we have a joint rates-credit scenario with Hull–White for the rates and Black–Karasinski for the credit components as in Chapter 8. If we wish to represent the evolution of the credit curve through a forward credit intensity, we can ignore the dependence of the credit calibration process on the rates process and use directly the results of the previous two sections, incorporating any correlations into the state variable x. If, on the other hand, we wish to represent the credit curve through a forward credit spread such as is needed to compute stochastic discount factors, we need to use the joint rates-credit model approach of Chapter 8. We include here the necessary calculations for the case where both the credit and the rates processes are represented as single-factor.

Using the notation there defined we find that, analogous to (15.31) but making use of the risky bond price formula (8.49) rather than the risk-free bond price, the instantaneous credit spread $s^T(x_\lambda, t)$ associated at time t with forward time $T > t$ is defined by

$$\begin{aligned} f^T(x_d, t) + s^T(x_\lambda, t) &= -\frac{\partial}{\partial T} \ln V_F^T(x_d, x_\lambda, t) \\ &= \bar{r}(T) + \frac{\partial \mu^*(x_d, t, T)}{\partial T} + \Lambda_1(x_\lambda, t, T) - \Delta\Lambda_1(x_\lambda, t, T) + \mathcal{O}(\epsilon^2), \end{aligned} \tag{15.51}$$

where we define

$$\Delta\Lambda_1(x_\lambda, t, T) = \int_t^T \phi_d(t_1, T)\Sigma_{d\lambda}(t, t_1)\Lambda_1(x_\lambda, t, t_1)e^{-B_d^*(t_1,T)\Sigma_{d\lambda}(t,t_1)}dt_1, \tag{15.52}$$

whence we deduce

$$s^T(x_\lambda, t) = \Lambda_1(x_\lambda, t, T) - \Delta\Lambda_1(x_\lambda, t, T) + \mathcal{O}(\epsilon^2). \tag{15.53}$$

Second order corrections can also be derived, but the resultant expressions are quite lengthy and unlikely to be needed in practice. Notice that, in the event that there is zero rates-credit correlation, we have $\Delta\Lambda_1(\cdot) = 0$ and the instantaneous credit spread can be identified with the credit default intensity applicable in the event of deterministic rates.

CHAPTER 16

Model Risk Management Strategies

16.1 INTRODUCTION

Much effort is currently being invested into managing the risk faced by financial institutions as a consequence of model uncertainty. One strand to this effort is an increased level of regulatory scrutiny of the performance of the model validation function, both in terms of ensuring that adequate testing is performed of all models used for pricing and risk management purposes and of enforcing a governance policy that only models so tested are so used. As is stated in the Federal Reserve's Supervision and Regulation Letter of US Federal Reserve [2011]

> An integral part of model development is testing, in which the various components of a model and its overall functioning are evaluated to show the model is performing as intended; to demonstrate that it is accurate, robust, and stable; and to evaluate its limitations and assumptions.

Another concern is model risk monitoring and management. Here the idea is that, having validated models and examined the associated uncertainty, the risk department should monitor and report on the risk faced by a financial institution, ideally so that senior management can, based on "risk appetite", make informed decisions about model usage policy. According to US Federal Reserve [2011]

> Validation activities should continue on an ongoing basis after a model goes into use to track known model limitations and to identify any new ones. Validation is an important check during periods of benign economic and financial conditions, when estimates of risk and potential loss can become overly optimistic and the data at hand may not fully reflect more stressed conditions.... Generally, senior management should ensure that appropriate mitigating steps are taken in light of identified model limitations, which can include adjustments to model output, restrictions on model use, reliance on other models or approaches, or other compensating controls.

Here the notion of best practice is less well established, in particular because different institutions adopt different approaches to measuring and reporting model risk. In what probably remains the most definitive book[1] on the subject, Morini [2011] asserts

> You will see that not even among quants there is consensus about what model risk is.

Indeed there are currently regular industry events held at which practitioners and managers from financial institutions share and discuss their views on current best practice and how this should evolve. It is not therefore possible, at least for the moment, to enforce specific regulatory standards in this area, although regulators do take an interest in how banks perform the model risk governance function.

Central to the task of monitoring and managing model risk or uncertainty is the challenge of how to measure it. Current practice tends to be a mix of qualitative and quantitative metrics. While the former are easier to implement, the latter are preferable in terms of the level of control which can be exercised, particularly if the model risk can be quantified in monetary terms. However, the fact that no commonly agreed methodology has emerged and such methodologies as have been proposed tend not to lend themselves to implementation by practitioners means that it has not been easy to make progress in this area.

A common approach taken by financial institutions has been to consider the reserves taken by the finance function to account for model parameter and/or calibration uncertainty as a proxy measure of model risk. This is arguably less than satisfactory for a number of reasons, not least that the purpose of reserves is to provide a protective buffer against, rather than a precise measure of, model risk.

The approach set out below represents a compromise between rigour and practicality to furnish model risk metrics against which risk appetite can be compared. We consider specifically rates-credit correlation risk in relation to credit derivatives pricing and/or CVA calculations (so-called "wrong-way risk"), making particular use of the results obtained in Chapter 8. However, we suggest that the methodology is applicable more widely to other types of model risk and a wider class of financial instruments and models, using results from other parts of this book.

We begin in §16.2 by reviewing previous methodologies which have been proposed for the quantification of model risk, before formally outlining our own proposed approach. In §16.3, expressions for the PV of semi-exotic credit derivatives, specifically credit-contingent interest rate swaps (including with capped or floored LIBOR) and contingent CDS with an interest rate swap underlying are used in conjunction with those developed in §16.2 to assess the level of model risk associated with the uncertain parameter(s). Finally in §16.4, we present some suggestions of directions in which the ideas presented could be further developed.

---

[1]It should be mentioned that the author in his book eschews the idea that any one book should aim to be definitive.

16.2 MODEL RISK METHODOLOGY

16.2.1 Previous Work

A number of authors have previously visited the question of what constitutes an appropriate methodology for the quantification of model risk in pricing financial derivatives. In his pioneering work on the subject, Cont [2004] proposes two approaches. In the first, a family of plausible models is envisaged, each calibrated to all relevant market instruments then used to price a given portfolio of exotic derivatives. The degree of variation in the prices which are observed provides a measure of the intrinsic uncertainty associated with modelling the price of the portfolio. A second approach, taking account of the fact that not all models are amenable to calibration to market instruments, compares the models by penalising them for the pricing error associated with calibration instruments. The pricing errors for multiple instruments can be combined using various choices of norm, giving rise to a number of possible measures of model risk.

While intuitively attractive, neither of these approaches appears to have been adopted by practitioners. This is likely a consequence of the cost of implementing multiple models and re-pricing under them. Financial institutions usually have only a very few models implemented, often just one, capable of pricing a given exotic option. Furthermore, regulatory pressure has recently been towards standardising pricing of financial derivatives by restricting or even reducing the size of the set of available models, which fact mitigates against the adoption of the kind of approach envisaged by Cont [2004].

Subsequently, Glasserman and Xu [2014] proposed an alternative approach based on maximising the model error subject to a constraint on the level of plausibility. The approach starts from a baseline model and finds the worst-case error that would be incurred through a deviation from the baseline model, given a precise constraint on the plausibility of the deviation. Using relative entropy to constrain model distance leads to an explicit characterisation of worst-case model errors. In this way they are able to calculate upper bounds on model error. They show how their approach can be applied to the problems of portfolio risk measurement, credit risk, delta hedging and counterparty risk measured through credit valuation adjustment (CVA).

Although this approach has the attraction of a rigorous definition and, according to the authors, is amenable to convenient Monte Carlo implementation, it has the disadvantage that an entropy constraint specified *a priori* is not the sort of concept which risk managers are likely to be comfortable with in defining or expressing risk appetite. Yet it is central to the whole approach. Furthermore, the method has the disadvantage that it probably offers too much laxity in allowing the joint probability distribution function governing risk factors to vary freely subject only to the entropy constraint. Many of the perturbed distributions, including those giving rise to worst-case errors, would likely be deemed "unrealistic" by practitioners for reasons which cannot easily be encoded through entropy considerations. An approach which allows the user to be more specific about what is believed to be "known" and with what degree of certainty using a parametrisation more closely related to market variables would probably be preferred.

For example, the consensus among practitioners might be that the "best" interest rate model would be somewhere between a normal and a lognormal process. But under the proposal of Glasserman and Xu [2014], if a Hull–White (normal) model were chosen as the baseline, deviations towards lognormal and away from it would be penalised equally. Yet, we are really only interested in assessing the impact of the former.

Soklakov [2015] independently developed a not dissimilar entropy-based approach which he termed quantitative structuring on the basis that it grew out of an attempt to optimise product design to exploit perceived model deficiencies inherent in market prices: the original problem was then turned on its head to ask instead what are the expected returns which could be made by exploiting a given model deficiency through investing in a portfolio or structured product designed to exploit the perceived model weakness maximally. The method takes advantage of the fact that this portfolio has a payoff given precisely by the log of the ratio of the terminal values of the pricing kernels associated with the two models. With this knowledge, the annualised expected returns on the portfolio can be calculated and a precise quantitative assessment of model risk made. The beauty of this approach is that it allows a worst-case assessment to be made for the model as a whole in relation to any products for which the model could be deemed appropriate. The drawback is of course that it allows the comparison to be made only in relation to one alternative model.

More recently, Skoglund [2019] adapted the method of Glasserman and Xu [2014], applying it to scenario calculations such as are used in credit loss forecasting. He argued that the more qualitative methods generally employed by financial institutions are increasingly being seen by regulators as inadequate, while the financial institutions find themselves being unduly conservative in the setting of provisions on account of the lack of robust quantitative assessments of model risk (see further below).

In his review of the subject Morini [2011], while lamenting the paucity of the model risk literature, comes down against excessive use of mathematical formalism and numerics which can serve to obscure the all-important link between specific modelling assumptions and the variability of prices that can emerge therefrom and advocates a middle path between that and "formal compliance or simple techniques to produce numbers that are acceptable to put in reports, but lacks [sic] the quantitative approach that would be needed to understand models deeply". A useful insight into the sorts of techniques that are currently used to put numbers into reports has been provided by Joshi [2017].

Along the latter lines, Brotcke and Brastow [2019], building on the earlier work of Jacobs Jr. [2015], have recently set out a proposal wherein an aggregate risk score is calculated based on a combination of quantitative and qualitative measures. This, they point out, is in line with the stipulations of US Federal Reserve [2011] and furthermore reflects the authors' experience conducting supervisory reviews for the US Federal Reserve. They propose summing a "model robustness index" score, providing an *a priori* assessment of the model's risk, and a "model stability index" score which takes into account how the model performs once in use. However, in a review of their proposal, Marlin [2018] cites a number of practitioners who cast some doubt on its practicality and indeed notes that the authors themselves acknowledge that practitioners don't know how to quantify the capital that should be held to protect against model risk other than to say they take a "conservative" approach. Another issue is the subjectivity of the weights which must be attached to incommensurable component scores to obtain an aggregate score. It remains to be seen whether the proposed approach achieves traction in practice.

We look in our treatment below to avoid these issues of subjectivity and incommensurability of index scores, following the suggestion of Skoglund [2019] and Soklakov [2015] to measure model risk instead in financial terms. We look to build to some extent on the basic philosophy of Cont [2004], but simplifying the methodology in compliance with the advocacy of Morini [2011] and avoiding the prohibitive cost of implementing multiple numerical models. We suggest that key to making progress is the ability to assess, at least to a good approximation, the impact of more advanced model features without necessarily having to implement them explicitly in a fully working model.

To this end, we propose that asymptotic analysis which has in the author's view been under-used in risk management offers a fruitful way forward, certainly in the context of credit derivatives pricing with which we are mainly concerned. A key advantage here is that the output of the model risk assessment process is in the form of analytic formulae rather than numerical routines. The relative transparency of the former will often furnish insight about which model configurations and inputs give rise to the greatest degree of uncertainty in terms of output prices. The alternative approach which is typically followed in model risk analysis is to sample the phase space of all possible market conditions, model parameterisations and product characteristics in a generally rather unsystematic way and infer conclusions from such data as are gleaned in the process. An obvious drawback of this approach is that there are no guarantees that the worst cases where the potential discrepancies are largest are uncovered; or how representative the numbers in the dataset are of the phase space which has been "sampled". This is of course in addition to the drawback that the model needs to be implemented incorporating all possible features, a not insignificant cost, before its performance can be investigated and evaluated in this way.

We suggest that a further reason why the model risk methodologies which have been proposed in the literature appear to have had limited traction in financial institutions lies in the organisational structure of those institutions. Specifically it is an issue that authority to make judgements in relation to which models are used, how they are configured and calibrated and how model risk is assessed is inevitably devolved across multiple functions: front office, market risk, model validation, finance, CVA desk, etc. For that reason we propose that a partitioned approach is taken whereby questions about how price-relevant model parameters are assigned and how the uncertainty associated with these is assessed can be considered separately from issues around how their values and assumed uncertainty levels (or distributions) impact on prices. Our focus in this chapter will by choice be on the latter. We note in this context that a further practical advantage of our proposed approach over the more mathematically sophisticated approaches of Glasserman and Xu [2014] and Skoglund [2019] is that the intuition of practitioners tasked with the responsibility to assess parameter uncertainty levels is better attuned to more immediate parameters like correlation than the more abstract concepts employed by theoreticians.

16.2.2 Proposed Framework

We choose to work here with rates-credit correlation uncertainty since this allows us to exploit a number of the results we have derived earlier to illustrate conveniently the utility of the method proposed below. But we would emphasise that the approach taken is not restricted to such and could indeed be applied to any model parameter, the uncertainty associated with which has a non-trivial but at the same time not overwhelming impact on pricing or risk calculations.

We formally state the problem we are looking to address as follows. Consider a model $\mathcal{M}(s, \rho)$ which we wish to use as the basis for pricing a portfolio Φ containing derivatives D_k, $k = 1, 2, \ldots, m$. Here $s = (s_1, s_2, \ldots, s_n)$, with s_i the value of the credit spread (suitably defined for a given issuer) associated with maturity T_i, $i = 1, 2, \ldots, n$, and ρ the correlation between rates and credit (previously denoted $\rho_{d\lambda}$), the appropriate value of which is uncertain or unknown and furthermore *not* readily ascertainable from market data, or else not in practice modelled. We wish to consider and indeed quantify, at least to a first level of approximation, the dependence of the portfolio price on the correlation parameter.

To this end we consider the calibration at time $t = 0$ of credit spreads in the model to a vector of market prices $p = (p_1, p_2, \ldots, p_n)$ for calibration instruments $\{\mathcal{I}_1, \mathcal{I}_2, \ldots, \mathcal{I}_n\}$. Let us express the result of such calibration for an assumed value of ρ formally as

$$s = f(\rho; p) \tag{16.1}$$

for some $f(\cdot; p) : [-1, 1] \to \mathbb{R}^n$. Since the market instrument prices are considered fixed for the time $t = 0$ of interest, we shall for convenience generally omit the explicit dependence on p_i in the following, in particular writing component-wise simply $s_i = f_i(\rho)$. There may be other market instruments to which the model is calibrated but, if the generated prices of these are not sensitive to ρ (or only very weakly so), we need not consider them explicitly in our analysis here.

Let us then denote the price calculated for derivative D using model $\mathcal{M}(s, \rho)$, thus calibrated by $V(D; \mathcal{M}(s, \rho))$. Let us further introduce the shorthand notation

$$V_k(\rho) = V(D_k; \mathcal{M}(f(\rho), \rho)). \tag{16.2}$$

From the examples considered in Chapter 8, we see that the dependence of credit derivatives prices on ρ tends to be well captured as a linear function thereof.[2] An appropriate measure of the model risk associated with pricing the derivative portfolio with an assumed value $\rho = \rho_0$ is on this basis obtained by use of the linear approximation

$$R(\Phi; \rho_0, \Delta\rho) := \Delta\rho \sum_{k=1}^{m} \left. \frac{\partial V_k(\rho)}{\partial \rho} \right|_{\rho=\rho_0} \tag{16.3}$$

[2]For other choices of model parameter than ρ, this will often still tend to be the case on the basis that the uncertain/unmodelled parameter will be of secondary importance; if this were not so, the consequent high degree of uncertainty introduced into pricing would compromise the utility of the pricing algorithm.

with $\Delta\rho$ an estimate of the level of uncertainty or inaccuracy associated with the representation of the parameter ρ. Performing the required differentiation on (16.2), we see

$$\left.\frac{\partial V_k(\rho)}{\partial \rho}\right|_{\rho=\rho_0} = \left.\left(\sum_{i=1}^{n} \frac{\partial V(D_k; \mathcal{M}(s;\rho))}{\partial s_i} f_i'(\rho) + \frac{\partial V(D_k; \mathcal{M}(s;\rho))}{\partial \rho}\right)\right|_{s=f(\rho),\ \rho=\rho_0} \tag{16.4}$$

We seek a convenient practical means of determining $f_i'(\rho_0)$. To that end we note that the ith calibration condition can be expressed as

$$V(\mathcal{I}_i; \mathcal{M}(s;\rho)) = p_i, \tag{16.5}$$

leading by the same token to

$$\left.\left(\sum_{j=1}^{i} \frac{\partial V(\mathcal{I}_i; \mathcal{M}(s;\rho))}{\partial s_j} f_j'(\rho_0) + \frac{\partial V(\mathcal{I}_i; \mathcal{M}(s;\rho))}{\partial \rho}\right)\right|_{s=f(\rho),\ \rho=\rho_0} = 0. \tag{16.6}$$

Here we assume that the model is bootstrapped by applying the calibration conditions in order of maturity, whence there will be no dependence of the price of $\mathcal{I}_i$ on s_j for $j > i$ The partial derivatives in this equality can be computed conveniently by use of the asymptotic modelling approach described below. From this, the values of $f_i'(\rho_0)$ can be inferred recursively. Substituting in (16.4) and then (16.3) gives rise to our representation of the model risk. On the basis of our assumption of approximate linear dependence of prices on ρ over the range of interest, we propose that our evaluations of $f_j'(\rho_0)$, with typically $\rho_0 = 0$, can consistently be used in place of $f_j'(\rho)$.

Our suggestion here is that, if we can derive analytic approximations to instrument prices taking into account the uncertain model parameters, this opens the way to obtaining analytic representations of the partial derivatives in (16.4) and so to obtaining an estimate of the model risk more conveniently and in a more transparent form than otherwise.

16.2.3 Calibration to CDS Market

If we consider our model to be calibrated to risky bond prices, the calibration is at this stage completely specified, at least to second order accuracy. In particular, we see that $f_i'(\rho) = 0$ in (16.4), simplifying our task.

Alternatively, if, as is often the case, the calibration is to a term structure of CDS rates, we can take the market prices p_i associated with maturities T_i to be zero and the associated market instruments to be ATM CDS. Let us further suppose that the function $\overline{\lambda}(t)$ can be taken as piecewise constant between the T_i, given say by

$$\overline{\lambda}(t) = \lambda_i, \quad t \in (T_{i-1}, T_i] \tag{16.7}$$

with $T_0 \equiv 0$. We can then take the s_i introduced in section (16.2.2) above to be given by

$$s_i T_i = \sum_{j=1}^{i} \lambda_j (T_j - T_{j-1}). \tag{16.8}$$

Inference of the $f_i'(\rho)$ is then straightforward, but our task is simplified if we suppose $\lambda = \mathcal{O}(\epsilon)$ and are willing to consider only the leading order impact of (re-)calibration, whence we can neglect the $\mathcal{O}(\epsilon^2)$ indirect impact of the λ_i through the (risky) discount factors in favour of their $\mathcal{O}(\epsilon)$ direct impact in the context of default-driven payoffs.[3] A straightforward calculation gives rise to the conclusion that

$$f_i'(\rho) \approx -\frac{T_i - T_{i-1}}{\rho T_i} \frac{\int_0^{T_i} B(0,u)\Delta\lambda(u)du}{\int_{T_{i-1}}^{T_i} B(0,u)du} \tag{16.9}$$

with expected $\mathcal{O}(\epsilon)$ relative errors.[4] Equipped with this additional information we are in a position to assess the model uncertainty associated with other derivative types priceable by our model.

16.3 APPLICATIONS

We illustrate our approach now with some examples. We will make use mainly of the rates-credit hybrid model introduced in Chapter 8, specifically the pricing kernel (8.14) and the results in §8.3 for risky cash flows, risky LIBOR flows and default-contingent cash flows, where the interest rate model is Hull–White and the credit model Black–Karasinski.

16.3.1 Interest Rate Swap Extinguisher

We start with the case of the interest rate swap extinguisher considered in §8.3.3 above. By this is meant an interest rate swap where the cash flows are contingent on survival of a named debt issuer. Suppose that the payment periods for both legs of the swap are $[t_{i-1}, t_i]$, $i = 1, 2, \ldots, N$ and the fixed coupon rate c. The extension of the calculation if payments are not synchronised is trivial. The fair price of a payer extinguisher will be

$$PV_{Extinguisher} = \sum_{i=1}^{N} \left(PV_{LIBOR}^{(i)} - PV_{Coupon}^{(i)} \right) \tag{16.10}$$

where, to first order in ϵ

$$PV_{Coupon}^{(i)} \sim B(0, t_i) c \delta(t_{i-1}, t_i), \tag{16.11}$$

$$PV_{LIBOR}^{(i)} \sim B(0, t_i) \left(\frac{1 - \phi_L(t_{i-1}, t_i)}{D(t_{i-1}, t_i)} - 1 \right), \tag{16.12}$$

with $\phi_L(\cdot, \cdot)$ given by (8.59).

[3]We have already implicitly made this assumption in assuming above that the s_i are independent of p_j for $j < i$.

[4]The errors can in addition be expected to approximate to near zero since the calibration swaps are assumed to be at the money, whence the (risky) discounting affects both legs almost equally.

It is from here a straightforward matter of differentiation to quantify the model uncertainty associated with the parameter ρ. For the coupon flows there is no such dependency to leading order. For the LIBOR flows, we have

$$\frac{\partial PV^{(i)}_{LIBOR}}{\partial \rho} \sim -\frac{B(0,t_i)\phi_L(t_{i-1},t_i)}{\rho D(t_{i-1},t_i)} \tag{16.13}$$

and, again ignoring the higher-order indirect impact of the λ_j through the (risky) discount factors, we obtain

$$\frac{\partial PV^{(i)}_{LIBOR}}{\partial \lambda_j} \approx -\frac{B(0,t_i)\phi_L(t_{i-1}\vee T_{j-1},(t_i\vee T_{j-1})\wedge T_j)}{\lambda_j D(t_{i-1},t_i)}. \tag{16.14}$$

From (16.4), we infer that, if the uncertainty associated with ρ is $\Delta\rho$, the model uncertainty associated with an interest rate swap extinguisher calibrated to risky bond prices is

$$\text{Uncertainty} \approx \Delta\rho \left| \sum_{i=1}^{N} \frac{\partial PV^{(i)}_{LIBOR}}{\partial \rho} \right| \tag{16.15}$$

and, if calibration is to CDS rates

$$\text{Uncertainty} \approx \Delta\rho \left| \sum_{i=1}^{N} \left(\sum_{j=1}^{n} \frac{\partial PV^{(i)}_{LIBOR}}{\partial \lambda_j} f_j'(\rho) + \frac{\partial PV^{(i)}_{LIBOR}}{\partial \rho} \right) \right|, \tag{16.16}$$

with $f_j'(\rho)$ given by (16.9). Notice that in the latter case, the impact of calibration adjustment is such as to *reduce* the overall uncertainty (for either a payer or a receiver swap), so ignoring it would be to take a conservative approach.

Capped LIBOR flows. We consider also the impact of capping the LIBOR flow in the extinguisher swap at some level $K > 0$. The pricing problem we considered in §8.3.4. From (8.73), we see that the impact of the cap is to change the value of the LIBOR flow from that given by (16.12) to

$$PV^{(i)}_{CappedLIBOR} \sim B(0,t_i)\left(\frac{1-\phi_L(t_{i-1},t_i)}{D(t_{i-1},t_i)} \Phi(d_2(\xi^*,0)) - \kappa^{-1}\Phi(-d_1(\xi^*,0)) \right), \tag{16.17}$$

using the terminology defined in §8.3.4. Otherwise the calculation for the correlation uncertainty proceeds exactly as above. The adjustment for floored LIBOR is straightforward.

16.3.2 Contingent CDS

We consider next a contingent CDS on an interest rate swap. Taking the payment periods to be the same as in the previous example, the cost (PV) of protection purchased at $t = 0$ on a payer swap is given by

$$V_{\text{Protection}} \sim (1 - R) \sum_{i=1}^{M} V_i, \tag{16.18}$$

with V_i given by (8.90), but interpreting

$$\kappa_i := \frac{1}{1 + c\delta(t_{i-1}, t_1)}. \tag{16.19}$$

It is again a matter of straightforward differentiation to obtain an expression for the correlation risk associated with this modelling approach. We obtain

$$\text{Uncertainty} \approx (1 - R)\Delta\rho \left| \sum_{i=1}^{N} \left(\sum_{j=1}^{n} \frac{\partial V_i}{\partial \lambda_j} f_j'(\rho) + \frac{\partial V_i}{\partial \rho} \right) \right|. \tag{16.20}$$

As can be seen, the main impact will be through differentiating $\Sigma_{d\lambda}(0, \cdot)$ w.r.t. ρ. Note, particularly in the case where n is large, it may be expedient to compute the credit sensitivities by numerical differentiation, rather than attempting to obtain them analytically as in (16.14) above.

16.4 CONCLUSIONS

We have proposed a framework for the quantification of model risk in credit derivatives pricing in circumstances where the correlation between rates and credit is either uncertain in its value or not included in the calculation. We considered in particular the cases of a) an interest rate swap extinguisher (including with capped LIBOR flows) and b) a contingent CDS on an interest rate swap underlying. We derived analytic expressions for the model risk as a function of the degree of uncertainty associated with the correlation, under an asymptotic assumption of the interest rate and the credit default intensity being small and taking into account the potential impact of correlation on model calibration. We propose that the results obtained are accurate enough for practical purposes.

Although the cases considered here involve rather simple modelling considerations, we suggest that the approach advocated has much wider application, including for parameters other than rates-credit correlation in other multi-factor models. In particular, it is possible to look at asymptotic modelling involving also the price of a spot underlying such as an equity, an FX rate or an inflation rate, using the formulae derived in Chapters 9–12. The spot underlyings could further be assumed to jump in value contingent on default, whence the model uncertainty associated with uncertainty in the expected jump size can also easily be obtained as an analytic expression. An example of such a calculation is given by Turfus [2018d], who considers the uncertainty in pricing a quanto CDS where the protection amount is capped in a currency different from that of the notional under the assumption that the model is calibrated to reproduce the CDS spreads for both currencies correctly.

CHAPTER 17

Machine Learning

17.1 TRENDS IN QUANTITATIVE FINANCE RESEARCH

17.1.1 Some Recent Trends

Every so often an idea rips through the quantitative finance research community like a hurricane, turning careers on their heads and causing consultants to re-badge themselves with new credentials which will qualify them for the new roles for which financial institutions are seeking to recruit. A couple of decades ago, perturbation methods were the new kids on the block, with the SABR model of Hagan et al. [2002] sweeping before it the previous wisdom that only exact analytic solutions were worthy of consideration as alternatives to full numerical solutions. The interest in the pioneering asymptotic analyses of Hagan et al. [2002] and Fouque et al. [2000] was driven mainly by an aspiration to be able to calibrate models efficiently in the presence of local-stochastic volatility, in the absence of exact analytic formulae such as Black–Scholes for liquid option prices (and of the levels of computational power available today).

In the wake of the credit crunch of 2007, the focus was increasingly on dealing with regulation and finding efficient ways of performing the calculations which needed to be performed repeatedly to comply with them. A concomitant increase in the focus on counterparty default risk led to controversies over discrepancies between different discounting and funding curves, which fuelled the creation of a cottage industry referred to generically as XVA, with the "X" representing a veritable alphabet soup of different value adjustments: "C" for counterparty (or credit); "D" for debit; "F" for funding; "L" for liquidity; "M" for margin; "T" for tax; and "K" for capital ("C" already having been assigned). The issue of how to integrate all these into a unified view without engaging in double counting remains a vestigial problem which will in likelihood never be solved.

In more recent years the arrival of bitcoin sparked a huge upsurge of interest in the associated blockchain ledger technology [Antonopoulos, 2017]. That interest has subsided somewhat recently, as has the bitcoin price, from its peak of nearly 20,000 USD at the end of 2017, in the wake of some of the overblown predictions of bitcoin overturning the existing economic order and disintermediating the banking system in short order coming up against the harsh reality of the scale of the challenges which would have to be overcome for that to happen.

17.1.2 The Arrival of Machine Learning

Undoubtedly the latest and most disruptive "big thing" in the world of quantitative finance is machine learning, also commonly referred to under the titles *deep learning* and *neural networks*, although the latter is strictly a subset of machine learning.[1] The ideas of machine learning go back, arguably, to the beginnings of computer science, but the field has only come into its own in recent years with the huge advances in the level of computing power which is readily available.

Early successes came in its application to pattern recognition (faces, voices, handwriting, images). Such use is typically in the realm of supervised learning, wherein a learning algorithm is presented with data and told what the "right" answer is for each dataset. The machine then has to evolve an algorithm enabling it to identify traits within the data which discriminate between cases of interest; this can ultimately be applied to new data outside the initial training set. The types of task addressed by supervised learning have evolved rapidly in recent years, leading to huge advances in the realm of robotics, where machines effectively programme themselves to perform complex tasks, to the point where vehicles have become self-driving and planes are able to fly themselves.

Another important area is data mining which usually adopts a more unsupervised approach. Here the aim is to detect trends and properties hidden in data using statistical and probabilistic techniques. This has captured the popular imagination through the likes of Google and Amazon who were able, through detecting patterns latent in customer/user data, to extract useful information about their preferences, which information could be used to inform marketing strategies and targeted advertising. This has of course proved a very lucrative business proposition, to the point where the collection and exploitation of data has become the main business driver for an increasing number of technology companies.

The question which naturally arose was whether traders operating in finance and commodity markets could use similar technologies to improve their trading strategies. It is hard to know exactly when this took off as much of the early work was proprietary and/or *ad hoc*, so not visible on the general radar. But there is certainly evidence over the last ten years of a rapidly growing interest shown by financial engineers and traders, with an increasing number of research papers starting to appear on the subject.

Both main areas of application in this direction have been in the realm of data mining. First, there is algorithmic trading, mainly in FX, where interest can be traced back to the early 2000s. Here the machine itself becomes the trader, and the main purpose

[1]The class of genetic or evolutionary algorithms which are based around the biological principle of natural selection are to be distinguished from neural networks whereby a more systematic learning strategy tends to be employed based on a carefully crafted internal architecture, the guiding principle again being biological, but this time mimicking the architecture and activity of the brain.

of the algorithm is to be able to respond to and exploit in real time signals encoded in the trading data faster than a human being could do. Another increasingly important area is the development of optimal portfolio trading strategies whereby trends latent in extended time series of market data are detected through intensive numerical investigation by a deep-learning algorithm and used to infer profitable trading strategies, exploiting the insights which these algorithms convey. Naturally, the latter idea has been of greater interest on the "buy side", although investment banks and brokers on the "sell side" have taken an active interest in algorithmic trading.

More recently, mainly in the last two or three years, supervised learning approaches have also started to make inroads into the world of financial engineering following the suggestion that the work of computationally expensive Monte Carlo and finite difference engines, used to calculate the prices and manage the risk of financial products, could be replicated using neural networks, which, having been trained adequately for the purpose, could perform the calculations more efficiently. This offers the benefit of huge cost savings, particularly in a risk management and regulatory context where risk and pricing engines are run repetitively across the bank's portfolios. It is further envisaged that, by learning from market data and prices directly, rather than through the agency of existing models calibrated thereto, deep-learning algorithms could even improve on their performance.

17.2 FROM PRICING MODELS TO MARKET GENERATORS

The engagement with machine learning in this latter context has tended to be more focussed on neural networks than the evolutionary-type algorithms typically used for unsupervised learning. Most of the work in this direction published thus far has been of a preliminary and exploratory nature, although a few commercial companies have already been started offering services along these lines. An important early proof-of-concept was reported by Ferguson and Green [2018]. They trained a neural network to price a call option on a worst-of basket of six stocks in a Black–Scholes framework (with flat implied volatility for each stock). Because of the relatively high dimensionality, this is a challenging task even for a Monte Carlo engine, an accuracy of 99% being achieved only with the use of up to ten minutes of CPU time. Nonetheless, the authors were able to train the neural network to provide results of comparable accuracy, making use of less than 6 milliseconds of processor time on a GPU. The main downside of their approach was that the one-off training of the network for this task took a week of dedicated processing on a 24-core server.

Similar contributions were made around the same time by a number of other authors. De Spiegeleer et al. [2018] considered American and barrier options in a Black–Scholes framework. McGhee [2018] and Bayer and Stemper [2018] considered vanilla options, the former in in a SABR stochastic volatility framework and the latter in Heston stochastic volatility and Bergomi rough volatility frameworks.

Building on this work, an important further contribution was made in a recent paper by Horvath et al. [2019], which earned the authors the Risk.net Rising star in quant finance award the following year. Their key strategy was to build on the observation that it was much easier to train a neural network to reproduce Black–Scholes implied volatilities for vanilla European options than the associated prices, on the basis that the implied volatility surface is reasonably flat by comparison. Of particular interest was the pricing of options calculated for a rough volatility model, since these are very expensive to compute, rendering the task of model calibration very time-consuming.

Denoting the implied volatility for a given equity underlying by $\sigma_{\text{B–S}}(K, T)$, associated with options with strike K and maturity T, the key market data input to a pricing model is the shape of this volatility surface for all strikes and maturities considered to be in scope. A neural network then needs to be trained, given a series of data points $\sigma_{\text{B–S}}(K_i, T_j)$, $i = 1, \ldots, n$, $j = 1, \ldots, m$, to return the value of $\sigma_{\text{B–S}}(K, T)$, which the rough volatility model would return in the event that the volatility surface was not one of those in the original data set. To this end, a large number N (in practice, $N = 40{,}000$ or $N = 80{,}000$) of representative volatility surfaces were generated using the target model, to serve as training data for the neural network.

The authors further observe that if, rather than trying to fit points on the volatility surface individually, the volatility surface itself, or rather the grid of points $\sigma_{\text{B–S}}(K_i, T_j)$, is taken to be the unit of output, the neural network can be trained more easily as the proximate nature of points with similar values of K and T means that they have similar levels of implied volatility, a fact the deep-learning algorithm was able to discover and take advantage of. The accuracy obtained was found to be comparable with the Monte Carlo accuracy inferred from the calculations in the original model. This led the authors to conclude the feasibility of replacing the calibration routine for rough volatility and other models with more efficient neural network-based algorithms.

In a slightly different direction, Kondratyev [2018] proposed a machine-learning approach as an alternative to the current practice of generating interest rate or other forward curve scenarios, using the standard financial models (see above) employed for many market risk and XVA calculations. He suggested that more realistic synthetic scenarios for the evolution of forward curves could be obtained by training a neural network on past time series. This idea was followed up by Kondratyev and Schwarz [2020] who introduced the concept of a *market generator*. The idea here was to go one step further. Rather than devise and calibrate pricing models to co-evolve multiple market variables in line with realistic distributions as part of a Monte Carlo simulation from which prices could be derived, instead a neural network – specifically a Restricted Boltzmann Machine (RBM) – could be trained to generate realistic distributions, learning directly from time series data. Further refinements of this data-driven scenario-modelling approach have recently been made by Kondratyev et al. [2020], who show how the RBM is particularly well suited to this task as it is able to learn the essential properties of a distribution from a relatively small data set and tends to avoid the twin perils of overfitting and allowing undue influence of outliers in the data set.

This nascent line of research, if the claims are to be believed, could potentially revolutionise the world of quantitative finance, challenging the conventional wisdom of modelling market variables through stochastic processes calibrated to market data and instead inferring evolutionary processes directly from data.

17.3 SYNERGIES WITH PERTURBATION METHODS

What follow are a few scattered thoughts of the author's about ways in which perturbation methods, and in particular some of the methods described in preceding chapters, might usefully complement machine-learning techniques, particularly in the risk management of financial products. As we are still in the early days of the development of machine-learning techniques in this context, our suggestions are necessarily provisional but may come in useful as the narrative unfolds.

17.3.1 Asymptotics as Control Variates

An interesting recent development has been the suggestion by Antonov et al. [2020] of a way in which asymptotic analysis can be explicitly combined with machine learning to their mutual advantage. The basic idea is that, if an approximate asymptotic pricing formula is known for a given product and it is wished to train a neural network to replicate the price rapidly, the asymptotic formula can be used as a control variate for the calculation. In the first instance, rather than the neural network being trained to find the price, it is trained to find the difference between the correct price and the asymptotic estimate. The difference should be small, and remain so across a wide parameter range, so even if the relative error in the machine-learned algorithm is not particularly low, when the price estimate is constructed by adding the asymptotic price to the (small) machine-learned difference, the relative error in comparison to this will usually be minimal.[2]

While this use of a control variate certainly ought to improve the rate of convergence of the machine-learned algorithm to the desired solution, this is not the main point of the introduction of the asymptotic solution by Antonov et al. [2020]. Rather, they seek also to address another concern, namely the well-known issue of the typically less-than-graceful failure of such algorithms when they are used with input parameters outside the space for which the training data provided coverage. This is a concern if the algorithm is to be used for risk management purposes, wherein stress scenarios are often specified, with market parameters taking extreme values far from current market levels. The solution they propose is effectively to substitute in the asymptotic approximation in place of the machine-learned algorithm in the region beyond its domain of validity. This turns out to be a non-trivial problem. The authors address it by representing the asymptotic solution through a relatively coarse interpolating spline with the property that it approaches zero at the boundary of the domain of validity, so that there is a smooth transition to the asymptotic solution outside that boundary.

In selecting training data, they propose that problems associated with the high dimensionality of the state space can potentially be addressed by use of a Monte Carlo

[2]What is being done here is arguably not very different from the trick of training on the Black–Scholes implied volatility rather than the price. Effectively, in that case, we are using the Black–Scholes formula as a control variate, except in that we also apply the inverse of the Black–Scholes formula as a way of scaling the result as a non-dimensional quantity.

approach, choosing points in the core region of the four-dimensional phase space for use in the learning process randomly rather than at regular intervals, as is commonly done, and thus helping to avoid the "curse of dimensionality". We shall return to this point below.

Examples are provided applying the technique to vanilla option pricing, both in the Black–Scholes framework (as a proof of concept) and in a SABR context, where the difference made by using the asymptotic formula is remarkable, especially in the high-volatility, high-strike régime where the SABR implied volatility rises very sharply. The authors suggest that the technique could be applied making use of other existing asymptotic formulae, and others again which might be derived by using currently available tools of asymptotic analysis. They do not specify further, but we would venture that many of the formulae set out in the preceding chapters of the present work would serve as possible candidates; and the techniques there described can certainly be used to derive many more results than we have been able to include here.

We would further suggest that these techniques, which are particularly versatile in deriving formulae for more complex/exotic products that depend on multiple stochastic underlyings, usefully complement the more mainstream work which has tended to focus heavily on pricing vanilla options in more complex/exotic models. We do not go into any detail here, but it is also possible to apply the techniques described above to the Heston stochastic volatility model replicating the second order results of Alòs et al. [2015] and on that basis to extend, if needed, many of the above results to incorporate stochastic volatility (and therefore smile and skew). A strategy similar to that adopted in §13.4 can also be applied to path-dependent Asian options. In short, if asymptotics and machine learning are to be seen as partners going forward in the way Antonov et al. [2020] envisage, there should be plenty of scope in that project for the ideas we have set out in this book.

17.3.2 Data Representation

One of the main challenges to be faced and overcome, if machine-learned pricing algorithms are to replace those currently used for risk management, is determining how best to represent market data to the machine, particularly when it is in the form of curves, surfaces and even hypersurfaces, such as swaption volatility cubes. This is an area to which surprisingly little attention appears to have been paid. We suggest here that a useful starting point is to scale parameters appropriately. One of the reasons we considered implied volatility to be so much better as a target for learning is because, unlike price, which has dimension (currency) and can consequently vary over a very wide range of values, annualised implied volatility is a pure number and, furthermore, tends to take rather similar values over a fairly large range of commonly referenced equity underlyings. This is true equally when implied volatility is an input as when it is an output.

Similarly, if in training a network to price equity options the spot price S_0 of the equity is scaled out by focussing on implied volatilities, it is worth being consistent and scaling other price-dependent parameters, such as the option strike price K with S_0, by specifying instead a single moneyness parameter, say $m = \ln(S_0/K)$. One can argue that the network can work out for itself that S_0 and K are not really independent parameters. But in order to train the network, say by specifying 8 different strike levels and 8 different equity price levels, we have potentially increased the number of training cases by a factor of 64, rather than just 8. If the cost of calculating each data point used for training purposes is high, such costs can quickly mount up. Further, we would lose a lot of the aforementioned benefit of embedding the moneyness dependence into a grid, by diluting it across multiple training data sets with different values for S_0 specified in each. The levels of barriers in barrier options can, of course, be usefully scaled in a similar way.

In the case of interest rate and credit derivatives, a similar approach can be taken for swaption pricing, specifying the strike through a moneyness level, scaling K with the current ATM swap (or CDS) rate. Managing swaption volatilities demands a little more effort. Prices (or the associated implied volatilities) will depend potentially on the moneyness, the time T to maturity of the option *and* the time τ to maturity of the underlying reference swap. Hence, we have inputs and outputs of the form $\sigma_{\text{B-S}}(m, T, \tau)$. For European swaptions this involves only the addition of an extra dimension. For Bermudan swaptions, however, there is the complication of a non-local dependence on the volatility surface, with early exercise options having shorter associated T values and correspondingly longer τ values, which will render the learning a little harder. Because both legs of the swap are impacted by the same discounting, the exercise criteria will be little affected by the level of the forward swap curve. So we can reasonably expect that this will, in and of itself, affect the training very little. However, the *shape* of the forward swap curve will remain relevant, because it will affect the moneyness of the early exercise options. So, an adequate sample of representative curve shapes will need to be provided amongst the training data, which requirement will increase the dimensionality of the problem further.

As we observed previously, little appears to have been written in the literature thus far about how to select representative curve (or surface) *shapes* in preparing the training data sets. In the case of Horvath et al. [2019], two specifications are considered for the forward variance curves specified in the training sets: constant and piecewise constant. In the former case, values between 1% and 16% are used; in the latter case curves have 8 sections, each with a value in the range 1–16%. Inevitably, all possible combinations cannot be considered in training, so a sampling process is needed, something the authors do not elaborate on in their paper.

What is clear is that not all curve or surface shapes are important for "real world" use of a machine-learned pricing algorithm. On the other hand, as pointed out by Antonov et al. [2020], a major use of these algorithms is likely to be in stress-testing for market risk purposes, where extreme scenarios far from current market conditions are considered; indeed, the values computed in these low-probability scenarios will often drive the risk metrics under the new Basel III financial regulation. Choosing the "right" scope for the variation of market data curves away from current levels necessarily involves a judicious choice between allowing too little variation away from current market levels, resulting in poor representation for extreme scenarios, and too much variation, resulting in possible degradation of the performance of the algorithm in normal market circumstances, as a consequence of the algorithm having to compromise accuracy in seeking to fit to a wider range of inputs.

We outline briefly a strategy which could be adopted for the selection of representative interest rate (or credit default intensity) forward curves. As pointed out in §15.2, evidence presented by Keller-Ressel [2019] suggests a two-factor short rate model is capable of giving rise to a fairly rich typology of curves, even with those parameters kept constant and an initial flat curve assumed. On this basis, we propose the use of the two-factor Black–Karasinski model, introduced in §15.5, which relies on a parsimonious 5 configurable parameters, $\sigma_x(t)$, $\alpha_x(t)$, $\sigma_y(t)$, $\alpha_y(t)$ and $\rho(t)$, setting them to a representative selection of (constant) values. For suitably correlated Ornstein–Uhlenbeck variables x_t and y_t at time $t > 0$, we can then conveniently generate forward curve realisations as $f_t(T) = f^T(x_t, y_t, t)$ using (15.50). By making random draws for x_t and y_t and considering various t-values up to some suitable threshold and applying them to a representative selection of initial curve shapes (possibly for a single currency or CDS rate, or else for a multiplicity of target currencies or CDS rates), we can sample the associated phase space of curve shapes as exhaustively as we choose. To facilitate a sufficiently uniform level of sampling, we can take advantage of low-discrepancy Sobol sequences rather than use the usual pseudo-random numbers. The training set can be conveniently extended as needed, simply by performing more draws for x_t and y_t and generating new curve shapes. The curves generated in this way can then be represented to the neural network in the same way as they are presented to the pricing algorithm being replicated, say as a table of swap rates associated with different maturities.

The advantage here of using Black–Karasinski lognormal volatility rather than Hull–White normal volatility is again that a suitable scaling is incorporated from the outset. Normal volatilities would have to scale with the forward rate, meaning that different representations of $f_t(T)$ would have to be developed for each different initial curve level considered. Note also that negative interest rates can be conveniently handled by including a suitable negative value for $s(t)$ in (15.32).

In general, there is no "right" answer to the question of how to choose representative curve and surface shapes. An initial data set of previously realised configurations from past market data time series is obviously a good place to start. In likelihood these will have to be supplemented by synthetic data to fill out the phase space adequately for the trained network to be able to handle any case the market may throw up in the future. How this synthetic data should be generated, how much should be generated/used, how far data should be stressed beyond typical market levels, and what weight should be given to such stressed data are all questions to be addressed; they will undoubtedly remain to some extent a matter of skill and judgement and depend on the priority of the user and the nature of the use case. Of course, advocates of the market generator approach would likely argue that the generation of suitable synthetic market data is a task best fulfilled making use of a machine-learning approach, rather than relying on expert human judgement.

Another question we consider briefly before concluding this discussion is, having generated a sufficiently large amount of synthetic market data, how much of it really needs to be used in training? The law of diminishing returns will apply insofar as each time we double the amount of training performed a smaller increment in accuracy will tend to result. Bachem et al. [2017] discuss this problem, making use of the concept of "coresets." These are defined as subsets of the full data set available for training, and have been shown by statistical analysis to be most important in improving the quality of the final results attained by the network. More precisely, they are provably competitive under some metric with results obtained by training on the full data set. This idea arose originally from earlier application of machine learning to problems in computational geometry. It seems not unlikely that the same considerations will in time be taken into account in a financial engineering context.

Bibliography

E. Alòs, R. De Santiago, and J. Vives. Calibration of stochastic volatility models via second-order approximation: the Heston case. *International Journal of Theoretical and Applied Finance*, 18(6):1550036, 2015.

K. I. Amin and R. A. Jarrow. Pricing Options on Risky Assets in a Stochastic Interest Rate Economy. *Mathematical Finance*, 2(4):217–237, 1992.

L. Andersen and D. Buffum. Calibration and Implementation of Convertible Bond Models. *Journal of Computational Finance*, 7(2):1–34, 2003.

L. B. G. Andersen and V. V. Piterbarg. *Interest Rate Modeling, Volume 2: Term Structure Models*. Atlantic Financial Press, 1st edition, 2010. ISBN 978-0984422111.

A. M. Antonopoulos. *Mastering Bitcoin: Programming the Open Blockchain*. O'Reilly Media, 2nd edition, 2017.

A. Antonov and M. Spector. General Short-Rate Analytics. *Risk*, April:66–71, 2010.

A. Antonov, M. Konikov, and M. Spector. *Modern SABR Analytics: Formulas and Insights for Quants, Former Physicists and Mathematicians*. Springer, 2019. ISBN 978-3030106553.

A. Antonov, M. Konikov, and V. Piterbarg. Neural networks with asymptotics control. Research paper, SSRN, 2020. URL https://ssrn.com/abstract=3544698.

A. Arnal, F. Casas, and F. Chiralt. A general formula for the Magnus expansion in terms of iterated integrals of right-nested commutators. *Journal of Physics Communications*, 2(3):035024, 2018. URL http://iopscience.iop.org/article/10.1088/2399-6528/aab291.

O. Bachem, M. Lucic, and A. Krause. Practical Coreset Constructions for Machine Learning. Research paper, ETH Zurich, 2017. URL https://arxiv.org/pdf/1703.06476.pdf.

G. S. Bakshi and Z. Chen. An Alternative Valuation Model for Contingent Claims. *Journal of Financial Economics*, 44(1):123–165, 1997.

Bank for International Settlements. Fundamental review of the trading book: a revised market risk framework. Consultative Document, Basel Committee on Banking Supervision, 2014. URL http://dx.doi.org/10.2139/ssrn.158630.

C. Bayer and B. Stemper. Deep calibration of rough stochastic volatility models. Preprint, arxiv.org, 2018. URL https://arxiv.org/pdf/1810.03399.pdf.

I. Beyna and U. Wystup. Characteristic functions in the Cheyette interest rate model. *CPQF Working Paper Series*, 28, 2011. URL http://hdl.handle.net/10419/44996.

F. Black. Interest rates as options. *The Journal of Finance*, 50:1371–1376, 1995.

F. Black and P. Karasinski. Bond and Option Pricing when Short Rates are Lognormal. *Financial Analysts Journal*, 47(4):52–59, 1991.

F. Black and M.S. Scholes. The pricing of options and corporate liabilities. *Journal of Political Economics*, 81:637–654, 1973.

A. Brace, D. Gatarek, and M. Musiela. The market model of interest rate dynamics. *Mathematical Finance*, 7(2):127–155, 1997.

D. Brigo and F. Mercurio. *Interest Rate Models—Theory and Practice: With Smile, Inflation and Credit*. Springer Finance, 2nd edition, 2006. ISBN 978-3540221494.

D. Brigo, N. Pede, and A. Petrelli. Multicurrency Default Swaps: Quanto effects and FX devaluation jumps. *International Journal of Theoretical and Applied Finance*, 22(4):1950018, 2019.

L. Brotcke and R. Brastow. Assessment of model risk in the aggregate: Contribution of quantification. *Journal of Risk Management in Financial Institutions*, 1:29–58, 2019.

L. Capriotti. The Exponent Expansion: An Effective Approximation of Transition Probabilities of Diffusion Processes and Pricing Kernels of Financial Derivatives. *International Journal of Theoretical and Applied Finance*, 9(7):1179–1199, 2006.

L. Capriotti and B. Stehlíkova. An Effective Approximation for Zero-Coupon Bonds and Arrow–Debreu Prices in the Black–Karasinski Model. *International Journal of Theoretical and Applied Finance*, 17(6):1450037, 2014.

P. Carr and L. Wu. Stock Options and Credit Default Swaps: A Joint Framework for Valuation and Estimation. *Journal of Financial Econometrics*, 4(8):409–449, 2010.

T.-K. Chung and J. Gregory. CVA wrong-way risk: calibration using a quanto CDS basis. *Risk*, July:1–6, 2019.

T. K. Chung and Y. K. Kwok. Equity-credit modeling under affine jump-diffusion models with jump-to-default. *Journal of Financial Engineering*, 1(2):1450017, 2014.

R. Cont. Model Uncertainty and its Impact on the Pricing of Derivative Instruments. Working paper, Finance Concepts, 2004. URL https://ssrn.com/abstract=562721.

E. Cortina. Modeling Defaultable Bonds with Mean-Reverting Log-Normal Spread: A Quasi Closed-Form Solution. Working Paper, FAMAF, 2007. URL http://www.famaf.unc.edu.ar/torres/trabajosparapublicacion/06-finanzas_cuantitativas/06-finanzas_cuantitativas-01.pdf.

J. C. Cox, J. E. Ingersoll, and S. A. Ross. A Theory of the Term Structure of Interest Rates. *Econometrica*, 53:385–407, 1991.

C. Cuchiero, C. Fontana, and A. Gnoatto. Affine multiple yield curve models. *Mathematical Finance*, 29(2):568–611, 2019.

Q. Dai and K. J. Singleton. Specification analysis of affine term structure models. *Journal of Finance*, 50:1943–1978, 2000.

A. Daniluk and R. Muchorski. Approximations of bond and swaption prices in a Black–Karasinski model. *International Journal of Theoretical and Applied Finance*, 19(3):1650017, 2016.

M. A. H. Dempster, J. Evans, and E. Medova. Developing a Practical Yield Curve Model: An Odyssey. Working Paper, SSRN, 2012. URL https://ssrn.com/abstract=2304372.

P. Donati and F. Donati. Modeling and forecasting the yield curve under model uncertainty. Working Paper 917, European Cantral Bank, 2008. URL https://www.ecb.europa.eu/pub/pdf/scpwps/ecbwp917.pdf.

P. Ehlers and P. Schönbucher. The Influence of FX Risk on Credit Spreads. Working Paper 214, NCCR FINRISK, 2004. URL http://www.nccr-finrisk.uzh.ch/media/pdf/wp/WP214_5.pdf.

R. EL-Mohammadi. BSWithJump Model And Pricing Of Quanto CDS With FX Devaluation Risk. Working Paper 42781, MPRA, 2009. URL https://mpra.ub.uni-muenchen.de/42781/.

C. Fenger. Credit Quanto Spreads. Working Paper, SSRN, 2016. URL https://ssrn.com/abstract=2645739.

R. Ferguson and A. D. Green. Deeply Learning Derivatives. Research paper, SSRN, 2018. URL https://ssrn.com/abstract=3244821.

Fintegral and IACPM. Making the Most of XVA: Practitioner Perspectives. White paper, IACPM, 2015. URL http://iacpm.org/wp-content/uploads/2018/06/IACPM-Fintegral-Making-the-Most-of-XVA-2018-White-Paper.pdf.

P. Fouque, G. Papanicolaou, and K. R. Sircar. *Derivatives in Financial Markets with Stochastic Volatility*. Cambridge University Press, 2000.

P. Fouque, G. Papanicolaou, K. R. Sircar, and K. Sølna. *Multiscale Stochastic Volatility for Equity, Interest Rate, and Credit Derivatives*. Cambridge University Press, 2011.

R. Geske. The Valuation of Compound Options. *Journal of Financial Economics*, 7:63–81, 1979.

P. Glasserman and X. Xu. Robust risk measurement and model risk. *Quantitative Finance*, 14:29–58, 2014.

O. Grishchenko, Han X., and V. Nistor. A Volatility-of-Volatility Expansion of the Option Prices in the SABR Stochastic Volatility Model. Working Paper, SSRN, 2014. URL https://ssrn.com/abstract=2374004.

A. Gulisashvili, B. Horvath, and A. Jacquier. Mass at Zero in the Uncorrelated SABR Model and Implied Volatility Asymptotics. Working Paper, SSRN, 2016. URL https://ssrn.com/abstract=2563510.

P. S. Hagan, D. Kumar, and D. E. Lesniewski, A. S. and Woodward. Managing Smile Risk. *Wilmott Magazine*, July:84–108, 2002.

P. S. Hagan, A. S. Lesniewski, and D. E. Woodward. Probability Distribution in the SABR Model of Stochastic Volatility. In P. K. Friz, J. Gatheral, and A. Gulisashvili, editors, *Large Deviations and Asymptotic Methods in Finance*, volume 110 of *Springer Proceedings in Mathematics and Statistics*, pages 1–35. Springer, 2015. URL http://www.lesniewski.us/papers/working/ProbDistrForSABR.pdf.

D. C. Heath, R. A. Jarrow, and A. J. Morton. Bond Pricing and the Term Structure of Interest Rates: A New Methodology for Contingent Claims Evaluation. *Econometrica*, 60(1):77–105, 1992.

S. Helgason. Sophus Lie, the mathematician. Working Paper, ResearchGate, 1994. URL https://www.researchgate.net/publication/251260625_Sophus_Lie_the_mathematician.

M. P. A. Henrard. Explicit Bond Option and Swaption Formula in Heath–Jarrow–Morton One Factor Model. Research paper, SSRN, 2003. URL https://ssrn.com/abstract=434860.

M. P. A. Henrard. Overnight Indexed Swaps and Floored Compounded Instrument in HJM One-Factor Model. Research paper, University Library of Munich, 2004. URL https://ideas.repec.org/p/wpa/wuwpfi/0402008.html.

M. P. A. Henrard. Skewed Libor Market Model and Gaussian HJM explicit approaches to rolled deposit options. *The Journal of Risks*, 9(4), 2007. URL https://ssrn.com/abstract=956849.

M. P. A. Henrard. LIBOR Fallback and Quantitative Finance. *Risks*, 7(3):88, 2019. URL https://doi.org/10.3390/risks7030088.

T. S. Y. Ho and S.-B. Lee. Term Structure Movements and Pricing Interest Rate Contingent Claims. *Journal of Finance*, 41(5):1011–1029, 1986.

B. Horvath, A. Jacquier, and C. Turfus. Analytic Option Prices for the Black–Karasinski Short Rate Model. Working Paper, SSRN, 2017. URL https://ssrn.com/abstract=3253833.

B. Horvath, A. Muguruza, and M. Tomas. Deep learning volatility. Research paper, SSRN, 2019. URL https://ssrn.com/abstract=3322085.

J. Hull. *Options, Futures, and Other Derivatives*. Pearson, 10th edition, 2018. ISBN 978-0134631493.

J. Hull and A. White. Pricing Interest Rate Derivative Securities. *The Review of Financial Studies*, 3:573–592, 1990.

A. Itkin, V. Shcherbakov, and A. Veygman. New Model for Pricing Quanto Credit Default Swaps. *International Journal of Theoretical and Applied Finance*, 22(3):1950003, 2019.

M. Jacobs Jr. The quantification and aggregation of model risk: perspectives on potential approaches. *Int. J. Financial Engineering and Risk Management*, 2(2):124–154, 2015.

F. Jamshidian. An Exact Bond Option Formula. *The Journal of Finance*, 44(1):205–209, 1989.

F. Jamshidian. LIBOR and swap market models and measures. *Finance and Stochastics*, 1(4):293–330, 1997.

R. A. Jarrow and Y. Yildirim. Pricing Treasury inflation protected securities and related derivatives using an HJM model. *Journal of Financial and Quantitative Analysis*, 38:337–359, 2003.

N. Jobst and S. A. Zenios. Extending Credit Risk (Pricing) Models for the Simulation of Portfolios of Interest Rate and Credit Risk Sensitive Securities. Working Paper, Wharton Financial Institutions Center, 2001. URL https://econpapers.repec.org/paper/woppennin/01-25.htm.

A. Joshi. *Managing Risk of Financial Models: A Smart and Simple Guide for the Practitioner*. CreateSpace Self-Publishing, 2017. ISBN 978-1976510342.

T. Kato. *Perturbation Theory for Linear Operators*. Springer-Verlag, 2nd, reprinted edition, 1995.

M. Keller-Ressel. Total positivity and the classification of term structure shapes in the two-factor Vasicek model. Research Paper, Cornell University, 2019. URL https://arxiv.org/abs/1908.04667.

Y. Kim and N. Kunitomo. Pricing Options under Stochastic Interest Rates: A New Approach. *Asia-Pacific Financial Markets*, 6:49–70, 1999.

A. Kondratyev. Curve Dynamics with Artificial Neural Networks. *Risk*, 31(6), 2018.

A. Kondratyev and C. Schwarz. The Market Generator. Research paper, SSRN, 2020. URL https://ssrn.com/abstract=3384948.

A. Kondratyev, C. Schwarz, and B. Horvath. Data Anonymisation, Outlier Detection and Fighting Overfitting with Restricted Boltzmann Machines. Research paper, SSRN, 2020. URL https://ssrn.com/abstract=3526436.

M. Lorig, S. Pagliarani, and A. Pascucci. Explicit Implied Volatilities for Multifactor Local-Stochastic Volatility Models. *Mathematical Finance*, 27(3):926–960, 2017.

A. Lyashenko and F. Mercurio. Looking Forward to Backward-Looking Rates: A Modeling Framework for Term Rates Replacing LIBOR. Research paper, SSRN, 2019. URL https://ssrn.com/abstract=3330240.

W. Magnus. On the exponential solution of differential equations for a linear operator. *Comm. Pure and Appl. Math.*, VII:649–673, 1954.

R. Mallier and A. S. Deakin. A Green's Function for a Convertible Bond Using the Vasicek Model. *Journal of Applied Mathematics*, 2(5):219–232, 2002. URL http://citeseerx.ist.psu.edu/viewdoc/summary?doi=10.1.1.485.2018.

S. Marlin. The disputed terrain of model risk scoring. *Risk*, November:29–58, 2018.

W. A. McGhee. An artificial neural network representation of the SABR stochastic volatility model. Preprint, SSRN, 2018. URL https://ssrn.com/abstract=3288882.

M. Y. Melnikov and Y. A. Melnikov. Construction of Green's Function Solutions for the Black–Scholes Equation. *Electronic Journal of Differential Equations*, 153:1–14, 2007.

F. Mercurio. A LIBOR Market Model with Stochastic Basis. Research paper, SSRN, 2010. URL https://ssrn.com/abstract=1583081.

F. Mercurio. A Simple Multi-Curve Model for Pricing SOFR Futures and Other Derivatives. Research paper, SSRN, 2018. URL https://ssrn.com/abstract=3225872.

R. C. Merton. Theory of Rational Option Pricing. *The Bell Journal of Economics and Management Science*, 4(1):141–183, 1973.

R. C. Merton. Option Pricing when Underlying Stock Returns are Discontinuous. *Journal of Financial Economics*, 3:1255–144, 1976.

A. Meucci. Review of Statistical Arbitrage, Cointegration, and Multivariate Ornstein–Uhlenbeck. Working paper, ARPM - Advanced Risk and Portfolio Management, 2010. URL https://ssrn.com/abstract=1404905.

K. R. Miltersen, K. Sandmann, and D. Sondermann. Closed form solutions for term structure derivatives with log-normal interest rates. *The Journal of Finance*, 52(1):409–430, 1997.

M. Morini. *Understanding and Managing Model Risk: A Practical Guide for Quants, Traders and Validators*. Wiley Finance, 2011.

C. R. Nelson and A. F. Siegel. Parsimonious Modeling of Yield Curve. *Journal of Business*, 60:473–489, 1987.

L. Ng. Numerical procedures for a wrong way risk model with lognormal hazard rates and Gaussian interest rates. *International Journal of Theoretical and Applied Finance*, 16(8):1350049, 2013.

S. Pagliarani and A. Pascucci. Analytical approximation of the transition density in a local volatility model. *Central European Journal of Mathematics*, 10(1):250–270, 2012. URL https://ssrn.com/abstract_id=1856043.

J. Pan and K. J. Singleton. Extending Credit Risk (Pricing) Models for the Simulation of Portfolios of Interest Rate and Credit Risk Sensitive Securities. Working Paper, Massachusetts Institute of Technology, 2007. URL http://www.mit.edu/junpan/sovrev.pdf.

A. Pascucci. *PDE and Martingale Methods in Option Pricing*. Bocconi University Press, 2011.

S. Peterson, R. C. Stapleton, and M. G. Subrahmanyam. A Two-factor Lognormal Model of the Term Structure and the Valuation of American-Style Options on Bonds. Working paper, ResearchGate, 1999. URL https://www.researchgate.net/publication/2424239_A_Two-factor_Lognormal_Model_of_the_Term_Structure_and_the_Valuation_of_American-Style_Options_on_Bonds.

M. Realdon. A Two Factor Black–Karasinski Credit Default Swap Pricing Model. *Icfai Journal of Derivatives Markets*, IV(4), 2007. URL https://ideas.repec.org/p/yor/yorken/07-25.html.

D. Redfern and D. McLean. Principal Component Analysis for Yield Curve Modelling: Reproduction of out-of-sample yield curves. White Paper, Moody's Analytics, 2014. URL https://www.moodysanalytics.com/-/media/whitepaper/2014/2014-29-08-PCA-for-Yield-Curve-Modelling.pdf.

V. Russo, R. Giacometti, and F. J. Fabozzi. Closed-Form Solution for Defaultable Bond Options under a Two-Factor Gaussian Model for Risky Rates Modeling. *The Journal of Derivatives*, Winter, 2020. URL https://doi.org/10.3905/jod.2020.1.104.

N. Santean. The hitchhiker's guide to the risk-neutral galaxy. Research paper, SSRN, 2020. URL https://ssrn.com/abstract=3377470.

P. Schönbucher. A LIBOR Market Model with Default Risk.Working Paper, SSRN, 2001. URL https://ssrn.com/abstract=261051.

P. Schönbucher. A Tree Implementation of a Credit Spread Model for Credit Derivatives. *Journal of Computational Finance*, 6:113–125, 2002.

J. Skoglund. Quantification of model risk in stress testing and scenario analysis. *Journal of Risk Model Validation*, 13(1), 2019.

A. Soklakov. Model Risk Analysis via Investment Structuring. Working Paper, SSRN, 2015. URL https://www.ssrn.com/abstract=2639369.

J. De Spiegeleer, D. Madan, S. Reyners, and W. Schoutens. Machine learning for quantitative Finance: Fast derivative pricing, hedging and Fitting. Research paper, SSRN, 2018. URL https://ssrn.com/abstract=3191050.

L. Tchuindjo. Pricing of Multi-Defaultable Bonds with a Two-Correlated-Factor Hull-White Model. *Applied Mathematical Finance*, 14:19–39, 2007.

F. Tourrucôo, P. S. Hagan, and G. F. Schleiniger. Approximate Formulas for Zero-Coupon Bonds. *Applied Mathematical Finance*, 14:107–226, 2007.

C. Turfus. Analytical Solution for CVA of a Collateralised Call Option. Working Paper, ResearchGate, 2016. URL https://www.researchgate.net/publication/311768471_Analytical_Solution_for_CVA_of_a_Collateralised_Call_Option.

C. Turfus. Analytic Swaption Pricing in the Black–Karasinski Model. Working Paper, SSRN, 2018a. URL https://ssrn.com/abstract=3253866.

C. Turfus. Exact Arrow–Debreu Pricing for the Black–Karasinski Short Rate Model. Working Paper, SSRN, 2018b. URL https://ssrn.com/abstract=3253839.

C. Turfus. Closed-Form Arrow–Debreu Pricing for FX and Inflation Options with Hull–White Stochastic Rates. Working Paper, SSRN, 2018c. URL https://ssrn.com/abstract=3261601.

C. Turfus. Analytic Pricing of Quanto CDS. Working Paper, ResearchGate, 2018d. URL https://www.researchgate.net/publication/325070862_Analytic_Pricing_of_Quanto_CDS.

C. Turfus. Perturbation Expansion for Arrow–Debreu Pricing with Hull–White Interest Rates and Black–Karasinski Credit Intensity. Working Paper, SSRN, 2018e. URL https://ssrn.com/abstract=3287910.

C. Turfus. Closed-Form Arrow–Debreu Pricing for the Hull–White Short Rate Model. *Quantitative Finance*, 19(12):2087–2094, 2019.

C. Turfus and A. Shubert. Analytic Pricing of CoCo Bonds. *International Journal of Theoretical and Applied Finance*, 20(5), 2017. URL https://ssrn.com/abstract=3420977.

C. Turfus and A. Shubert. Two-Factor Black–Karasinski Pricing Kernel. *Risk*, 2020. URL https://ssrn.com/abstract=3420977.

US Federal Reserve. SR11-7: Guidance on Model Risk Management. Supervision and Regulation Letters, Division of Banking Supervision and Regulation, 2011. URL https://www.federalreserve.gov/supervisionreg/srlettesr1107.htmrs/.

R. J. Van Steenkiste and S. Foresi. Arrow–Debreu prices for affine models. Working Paper, SSRN, 1999. URL http://dx.doi.org/10.2139/ssrn.158630.

O. Vasicek. An equilibrium characterization of the term structure. *Journal of Financial Economics*, 5:177–188, 1977.

Index